ALGERIA

ALGERIA

ANGER OF THE DISPOSSESSED

MARTIN EVANS AND JOHN PHILLIPS

YALE UNIVERSITY PRESS

NEW HAVEN AND LONDON

For information about this and other Yale University Press publications, please contact:

U.S. Office:	sales.press@yale.edu	yalebooks.com
Europe Office:	sales@yaleup.co.uk	www.yaleup.co.uk

Maps designed by Chartwell Illustrators, Surrey
Text design by Roger Hammond
Set in Adobe Garamond by SX Composing DTP, Rayleigh, Essex
Printed in Great Britain by St Edmundsbury Press Ltd, Bury St Edmunds

Library of Congress Cataloging-in-Publication Data

Evans, Martin, 1964–
   Algeria: anger of the dispossessed/Martin Evans and John Phillips.
      p. cm.
   Includes bibliographical references and index.
   ISBN 978–0–300–10881–1 (alk. paper)
   1. Algeria—History—1962–1990. 2. Algeria—History—1990– 3. Islam and politics—Algeria. I. Phillips, John. II. Title.
   DT295.5.E92 2007
   965.05—dc22

2007021010

A catalogue record for this book is available from the British Library.

10 9 8 7 6 5 4 3 2 1

CONTENTS

ACKNOWLEDGEMENTS

First, we would like to acknowledge with gratitude the financial support for Martin Evans of the Arts and Humanities Research Council, the British Academy and the Centre for European and International Studies Research at the University of Portsmouth; and for John Phillips of the Society of Authors.

Thereafter, many friends and colleagues have helped our research and we would like to thank our editors at Yale Robert Baldock and Phoebe Clapham, Martin Evans' agent Bill Hamilton, Matthew Campbell and Peter Conradi at the *Sunday Times*, Richard Beeston at *The Times*, Abdelhamid Aoun and Clive Myrie at the BBC and Peter Furtado and Charlotte Crow at *History Today*; also Hannah Abbo, Robert Aldrich, Martin Alexander, Catherine Barry, Michael Brett, Tony Chafer, Elizabeth Colton, John Cornwell, Jan-Georg Deutsche, Calum Evans, John Evans, Skye Evans, Emmanuel Godin, Azzedine Haddour, Houria Hammoudi-Honey, Mohammed Harbi, George Joffe, Douglas Johnson, Rod Kedward, John King, Zineb Lalaouine, Aidan Lewis of the AP in Algiers, Andrew Lycett, Sean MacCarthaigh, Margaret Majumdar, Gordon Marsden, Gilbert Meynier, Samia Mitchell, Brendan Murphy, Lucy Noakes, Gerry O'Connell, Sabreah Oughton, Valerio Pellizzari, Charles Ridley, Fr. Armand Rivaux, Lydia Aït Saadi, Brendan Simms, Ronald Singleton, Archbishop Henri Teissier, Natalya Vince, Sabaah Wali and Philip Willan.

LIST OF ABBREVIATIONS

AIS	Armée Islamique de Salut (1994–7)
ALN	Armée de Libération Nationale (1954–62)
AML	Association des Amis du Manifeste et de la Liberté (1944–5)
ANP	Armée Nationale Populaire (1962–)
CCE	Comité de Coordination et d'Exécution (1956–8)
CIA	Central Intelligence Agency (US)
CNN	Conseil Consultatif National (1992–4)
CNRA	Conseil National de la Révolution Algérienne (1956–62)
CNT	Conseil National de Transition (1994–7)
CTRI	Centre Territorial de Recherche et d'Investigation
DECs	Délégations Executives Communales
DRS	Département du Renseignement et de la Sécurité (1990–)
ENA	Etoile Nord-Africaine (1926–37)
FFS	Front des Forces Socialistes (1963–)
FIDA	Front Islamique pour le Djihad en Algérie
FIS	Front Islamique du Salut (1989–92)
FLN	Front de Libération Nationale (1954–)
GIA	Groupe Islamique Armé
GIS	Groupe d'Intervention Spéciale
GPRA	Gouvernement Provisoire de la République Algérienne (1958–62)
GSPC	Groupe Salafiste pour la Prédication et le Combat (1998–2007)
HCS	Haut Conseil de Sécurité
HCE	Haut Comité d'Etat
ISI	Interservice Intelligence (Pakistani secret services)
LADDH	Ligue Algérienne de Défense des Droits de l'Homme (1985–)
LIDD	Ligue Islamique de la Daâwa et du Djihad
MAOL	Mouvement Algérien des Officiers Libres (1997–)
MCB	Mouvement Culturel Berbère (1968–)
MDA	Mouvement pour la Démocratie en Algérie (1984–)
MDS	Mouvement Démocratique et Social (1999–)
MIA	Mouvement Islamique Armé

MN	Mouvement Ennahda
MNA	Mouvement National Algérien (1954–62)
MRN	Mouvement du Rénouveau National
MSP	Mouvement de la Société pour la Paix
OAS	Organisation de l'Armée Secrète (1961–2)
OAU	Organization of African Unity
OPEC	Organization of Petroleum Exporting Countries
OS	Organisation Spéciale
PAGS	Parti de l'Avant-Garde Socialiste (1966–93)
PCA	Parti Communiste Algérien (1936–66)
PPA	Parti du Peuple Algérien (1937–54)
PRS	Parti de la Révolution Socialiste (1962–82)
PT	Parti des Travailleurs (1974–)
RCD	Rassemblement pour la Culture et la Démocratie (1989–)
RND	Rassemblement National Démocratique (1997–)
RPN	Rassemblement Patriotique National
SM	Sécurité Militaire
SONATRACH	Société Nationale pour le Recherche, la Production, le Transport, la Transformation et la Commercialisation des Hydrocarbures
UGTA	Union Générale des Travailleurs Algériens

GLOSSARY

All terms are Arabic unless otherwise stated

amazigh (pl. *imazighen*)	free man: the term used by contemporary Berbers to describe themselves
bachaga	regional leader in the Ottoman and French systems
bida	unacceptable innovation in Islamic doctrine
cadi	judge
caïd	local governor/tax collector
djemaa	council of elders
emir	one who commands. Often used to refer to the leader of an Islamic group
fatwa	a legal opinion on a religious question issued by a recognized Muslim scholar
fitna	division within the Muslim community
haram	forbidden by Islamic law
hogra	humiliation
hadj	pilgrimage to Mecca
harki	Muslim auxiliary who fought in the French army during the war of liberation. For all post-independence regimes the word has been synonymous with 'traitor'
hizb	political party
hizb fransa	'the party of France': a pejorative term referring to Algerians supposedly defending the interests of the former colonial power
jahiliya	the state of ignorance that existed before the arrival of Islam
jihad	effort, struggle, a legitimate war
Majlis al-Shura	Consultative Council
marabout	holy man
raï	literally means 'opinion'; musical genre that emerged from Oran
Salafist	member of the Muslim revivalist movement *salafiya*, based on the idea of a return to the ideas and practices of early Islam
sharia	Islamic law
sheikh	elder, religious leader
sherif	member of family descended from the Prophet
shura	consultation
Sufism	mystic tradition within Islam
Tamazight	the Berber language
ulama (pl. *ulema*)	group of religious scholars
umma	the community of Muslim believers
wilaya	an administrative region: during the war of liberation the FLN divided Algeria into six such regions

LIST OF ILLUSTRATIONS

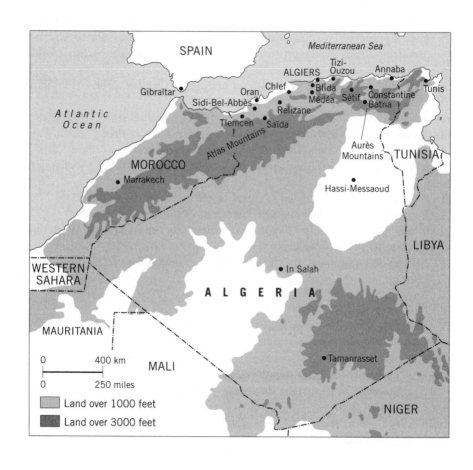

PREFACE

Why Algeria?

LYING ON THE southern shores of the Mediterranean, Algeria is a vast country, the second largest in Africa and indeed the eleventh largest in the world.* Bordered by Morocco to the west, Tunisia and Libya to the east and Mauritania, Mali and Niger to the south, Algeria is a land of dramatic physical extremes where vertiginous gorges and snow-capped mountains compete with tangerine groves, marshy plains and vast tracts of the Sahara desert. It is by any stretch of the imagination a singular landscape, beautiful, beguiling, bewildering, which down the centuries has formed a historical crossroads between Islam and Christianity, Africa and Europe, the First World and the Third.

At the beginning of the twenty-first century, the notion that Algeria represents an adjacent 'other' is just as prevalent as it has ever been. Most obviously, this impression is derived from the train of events since 11 September 2001 and all the attendant speculation about the 'clash of civilizations'. Equally, however, it stems from the pressure of economic migration from the poor South, and here one fact is vital: for Algeria's 33.3 million Muslim inhabitants, one of the fastest-growing populations in the world, Europe is just two hours away by plane, and large numbers covet a better life in the rich North.

Algeria occupied the world headlines between 1954 and 1962 with the national liberation struggle against French rule. Immortalized in Gillo Pontecorvo's 1966 film *The Battle of Algiers*, this was one of the bloodiest and most protracted wars of decolonization, with no quarter given by either side. When independence was finally won this was rightly seen across the globe as a momentous event. Yet almost at once Algeria was forgotten, as the world's gaze shifted to the Vietnam War, the events of May 1968 in France, and the Soviet invasion of Czechoslovakia. Beyond France, reports on Algeria tended to be sporadic, largely because from a news perspective, with independence attained, the story was over.

Algeria only returned to the world media spotlight in the late 1980s, with the rise of the political Islamist party the Islamic Salvation Front (FIS). In

*Algeria covers some 900,000 square miles. Sudan is the only African country to be bigger.

January 1992 the army cancelled elections which the FIS was poised to win and the country soon descended into violence as young Islamist guerrillas took to the hills to fight the military regime. A cycle of terrorism and counter-terrorism ensued, creating a spiral of uncontrollable events that grew ever more savage. The ferocity and frequency of bombings, shootings and ambushes turned whole swathes of the country into a maze of military checkpoints, concrete blast walls and razor wire. The second Algerian war had begun.

During late 1997 and early 1998 Algeria turned bloody beyond belief. Suddenly to the outside world the place became not so much a country but an event, a maelstrom of violence where whole villages were wiped out in the hinterland of the capital. Three hundred ordinary civilians were massacred in Raïs on 28 August 1997, followed by five hundred in Béni-Messous on 5 September, four hundred in Bentalha on 22 September, then five hundred more in the three villages of Meknessa, Souk El-Had and Had Chekala on 4 January 1998. By this point the area south of Algiers, dubbed 'the triangle of death' by locals, amounted to one huge killing field as groups of hooded men returned night after night to carry out murder, mutilation, disembowelment and systematic rape. In 1999 even the government was forced to admit that the conflict had led to a hundred thousand dead, that is, on average, five hundred people every week, with many more maimed, injured and traumatized. Independent experts suggest the figure is more like two hundred thousand.

By autumn 1997 the sheer scale of the violence in Algeria had become impossible for the international community to ignore. On 30 September Mary Robinson, the UN High Commissioner for Human Rights, made a public plea calling for an end to bloodshed. Two weeks later four human rights organizations – Amnesty International, Human Rights Watch, the Fédération Internationale des Ligues des Droits de l'Homme and Reporters sans Frontières – called for a special UN session on Algeria and the establishment of an independent international inquiry into the massacres, a demand that was backed up by the United States on 5 January 1998. On 19 January a European Union delegation made a visit to see the situation on the ground.

In the midst of all this international attention there was much that was puzzling. Why, for example, was the army incapable of intervening to protect its citizens even though some units were stationed in barracks just a few hundred yards away from the massacres? Why had kidnappers been able to abduct a group of mostly elderly Roman Catholic monks from their monastery at Tibhirine under the noses of soldiers deployed at a nearby post? Some began to ask if insiders within the military regime were manipulating the bloodshed in order to sabotage any attempts at dialogue with the Islamist guerrillas.

The aim of this book is to scrape away at the layers of confusion and obfuscation in order to reveal the causes of this violence. We want to go beyond stereotypes which interpret the conflict as the consequence of a pathological Oriental mindset, the simple battle between secularists and Islamists or the inevitable failure of the post-independence regime. There is nothing inevitable or predetermined about Algeria. Instead, the country's tragedy has to be understood as the product of a specific and complex historical context filled at every point with alternative possibilities and counter-factual scenarios.

This book is an exploration of the connections between past and present, where the injustices and horrors of yesteryear are engraved upon people's minds and have powerful influences on what happens next. The introduction and first four chapters will chart the country's long historical roots, examining the complicated relationship between the pre-colonial, colonial and post-colonial periods, whilst chapters four to eight will focus on post-1988 Algeria, analysing in detail the twists and turns of the unfolding conflict.

The book is also a dialogue between a historian and a journalist, both of whom have extensive first-hand experience of North Africa and Algeria. Both authors see Algeria as a microcosm of the contemporary world: a country which is grappling not just with religious terrorism and the legacy of colonialism but also with huge economic inequalities and a difficult transition to democracy.

Finally, the book sets out to put Algeria into a wider perspective. In January 2003 Algerian Islamists were arrested in north London, accused of plotting a ricin attack on the London Underground, an event that was exploited to the hilt by Tony Blair in his justification for the invasion of Iraq. The clampdown on Islamist activists that followed was met with ironic applause from governments in Algiers and Paris who had long accused Britain of turning a blind eye to religious extremists, from which London had gained the soubriquet 'Londonistan'. Algeria is not elsewhere, a distant French enclave of no real interest. What happens in Algeria has deep ramifications. The history of Algeria reminds us of a basic but fundamental truth, namely that in the contemporary world no country is an island.

Martin Evans, Portsmouth
John Phillips, Rome
March 2007

Raffet pinxit

Rouargue sculp.

The capture by the French of the Algerian city of Constantine in 1836, as depicted in a popular
engraving by Rouargue following a drawing by Raffet

The Role of the Past in Algerian History

O N 14 JUNE 1830 a small French force waded ashore at first light at Sidi-Ferruch, a beach some twenty miles to the west of Algeria's capital, Algiers. This spot had been chosen as the bridgehead for invasion because it was sheltered and the water was so shallow, and during the next few days the French landed an impressive force of 37,000 men and 91 artillery pieces, its largest expedition since the Napoleonic campaign. Meticulous planning, combined with strength of numbers, led the military leaders to predict a walk-over and such was the weight of expectation that members of French high society hired pleasure boats to observe the naval bombardment of the Algerian coastline.

It was a hubris that was well placed. En route to the capital the French met little resistance, quickly routing a ramshackle force of 35,000 Ottoman troops at Staouéli on 19 June, the only serious military engagement of the whole campaign. By 5 July Algiers had capitulated, at which point the invading troops were given a free hand to pillage the casbah for jewels, art and treasure. Flushed with a triumph which he knew would earn him a marshal's baton, the expedition's leader, the ultraconservative General Bourmont, congratulated his men on a campaign that had lasted just twenty days and cost a mere four hundred casualties. As intended, it had brought about the destruction of the Ottoman regency that, in Bourmont's words, had been a 'thorn in the side of Europe for three centuries' through its sponsorship of the Barbary pirates operating from Algeria's ports.

In retrospect the invasion of Algeria was an event of enormous international significance. This was the first Arab country to be annexed by the West, and June 1830 set the pattern for the way in which the Arab world was to be carved up by Britain and France over the next hundred years. But at the time it was not part of a grand design for systematic imperial expansion.

French policy itself was muddled and confused. Even though the military had forecast an easy victory there were no plans in place about what to do next and over the following few years military men and politicians would argue endlessly over the best course of action: withdrawal, limited control of the major coastal towns or full-blown occupation.

The immediate pretext for the invasion was revenge for an incident in 1827 when the Dey of Algiers, Khodja Hussein, angry at the French refusal to repay loans from the Napoleonic wars, attacked the French consul with a fly whisk, shouting: 'You are a wicked, faithless, idol-worshipping rascal.' The French newspapers were enraged. National honour, the *Gazette de France* told its readers, had to be avenged; Algiers, routinely described as a 'nest of pirates', had to be taught a lesson. Egged on by the press, the French began a naval blockade of the Algerian coast, but for all the talk of prestige their real motivations were political, economic, religious and cultural. Politically, the Algerian adventure was a cynical attempt to divert attention away from King Charles X's weak and unpopular regime. Economically, French traders wanted to expand outwards from the trading posts they had already established on the Algerian coast at La Calle and Bône. For them Algeria was an alluring prize. As well as being a country of enormous untapped economic potential it was viewed as a place of fabulous wealth, an image that was fuelled by the legend of the casbah treasure, the gold that had been plundered over the previous three centuries by the pirates operating out of Algiers.

In religious terms, the Mediterranean was still seen as a zone of confrontation between Christians and Muslims, a mental image that was reinforced under the restored Bourbon monarchy by a wave of nostalgia for the Crusades. In the writings of Joseph-François Michaud, whose *Histoire des Croisades* was published in the last years of the Napoleonic Empire and became immensely popular, the Crusades were held up not only as a model of true religious devotion, but also as the first expression of France's national grandeur, and hence the invasion of Algeria was trumpeted as a victory over Islam.[1] In fact when Charles X formally announced the invasion to the National Assembly on 2 March 1830, he justified the enterprise explicitly on religious grounds.[2] For him, he solemnly told the seated deputies, French intervention was about the spread of Christianity:

> In the midst of the grave events that have preoccupied Europe, I was obliged to suspend the effect of my just resentment against a Barbary power; but I can no longer allow to go unpunished the grave insult to my flag; the resounding redress that I hope to obtain in satisfying the honour of France will with the Almighty's help turn to the profit of Christendom.[3]

Finally, there was the cultural dimension. Dynamic, modern and vibrant, France conceived of itself as a coherent nation state with a superior culture. In contrast the Ottoman regime was looked down upon as a failed state. Although it had been a threat during the sixteenth century, when Algiers sponsored the corsairs that regularly attacked European shipping in the Mediterranean, by the beginning of the nineteenth century the country had become, in French eyes, terminally unstable. The Ottoman sultan in Istanbul was clearly too weak and too distant to offer protection, the regime was no longer able to contain the regular uprisings of autonomous tribal groups, the economy was increasingly falling under the domination of European financiers and the regency itself was riven with infighting. Little wonder that Algeria was seen as an inviting target for colonization.

For all Charles X's talk of religious and military glory the Algerian adventure failed to prevent the demise of the Bourbon monarchy, which was overthrown only a month later in the July Revolution, and still less did it lead to an easy victory. Just because the native population welcomed the overthrow of the Ottomans it did not mean that they wanted to be ruled by the French, and by 1832 France was bogged down in a bloody war of occupation. Not until 1847 did Algerian resistance begin to be overcome, whereupon the country set its feet on the road that eventually led to its assimilation as an integral part of France, in theory no different from Normandy or Brittany. It was a fateful step because, as subsequent settlers never tired of telling their mainland compatriots, this meant that Algeria was an older part of France than Savoy, which was only received from Italy in 1859. Henceforth generations of French schoolchildren would be told that France was divided by the Mediterranean like Paris divided by the Seine. The end result was the most extreme form of colonization: by having the land and culture of its native population taken away Algeria was to be made French. It was a brutal process which ultimately led to the counter-violence of the war of liberation between 1954 and 1962 and which has continued to frame Algerian politics ever since.

■ ■ ■

These are the basic historical facts about the 1830 invasion. However, what is significant here is not the finer detail of the French landing but its mythic potential; the way in which over time, and by accretion, this event has been transformed into the starting point for multiple, differing, and often utterly opposed interpretations of Algerian history. It has become a totem for an array of national and religious narratives, each of which tells a very different story about the significance of 1830 in terms of the origins and meaning of Algerian history. What animates these narratives is disagreement not only about what happened in the past, but also about what is happening in the present and what will happen in the future. Past, present and future are seen as one and have played a key role in justifying all kinds of violence. Thus, the past in Algerian history has been invoked to legitimize not just the appropriation of land by colonialism, but also the war of national liberation as well as Islamist and anti-Islamist violence.

In the case of the French colonial narrative, 1830 was the starting point of history. Before colonization Algeria had been an empty space devoid of civilization. Through an industrious and pioneering spirit the French settlers transformed this arid landscape: by draining plains, establishing vineyards and introducing new agricultural techniques, they made the desert bloom. It was a potent mythology, one akin to that of the settlers in nineteenth-century Australia or early Zionists in post-1948 Israel, and a continuous contrast was made between the lazy, unproductive natives on the one side and the resourceful settlers on the other. The fact that the settlers had tamed such a harsh environment showed why they, and not the local population, had a right to own the land.[4]

There is no better vantage point for understanding the assumptions that underpinned colonialism than Eugène Delacroix's 1834 painting *Women of Algiers*, which now hangs in the Louvre. The painting resulted from an expedition which Delacroix made to Algeria and Morocco in 1832 at the behest of the Comte de Mornay, who wanted him to act as the artist accompanying his diplomatic mission to the Sultan of Morocco, with whom France was seeking an alliance.[5] Delacroix was overwhelmed by the aesthetics of the landscape, above all how the light differed from that of the North, and during the course of the whole trip he filled seven notebooks with hundreds of drawings and sketches.[6]

The painting itself was of three French models dressed in North African costumes, based upon poses of Muslim women that Delacroix had sketched in Algiers, and it would be no exaggeration to say that this image has assumed an iconic status in terms of France's vision not just of Algeria, but of the whole of North Africa. Delacroix's aesthetic preoccupations are obvious – this is a seductive image dominated by the effect of colour and light – and so too are his cultural assumptions. In portraying the Algerian women as submissive, sensual and inviting, he is implicitly saying that the country is a place of fertile riches and therefore ripe for colonization.[7]

At the end of the nineteenth century this mythology was reformulated and the settlers came to see themselves as the inheritors of the Roman Empire, taking up the Latin achievement which had fallen under abeyance with the Arabs.[8] Writers such as Emile Gautier conjured up the image of the Roman Empire as a stable and prosperous civilization, *pax romana*, which was violently overturned by the Arab invasion of the seventh century.[9] This narrative simplified the complexities of North African history; the Vandal invasion was ignored, as was the re-conquest by the Byzantine Empire, in order to leave an overriding image of the Arab invasion as the North African equivalent of the ravages of Genghis Khan. For Gautier the Arab conquest was a disaster of apocalyptic proportions because it led to the triumph of a lower form of civilization in which nomads predominated over settled peoples, pastoral over agricultural, the tent over the house, the tribe over the family. From then on North Africa was shrouded in darkness, awaiting the return of Latin civilization in the guise of French colonialism. Seen through this lens, 1830 was an act of liberation, through which France was bestowing the benefits of good rule, medicine and science on the southern shores of the Mediterranean.

In contrast, the National Liberation Front (FLN), which led the war against the French between 1954 and 1962, saw 1830 as the starting point of the national liberation struggle.[10] From the beginning, FLN doctrine claimed, the native population opposed the colonial occupation, inaugurating a long fight for independence which finally ended 132 years later. Through victory the FLN allowed Algerians to recover an uncomplicated Arab-Islamic identity. By fusing the FLN and the people into one, this narrative reduced complex history to a narrative of heroes and villains. It was an extremely simple story of heroic resistance led by the FLN; those who collaborated with the French were traitors to their religion and nationality, while the contribution of rival political organizations was ignored. Algerian resistance was conjured up as a single political force, at once historically continuous, socially cohesive and ideologically consistent, which began in 1830 and continued until the decisive leadership of the FLN brought victory in July 1962. Significantly too, this official memory became highly militarized after the coup of 19 June 1965 which overthrew Ahmed Ben Bella and brought Colonel Houari Boumediène to power. As Boumediène never tired of telling his officers, the army had not just cast off colonialism, it had humiliated a NATO power, the fourth most important military force in the world, and become an example to the rest of the Arab world. The army was now seen to incarnate the war of liberation: embodying the nation's most sacred values and rooted in the struggle of the people, it was the spine of the revolution, and the key dates in the war became the basis of an official calendar, a cycle of military commemorations that regularly reminded the population who held power and why.

This official memory was highly anonymous. Indeed, it became a standard joke that the only veterans who were publicly mentioned were those who had been killed during the war, as individuals were airbrushed out in the name of a faceless populism. According to the official FLN slogan, inscribed on every government building, the war had been fought 'by the people and for the people' and the end result was a paradox in the sense that the past was everywhere, while history as a critical discipline was absent. Reverence replaced understanding as this single narrative – militarized, anonymous, populist and divorced from any precise context – was religiously transmitted to the new post-colonial generation.

Despite its selective memory and calculated deceits, the official view had an enormous hold until the 1980s, largely because it dovetailed with the experience of the ordinary populace. Algerians were only too aware of how colonialism had been based on racism and exclusion and for this reason the FLN enjoyed an enormous amount of popular legitimacy. Even so the official monopoly of history was challenged from two significant directions.

The first of these was the Islamist challenge, which can be traced through the extraordinary career of Sheikh Abdelatif Soltani. Born in 1902, Soltani was formed by the Association of Algerian Ulema, a movement of religious clerics that was established in 1931 in Constantine in the eastern part of the country. Quietly spoken and plainly dressed, Soltani was instrumental in developing close links with the Muslim Brotherhood in Egypt, which had been founded by Hassan al-Banna in 1928 and was dedicated to the reconstruction of Islamic society on the basis of the texts and traditions dated back to the time of the Prophet Mohammed.[11]

Although suspicious of the political leadership, Soltani felt that the FLN had to be supported in order to Islamicize society from within. However, given the tactical nature of this alliance, it is not surprising that once independence had been achieved in July 1962 he quickly fell out with the FLN regime which he saw as too socialist, too secularist and too Western.

Soltani was angered by the notion that Algeria might have won the war militarily but lost it culturally and this led him to found, along with Abassi Madani and Ahmed Sahnoun, the association al-Qiyam ('Values') in 1963.[12] He was especially incensed by what he saw as the lax morality of the post-independence regime. The continued sale of cigarettes and alcohol, as well as the prominent presence of women on the military parades of 1 November 1965, dressed, in Soltani's opinion, in a scandalous fashion, were symbolic of the continued dominance of Western values and showed just how far Algeria was under attack from the inside. In calling for a reassertion of true Islamic values Soltani reminded Muslims that a true jihad had an internal as well as an external dimension. Soltani emphasized that the war of liberation was not just about the physical expulsion of the French but also the cleansing from Western practices, notably alcohol, smoking and co-education. This interpretation of the true meaning of the war of liberation would be at the core of the Islamist movement throughout the 1980s and early 1990s.

The second challenge to the official interpretation of history came from the Berber movement, whose emergence encapsulates the most controversial issue in Algerian politics and history: what is the ethnic composition of the Algerian population and where do they come from? The original inhabitants in North Africa emerged from two independent Stone Age cultures, the Neolithic Caspian and the Caucasoid Proto-Hamites, which arrived from Egypt and western Asia respectively between 10,000 and 5000 BC. Thus, it was their descendants whom the Phoenicians encountered when they established a series of trading settlements along the coast in 1100 BC. Collectively, Greek sources referred to them as *barbaroi*, a name used for any people who did not speak Greek, which in turn was taken up by the Romans and the Arabs. This is the origin of the term Berber, although Berber activists prefer to talk about *Imazighen*, meaning 'free men', a term derived from their own language, Tamazight. Today the legacy of Berber culture is self-evident throughout Algeria with the Kabyles in Kabylia, the Shawiya in the Aurès region, the Mozabites around Ghardaïa and the Tuaregs in the Saharan Hoggar region, in total about 20 per cent of the population, all speaking a variant of the Berber language. Significantly, their existence challenges the official post-independence conception of Algeria whereby the government, determined to counteract the years of colonialism, asserted that the native population was culturally, linguistically and ethnically Arab; a monolithic understanding of the nation that, by ignoring the Berber issue, placed Algeria at the centre of the Arab world.

Demands for the recognition of Berber rights provoked the train of events which led to the 'Berber spring', one of the most significant events in post-independence Algeria. The spark was the banning of a public meeting on 19 March 1980 with Mouloud Mammeri, professor of anthropology and champion of Berber culture, in Tizi-Ouzou, the capital of Kabylia. Such censorship provoked protests which erupted into a general strike across the region, during which the protestors drew an explicit parallel with the 'Prague spring' to underline their struggle for self-expression and human rights.[13]

As such the 'Berber spring' challenged the fundamental tenets of all the post-1962 regimes. By denouncing the FLN definition of the Algerian people as far too narrow, it was characterizing the notion of an Arab-Islamic identity as an imposition. This authoritarian approach to history, Berber activists continued, reflected the state's anti-democratic and anti-pluralist character. The Berber spring also looked at the war of liberation from a new angle. By underlining the manner in which the resistance fighters in Kabylia had borne the brunt of the French violence between 1954 and 1962, Berber activists were claiming that the internal resistance had been betrayed by the army of the frontiers which had just sat tight in Morocco and Tunisia until independence.[14]

Although the Berber spring was essentially a Kabyle affair, the Berber issue raised the question of where Algerians came from and this issue, perhaps more than anything else, reveals why the Algerian past is a battleground. In the nineteenth century French ethnographers tried to argue that the Berbers were descended from Indo-Europeans in order to differentiate them from the Arabs.[15] The likes of Gautier took the view that the Berbers of the mountains were much closer in mentality to, say, the French peasantry in the Auvergne. It was a classic divide-and-rule policy that, like the one followed by the Belgians in Rwanda which distinguished the Hutus from the Tutsis, has left a poisonous legacy. For the Algerian regime such distinctions were anathema. Anybody who subscribed to them was an agent of French neo-colonialism who was trying to weaken the Algerian nation from the inside. Such vitriol became a reflex action for the regime and was encapsulated in the infamous Arabic slogan *hizb fransa* ('the party of France'). On these grounds the Berber movement was stigmatized as inauthentic and foreign, and derided as a conduit for French ideas of secularism, feminism, liberalism and socialism which were corroding the country's Islamic identity, an accusation also taken up by the Islamists.

Although Islamists and Berberists come from opposite ends of the political spectrum their understanding of history is united by the common theme of confiscation at independence. Both agree that in 1962 Algerians were duped by a corrupt minority only interested in power and personal aggrandizement. Both agree that the FLN was a fissiparous phenomenon, containing competing tendencies and groups. Both agree too that the FLN was profoundly changed by the war, the noble intentions of November 1954 sullied by the grubby reality of post-independence politics. This attitude took hold at a popular level during the 1980s, when ordinary Algerians lamented that 'the FLN of the war was not the FLN of independence'.

The colonial narrative, the official narrative, the Soltani narrative and the Berber narrative: these four examples demonstrate just how far interpretations of Algerian history are hopelessly entangled with politics and ideology.[16] History is inextricably bound up with contemporary politics and for this reason it has been open to abuse, misuse and fabrication. In each narrative, historical truth has been skewed by the ideological concerns of the present where, to put it crudely, good history is that history which is good for 'our country', 'our political party', or 'our religious movement'. Yet it is too simplistic to dismiss these narratives as a tissue of lies. They are a compound of truth and fiction where each narrative takes the basic facts before pulling them in different directions. Moreover, these narratives have been able to mobilize people because they do connect with their experience. They play on key aspects of the culture, above all the Islamic references which are the cornerstone of Algerian life, as a way of legitimizing themselves, giving the impression that they are the natural outcome of long historical narratives stretching back hundreds or even thousands of years.

The French philosopher Ernest Renan, in a lecture given in 1882, famously argued: 'forgetting, even getting history wrong, is an essential factor in the formation of the nation, which is why the progress of historical studies is often a danger to nationality'. Nowhere has this adage been more true than in post-independence Algeria.[17] The function of history for the regime was neither truth nor scholarship. The population was discouraged from a critical historical consciousness because history had just one usage: to construct a heroic narrative that legitimized the post-independence regime and built a clear national identity.

This meant that historical scholarship was tightly controlled. Mohammed Harbi, an FLN veteran who was imprisoned by Boumediène after the June 1965 coup, had his historical research explicitly censored.[18] As an academic working in exile at a Paris university he set out to give Algerians back their history through the publication of a series of books and key documents. In doing so he argued that all the talk of liberation was a mirage; in reality the war against the French had allowed the army to take power. In reply, the Algerian government vilified him as a lackey of colonialism: after all, by publishing in France, was he not just handing over ammunition to the enemy?

Abdelmalek Sayad collaborated with the French sociologist Pierre Bourdieu to produce an ethnographical study of the Kabyle region in the early 1960s.[19] He has also done extensive work on Algerian immigration in France. In a series of interviews he has talked about the tension between history, origins and national myths. Moments of dramatic crisis, such as the one Algeria is undergoing at the moment, reveal, he argues, the greatest need for rigorous historical research. He explicitly equates the miserable state of the historical profession in Algeria with the social deprivation of the population. What, he asks, does it say about a country that it is not mature enough to face up to the complexities of the past and break free of mythologies, not just of the colonial but also of the pre-colonial period? Sayad underlines the narrow constraints of the FLN narrative, which was fundamentally a response to the colonial narrative, a counter-narrative that fed off the myths of colonialism and was nurtured by it. Characterized by a strong sense of hagiography, this counter-narrative became disorientated when it lost the colonial enemy in 1962. Consequently the post-colonial state had to continually conjure up the spectre of neo-colonialism in the guise of the *hizb fransa* ('the party of France'). Paradoxically, too, this counter-narrative was a mirror image of French nationalism. Like French nationalism it set out to fashion a strong attachment to the idea of the Algerian republic through a series of rituals and commemorations which put the nation beyond any historical analysis.

For all these reasons Sayad makes an impassioned plea for a re-examination of this nationalism in a critical light. It has to be understood as the product of a particular context; otherwise Algerians will have no real idea of their historical origins. Moreover, research must break out of the colonial and FLN chronologies whereby 1830 is the starting point for history. The complexities of the pre-1830 period are vital to understanding of contemporary Algeria and in this respect, Sayad continues, discussion of the period before Islam must not mean that one is immediately accused of being a neo-colonialist reverting to colonial ideas of Latin Algeria. Like Tunisia with Carthage and Egypt with the pharaohs, Algeria must integrate this past into the national history.

Taking Sayad's comments as a starting point, the first chapter of this book will provide an overview of the pre-colonial period. By highlighting grand sweeps we want to stress a particular set of connections between the past and present. On one level this might seem obvious, but since so much of Algeria's history has been shrouded in taboo it is critically important. Although broad in comparison with the detail of the subsequent chapters, this is not an exotic backdrop before we get to the main section of the book. By showing how history, even history going back ten thousand years, is still determining events in contemporary Algeria, this next chapter frames the rest of our study in a fundamental way.

CHAPTER ONE

Dissident Landscape

BEFORE THE SIXTEENTH century Algeria did not exist. Successive invasions – Phoenician, Roman, Vandal and Arab – had each left their cultural and genetic imprint, but what brought the country into being as a separate state was three centuries of Ottoman rule. Beginning in 1529, the Ottoman Regency knitted the North Africa region into a unified territorial identity, laying the foundation for an enduring entity which the French and the post-1962 Algerian state took over.

The event which led to the establishment of Ottoman power was the fallout from the overthrow of the last outpost of Islamic Spain in Granada in 1492. Exhilarated with victory, symbolized by the expulsion of Jews and Muslims, the newly united Spanish kingdom now took the Reconquest across the Mediterranean and launched naval attacks on North Africa. Fearful of further defeats, Muslims petitioned the Ottoman Turks for support, specifically calling on the Barbarossa brothers, Aruj and Khair ed-Din based on the island of Jerba off the coast of Tunisia, to come to their aid. This made North Africa the front line between Catholic Spain and the Ottoman Empire and the Barbarossa brothers established a chain of strong points along the coast to halt Spanish expansion. However, once the Spanish onslaught had been repelled the way was open for Ottoman domination and the Barbarossa brothers used these bases to take Algiers in 1529 before expelling the local rulers, the Hafsids, from Tunis and Kairouan.

Thus began Ottoman rule which, although initially confined to the city-state of Algiers, progressively established its own administrative, tax-collecting and judicial authority throughout Algeria. The regime's legitimacy was derived from its struggle against Christendom, its warrior origins and the prestige of the Ottoman power as the great theocratic empire of Islam. In administrative terms Algiers was at the apex of the system, whilst the rest of the country was divided into three regions: Constantine, Mascara and Titteri. Crucially, although the Ottomans made alliances with local elites, their very foreignness, as an elite perpetually recruited from abroad, enabled them to cement the

Regency's unity by keeping power for themselves as a group rather than as individuals. As a result the three administrative regions were never allowed to break off and establish their own provincial states.

Under the Regency Algiers rose to become the most important centre of Ottoman power in the western Mediterranean, its power radiating over the whole of the North African coast. Tlemcen was taken in 1551, Bougie in 1555, whilst the 1580 treaty between the Ottoman sultan and Philip II of Spain transformed Morocco into a buffer state. In this way the geographical dimensions of Algeria took on a precise shape which the local population gradually began to identify with, even if they continued to define themselves in religious rather than national terms.

Prior to this point 'Algeria' must be talked about in inverted commas. It was simply central North Africa, traversed by the east–west route along the high plains and by coastal traffic along the sea. As a result, the Phoenician-Carthaginian occupation spread by sea along the coast from east to west, and the Roman occupation by land, again from east to west. The Arab invasion in the seventh century did likewise, whilst the two great mediaeval Muslim Berber dynasties – the Almoravids and Almohads – advanced from west to east. By the end of the Middle Ages 'Algeria' was in consequence a large and unstable area where the small family, the village and the tribe were the basic units of society. Sandwiched between Tunisia and Morocco, where the impetus to state formation had begun in the eighth and eleventh centuries respectively, 'Algeria' did not have any major centres of power to rival Kairouan in the east or Fez or Marrakesh in the west. Algiers was a minor port, and only accidentally the bridgehead for the Ottoman conquest.

For this reason, before the sixteenth century 'Algeria' was bound up with the broader patterns of North African history, interacting with the Mediterranean, Europe and the Middle East as part of a wider region. Yet, in the colonial and post-colonial periods opposing groups have looked back to this long pre-Ottoman past in the search for pure and authentic Algerian origins. They have seized upon specific episodes and figures to create a collective national identity. They have distilled history in order to manufacture unbroken chains of meaning that link past, present and future. What values, therefore, have been inscribed on the past and how has it been exploited for ideological and political purposes?[1]

In the first instance there is the landscape, which in Algeria is made up of the sea, the intermittent coastal plains, the Tell Atlas and Saharan Atlas mountain ranges, the high plains to the south and the inhospitable desert where summer temperatures can soar to 55°C. Given that there has never been a large-scale fishing industry along the North African coast, Algiers did not emerge as a major port until the sixteenth and seventeenth centuries, when it became a base for the Muslim corsairs to prey upon European shipping and shorelines. Similarly, the intermittent coastal plain was historically a zone of marshland, flooding and deadly malaria, with the result that the population was traditionally concentrated in the healthy uplands.

In contrast, the huge Tell Atlas Mountains, with some peaks rising to over 2,000 feet, have always been self-sufficient for the essentials in life. The climate of the northern Tell Atlas is Mediterranean, with high rainfall meaning that the land can be used to sustain not just sheep and goats, but also olives, wheat and dates. Grass and trees grow thickly and the mountains have been likened to island republics flanked by the sea and the plains on one side and the desert on the other.[2] There are few rivers that can be used for irrigation, so it is the volume and timing of rainfall that determine settlement patterns. Nearer to the sea the mountains soften with a string of smaller summits.

Statements about 'national character' are little use to the historian. It is nonetheless true that the landscape moulds life, fashioning social practices and traditions which become deeply embedded within society. In Algeria's case the physical separation of the plain and the mountains has been transformed into a cultural and political one. The plain was marked out by the flow of armies and trading as it interacted with the broader Mediterranean world. Looking out to the sea, the people of the coast developed a whole set of ingrained prejudices about the mountains. They were seen as sinister and foreboding, to be avoided at all costs. In contrast, the people of the mountains conceived of their landscape as a refuge from authority. The mountains functioned as natural obstacles where the power of the plain stopped abruptly and the end result was a Berber society that was fiercely independent. The Arabs made a fundamental divide between *Bled el Makhzen*, 'the lands of the government', and *Bled es Siba*, 'the lands of dissidence', and each colonizing power in turn found it difficult to subdue the mountain populations.

Greek accounts distinguished these mountain inhabitants as a turbulent, fair-skinned people who spoke a remote Libyc language. Under Masinissa, the Numidian king whose Berber realm covered what is essentially modern Algeria, tribes and villages were linked to his central power through the payment of a regular tribute. Modelling himself on Alexander the Great during a sixty-year reign that lasted until his death in 148 BC, Masinissa aimed to establish an Hellenic-style state, thereby demonstrating that Berber culture was not a static entity, but one transformed through its interaction with the wider Mediterranean world. Below the level of the monarchical elite the Berbers continued to be a disparate people. Defined by clans, lineages, tribes and families, they placed great emphasis on self-reliance as a response to insecurity and weak government and in the long term this impeded the establishment of a state with a sophisticated administrative structure. Faced with outside authority these tribes jealously guarded their own territory, living by their own customary law whereby the village came together to decide important matters through the village councils.[3] Naturally egalitarian, in so far as they recognized the equality of the male heads of the various families, these councils covered all aspects of life, but in particular the resolution of feuds.

Of course there is nothing specifically Berber about this. It is a pattern of autonomy that is deeply embedded within the mountains that encircle the Mediterranean, as Noel Malcolm has shown with regard to Kosovo.[4] Together, however, these traditions instilled a strong sense of place. This was a mountain culture where the knowledge of the landscape – its hiding places and natural fortresses – was passed down from generation to generation and used against the Romans, the Arabs, the Ottomans, the French and the post-independence state. It is the world of the outlaw and the rebel. It is the world of defiant tribes who embraced dissident forms of both Christianity and Islam. It is the world of the *maquis*, the armed resistance known as the 'lions of the mountains', fighting in the face of overwhelming odds against the French army. It is very much a man's world, where by tradition great stress has been placed upon honour and respect for arms.

This defiance explains the long and determined resistance to the Phoenician-Carthaginian occupation between 1100 and 146 BC. It also explains the opposition to Roman rule symbolized by the legend of Jugurtha, Numidian king and grandson of Masinissa, whose battle with Rome was immortalized by the Roman historian Sallust.[5] In his account, written some sixty years after the events he described, Sallust painted Jugurtha as a Herculean figure famed for his prowess on the battlefield, the idol of his soldiers and the terror of the enemy. Jugurtha had no desire to be dominated by Rome and in 112 BC he executed some Romans, possibly traders, living at Cirta (modern Constantine). Furious, the Senate orded revenge, but Jugurtha fiercely resisted the ensuing invasion. Confronted with a lightly equipped and elusive foe, the Roman legionaries, weighed down with heavy equipment and suffering from the heat, found it hard to land a decisive victory and the campaign dragged on for some seven years until Jugurtha was taken captive and brought in chains to Rome.

Jugurtha died a prisoner in 104 BC but his memory endured down the ages and underwent a revival during the 1940s and 1950s as the nationalist movement appropriated him as an inspirational figure for the anti-colonial struggle. Mohammed Sahli's 1947 study, *Le Message de Yougourtha*, was crucial in establishing a modern cult, whereby Jugurtha became a reference point for a new generation of militant anti-colonialists like the writer Kateb Yacine. In his 1956 novel *Nedjma* Kateb invoked Jugurtha as one of the ancestors of the Algerian nation, incarnating the spirit of resistance at the heart of Algerian history;[6] likewise, the National Charter of 1976 traced the origins of the modern nation back to the Numidian king. However, the truth is that Jugurtha's afterlife as national icon challenges any singular narrative of Algerian history. After all, as a pagan Berber, his identity is at odds with the official Arab-Islamic definition of the nation that prevailed in post-independence Algeria.

Roman colonization really took off in 46 BC after Julius Caesar won the battle of Thapsus (in modern Tunisia) against his rival Pompeius. For the next two centuries North Africa became one of the most stable provinces in the Empire – Rome's breadbasket, supplying two-thirds of the grain requirement. Roman rule led to the creation of two separate societies: Romanized Africans, who were wealthy and limited to the towns and coasts, and the native population who were poor and rural. No attempt was made to bring the mountains under Roman control and the alienation of the Berber population was a key factor in the eventual disintegration of imperial power.

By the time of the Emperor Constantine's conversion in AD 312, Christianity already had deep roots in North Africa, and a generation later it produced one of the major figures of late antiquity: St Augustine. Born in Thagaste, modern-day Souk Ahras on the border between Algeria and Tunisia, in AD 354, into a down-at-heel but nevertheless well-respected Roman family, St Augustine's early life was notoriously dissolute – he was a regular frequenter of brothels during his student days at Carthage – before his midlife conversion to Christianity. From then on he became a tireless champion of the Church, as he set out to reconcile the philosophies of Ancient Greece and Rome with the precepts of the Christian faith, a spiritual journey that produced two literary and religious masterpieces – *Confessions*, the world's first autobiography, and *City of God*, in which he outlined the argument that humanity lives in one of two cities: the city of God, symbolized by Jerusalem, or the earthly city, symbolized by Babylon.

Son of a Berber mother, the deeply committed Monica who was pivotal in bringing her son round to the Christian faith, St Augustine encapsulates the controversy over the place of Christianity in Algerian history. Under French rule Cardinal Lavigerie, the archbishop of Algiers from 1867 until 1892, tried to use the memory of St Augustine to reclaim Algeria as a Christian land and made attempts to convert the Berber population. Conversely, André Mandouze, a member of the French Resistance during the Nazi occupation, who supported the Algerian war of liberation and was briefly the rector of Algiers University, has invoked St Augustine in a very different way.[7] As a leading expert on St Augustine, he has argued, like Sayad, that Algerian history must not be trapped by either the nationalist or colonial narratives.[8] The figure of St Augustine, Mandouze feels, points to the deep roots of Christianity in Algeria and lays the basis for a multi-cultural and multi-faith society. Elsewhere, Kateb Yacine and the contemporary Algerian writer Assia Djebar have also looked to St Augustine as one of the founders of the Algerian nation, whilst in 2001 a major international conference in Algiers set out to officially recognize the saint as a key figure in Algerian history.[9] President Bouteflika himself chose to address the conference, making a symbolic statement about the place of Christianity as part of the fabric of Algerian culture. Whilst studiously ignoring St Augustine's Berber origins, he sought to lay claim to the saint as an Algerian who belongs as much to Islam as he does to Christianity.

Of course, to present St Augustine as one of the fathers of the modern nation is an anachronism, since in his time the country did not even exist. Nonetheless he referred to himself as an African and, more importantly, he had a close affinity with the mountains that have marked so much of Algerian culture. The nearby Medjerba range separated him off from the sea, whilst the Aurès chain to the south sealed him off from the Sahara desert. These mountains formed the backdrop to his mental landscape; they were symbolic of God's constant presence in the world or of the skyward reach in Saint John's Gospel.

St Augustine died at the age of seventy-six in AD 430, his life spanning the decline and fall of the Empire as Roman rule in North Africa was overwhelmed by the Vandal invasion. The Vandals in turn were pushed out by the resurgent eastern half of the Roman Empire – its capital Byzantium – which successfully invaded in AD 533. Yet, despite the Byzantines' attempt to construct a massive chain of fortresses, the Berbers were just too strong to be quelled. Soon North Africa was too remote from Byzantium to be of prime concern and in 646 the prefect Gregory declared the province independent.

One year later, however, Gregory was defeated and killed as the first wave of Arab invaders arrived from the east. This began the most far-reaching episode of the pre-Ottoman period: the arrival of Islam, which in 647 was less than fifty years old.

■ ■ ■

This expedition, part of the astonishing expansion of Islam in the century after the Prophet Mohammed's death in 632, probably did not have any real religious influence on the local population. The Arab leader Oqba Ibn Nafi left no garrison forces and was himself killed near Biskra in modern Algeria. Some Berbers did enlist in the Arab armies, but there was also enormous resistance during the rest of the seventh century, led by the Jewish queen Dihya Kahina who united Christians, pagans and Jews. Symbolizing the valour of the peoples of the Aurès Mountains, she was a dramatic figure, much like Boudicca in British history, whose flowing hair, warrior instincts and magical powers – she supposedly had the gift of second sight – made her a natural leader. After her eventual defeat and killing, her Berber tribes were obliged to become Muslim and hand over twelve thousand horsemen, led by Kahina's two sons, who allied themselves with the Arabs in the ongoing holy war.

For this reason the Kahina story, as told down the centuries, assumed a prophetic status. By concluding with her sons' conversion, it came to symbolize the inevitable triumph of Islam, thereby demonstrating the key to the Arabs' final success: the universal doctrine of Islam as a religion. Whereas during the classical period the Berbers had, for the most part, been seen as permanently beyond the pale of civilization, now, in theory at least, they were able to become part of God's community as equals. This, as Michael Brett and Elizabeth Fentress have rightly emphasized, was nothing short of a revolution.[10] Seen as Muslims, the Berbers were identified as a people for the first time and elevated into a branch of the human race descended from Noah and his sons.

The Kahina legend encapsulates the historical controversy surrounding the arrival of the Arabs: was it a conquest or a new religious dawn based on an egalitarian credo that all Muslims are brothers and sisters who form one single religious entity? Although it took a century for the Arabs to quell the Berbers, once they had succeeded the subsequent process of Islamicization was more thorough than anything the Romans achieved.

The post-independence state saw the arrival of Islam as *the* crucial event in the formation of an Arab-Islamic identity which is the spine of modern Algeria. Anything that predated Islam was dismissed as pagan ignorance, while the Roman period was a form of colonial oppression which merely anticipated the savagery of French rule. In contrast, the Berber historian Samy Hadad argues that the numbers of Arabs in the seventh century were relatively small, and that Algerians have been deliberately alienated from their true ethnic roots for political reasons.[11] In his eyes Algerians are for the most part not Arabs but Arabized Berbers, and it is vital to recognize the Berber component of the Algerian nation.

Crucially too, official history has skated over the fact that Islamicization and Arabization were not immediate. It was a process, and for all the talk of Islamic equality tensions between Berber converts and the Arabs were present right from the start. Some Berbers were resentful at Arab domination, and felt that the Arabs looked down upon them as unable to rule. For this reason many Berbers embraced Kharijism, the first dissenting sect in Islam, which sprung up in the Arabian peninsula in the seventh century. Supporters of Kharijism were hostile to central government. They also believed that sincere faith, not race, should be the only criterion for religious leadership and this egalitarianism appealed to the Berber mindset; a way of accepting Islam but rejecting Arab rule.[12]

If dissent was one way in which Islam and Arab culture were becoming rooted within North African society, the other was to be the invasion by the Banu Hillal, a nomadic tribe of Syrian origin, in 1051. Theirs was the classic pattern of Arab politics and warfare: nomadic tribes united around a specific military objective and the local population were no match for this concerted onslaught. As the Banu Hillal swept westwards, they destroyed all in their path; devastating the agricultural lands with their goats and their flocks until they eventually ran out of steam when they reached the southern oases. In the meantime each chieftain registered lordship over the passing villages by leaving a headdress as a sign of possession.

As for so many interpretations of the Algerian past it is impossible to separate politics and history. Within Arab oral accounts the Banu Hillal story became the stuff of legend. Their journey to the west and conquest of North Africa assumed the status of an epic narrative which was recited down the ages in a mixture of poetry and rhyming prose.[13] In contrast the mediaeval Arab historian Ibn Khaldoun compared them to a plague of locusts and considered their impact on North African society to be a disaster.[14] Similarly, nineteenth-century French historians deliberately conflated the Banu Hillal with the arrival of Islam and the end of civilization. Yet, despite these different points of view there is no doubt about the long-term significance of the Banu Hillal for North Africa. In their aftermath there was a dramatic shrinkage in power of the cities, which were reduced to a few isolated centres dotted along the coast. The countryside meanwhile fell under the control of nomads, as the infrastructure of roads and cities which had helped to keep the region unified since Roman times fell apart. Finally, in linguistic terms Hillalian Arabic now became the predominant language on the plains.

The turmoil caused by the arrival of the Banu Hillal, combined with shifting power struggles in Muslim Spain, created a power vacuum that led to the emergence of the two great Berber dynasties of the Middle Ages – the Almoravids and the Almohads – which together lasted from 1054 to 1212. Both came from the south and both were motivated by religion, aiming to purify Islam of the decadent ways that were, in their eyes, being promoted by the wealthy Andalusian Muslims of Spain. The impetus for the movement came from local leaders who, having made the pilgrimage to Mecca, returned with a desire to end the widespread abuse of orthodox practices. In particular, they denounced the drinking of palm wine, playing licentious music and the taking of more than four wives. It was a simple, rigorous and puritanical form of Sunni orthodoxy that soon gained a considerable following. Together the two dynasties lasted a century and a half, creating an empire that at one point stretched right across the Maghreb to Libya, south to Senegal and Ghana and north into Spain.[15] The memory of these mediaeval empires is very significant in contemporary North Africa, and since the late 1950s Moroccan nationalists have used them to lay claim to areas in Mauritania and Algeria.

Three further factors should be stressed. First, the religious zeal of the Almoravids and the Almohads intensified the spirit of confrontation between Islam and Christendom. The awareness that Christendom was under attack in Spain was one of the reasons behind the launch of the Crusades in 1095 by Pope Urban II at a great council meeting of clergy and nobles at Clermont in France. Consequently, although the Crusades in the Middle East ultimately ended in ignominious failure, in Spain the part played by Christian knights, most importantly the Knights Templar and the Order of Santiago, was crucial in changing the balance of power, and by the end of the thirteenth century only the kingdom of Granada remained in Muslim hands. Secondly, the Almoravids and the Almohads completed the Islamicization of North Africa. The fact that these nomadic movements were Berber-led took the Muslim religion far beyond the pale of early Islamic civilization in North Africa. By now, Islamic rule extended far to the south of the line of Roman rule. Thirdly, the Almoravids and Almohads left a significant mark on a pattern of Islamic politics, by rousing ordinary Muslims to challenge their masters who were denounced as having turned away from the purity of the Islamic faith. In this approach there must be no compromise, and for the contemporary Moroccan political writer Fatima Mernissi the tradition of revolt against unbelief and despotism has been an enduring model of Islamic politics.[16]

The cumulative impact of the Almoravids and the Almohads underlines how, in religious and cultural terms, the arrival of the Arabs was a revolution. Although it is probably right to talk about an Arab invasion, it is striking how quickly Islam put down such deep roots. Indeed, the more or less total

Islamicization of the populace took just over two hundred years. In part, this was because Byzantium was discredited, but more than anything it was because the local population's tribal and family structures were similar to those of the Arabian peninsula, which made for a natural affinity between the Arab and Berber way of life. Furthermore, the simplicity of Islam – there being no church acting as an intermediary – along with the promise of booty and the desire to avoid taxation, explains why conversions took place on such a large scale. The surviving Punic language of the Carthaginians was also closely related to Arabic and its continued usage eased the Arabization process.

But Arabization and Islamicization were not identical. The Berbers might have embraced Islam but they were still resentful towards Arab rule. The Arabs became associated with the plains and the Berbers with the mountains, although the Islamic customs and practices that now became the bedrock of the local identity did much to blur these distinctions. Islam, with its division between the 'land of Islam' and the 'land of war', marked out a strong sense of place and became the way in which the local populations defined themselves of Arab culture against the *roumi*, the Arabic for 'outsiders' derived from the word Roman which became synonymous with Christian.[17]

North Africa, therefore, would be forever linked to the culture and politics of the Arab world. Yet those Arabs who were the spearhead of the advancing armies were small in number and inevitably intermarriage with non-Arabs led to a dilution of Arab culture. From this point on, personal names became very important as a guide to an identifiable genealogy and those descended from the Arab lineage carried enormous prestige. Those whose ancestors were religious leaders (sheikhs), saints (marabouts), or had made the pilgrimage to Mecca (*hadji*) could always explicitly identify them as such; those who claimed the name 'Sharif' purported to be able to trace their lineage right back to the prophet Mohammed. By the tenth century Latin was replaced by Arabic in all the romanized areas of North Africa as the Latin and Greek population of the cities withdrew to Spain and Sicily. Meanwhile, the Berber languages were transformed through intermingling with Arabic and some Berber scholars began writing in Arabic script. Jewish presence, implanted in North Africa since the arrival of the Phoenicians, continued as the Jews were accorded protected status as 'people of the book'. In return for a tax they were allowed to continue practising Judaism.

Ever since, North Africa has been characterized by religious homogeneity. With the suppression of Shi'ism in the eleventh century North Africa, unlike the Middle East, would not be plagued by the Shia–Sunni split. And unlike in the Middle East, there would be very few Christian Arabs in the Maghreb.

The Malikite school of theological thought became rooted throughout North Africa and was the mainstay of legal administration, education and state legitimization until the nineteenth century. Arab and Muslim culture now saturated all aspects of North African life and rituals, from the daily call to prayer, to the Qur'an, Islamic architecture and the lunar calendar. Instinctively the local population looked to the east, as well-established pilgrimage routes led the way to Mecca. Equally, the life of Mohammed was held up as a model and thereafter his example, in particular the desire to create a new virtuous society along the lines of the early Caliphate, would fuel politics and religion right up to the present day.

As the language of Qur'an, Arabic now carried huge prestige within North African society. However, Arabic was not only the language of religion, but also of administration, trade and commerce. Islam was the basis of a huge common market which stretched from the Atlantic to India and the economic revolution brought about by the Arabs – the largest worldwide economic bloc until the sixteenth century – did as much as religion to spread their language. The Berbers welcomed the establishment of market towns along trade routes because they too wanted to benefit from this wider economic community.

Collectively Arabic and Islam cultures became a cement that transcended tribes and fostered a sense of belonging to a wider Muslim community: the *umma*. Even so, within North Africa different strands of Islamic practices developed. On the one hand was orthodox Islam, which was essentially urban-based and placed great stress on scripture and learning. On the other was rural Islam, which fused Muslim beliefs with local practices such as the evil eye and the belief in the divinity of nature. The clearest expression of this rural Islam was Sufism, which emerged during the twelfth century. Operating outside the official structures of the mosque, Sufism was a mystical theology that fostered the cult of local saints, known as marabouts, and their tombs.[18] Fusing philosophical contemplation with rituals which involved ecstatic experiences, Sufi mystics enjoyed the *baraka* – a blessing that marked them out as friends of God – and became associated with miraculous power and the gift of second sight. Sufism swiftly became the predominant form of Islam within the countryside and Sufi orders were centred on *zawiyas* (refuges). As such they began to rival the mosque and tensions have existed between these two strands of Islam ever since. In the 1830s the Sufi orders would lead the resistance to the French invasion, but during the 1930s they would be attacked by the Association of Algerian Ulema on the grounds they perpetuated pagan prac-tices and acted as servile agents of the colonial regime. Similarly, in the early 1990s Islamists would desecrate saints' tombs on the grounds that these saints were being associated with God; whilst at the opposite end of the spectrum the present Algerian state, which had traditionally looked down upon Sufism, began to promote it as a rival to political Islam.

Yet, if the Muslim religion now defined the daily rhythm of life in North Africa, after the Almoravids and the Almohads Muslim dynasties in the region rose and fell at a bewildering rate. There was a momentary revival in the latter part of the fourteenth century but after that Muslim dominance went into terminal decline, climaxing in the capitulation of Islamic Spain in 1492. This explains why the local population looked to the Ottomans for protection in the early sixteenth century.

OTTOMAN RULE

When the war against Spain ended in 1580 direct Ottoman rule was allowed to lapse. So, although a tribute was sent to Istanbul in exchange for the sultan's political support, real power quickly resided with the Agha, the chief officer of the Turkish military elite (the janissary), who in 1689 became the head of state (Dey) elected by a council (*diwan*). It was this system that ruled Algeria until the French invasion in 1830. There was a dual Muslim judicial system with Hanafite law for the Turkish elite and the Malikite school of law for the local population.[19] It was during the Ottoman period that the various Sufi orders really took root. The most important of these were the Rahmaniya in Kabylia, the Tijaniya in the Sahara, the Darqawa in the Oran and the Qadiriya, a local offshoot of the more widespread Shadhiliya, each of which played a key role in giving the rural population its Islamic identity during the seventeenth century.

The purpose of the regime was the extraction of profit through military force. In this respect the Turkish military corps had the right to collect taxes, whilst the sons of soldiers and local women, known as *kulughlis*, worked for the administration as civil servants. The Dey administered Algiers, exerting power through the command of the janissary garrison, the *kulughlis*, auxiliaries and loyal tribes. Outside of Algiers the rest of the country was divided into three regions, Constantine, Mascara and Titteri, which were each governed by an individual known as a bey who, aided by lieutenants (*calipha*), was expected to bring in taxes on a fixed day to Algiers. Below the three beys the *cadis* (judges) and *caids* (tax collectors) functioned as a bridgehead between rulers and ruled, controlling the local tribal leaders, levying taxes, settling judicial disputes. The towns meanwhile administered themselves with many of the inhabitants being refugees from Andalusia, including part of the Jewish population, which ran small businesses. In general there was much mutual suspicion between the towns and the countryside. The urban populace looked down upon the countryside as uncouth and uncivilized, and in turn were hated by the tribes.

Beyond zones of direct administration the Ottoman regime singled out tribal leaders, known as *bachagas*, who in exchange for status and privileges acted as administrators and supplied fighting men. The Ottoman system was based on clientelism and relied upon creating privileged tribes that were formed by the consolidation of smaller groups. This then allowed the Ottoman regime to play a classic divide-and-rule strategy by playing off one tribe against another. On top of this the Ottomans actively encouraged the Sufi orders by giving them judicial positions and tax revenues, as well as money to endow mosques and tombs. Thus, an essentially egalitarian lineage society was transformed into a hierarchical one linked to Ottoman authority in Algiers.

The Ottomans controlled the roads, passes, towns and the plains and anyone wishing to trade or work in a marketplace required a permit issued by the authorities. This was particularly effective in the Kabyle region, where the local economy relied upon the sale of olives, figs and handmade products for survival. However, beyond the plains Ottoman power stopped abruptly. Whole regions escaped control and in the face of Ottoman attempts to extract yet more taxes there were frequent rebellions.

Privateering was the most lucrative enterprise for the Ottoman state. Not only did corsairs operating out of Algeria seize ships at sea, they also kidnapped Europeans and held them to ransom.[20] During the seventeenth century some one million Europeans were enslaved, with the result that the image of the brutal Barbary coast became deeply embedded within the Western psyche. The depiction of sadistic Muslim corsairs became the staple of popular prints, literature and music, as in the case of Rossini's 1813 comic opera *The Italian Girl in Algiers* which recounted the captivity of a group of Italians by a lecherous sultan.

Ottoman rule was beset with factional struggles amongst the janissaries. The resultant power struggles meant that between 1671 and 1830 fourteen out of the twenty-eight Deys were assassinated. But despite this instability the Ottoman regime did have all the hallmarks of a functioning state. During the seventeenth century the Dey concluded treaties with the European powers by which they paid a tribute to the Dey to restrain piracy. Similarly, the regime lent money to the European powers – as we have already seen, the failure of the French to repay loans from the Napoleonic wars was the origin of the then Dey's angry exchange with the French consul in 1827 that provoked the invasion three years later. All the same, the Ottoman state entered into a terminal crisis during the eighteenth century when a steep decline in privateering and trade produced ever-increasing instability. So, whilst there were 35,000 Christian captives in Algiers at one point in the seventeenth century, there were only 1,200 when the British admiral Lord Exmouth bombarded the city on 27 August 1816 in an attempt to end the Dey's slavery practices. To compensate for falling revenue the Dey increased taxation of the countryside. In the short term this policy might have shored up Ottoman finances but in the long term it was a disaster. The regime came to be bitterly resented by the local population and there were large-scale rebellions by the Sufi orders. This in turn explains why Ottoman rule collapsed so quickly in 1830.

Nonetheless, the significance of the Ottoman period for subsequent Algerian history must be underlined. The period defined the territorial identity of the country and therefore created the basis for the Algerian nation state as a geopolitical entity. Furthermore, even if swathes of the country were beyond direct Ottoman control, it did function as a state. For this reason the Ottoman period was invoked by the national liberation movement between 1954 and 1962 to refute the settlers' assertion that Algeria was a blank space waiting to be colonized. The Ottoman achievement was that they fashioned a unified entity which prevented the country from falling under Christian domination.[21] In this sense much of the nationalist discourse saw the liberation struggle not as a revolution but as a return to independence. Importantly too, during the 1980s and early 1990s the Ottoman regime was also invoked by Islamists, who called for a return to a pre-1830 ideal that saw Algeria as a religiously unified entity which, post-1830, had become contaminated by French ideas.

The Ottoman experience has left a lasting legacy in terms of the pattern of rule. It bequeathed a model of court politics that still marks Algerian politics because, as Luis Martinez has underlined, the period produced a mercenary attitude towards the state.[22] For both caïd and corsair, the state was conceived as a route to personal enrichment and prestige, where the goal was not to create national wealth but to extract a levy from the population. As the French state adapted Ottoman structures, using the system of bachagas, cadis and caïds in order to rule the Algerian countryside, this mindset carried on over into the war of liberation, post-independence and the violence of the 1990s, where a range of actors continued to see the state as a structure to be colonized for their own interest. Martinez argues that much of what drives political divisions has to be understood not in terms of genuine ideological differences, but by the desire for power and to be a modern-day sultan.

Martinez's remarks remind us that Algerian history, like all history, is a palimpsest. Time is layered upon time so that one buried layer of history seeps through to the one above. A landscape which encouraged resistance to central authority, religion, Ottoman structures: the cumulative impact of these different layers is a past that is permanently present. In this way the complex pre-colonial period produced a web of deeply embedded cultural traditions which form the long-term context for the contemporary period.

CHAPTER TWO

Forced Marriage: French Algeria 1830–1962

With his long dark hair, trademark dark sunglasses and hard-drinking lifestyle, the Algerian singer Rachid Taha is every inch the modern rock star. Yet behind the swagger and the showmanship there is a unique and thoughtful talent, whether it be covering the Clash's 'Rock the Casbah' in Arabic or carefully reworking traditional North African songs in an effort to explore the trials and tribulations of being Algerian. Speaking on British television in 2005 the singer tried to convey the complexities of his personal identity by explaining that although he will be Algerian until the end of his days, on a day-to-day level he is French.[1]

The child of Algerian immigrants to France – his father crossed the Mediterranean from Oran in the 1970s – Rachid Taha's subtle and nuanced response spoke to many of his generation. This was the man who first shot to fame during the 1980s as the lead singer in an immigrant band, whose name Carte de Séjour (Residency Permit) was a provocative riposte to the rise of Jean-Marie Le Pen's far-right National Front. Carte de Séjour's video to their cover of Charles Trenet's 1941 hit '*Douce France*', an iconic song in the French popular canon, is one of the most subversive of all time; a statement about post-colonial society, it showed the band strumming in a late-night Parisian café, surrounded by old French couples serenely waltzing to the tune. Its message was that there was no going back. Whatever Le Pen might do or say, Algerian immigrants and their descendants are an inescapable part of France. Taha's music makes a profound statement about the complex interaction between the two countries, underlining not just the impact of Algerian culture in France but that of French culture on Algerians.

This intertwining of France and Algeria is a central aspect of the historian and activist Mohammed Harbi's personal memoir *Une Vie Debout*.[2] In one passage he recounts with striking honesty the feelings of his fellow FLN member Messaoud Guedroudj after the two of them had been smuggled across the frontier into northern France by Belgian anti-colonialists in the summer of 1956. Much to the astonishment of the Belgians, who believed that they were driving their charges into enemy territory, when the group stopped at a restaurant in Reims Guedroudj immediately became happy and relaxed. He explained that it was good to be on home soil, a reaction that made them all burst into laughter. Reflecting on the irony of this episode, Harbi argued that Guedroudj's attitude had to be understood as the result of a long marriage which, even if it was forced, could not fail to leave a lasting mark, producing myriad confused sentiments and allegiances in which love intermingled with hatred.

French rule in Algeria lasted for 132 years, as opposed to 75 years in Tunisia and 44 in Morocco, a depth and duration of colonial experience unique within the Arab world. Until the French invasion of 1830 the local population had been locked into the history and culture of the Middle East. Now, this East–West axis would be matched by the pull of a North–South equivalent.

The fact that Algeria was officially an integral part of France produced a whole series of paradoxes and contradictions for the native population. Multiple messages were given out to Algerians by the French wherein the image of 'France the colonizer' coexisted uneasily with 'France of the Rights of Man'. Was the French policy one of assimilation, transforming Algerians into equal citizens, or subjugation, keeping them down as disempowered subjects? This tension was present from the 1850s, when the French government first decided that the principle of representative government applied to the native population as inhabitants of France, even if this principle was scandalously manipulated by the French settlers to deny that population an effective voice. Indeed, it became the basis of a 1920s nationalist politics that was determined to show that Algerians were not to be excluded from the universal values of representative government.

After independence in 1962 the Algerian regime underlined the horrors of colonialism, insisting that the promise of equal rights was a lie; Algerians were never going to be treated as citizens. The Franco-Algerian relationship was seen as a straightforward story of injustice leading to revolutionary anger that had climaxed with victory in the war of liberation. Anger at colonialism became a cornerstone of official discourse and it has permeated all parts of

Algerian politics, most obviously the Islamist movement. Yet, as the examples of Rachid Taha and Mohammed Harbi show, the relationship between the two countries is much more complex and ambiguous. The 1789 ideals of 'liberty, equality and fraternity' and the principle of representative government, for example, had a genuine impact upon modern intellectuals and activists. By the 1920s Algerian political leaders had internalized these values. They applied them to their own situation and it was ultimately the belief that Algerians could not be denied these rights, above all the right to national self-determination, that brought an end to French Algeria in 1962.

Even if 'Colonial France' is rejected, the 'France of the Rights of Man' has continued to be a crucial reference point. Ironically, it has come to stand as the model by which many of today's younger Algerians, with no memory of colonialism but who watch French television on satellite, measure the Algerian system's claim to be democratic, popular and republican. Modern France is also seen to encapsulate the dream of a better economic life. It is the country to which the majority of young Algerians still want to emigrate; when President Chirac visited Algeria in 2003, he was greeted by thousands waving their passports at him and shouting 'Chirac, visa!' Many joke that if there was a referendum today they would vote for Algeria to return to French rule; a provocative comment that speaks volumes about their sense of post-colonial dispossession.

France, therefore, remains an omnipresent feature of Algeria. 'Colonial oppressor', 'country of human rights', 'consumer paradise': the contested historical relationship saturates political discourse from all points of view, making Algeria the most francophone of France's former territories, even though the government has always refused to join the International Francophone Organization, formed in 1970 to bring together French-speaking countries on the international stage.[3] Given this continuing impact upon the Algerian political imagination, the situation today cannot be understood without considering the context of French colonialism and its aftermath.

■ ■ ■

In the wake of the 1830 French invasion and the swift overthrow of Ottoman rule in Algeria, the main resistance came from the eastern part of the country in the form of a charismatic twenty-five-year-old holy man (*marabout*), Abd el-Kader. As part of the Qadiriya religious order and drawing upon the prestige of his Sharifian descent, Abd el-Kader proclaimed himself commander of the faithful and called for a jihad against unbelievers.[4] Dubbed the Algerian Cromwell by the writer Alexis de Tocqueville, Abd el-Kader explicitly fused religion and resistance and the extent of his success can be measured by the treaty of Tafna in 1837, whereby he was recognized as the sovereign over two-thirds of Algeria.

Theoretically this treaty laid the basis for the peaceful coexistence between an Arab state and the French territory, but the frontiers were ill-defined and this made the return to open warfare only a matter of time. So it was no surprise when just two years later the French launched an all-out war of conquest led by Marshal Thomas-Robert Bugeaud. The engravings from the period convey a man in his mid-fifties with a stern, ruddy face and greying temples. Proud of his peasant origins, Bugeaud was utterly relentless in the pursuit of victory. Gone were the ponderous columns that could be easily ambushed; in their place were light units that could pursue the enemy over rough terrain, hitting them again and again until they were defeated. Speaking before the National Assembly in 1840, Bugeaud was blunt about his aims: 'Wherever there is fresh water and fertile land, there one must locate *colons* [colonizers], without concerning oneself to whom these lands belong.'[5] Crops, mosques, *zawiya*s (Sufi refuges): in Bugeaud's eyes all were targets for reprisal as the army adopted a scorched-earth policy. Egged on by their commanders the ordinary soldiers gave no quarter, undergoing a brutalization process whereby atrocities, including the asphyxiation of five hundred men, women and children from the Ouled Riah tribe who had taken refuge in caves, became a routine fact of battle. Hounded on all sides, Abd el-Kader eventually surrendered on 23 December 1847 on a dark and rainy night in the hills just above Oujda on the frontier with Morocco. After imprisonment in France he was allowed to go into honourable exile in Damascus in December 1855.

French history books would extol Bugeaud as the founding father of French Algeria, the genius who opened the way for colonization.[6] For Algerians, though, his name lives on as a byword for brutality. Growing up in the village of El-Arrouch in the 1930s, Mohammed Harbi vividly remembers how his mother frightened him with stories about the ogre Bugeaud, who would come and eat him up if he did not go to sleep.[7] Conversely, although the French went some way to romanticizing Abd el-Kader as an honourable enemy, even building statues to him in the late 1940s, for Algerians he was always held up as the embodiment of anti-French resistance.[8] He was an inspirational figure for anti-colonial nationalists such as the writer Kateb Yacine and when his ashes were brought back to Algeria from Syria in 1967 this was a state occasion of huge symbolic importance.[9] It showed that Algeria was a fully fledged nation state with its own pantheon of heroes who, beginning with Abd el-Kader, formed a chain of authenticity which led ultimately to the FLN.[10]

Resistance flickered on until 1870. In the meantime the Second Republic in 1848 declared that it wanted to assimilate Algeria and give it political representatives in France. However, instability – Louis-Napoleon overthrew the Second Republic in a coup d'état on 2 December 1851 – meant that in practice Algeria became a fiefdom of the army, a fact that was symbolized by the formation of the Foreign Legion in 1831, with its headquarters at Sidi-bel-Abbès in eastern Algeria, some forty miles to the south of Oran. Confronted by a complex and heterogeneous society the army had to be pragmatic. On the ground it adapted the Ottoman system, looking for compliant local leaders amongst the caïds (tax collectors), cadis (judges) and bachagas (tribal leaders), who would raise taxes in return for special concessions such as the conservation of harvests and a cut of any tax yield. At the same time the army was not afraid to introduce major innovations and in February 1844 it created the specially designated Bureaux des Affaires Arabes to reach out to Muslims. The officers selected spoke Arabic and were familiar with the local culture, fashioning a strategy which, although highly paternalistic and based upon the principles of protection and domination, displayed a certain sympathy for the local population.

Such measures provoked the hostility of the first French settlers, who numbered 35,000 by 1849. They wanted to keep the native population in a state of subjugation and this was a running sore during the 1850s. Initially the settlers looked to Napoleon III's Second Empire, established on 2 December 1852, as an ally and welcomed his reassurances that Algeria was an extension of France which would be assimilated into the mother country. However, in September 1860 Napoleon performed a spectacular U-turn. He blocked colonization and three years later proclaimed the idea of an Arab Kingdom, stressing his affinity with Arab culture and talking about the notion of reconciliation between the two communities. Such pro-Arab talk transformed the settlers into staunch republicans and was emblematic of what became a deeply embedded psychology whereby Paris was a dirty word synonymous with pro-native sentiment.

For all the talk of reconciliation, the barriers within French Algeria were becoming rigidly defined during the Second Empire. A major step along this road was the sénatus-consulte of 1865 whereupon Algerians were treated as subjects rather than citizens. Under this definition Muslims were governed by Islamic law, and justice was left in the hands of Muslim judges (the cadis) rather than the French civil code. Ostensibly this arrangement was meant to protect local religion and culture, but in practice it acted as a barrier to assimilation because Muslims could only acquire French nationality by signing away the right to be governed, in non-criminal jurisdiction, by Islamic law, an act of apostasy few were willing to take. By 1936 only 2,500 had taken this step, enshrining a fundamental divide between the voterless subject and the full citizen which would be one of the basic causes of the war of national liberation.

With the dismantling of native society Muslims began to lose their traditional forms of support, such as the setting aside of stores of food for times of hardship, which made them very vulnerable to famine. But when in 1867 some three hundred thousand Muslims died of starvation, a catastrophe on a par with the Irish famine of 1847–51 in terms of the percentage of the total population that died, the settlers were quick to blame the army regime for being too indulgent towards traditional patterns of land holding, which were perceived as archaic and inefficient.

■ ■ ■

Like the rest of France, the settlers experienced defeat in the Franco-Prussian war of 1870–71 as a dreadful humiliation. Their only consolation was that the demise of the Second Empire opened the door to the extension of civil power since, with the proclamation of a republic in Paris on 4 September 1870, Algeria now sent deputies to the national assembly. In contrast such a prospect stirred up a rebellious mood in the Muslim population, a mood that was magnified still further by economic discontent, the widespread belief that French defeat by the Prussians had been a punishment from God, and the desire to recover independence. It was a highly charged atmosphere and what brought it to breaking point were the Crémieux decrees giving citizenship to the Jews on 24 October 1870. One local leader by the name of El-Mokhrani, a hitherto loyal Muslim, angrily declared, 'I will take orders from a French officer but from a Jew never,' and on 16 March 1871 he proclaimed a jihad against French rule.[11] Eight hundred thousand Muslims answered his call but there was no coordinated action and by the end of the year the rebellion had ended in ignominious failure.

What followed was an unmitigated disaster for the local population. Pro-rebellion tribes had their lands confiscated and their leaders were deported. Islam itself was subjected to a concerted attack: Arabic was officially categorized as a foreign language, Qur'anic schools put under surveillance, and pilgrimages to Mecca were tightly controlled, in an effort to insulate Algeria from the rest of the Muslim world.

If the Muslims were the losers, the winners were the settlers. From now on their interests were paramount, as ruthless colonization and republicanism went hand in hand.[12] The last quarter of the nineteenth century can be seen as the high point of settler power; the moment when they probably felt most secure about their long-term presence. This was because the Third Republic, established in 1870 and lasting until 1940, was held up as a superior civilization based upon science, progress, education and a strong sense of national identity. Marked by a strong affinity with the Enlightenment and the French Revolution, the values of the Third Republic were portrayed in France as universal truths that marked a new dawn not just for France but the whole world. The doctor and the teacher were the twin heroes of this civilizing mission, their task to battle against a Muslim society deemed to be 'other' by the settlers to this brave new world based upon science and technology.

The northern regions of Algeria were formally divided into three French departments in 1881 whilst the Sahara and the southern territories remained under the control of the French army, a Gallic-style Wild West portrayed so evocatively in the Louis Gardel novel *Fort Saganne*.[13] Within the French imagination the domain of the Foreign Legion was the Sahara, a place whose extreme temperatures and unforgiving landscape marked it out as the very edge of civilization.[14] As one old Foreign Legion song put it:

> Goodbye, Old Europe, may the devil take you.
> Goodbye, old country, for the burning sun of Algeria.
> We are the wounded from every war,
> The world's damned ones.
> We need sunlight and space, to rebuild our bodies.[15]

The role of the Foreign Legion was to protect this boundary between civilization and its opposite. As such the Legion was symptomatic of the frontier mentality, the sense of a way of life under siege, which became fundamental to the settlers' mindset.

It was in 1881 that Algeria was administered for the first time as an integral part of France. Now the territory came under the jurisdiction of the Ministry of the Interior rather than the Ministry of Foreign Affairs. In principle such an arrangement meant that Algeria was subject to the same laws of government as the rest of the Third Republic but in practice the territory was always a case apart. At the apex of French Algeria was the governor general who reported directly back to the Ministry of the Interior, and the singularity of these structures was underlined even further when on 29 December 1900 budgetary powers were devolved to a special assembly. This gave Algeria a measure of financial independence which would have been unthinkable in the regions of mainland France.

With the extension of civilian rule the second-class status of the Muslim population became the foundation stone of French Algeria and Muslims' exclusion was reflected at all levels of political representation. Each of Algeria's three departments sent two deputies to the National Assembly in Paris but only full French citizens, that is adult male settlers, had the right to vote. These deputies became the electoral base of the colonial lobby, a broad coalition of pro-colonial interest groups both within and without the National Assembly. Established in 1892, this quickly became a well-oiled political machine led by Eugène Etienne, parliamentary member for the Algerian department of Oran from 1881 to 1919, who achieved high office in the French government. Variously Minister of the Interior, Minister of War and Vice-President of the Chamber of Deputies, Etienne had razor-sharp political instincts and ensured that any measures that smacked of pro-Arab reforms were immediately quashed.

Back in Algeria, anti-Muslim discrimination was built into the electoral system. Elected settlers made up four-fifths of the membership of the three departmental councils established in 1875, whilst the Muslim contingent was composed of landowners hand-picked by the French authorities. At the level of the local councils the 196 *communes de plein exercice*, based upon the metropolitan model of a ruling mayor and elected municipal council, only allowed 5 per cent of the adult male Muslim population to vote until 1919 and even then the percentage of Muslim representatives could not exceed one-quarter. Similarly within the seven *communes mixtes*, which held sway in those areas that were predominantly Muslim, all Muslim representatives were appointed by the French administration.[16] The inferior status of Muslims was inscribed into the law with the introduction of the *Code de l'Indigénat* in 1881. This was a uniquely repressive set of rules that closely controlled the Muslim population and imposed harsh penalties for a multitude of infractions, including vague crimes such as being rude to a colonial official or making disrespectful remarks about the Third Republic. Abolition of the loathed *Indigénat* was to be a basic demand of all the various strands of the Algerian nationalist movement in the 1930s.

The last quarter of the nineteenth century witnessed a huge influx of settlers. Only a small percentage were rich. The vast majority were from poor backgrounds and for them Algeria represented a kind of El Dorado; a promised land where, by virtue of being French or given French citizenship, they enjoyed a rank, by virtue of their status compared to that of the native population, that they had previously lacked. Some came from the Midi where phylloxera had ravaged the wine crop; others were refugees from Alsace-Lorraine after the Prussian victory of 1871. The French were not always in the majority; over half of the 430,000 settlers living in Algeria in 1886 came from Spain, Italy or Malta. Three years later, on the hundredth anniversary of the French Revolution, they received French citizenship as a gift from the generous Third Republic.

The world which these settlers inhabited was a rugged, macho life dominated by physical pleasures of sport, the beach, the bordello and the drinking of pastis. Their self-image as heroic pioneers permeated all aspects of settler culture.[17] They had made the desert bloom through relentless endeavour and on this basis they felt they had a right to be in Algeria. They took great pride in the roads, the railways and the hospitals they had built and, to underline this point, made continual contrasts between pre-1830 and post-1830.

The settlers were determined that there must be no concessions to the native population and consistently sabotaged any political reform. In their eyes the local population only really understood force and had to be kept in a perpetual state of humiliation. In large part this intransigent psychology was derived from unease about their own lowly origins; the settlers' living standards were always significantly lower than those of mainland France and they held a widespread belief that other French people looked down on them as poor and uncultured. Such an inferiority complex explains why defence of their status over the Muslims became a cornerstone of their identity.

To make way for the settlers the local population was pushed to one side. The Warnier law of 1873 split up communally held land into individual lots so that it could be sold off more easily. The French authorities claimed that in the long term this would benefit Algeria because it opened the way for a free-market system; but in practice it was little more than a thinly veiled cloak for an all-out land grab and between 1871 and 1898 French settlers acquired one million hectares. It was a brutal process which by 1900 had broken the traditional indigenous leadership. Those who kept some power did so by carving out a position for themselves in the French administration. But the price of this survival was the loss of prestige, as much of the population dismissed such leaders as the 'old turbans', a pejorative term that marked them out as pro-French collaborators. The marginalization of the pre-colonial elites also levelled Algerian society, further strengthening a deeply rooted cultural egalitarianism and greatly reducing the importance of class-based politics. Such egalitarianism shaped the populism of the FLN and has continued to mark Algerian society ever since. Specifically it explains the mass resentment at the sharpening of class divisions at the end of the 1980s and the surge in support for Islamism which, in many respects, took over much of the traditional populism of Algerian nationalism.

Within Algeria the French authorities operated a divide-and-rule policy, making judgements, based upon ethnography and anthropology, as to which parts of the population were more open to French culture. The Jews were seen as the group that would be most easily assimilated, and they were given full citizenship in October 1870, one of the first acts of the Third Republic: Jewish emancipation had been a cornerstone of the French Revolution, going hand in hand with the values of republicanism. It was a decision that inevitably provoked resentment amongst Muslims.[18] The move also produced strong reactions within the settler community. Many saw it as the first step to Arab emancipation and there were anti-Jewish riots in Oran in May 1897, tinged by the belief that these newly freed Jews were engaged in a capitalist plot to exploit the poorest settlers. One year later Edouard Drumont, a vicious anti-semite, was elected as a parliamentary member for Algiers, to tumultuous acclaim.[19] Thereafter settler culture was marked by a strong strain of anti-semitism, and the legislation of the Second World War collaborationist Vichy regime, revoking the Crémieux decrees and turning Jews into second-class citizens, was warmly welcomed.

If the Jews were seen as the ethnic group closest in culture to the Third Republic, the ones seen as furthest away were the Arabs, whose way of life was categorized as mediaeval. Still dominated by religion, still dominated by tribal vendettas, still dominated by a nomadic lifestyle, they were viewed as an inferior, pre-political society. The French sought to make a distinction between the Arabs who arrived after the seventh century AD and the Berbers, the original population.[20] For many natives, such a distinction, given the fusion of Arabic and Berber culture over the subsequent centuries, made no sense. Nonetheless the French set out to court the largest Berber group, the Kabyles. The essence of what became known as the Kabyle myth was that the Berbers were Indo-European in origin and their mountain culture, based as it was on independence and hard work, made them much more akin to the peasants of the Auvergne than were the Arabs. Crucially. too, the authorities claimed that the Kabyle people's attachment to Islam was much more super-ficial, evidenced from the fact that Kabyle women were not veiled, polygamy was not practised and the cult worship of the *marabout*s, retaining as it did strong elements of pre-Islamic beliefs, was widespread. Much more deep rooted in Kabyle society was the tradition of democracy through the *djemma* (village councils) which, when added to the Kabyle people's linguistic and cultural cohesion, meant that that they were much further down the road to modernity. In short, the Berbers were seen as possessing the basic components for nationhood whilst the nomadic Arabs, still dominated by the stranglehold of Islam, were not.

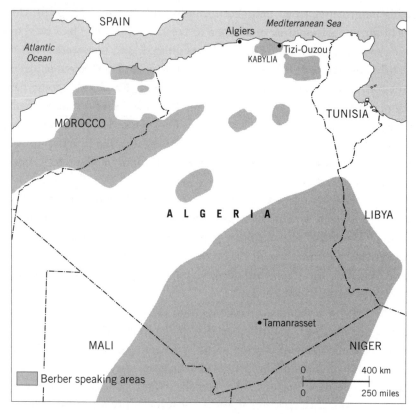

This policy was reflected in the large number of schools that were established in Kabylia, the extensive studies carried out by historians and ethnologists to prove that the Berber people shared a common origin with Europeans, and the strenuous efforts at encouraging the Berbers to rediscover their Latin-Christian heritage. Cardinal de Lavigerie, appointed as the archbishop of Algiers in 1867 at the age of thirty-eight, was the most outspoken advocate of the need to convert Berbers to Christianity. A larger-than-life character fired up by a militant energy, he set up Christian orphanages for Berber children and established the Society of African Missionaries, known as the White Fathers because of their Arab dress. Through such action he wanted to restore the lost age of St Augustine and to wrest North Africa from the shackles of Arab-Islamic culture.[21]

If divide and rule was one aspect of colonial policy, so too was an adaptation of the Ottoman system, especially in the remote mountains of the Aurès and Kabylia, where even as late as the 1950s some Algerians had never seen a French official. The mountains and plains represent a fundamental divide in Algerian history and this was no less true under colonialism. French authority and settler culture was based on the coast and under-government in the mountains, and the interior was a perennial weakness of the colonial regime. In these remote areas the French sought out intermediaries to act as the bridgehead between rulers and ruled. Some were ex-servicemen whose war record marked them out as loyal servants; some were local leaders who wished to ingratiate themselves with the colonial authorities; whilst others, as the titles *bachaga* (tribal leader), *cadi* (judge) and *caïd* (tax collector) suggested, were remnants of the Ottoman period. In 1919 the *cadi*s were formally organized into an administrative body as a way of strengthening surveillance over the Muslim population. Yet if many *cadis* felt that they were working on behalf of the local population, many too were appalling cheats and swindlers. Given the scale of illiteracy the scope for corruption was vast, with the result that the cheating *cadi*, exploiting his position in the colonial system to live off the fate of the peasantry, became a familiar hate figure within popular culture.

The French adapted Ottoman practices in other ways. Just one month after the landings in 1830 the Zouaous Berber tribe, which had always raised troops for the Dey, supplied 500 troops, known as *zouaves*, for the invasion force.[22] In 1856 the decision was made to channel this pro-French sentiment with the creation of three Algerian infantry regiments, and thereafter Muslim troops were to distinguish themselves on battlefields as far afield as the Crimea, Mexico and Madagascar. In the First World War 170,000 Algerians ignored the call of the Ottoman caliphate to rise up against their colonial masters and fought in the French army. In the Second World War Algerians formed the backbone of the French Army of Africa, supplying 250,000 troops for the Italian campaign between 1943 and 1945. They played a key role at the Battle of Monte Cassino and a moving plaque paying tribute to the fallen of the Algerian regiments can be seen on the walls of the beautiful church of St Louis des Français in Rome. In some cases part of the appeal was the promise of regular food and income. But if initially many saw the army as a way out of grinding poverty, many too came to see it as their home, equating loyalty to a particular regiment with loyalty to the French nation. The authorities soon came to look upon ex-servicemen as a pillar of support, to be trundled out at every available opportunity, as the photograph of loyal Muslim veterans saluting the tricolour became a familiar trope of colonial propaganda.

The expropriation of land forced huge numbers of Algerians to endure abject living conditions as the country became a tale of two economies sitting side by side. On the one side were the rich settlers whose huge enterprises, comprising some 2,350,000 hectares of the best land and using the latest agricultural techniques, produced wine and food for export; on the other the Algerian peasantry who were forced to maintain a subsistence economy based on archaic methods.[23] This way of life was unable to cope with the dramatic rise in population, which tripled in Algeria between 1856 and 1940 to 6.5 million, ironically due to the impact of French medicine in reducing infant mortality. By 1930 only 1 per cent of Algerians had a farm of more than 100 hectares, meaning that hunger became part of everyday life for the native population. When the country was hit very hard by the Great Depression in the 1930s the French ruthlessly protected settlers' interests, further intensifying the pauperization process which triggered a huge exodus of landless peasants from the interior to the major coastal cities. This great displacement of the population climaxed tragically with the 1937 famine, widely remembered amongst North Africans as the terrible year of hunger, when people literally dropped dead of starvation on the roadside. Some of the local authorities did introduce some relief measures, but most sent victims back to their place of origin, believing that Muslim Algerians followed a primitive way of life based upon tribes and religion which, because it could not compete, was predestined for extinction.

How to escape poverty became a fundamental question for Algerian society, a quest that was reflected in the large-scale drift to the towns; in the huge numbers of Muslims employed as cheap workers in agriculture; and in the beginning of Algerian immigration to France, which had totalled 92,000 by 1923.[24] All of this underlined just how far the Muslim way of life had become invisible within French Algeria. The fact that the cultivation of wine was offensive to most Muslim sensibilities did not enter into the equation because their culture did not matter. The end result was a fragile peace riven with tension, anger and resentment.

By 1926 the number of settlers had reached some 833,000, 15 per cent of the population, reaching just under one million by 1954. The richest settlers occupied the best agricultural land, whilst their poor counterparts were concentrated for the most part in the major towns and cities. In 1931 the settler population accounted for 69 per cent of the total population in Algiers, 79 per cent in Oran, 48 per cent in Constantine and 57 per cent in Bône. Of the settler population, 79 per cent had been born on Algerian soil. Their identity was bound up not only with the sense of being French, but also with a strong attachment to Roman Catholicism. Religious holidays, weddings, baptisms, the weekly mass: these rites separated the settlers from the Jewish and Muslim populations on a day-to-day basis. Their sense of superiority was reinforced in language. As a matter of course they addressed Muslims by the familiar *tu* rather than the polite *vous*, underlining their second-class status. Aline Charby, who grew up in a rich Catholic settler family in the 1940s, recalls how Arab servants were treated in a derogatory way.[25] She remembers too that racist expressions were normal in everyday parlance: Muslims were regularly referred to by pejorative terms such as *melon*, *raton* and *bougnoule*. The writer Marie Cardinal remembers, 'Our cleaning ladies were called Fatmas. We addressed them with the *tu* and they us as *vous*.'[26] The settlers themselves came to be known as '*pieds noirs*', 'black feet', a term they eventually used to identify themselves as well.

Culturally, religiously and linguistically, French Algeria was rigidly segregated, though not in the way that South Africa was during the apartheid regime. There were no special places reserved for Muslim or French on public transport. Instead, French Algeria was crisscrossed by a series of invisible barriers which could not be transgressed. Talking about his childhood in the 1940s, the Algerian writer Nabil Farès recalls that the level of demarcation was absolute. On the beach just outside Algiers everybody knew which was the French part and which the native part and there was no interaction between the two.[27] The main streets of the European quarter of Algiers, with their wide tree-lined boulevards, were particularly elegant. Yet not a stone's throw from the grand façades was a totally different world, the world of the casbah with its overcrowded housing and tiny trap-like streets. These were the two faces of every city: the one of French power and high society, and the other of poverty and squalor. There was virtually no intermarriage between the two communities. Nor did settler and Muslim mix much at school. Attempts to expand education for Muslims was blocked by the settlers, who feared that they might get ideas above their station. In 1890 only ten thousand Muslim children attended primary school, out of a population of 3.5 million. Admittedly this had risen to 1.2 million out of a population of nearly 7 million at the end of the Second World War but even by 1954 only one Muslim boy in five was attending school, a figure plummeting to one in sixteen of the girls.

The settlers were confident in the permanency of French Algeria and this self-confidence was reflected in the commemorations organized to mark the hundredth anniversary of the 1830 invasion. In Algiers the centenary was a glittering occasion. The main streets were adorned with tricolours, the statues and war memorials dressed in garlands and ribbons, whilst at Sidi-Ferruch there was a re-enactment of the original landing. To accompany the celebrations numerous books and pamphlets waxed lyrical about the forward march of colonization, claiming that the native population, immensely grateful for the way in which invasion had destroyed Ottoman domination, was now being won over to the French cause.[28] Yet this optimism was underpinned by a palpable sense of fear about the unstable pillars of French rule. In government circles many officials were only too aware of just how far they were outnumbered by the natives.[29] From their point of view statistics on population increase made alarming reading during the 1930s. Between 1926 and 1936 the Muslim population increased from 6 million to 7.2 million thanks to falling infant mortality and a rising birth rate. In comparison the increase in the settler population was much slower. By 1954 the ratio of Muslims to settlers had reached nine to one.

The imbalance between the two populations was striking, and reflected in a network of fears about Muslims. The perception of the natives as a seething mass, reproducing at will and motivated by a fanatical religion hell-bent on the destruction of Christianity, became deeply ingrained within the settler psyche.[30] The Algiers casbah in particular, whose sinewy alleys were so memorably portrayed in the opening scene of Julien Duvivier's 1937 gangster film *Pépé le Moko*, was viewed with trepidation because its teeming population was so chaotic and so uncontrollable. If not kept constantly under check it could erupt into violence and overrun the French quarter at any moment.

Of course, there were many currents of opinion within the settler community. Not all of them were out-and-out racists. There were people of goodwill who knew that something had to be done about the plight of the Muslim population. A small minority of settlers even sided with the FLN during the war of liberation and became Algerian at independence. However, the liberal strand of thought was best represented by the settler intellectual Albert Camus. Unquestionably the most famous writer to come out of French Algeria, Camus was born in 1913 into a poor family in Bab el-Oued in Algiers.[31] A member of the French Resistance, where he wrote for the clandestine paper *Combat*, after 1945 he became an icon of the intellectual existential left with his swept-back hair and brooding good looks, before his death in a car accident in 1960. A tireless supporter of reform, he tried to alert his compatriots to the famine conditions in Kabylia in 1938 through a series of articles in the communist-supporting daily *Alger Républicain*.[32] Even so, there were limits to Camus's liberalism. In his fiction, most famously in his 1942 novel *The Outsider*, the natives tended to be treated in generic terms and were always prone to violence and irrationality. Equally, Camus never rejected the French right to rule. When receiving the Nobel Prize for Literature in December 1957 in Stockholm, he was called upon by a member of the audience to give his views on the political situation in Algeria. He replied:

> It is with a certain repugnance that I give my views in public. I have always condemned terror. I must also condemn terrorism which operates blindly, in the streets of Algiers, and which one day could strike my mother or my family. I believe in justice, but I will defend my mother before justice.[33]

ALGERIAN NATIONALISM 1871–1954

After the failure of the 1871 rebellion it is possible to talk of a collective trauma. In the face of humiliation Muslims became sullen and resentful as Algerian society turned in on itself. A sense of paralysis was endemic as the vast majority became preoccupied with the minutiae of everyday life. But just because it was impossible to envisage how French rule could be defeated did not mean that the vast majority of Algerians accepted it. Instead Algerians found solace in religion as Islam came to be regarded as a bulwark, a safe haven that could not be overcome by colonialism. It is significant that very few Muslims took up French citizenship and that Lavigerie's attempts at conversion made very little impact. In 1908 some four thousand Algerians from Tlemcen, fearful of being called to fight fellow Muslims in Morocco, chose to follow the example of the Prophet and go into exile. In 1911 there was a massive wave of Muslim sympathy for the Ottoman resistance to the Italian invasion of Libya, while many middle-class Muslim parents, reticent about sending their children into the secular French education system, chose to send them to religious universities in Fez, Tunis or Cairo. For men who felt powerless in the face of French rule it became even more important to assert themselves over women, and in the domestic sphere they underlined the need for a strict adherence to Muslim values as a way of setting their families apart from the French.

In this sense Algeria can be seen as a microcosm of the Muslim and wider non-European world. During the nineteenth century Western Europe became the powerhouse of the world, the combination of technical innovation and economic power producing a dynamism that far exceeded anything previously known to humanity. The French Third Republic, marked by its belief in science and progress, saw itself as the standard bearer of this new civilization.

This raised the question of how Algerians should respond; was the civilizing mission about the imposition of an alien way of life or did it contain ideas and knowledge which could be adapted and appropriated by the Islamic world?

The scale of the French repression of the rising of 1871 meant that it took over half a century for an Algerian response to the French challenge to emerge. By the mid-1930s it is possible to define four distinct movements, the first of which can be characterized as assimilationist in outlook. The Young Algerians movement, inspired by the Young Turks movement in the Ottoman Empire, was drawn from a younger, urban middle-class membership as a direct response to the introduction of conscription for Algerians on 3 February 1912. Led by Emir Khaled, grandson of Abd el-Kader and a graduate of the French military academy in Saint-Cyr, the Young Algerians were fiercely critical of the old elite who were only too willing to fill up the Muslim seats on the representative councils.[34] The Young Algerians argued that in return for conscription the French must be prepared to give Muslims citizenship rights, and their 1912 Manifesto called for an end to the *Indigénat*, equal taxation, enlarged suffrage for Muslims and representation in the National Assembly.[35] The Muslim contribution to the war effort during the First World War strengthened the case for reform and on 4 February 1919 the government made it easier for certain categories of Muslim men – those who had served in the army, farmed land or rented urban property and who could read and write French – to request citizenship. The percentage of Muslim representatives on departmental and local councils was also raised to one-third. These were very modest reforms which fell far short of what the Young Algerians wanted. They nevertheless provoked the ire of the settlers, again underlinng the ongoing tension between Paris and Algiers, and Emir Khaled, who was elected to Algiers municipal council in 1919, became the target of a hate campaign which eventually forced him into exile in France in 1923.

Frustrating though this episode was, some of the Young Algerian movement continued to press their case, founding the Fédération des Elus Indigènes in 1926. This was not a political party as such but a coalition of independent elected officials drawn principally from the ranks of professional men, in particular doctors and schoolteachers. Deeply attached to what they saw as the progressive values of 1789, the Federation, in their inaugural conference in Algiers, called for native representation in parliament, the abolition of the *Indigénat* and the extension of full citizenship rights to Algerians. They had no illusions about what they were up against. Many had been subjected to racism and were only too painfully aware of the extent to which the settlers were resistant to political change. For these reasons they saw Paris as a tribune to appeal to, believing that reform would come from the mainland through an extension of citizenship rights to Muslims.

The personification of this movement was Ferhat Abbas, one of the most extraordinary figures to emerge in Algerian politics during the twentieth century.[36] Born in 1899 in the Constantine area, Abbas was a pharmacist by training and his family history was typical of that segment of the lower middle classes which had seized the opportunities for social advancement offered up by French rule. His father, born a peasant, had become a *caïd* and eventually a Commander of the Legion of Honour. Inspired by his father's example, Abbas did his secondary studies at the French lycée in Constantine and rose through the ranks of the colonial bureaucracy. His whole demeanour, from his slicked-back hair and sharp-fitting suits to the fact that he was ill at ease with Arabic and married to a French woman, was that of the well-heeled French bourgeois. For Abbas there was no contradiction between being French and Muslim, as he famously pronounced in an editorial on 27 February 1936:

> I will not die for the Algerian nation, because the notion of Algeria as a country does not exist. I have not found it. I have examined History, I have questioned the living and the dead, I have visited cemeteries; nobody spoke to me about it … One cannot build on the wind.[37]

The next strand within Algerian politics was part of a wider Islamic renaissance which had begun during the nineteenth century and drew upon the ideas of Jamal al-Din al-Afghani (1838–97), Mohammed Abduh (1849–1905) and Rashid Rida (1865–1935), three religious scholars who were determined to challenge the dominance of Western ideas.[38] Given the strength of Western imperialism, all three were in no doubt that reform was urgently needed but they concluded that Muslim countries could only become truly independent of the West through the reassertion of an Islamic identity. Within Algeria the influence of this current of thinking became discernible after the First World War when a group of religious thinkers called for urgent action to resist the growing impact of French and combat maraboutism. They wanted to put Arabic back at the centre of Algerian culture and in 1931 created a religious association which became generally as the Association of Algerian Ulema. From the outset the Association was led by arabophone clerics from traditional middle-class backgrounds. Many adherents were graduates of the Islamic universities of Zaytuna in Tunis and al-Azhar in Cairo, where they had come into the orbit of the theological thinkers from the Egyptian Brotherhood founded by the schoolteacher Hassan al-Banna in 1928.[39] The Egyptian

Brotherhood saw itself in the tradition of the modern reform movement initiated by al-Afghani. Many of the Algerian clerics were struck by the strident tone of the Brotherhood, which called above all for an end to foreign economic control and the establishment of an Islamic state based upon the *sharia*.

The Association's leader was Sheikh Abelhamid Ben Badis, who had been born in Constantine in 1889. Quietly spoken and a man of huge learning, Ben Badis had undergone his formal religious education in Tunisia and Egypt. Back in Algeria he brought together a circle of religious thinkers who founded two theological journals, *Al-Muntaqid* (The Censor) and *Ash-Shihab* (The Meteor) in 1925. For them the recovery of Muslim history was paramount as they wished to challenge the assumptions underpinning the 1930 centenary celebrations. It is no coincidence that Moubarak El-Mili's *Histoire de l'Algérie dans le présent et le passé* and Taoufiq al-Madani's *Livre de l'Algérie* were both published in 1931. Each was intended to hold up a mirror to the past and prove the existence of the Algerian nation, a nation that had once been very powerful and was now awaiting a resurrection. Moreover, through the recovery of Islamic history they wanted to inspire a new generation of Algerians who were mesmerized by the seeming invincibility of French power. The enduring message of the Association of the Algerian Ulema was the rediscovery of Algerian religion, language and history, a goal that was summarized in Ben Badis's famous formulation: 'Islam is my religion, Arabic is my language and Algeria is my country.'[40] This was a rejection of Ferhat Abbas's claim that the Algerian nation did not exist, a point that Ben Badis rammed home in April 1936:

> What is more, this Algerian and Muslim nation is not France … It does not want to become part of France. It could not become part of France if it wanted to. By language, by culture, by race, by religion it is far removed from France and does not want to integrate.[41]

Equally, Ben Badis attacked the folk Islam of the *marabout*s, denounced as heretical and as agents of the colonial administration. He also rejected any distinction between Berber and Arab. Instead, orthodox Islam was held up as the lifeblood of the Algerian people, the one force that transcended tribal divisions and would defeat the colonial game of divide and rule. In a 1936 letter Ben Badis was adamant:

> The sons of *Ya'rub* [the Arabs] and the sons of *Mazigh* [the Berbers] have been united by Islam for more than ten centuries. And throughout these centuries, they

have never ceased to be closely united with one another in bad times and good times, so that from ancient times they constitute one Algerian Muslim element whose mother is Algeria and whose father is Islam ... After all this, what force is capable of coming between them? ... They never did disunite when they were powerful, how could they now that others are holding power? By God, no! And all attempts to divide them will only serve to reinforce their unity and consolidate their bonds.[42]

Through a network of schools throughout the country, including the Ben Badis Institute in Constantine which trained Muslim teachers, the Association of Algerian Ulema had a profound impact on tens of thousands of Algerians until its dissolution by the French authorities in 1956. Condemning alcohol, tobacco, dancing and music, its members' puritanical outlook formed a whole generation for whom the sanctity of Algeria's Arab-Islamic identity would be the cornerstone of their beliefs. Indeed after 1962 much of the Association's theological perspective would be appropriated by the post-independence regime, and the annual commemoration of Ben Badis's death on 16 April 1940 quickly transformed him into a national hero.

If the Association of Algerian Ulema were cultural nationalists, political nationalism was represented by Messali Hadj (so named because he had been on pilgrimage to Mecca), the first political leader to call unequivocally for Algerian independence. Messali's significance cannot be overstated. Born in 1898 in Tlemcen in the western part of the country, the bearded Messali was an autodidact from a modest background whose tireless activism on behalf of the cause brought constant surveillance and regular bouts of prison. A formidable speaker – his speeches, usually delivered in a trademark fez, were greeted with chants of 'the great one' – by the early 1950s he was without doubt the symbol of Algerian nationalism.

After fighting in the French army during the First World War, Messali stayed on as a worker in Paris, where contact with the French labour movement gave him a clear grounding in modern politics and organization. Drawing on this experience he was instrumental in the foundation of the Etoile Nord-Africaine (ENA). Originally linked to the French Communist Party, the ENA set out to organize the large numbers of Algerians – over a hundred thousand by the mid-1920s – in the Paris region. By the end of 1927 Messali had severed links with the French Communist Party, thereby provoking a long-lasting suspicion between him and the communists, but the ENA in France had some 3,500 members and a radical and uncompromising programme. While stressing the centrality of Islam and Arabic to the Algerian national identity, the ENA specifically called for abolition of the *Indigénat*, freedom of the press, the creation of a National Assembly for Algeria, the withdrawal of all French troops and immediate independence; confiscated land had to be returned to the Algerian people and all industry nationalized. The ENA also stressed social egalitarianism and the importance of honour – *nif* – and national dignity, something that had been denied Algerians by colonialism. Not surprisingly, given the radical tone of its demands, the ENA was banned by the Paris authorities in 1929. Thereafter, confronted with constant surveillance, it would take herculean efforts on the part of Messali to keep the party alive.

The genesis of the ENA points towards the importance of immigration within modern Algerian nationalism. Immigrants, many from Kabylia, formed the bedrock of initial support for the ENA. Drawing upon their experience of contact with French political parties and trade unions, they modelled their organizational methods on the likes of the French Communist Party. Similarly Messali's ideology, underlining as it did Muslim values and social equality, resonated with the egalitarian society among Algeria's Muslims, which is why Islamo-populism became such a powerful feature not just of FLN nationalism in 1954 but Islamism in the 1990s.[43]

The final strand within national politics was the Algerian Communist Party. Officially created in 1936 out of the Algerian section of the French Communist Party, itself founded in 1920, the party initially drew support from settlers, although it did attract a significant number of Muslim members immediately following the Second World War.[44] A staunch defender of equal rights, the Algerian Communist Party fluctuated on the national question. In the 1920s the French Communist Party had unambiguously supported independence, but by 1936 the primary focus of communist rhetoric was on the international fight against fascism, and with this strategy in mind militant anti-colonialism was put on the back-burner.

In March 1939, in a speech given to members in Algiers, Maurice Thorez, the general secretary of the French Communist Party, redefined official policy and introduced the concept of Algeria as a 'nation in formation'. According to this formula Algeria was not yet a fully fledged nation, but a melting pot of some twenty races which were in the process of creating a nation. For Thorez the Algerian Communist Party was the most progressive force in Algeria because it was the only party which was uniting all the various races into one political organization. Thorez stressed two further themes: first the positive role played by the Third Republic in introducing values and ideas which were moulding the Algerian nation; and second the fact that, given the international fight against fascism, it was in the best interests of Algeria to remain under the protective wing of the Third Republic. Such a line of analysis led to a bitter argument with nationalists. For Messali and his followers the view that Algeria was not a nation but a piecemeal grouping of tribes and races smacked of an apology for colonialism. In return, the Algerian Communist Party stigmatized Messali as a fascist fifth columnist. Even so, and despite its relatively small membership and the fact that it subscribed to an atheist doctrine, the Algerian Communist Party continued to exert a significant influence, an influence that would continue in post-independence Algeria.

For each of these political groups the 1930s witnessed an upsurge in militancy, framed by the economic backdrop of the Great Depression. The massive increase in the Muslim population compared to the settlers, the Arabization of the countryside and the towns and cities of the interior, the widening gulf between the modern and the traditional economy, one dynamic and getting richer, the other underdeveloped and poor: all of these factors created a tense social situation in Algeria, exacerbating the political and economic exclusion of the Muslim population. Within this context the election of the anti-fascist Popular Front government in France in spring 1936 raised huge hopes for change. Metropolitan France witnessed mass demonstrations and factory occupations, while in Algeria Messali, amnestied by the new Popular Front regime, made a triumphant return and was acclaimed by the masses.

Such a welcome was symptomatic of a new radical mood. In the wake of the Popular Front's election victory, the Fédération des Elus, the Association of Algeria Ulema and the Algerian Communist Party came together to form the Algerian Muslim Congress, which acted as a pressure group on the new government. Two conventions in Algiers, in August 1936 and July 1937, forged a common platform which called for 'unity pure and simple with France, with the abolition of special structures, notably the *communes mixtes*, and the Government General'.[45] Messali supported the Muslim Congress for tactical reasons but still reiterated the demand for independence, a slogan which earned a tumultuous welcome from the crowds at the first Muslim Congress and underlined the fact that, with the urban lumpenproletariat and the impoverished rural masses as the base of his support, he was the rising star in Algerian politics.

The Popular Front government introduced a spectacular array of reforms. These included the raising of the school-leaving age to fourteen, the reorganization of the Bank of France, the nationalization of the arms industry and the appointment of a commission to investigate living conditions throughout the empire. Proposals to extend the voting rights of Muslims were brought before the National Assembly by Léon Blum, the prime minister, and Maurice Viollette, a former governor general of Algeria, in December 1936. Practically speaking, the voting reforms proposed by Blum's government were modest. Under its provisions just 25,000 out of six million Algerians would have been offered citizenship, but even this meagre legislation provoked the wrath of the colonial lobby within the Assembly. For the settlers it was the thin end of the wedge, another example of Paris liberals meddling in affairs which they did not understand, and all the worse because it was sponsored by a Jewish prime minister and a former governor general whose concern for the natives had earned him the soubriquet 'Viollette the Arab'. Consequently the colonial lobby did all they could to sabotage the bill. Confronted with such determined opposition Blum vacillated, with the result that when the Popular Front government finally collapsed in June 1938 the Blum-Viollette bill went with it.

The Muslim Congress supported the Blum-Viollette reforms. For the likes of Ferhat Abbas these reforms symbolized a fraternal France which through a grand gesture would open the way for assimilation. The year 1936 represents a watershed in the history of Algerian nationalism. Had it been possible to integrate the Muslim elite the divide between the two Algerias, between French and Muslim, might have narrowed. After that it would be very difficult to resuscitate assimilation as a credible way forward and this failure of reform led to the emergence of two political tendencies. On the one hand the supporters of Abbas continued to press for equal political rights, while on the other Messali Hadj mobilized his followers around the theme of militant nationalism.

In 1937 it was this second viewpoint which rapidly began to gain ground, especially amongst the working and lower middle classes in the large towns and cities. Uncompromising and radical, Messali asserted a new set of priorities with the slogan 'neither assimilation nor separation, but emancipation'. Most of all he underlined the need to learn the lessons of the Popular Front episode and change perspectives, arguing that faith in reform by the metropolitan Left was dangerously misguided. To support his argument Messali pointed to the fact that the Popular Front had not only reneged on electoral reform, but had led a policy of repression, dissolving the ENA in January 1937 on the grounds that it represented a threat to the territorial integrity of the Republic. When the ENA was reconstituted as the Parti du Peuple Algérien (PPA) this repression continued.

■ ■ ■

The outbreak of the Second World War in September 1939 left the nationalist leadership reeling from a blanket repression. The Algerian Communist Party and Parti du Peuple Algérien were banned, whilst Ben Badis was placed under house arrest. This repression intensified under the Vichy regime which emerged from the defeat of 1940 and was led by the octogenarian First World War hero Marshal Pétain. The settlers were delighted when the regime sentenced Messali to sixteen years' hard labour in March 1941, and gave equal welcome to the Jewish Statute of October 1940 and the revocation of the Crémieux decrees which transformed the Jewish population into second-class citizens. However, it is also important to remember that this was a period of complex ambiguities, where choices of action were far from clear. Ferhat Abbas volunteered for military service in September 1939 as a gesture of solidarity with the Third Republic. But the fall of France left him disillusioned and initially at least he saw an opportunity to press the Algerian cause within the Vichy regime. On 10 April 1941 he sent a detailed report to Pétain outlining the economic and social hardships suffered by Algerians. Forty years later he justified his action on the grounds that, at the time, he believed that Vichy had created a new climate which had the potential to transform old structures,[46] and that he was unaware of the extent to which Pétain was in the pocket of the colonial lobby. Similarly, following the logic that your enemy's enemy is your friend, some PPA members looked towards the Nazis as possible allies against the French, although it should be underlined that this was only a tiny minority. Overall, therefore, September 1939 until November 1942 was a time of confusion and fragmentation. The catalyst that radically transformed this situation came from outside, with the American landings in North Africa on 8 November 1942 which quickly overcame the resistance offered up by the French army and led to the liberation of Algeria from Vichy. This event provided the dramatic spur for the re-emergence of a dynamic national movement.

For Algerian nationalists the arrival of the Americans was significant for two reasons. First, it revealed the weakness of the French, who had definitively lost their aura of military invincibility. Second, it brought Algerians into contact with the new ideas contained within the Atlantic Charter. Signed by Winston Churchill and Franklin Roosevelt in August 1941, and trumpeted as a clear statement of democratic ideals directly opposed to Nazism, the Charter unambiguously asserted the rights of peoples to choose their own form of government. Churchill famously emphasized that the Charter only applied to Nazi-occupied Europe; he had no desire to oversee the liquidation of the British Empire. Even so the genie was out of the bottle and, assisted by the

American desire to distance themselves from the old colonial powers, the Charter's subversive implications soon became apparent to Algerians, who asked why there should be one rule for Europeans and another for non-Europeans and carefully drew upon the language of the Atlantic Charter to challenge the legitimacy of French rule. Towards the end of 1942 Abbas met the American envoy in Algiers, Robert Murphy, whose sympathetic response led him to present a shortlist of demands to the French and Allied authorities. Abbas specifically made the point that Algerian support for the war was not unconditional, but dependent upon the precise nature of the war aims: 'If this war were, as has declared the President of the United States, a war of liberation for peoples and individuals, without distinction of race or religion, Algerian Muslims would join, with all their strength ... in this liberating struggle.'[47]

Abbas and the leadership of the Fédération des Elus quickly followed up the meeting with Murphy with their Manifesto of the Algerian People in February 1943. Presented to Governor General Peyrouton at the end of March, this nine-page document catalogued Algerian demands, specifically the recognition of the Algerian right to self-determination. In response, and reflecting the weakness of the French, the Governor General called on the signatories to produce a comprehensive programme of reform.

The resultant platform, officially presented to the French authorities on 11 June 1943, called for a new beginning,[48] arguing that the imminent defeat of fascism offered up a unique opportunity to establish an Algerian nation where all, settler and native alike, would be treated as equals. This radical new language was underpinned by the enormous sacrifices being made by the Muslim soldiers who, with mainland France under occupation, made up 90 per cent of the Free French forces. The document argued that these soldiers needed to have the guarantee that in fighting for the liberation of France they were also fighting for the liberation of Algeria. Abbas reiterated this view in January 1944 when he warned the French authorities that the world, as in 1789, was experiencing a revolutionary epoch which, by extending democratic principles to the rest of the globe, represented the end of colonialism.[49]

During the spring of 1944 Abbas's hopes dissipated. Demands for independence were ignored and reforms introduced on 7 March, granting citizenship to 65,000 Algerians, were widely perceived as too little too late. Such frustration produced a militant atmosphere and led to the creation of the Association des Amis du Manifeste et de la Liberté (AML) in Sétif in Constantine on 14 March. Supported by Abbas, the Association of Algerian Ulema and the Parti du Peuple Algérien – though significantly not the Algerian Communist Party, which denounced the AML as a nationalist organization controlled by foreign powers – the AML's goal was the creation of 'an autonomous Republic federated with a renewed and anti-colonialist France'.[50] The AML quickly mushroomed into a genuine mass movement with a membership of a hundred thousand, but during the course of this expansion serious divisions began to appear, separating the leadership, which wished to remain within the letter of the law, from the grassroots dominated by the Parti du Peuple Algérien and committed to a radical fight against French rule. The latter soon came to predominate over the former, creating a combative anti-colonial approach which militants became impatient to put into action. At a special conference in Algiers on 2 April 1945 the vast majority of delegates voted not for an autonomous Republic federated to France, a formula seen to smack of compromise, but for the immediate creation of a separate Algerian parliament and government. In the remoter parts of Algeria, notably in Kabylia and Constantine, the PPA formed networks of paramilitary cells as the grassroots prepared for a military confrontation, which they saw as inevitable, even if the leadership regarded such action as rash and ill-advised.

By the end of April 1945 the tense climate was impossible to ignore. Not only was settler property attacked but wild rumours of an impending insurrection began to circulate in the major towns and cities. In an effort to seize the initiative the authorities deported Messali Hadj to Brazzaville on 23 April 1945. However, such a crude measure only served to heighten tensions, giving nationalists a precise grievance around which to mobilize. April, a month of acute economic hardship for Algerians, brought these tensions to near breaking point. A very bad harvest in 1944, compounded by a long, cruel winter, had led to famine conditions in the countryside. With nothing to eat, thousands of Algerians flocked from the interior to the major towns, thereby providing a ready-made audience for AML ideas. Economic deprivation and radical nationalism fed off one another and fuelled a climate of violence which was to have a tragic climax.

Large numbers of Algerians were self-consciously aware of what the defeat of Hitler's Germany represented and wanted to use the Victory in Europe celebrations to assert a separate national identity. Through an impressive show of force the AML aimed to make an explicit link between the victory over fascism and the end of colonialism. To this end 8 May witnessed huge demonstrations calling for independence across the country. Most passed off without incident but at Sétif events escalated out of control. There the march, which was scheduled to leave the main mosque at 9.15 a.m. and then follow the Avenue Clemenceau to the war memorial, was broken up by the police who intervened to tear down banners proclaiming 'Down with colonialism',

'Free Messali', 'Long live a free Algeria' and 'We want to be your equals'. This was the spark for a general and violent insurrection which engulfed the whole region. Over the next five days 103 settlers were murdered and another hundred wounded as groups of Muslims roamed the countryside with clubs, axes and knives. Faced with such a large-scale rebellion the French response was ferocious. Martial law was declared, the AML dissolved, Abbas and the moderate leadership imprisoned and the army given carte blanche to repress the rebellion. The violence dragged over several weeks as Senegalese and Foreign Legion units, aided and abetted by settler vigilante groups, killed and pillaged without discrimination. By the end the death toll, according to French statistics, was between 1,020 and 1,300, whilst Algerian nationalists have put the figure at 45,000. Significantly, whatever the truth, such repression was supported right across the political spectrum. Even the Algerian Communist Party and the French Communist Party denounced the uprising as the work of Nazi agents, a claim that was difficult to sustain given that Germany had just capitulated and that would be held against them for years to come by nationalists.[51]

For the French government Sétif demonstrated the authority of the French nation state determined to wipe away the stain of defeat and occupation. Conversely, the ferocity of Sétif created a new generation of Algerian nationalists. The writer Kateb Yacine, who experienced the repression first-hand as a sixteen-year-old, remembered Sétif as the politicizing moment of his life.

> My sense of humanity was affronted for the first time by the most atrocious sights … The shock which I felt at the pitiless butchery that caused the deaths of thousands of Muslims, I have never forgotten. From that moment my nationalism took definite form.[52]

It was a line in the sand, a point of no return, proof that even a France based upon Resistance principles was in the grip of colonialism. Such conclusions were symptomatic of this new generation, many of whom were demobilized soldiers who heard about Sétif some months after the event. Believing that they had been fighting for equality between settler and Muslim, they were horrified by the hypocrisy and double standards. For war veterans such as Ahmed Ben Bella and Mohammed Boudiaf, two future heads of state, news of Sétif turned them into instant anti-colonialists who rejected electoral politics, rejected assimilation and rejected the image of metropolitan France as a tribune of appeal. Confronted with the continued intransigence of the French authorities, they saw violence and direct action as the only way forward.

■ ■ ■

After the trauma of Sétif, Algerian politics took some time to reconstitute itself. On his release from prison Messali founded the Mouvement pour le Triomphe des Libertés Démocratiques. Uncompromising in its support for independence and the redistribution of land back to the Algerian peasantry, the Mouvement became known popularly as the 'pipa' or 'le parti des pauvres' ('the party of the poor'). In contrast, Ferhat Abbas drew a very different lesson from Sétif. The French response led him to the conclusion that violence was futile. The aims of the Manifesto could only be realized within the existing structure and with this strategy in mind he created the Union Démocratique du Manifeste Algérien in 1946, seeking to bring together those Muslims who were still committed to evolutionary change.

Initially Abbas's hand was strengthened by French attempts at reform. On 27 August 1947, the Fourth Republic National Assembly voted through a special statute for Algeria. Widely trumpeted as the foundation stone of reconciliation between the two communities, it made notable concessions to Muslim demands, including the abolition of the *communes mixtes*, the suppression of the military government of the Saharan territories, the acceptance of Arabic as an official language alongside French, the separation of Church and State for Muslims and the electoral enfranchisement of Muslim women. In tandem with these measures the statute introduced an elected assembly specifically for Algeria which would have the power not only to modify metropolitan law but also to vote in the budget and finance bills. However, the Algerian Assembly was based upon the principle of the double college whereby the settlers and the Muslims both elected sixty members. In effect this meant that the votes of nine Muslims were worth the vote of one settler and such an imbalance made many Muslims cynical about democracy. Moreover, the important reforms were never applied; when the Algerian Assembly was eventually dissolved in April 1956 the provisions of the statute had not even been discussed. On top of this the authorities tried to break the nationalist parties through corruption and intimidation. Elections were routinely rigged to prevent the Mouvement pour le Triomphe des Libertés Démocratiques from gaining seats and to ensure the election of loyal Muslims. Inevitably such flagrant abuses squeezed out liberals like Ferhat Abbas, meaning that their arguments carried less and less credibility.

The most militant Algerians, those now clearly committed to the armed struggle, were drawn to the Organisation Spéciale (OS), the paramilitary wing of the Mouvement pour le Triomphe des Libertés Démocratiques. Formed secretly during 1947, the nucleus of the Organisation Spéciale was a group of professional activists in their twenties who were drawn in the main from a literate artisan or middle-class background. Significantly they included Ahmed Ben Bella, Hocine Aït Ahmed, and Mohammed Boudiaf, all three of whom would become key figures in Algerian politics over the next fifty years.

Slim and athletic, Ben Bella, a merchant's son from Marnia on the Moroccan border, had been a promising footballer in his youth. Decorated in France in 1940 and again in Italy between 1943 and 1945, he rose to the rank of sergeant-major. However, returning to Algeria and learning about Sétif was the turning point for him. Disgusted by the stories of the violence, from that moment on he had one political goal: Algeria for Algerians. Resigning from the army, he gravitated towards electoral politics before going underground as a professional revolutionary sometime in 1947. Equally tall and imposing was Hocine Aït Ahmed. The son of a Kabyle lawyer, and a formidable orator, Aït Ahmed developed a reputation as a political animal who combined a formidable intellect with street-fighting prowess. Meanwhile Mohammed Boudiaf, another French army veteran, originated from the South Constantine area. Although afflicted since schooldays by chronic tuberculosis, he too was a tireless activist, ready to take on opponents with his fists if necessary. Little did the three men know when they immersed themselves in the anti-colonial cause that Ben Bella would be the first post-independence president and Boudiaf the fourth, whilst Aït Ahmed would be one of the major figures in oppositional politics.

Over the next two years the Organisation Spéciale trained up a clandestine army of some 4,500 men before mounting its first action: a masked attack on the main post office in Oran. By this point the Organisation Spéciale was being closely tracked by the French police, which launched a series of arrests in spring 1950. The capture of Ben Bella and the discovery of a series of carefully hidden arsenals were major blows and, although Ben Bella was able to subsequently escape to Cairo, the Organisation Spéciale had been effectively dismantled by 1951. For a time the nationalist movement seemed to have lost all sense of momentum, which created a mood of disillusionment that was compounded still further by bitter divisions within the Mouvement pour le Triomphe des Libertés Démocratiques. Here a group of young intellectuals, calling themselves the 'centralists' and headed by Hocine Lahouel, had become alienated by what they saw as Messali's dictatorial tendencies. This in turn had led them to create a new party which explicitly excluded Messali.

This internecine warfare was deeply depressing for those Organisation Spéciale militants still at large. For them it played into the hands of colonialism and reinforced their conviction that what was needed was a totally new organization which would prepare the way for an armed insurrection. This logic led directly to the formation of the Comité Révolutionnaire pour l'Unité et l'Action in March 1954 by Hocine Aït Ahmed, Ahmed Ben Bella, Mostefa Ben Boulaid, Larbi Ben M'hidi, Rabah Bitat, Mohammed Boudiaf, Mourad Didouche, Mohammed Khider and Belkacem Krim. The Comité Révolutionnaire met constantly during the rest of the year in Algiers and Berne in Switzerland. Its members were under no illusions about the scale of the task confronting them but their confidence was bolstered by the French defeat in Indo-China in May 1954 which, along with nationalist uprisings in Morocco and Tunisia, exposed the vulnerability of the Fourth Republic.

Such resolve cannot be divorced from the new international context. Decolonization was a dominant feature of the post-1945 world, a global phenomenon that happened with extraordinary speed. The formation of the Arab League, committed to Arab unity, by Egypt, Iraq, Lebanon, Saudi Arabia, Syria, Transjordan and the Yemen in March 1945; Indian independence from Britain in 1947; the Bandung Conference in Indonesia in April 1955, bringing together twenty-nine non-aligned countries from Africa and Asia which challenged the sharply divided choices of the Cold War: all these events gave confidence to the new generation of Algerian nationalists because they seemed to demonstrate that decolonization had an unstoppable logic. As more and more independent countries acceded to the United Nations it became a forum for militant anti-colonialism. The new generation of Algerian activists understood that any war would be won not militarily but diplomatically, by isolating the French on the international scene.

The Comité Révolutionnaire pour l'Unité et l'Action was renamed the Front de Libération Nationale (FLN) on 10 October 1954. Given that so many of its leaders were not only veterans of the French army but also activists from the Mouvement pour le Triomphe des Libertés Démocratiques, it is not surprising that they created a military-style structure, with the political wing, the FLN, complemented by its military equivalent, the Armée de Libération Nationale (ALN). Algeria was divided into six *wilayas* (administrative areas) to which was subsequently added the 'seventh *wilaya*', mainland France; whilst the substructures of the light company (*katiba*) of 100 men and section (*failek*) of 30 men were modelled on French military practice.

The FLN lost no time in organizing an insurrection, which they planned for 1 November 1954, the reasoning being that since it was All Saints' Day, a religious holiday, the colonial authorities were likely to be off guard. Few in number and poorly armed, the FLN centred their revolt in the Aurès

Mountains but with coordinated attacks across the country to give an illusion of strength. So at 1 a.m. in Batna a group entered the town and killed two sentries mounting guard at the gate of the regimental barracks; at 3 a.m. an attack on the French garrison to the east of Batna in Kenchela led to a protracted shoot-out where a French lieutenant was fatally wounded; while at 7 a.m. another group ambushed the Biskra-Arris bus in the Tighanimine gorges. In this last case the target was a prominent loyal *caïd*, Hadj Sadok, who was returning to Arris to warn the authorities of impending revolt. Stopped by a makeshift roadblock of boulders, Sadok was ordered off the bus by the guerrillas, along with a couple of newly married young French teachers, Guy Monnerot and his wife. On the roadside Sadok apparently reached for his pistol, at which point he was mown down by a burst of gunfire which also caught Guy Monnerot in the chest and his wife in the side. The bus driver was then told to drive Sadok's body into Arris, as a warning to the local population about the omnipresence of the rebellion, while the Monnerots were left to bleed to death.[53] The French were taken completely by surprise. Nobody had any idea what the FLN was or that this would be the start of an eight-year undeclared war.

Inspired by the Vietnamese nationalist leader Ho Chi Minh's dictum 'for every nine of us killed we will kill one – in the end you will leave', the FLN wanted to create an atmosphere of violence and insecurity that would be ultimately intolerable for the French, and bring Algeria to the attention of the world. Such logic was based upon a realistic appreciation of the military balance of power. The FLN leadership knew that they were pitting themselves against the fourth largest army in the world. Of course knowledge of the mountains would make the rebels difficult to beat, but there was no equivalent to the jungle of Indo-China; away from their mountain strong-holds, the open scrub and the vast desert expanses offered precious few military advantages to the guerrillas. Consequently their objective was to win a political victory. It was a single-minded strategy that recognized that favourable votes in the United Nations would matter even more than military success.

The attacks across the country were accompanied by a tract, broadcast on Radio Cairo, outlining the aims of the rebellion. As a clarion call to the Algerian people, embodying the spirit of November 1954, this has subsequently become a document of enormous historical significance.

To the Algerian people,
To the militants of the National Cause!

... After decades of struggle, the National Movement has reached its final phase of fulfilment.

... a group of responsible young people and dedicated militants, gathering about it the majority of wholesome and resolute elements, has judged that the moment has come to take the National Movement out of the impasse into which it has been forced by the conflicts of persons and influence, and to launch it into the true revolutionary struggle at the side of the Moroccan and Tunisian brothers ...

Our movement of regeneration presents itself under the label of:

NATIONAL LIBERATION FRONT

thus freeing itself from any possible compromise and offering to all Algerian compatriots of every social position and of all parties ... the goal of joining in the national struggle.

GOAL

National independence through:

1 restoration of the Algerian state, sovereign, democratic, and social, within the framework of the principles of Islam;

2 preservation of all fundamental freedoms, without distinction of race or religion.

INTERNAL OBJECTIVES

1 Internationalism of the Algerian problem.

2 Pursuit of North African unity in its national Arab-Islamic context.

3 Assertion, through the United Nations Charter, of our active sympathy towards all nations that may support our liberating action.

If these demands were met, the 1 November declaration stated, French cultural and economic interests would be respected and French people would have the choice of either retaining their own nationality, in which case they would be considered foreigners, or becoming Algerian citizens. The document was at pains to underline that the new ties between France and Algeria would be defined on the basis of equality and mutual respect.

The declaration underlines that the FLN had one overriding goal, national independence. The FLN was fighting for the right to national self-determination, a secular concept derived from the French Revolution and enshrined within the 1948 United Nations Charter; but in doing so it wanted to recover the Arab-Islamic identity of the Algerian people. By lionizing Islam, Arabism and the 'people' in these terms the FLN was taking over Messali

Hadj's Islamo-populism lock, stock and barrel, unsurprisingly given the political milieu in which the organization had been formed.

The language of the FLN was a synthesis of secular and religious values and the meaning and significance of the 1 November declaration has been bitterly contested ever since. Utterly opposed groups have all laid claim to the heritage of November 1954; the starting point for the 1989 Constitution was that all parties had to comply with the values of November 1954,[54] while the Islamists have cast themselves as the true inheritors of November 1954, arguing that the original FLN was committed to the creation of a truly Islamic society. These competing interpretations have made a heavy contribution to the violence of the last two decades.

THE WAR OF LIBERATION, 1954–62

Retrospectively, 1 November 1954 is seen as the beginning of the Algerian War.[55] What followed was one of the longest and bloodiest wars of decolonization, with merciless atrocities committed by both sides.[56] The French resorted to torture and summary execution; the FLN practised decapitation, mutilation and throat-cutting. Beyond the complex, even bewildering, details it is vital to highlight the connections between the past and present because so much of what is happening in contemporary Algeria is only explicable in terms of that war.

For the FLN the early phase, lasting from November 1954 to the end of 1955, was one of bare survival. On 12 November the interior minister, François Mitterrand, told the National Assembly that Algeria was an integral part of France. His hard-hitting language was soon backed up by military repression and thereafter the FLN units were hard pressed on all sides. The FLN had hoped that 1 November would spark off a general uprising, but in practice the Muslim population, the memory of Sétif etched in their minds, were cautious. They preferred to wait on events and the FLN had to resort to violence and intimidation to make them compliant. The national liberation movement might have projected the image of mass struggle but the cornerstone of the FLN strategy was control of the native population. People had to know that betrayal would result in immediate retribution. To underline this the FLN struck out at pro-French Muslims, dismissed contemptuously as *béni-oui-oui* (yes men). Consequently Algerian administrators, politicians and anybody disobeying Muslim rules of conduct all ran the risk of throat-cutting, mutilation or assassination as the FLN imposed itself as the sole nationalist force. The FLN also made it clear that other political parties had to dissolve themselves and their members rally to the FLN on an individual basis. Thus, Ferhat Abbas went over to the FLN in January 1956, as did the Association of the Algerian Ulema, formally banned by the authorities in April 1956. After prolonged negotiations Algerian Communist Party members were integrated into the FLN although the party itself continued to operate as a separate entity.[57] The one major exception was Messali Hadj, who rejected the predominance of the FLN and launched his rival organization, the Mouvement National Algérien (MNA). The FLN's predominance was almost total, and they achieved a major coup on the international front by being allowed to have observers at the Afro-Asian conference at Bandung in Indonesia in April 1955.

The second phase of the war lasted from the general election of 2 January 1956 to May 1957 and the end of the Battle of Algiers. Given the spiral of violence and counter-violence the elections took place in a highly charged atmosphere. The big shock was the breakthrough on the extreme right of the populist rabble-rouser Pierre Poujade, whose party won 11.6 per cent of the vote and 51 seats. With the French Communist Party winning 25.8 per cent of the vote, the Socialists 14.9 per cent, the Radicals 14.3 and the Christian Democrats 11.3 per cent, there was no clear winner.[58] After three weeks of political bargaining it became clear that the only group capable of forming a government was the Republican Front – a coalition of Socialists, Radicals and left-wing Gaullists – and on these grounds President Coty entrusted Guy Mollet, the Socialist Party leader, with the premiership on 26 January.

Mollet was a Marxist Anglophile and veteran of the French Resistance, deeply attached to republican values and fiercely anti-clerical. During the election he had campaigned upon a platform of peace in Algeria, and at one point described the burgeoning war as 'idiotic and without end'. Not surprisingly, therefore, he got a rough ride when he visited Algiers on 6 February. The settler crowd bombarded him with tomatoes and rotten eggs, an experience that left him badly shaken. Hitherto ignorant of Algeria, Mollet was shocked to discover that the majority of settlers were not rich colonialists but ordinary workers, many of whom voted socialist. This made 6 February into a conversion experience and henceforth Mollet saw the whole issue through the prism of the 1930s appeasement era: as for so many other socialists the memory of Munich made him feel guilty and he became determined not to repeat the same mistake again. From now on the conviction that the settlers must not be sold out, as the Czechs had been to Hitler in 1938, became an official government mantra. This world view was bolstered still more by the belief that what was taking place in Algeria was a battle between the universal civilizing mission of the French Republic and an Arab nationalism that was religiously fanatical in character. There would be no negotiations with terrorists who threatened the sanctity of the Republic.

To reassure settlers Mollet introduced a series of hardline measures. On 12 March 1956, the National Assembly, including the Communist deputies, voted in special powers, in effect giving the army a free hand to break the rebellion; the Algerian Assembly was dissolved and the army reservists recalled, meaning that by the end of the year there were 400,000 soldiers in Algeria. In theory the intention was to pacify the country, ridding it of terrorism and preparing the way for elections, but in practice the logic of military confrontation came to dominate, producing a cycle of violence and counter-violence which it would prove impossible to escape from. The government of the Republican Front caved in again and again to the military. Determined not to lose as in Indo-China and fearing that the government was involved in secret negotiations with the FLN, on 22 October the army forced a plane taking FLN leaders including Ben Bella, Boudiaf and Aït Ahmed to Tunis to divert to Algiers, in a bid to decapitate the rebellion. Unable to resist, they were led away by police to begin five and a half years of imprisonment. Meanwhile Mollet, angry though he was at the way in which the army had bypassed the government, sanctioned the action. On 31 October came the Suez crisis. The Republican Front, in alliance with Britain, attacked Egypt, spurred on by a conviction that President Nasser's Egypt was the real force behind the FLN, a 'Muslim Mussolini' leading a new pan-Arab imperialism that had to be stopped. Worldwide outrage, led by the US and the Soviet Union, led to a withdrawal one week later. However, such humiliation merely redoubled the army's desire to show that it was still master in Algeria.

The arrival of the reservists meant that the FLN was under enormous pressure during the course of 1956. In August 1956 its leaders decided to relieve the rural guerrilla units by changing tack and launching a campaign of indiscriminate terrorism in Algiers. Responding to a bomb placed in the Muslim quarter by rogue elements in the French police, on 30 September three women operatives, Zohra Drif, Djamila Bouhired and Samia Lakhdari, dressed as French women in order to pass through French checkpoints out of the casbah. Their bombs, placed in two fashionable cafés frequented by settler students, caused mayhem and left three people dead and some fifty wounded. Then the stakes were upped still further by the assassination of Amédée Froger, the mayor of Boufarik and President of the Federation of Mayors of Algeria on 28 December, allegedly by Ali Ammar, a twenty-six-year-old former casbah under-world pimp recruited by the FLN whilst in prison and nicknamed 'Ali la Pointe'.

Angry at the way in which the FLN could seemingly strike at will, an angry settler mob went on the rampage in Algiers, lynching Muslim men and attacking Muslim women with iron bars. The Battle of Algiers had begun and, as law and order broke down, the government handed over police powers to General Massu, the commander of the crack 10th paratrooper division, with instructions to break the FLN by any means necessary. In the alleyways, cellars, sewers and tunnels that make up the notorious casbah the paratroopers and the FLN fighters fought out a deadly game of hunter and hunted. Faced with a network of tightly-knit urban guerrillas the army resorted to torture on a systematic scale to extract information, including fitting electrodes to genitals, and during the next ten months 3,024 prisoners disappeared.[59] Grisly though these methods were, they did yield success and by October 1957, when Ali la Pointe, by now the last remaining leader, was blown up in his hiding place in the casbah, the FLN networks had been dismantled. Nonetheless the outcry over the methods left France isolated on the international scene. As the *Le Monde* journalist Jean Lacouture later recalled, France had won militarily but lost politically, and this was to be the story for the rest of the war.[60]

The fall of the Mollet government on 21 May 1957 inaugurated the third phase of the Algerian War, which lasted until September 1959 and witnessed the end of the Fourth Republic and the return to power of General Charles de Gaulle in May 1958. After Mollet the Fourth Republic entered what was to become a terminal crisis. Governments were little more than a reshuffling of ministries between Socialists, Christian Democrats and Radicals, each of which was overwhelmed by events in Algeria. Eventually President Coty tried to stop the rot by calling upon the Christian Democrat Pierre Pflimlin to form a government. But this only brought matters to a head because Pflimlin had made no secret of his support for negotiations and his appointment on 13 May 1958 provoked demonstrations in Algiers. The fear of being sold out to the FLN by Paris politicians led to settlers trashing the governor general's office and General Massu formed a Committee of Public Safety. A tense standoff between Paris and Algiers ensued, which took on a new direction when General Salan, the army commander-in-chief in Algiers, shouted 'Vive de Gaulle' from the balcony of the governor general's building on 15 May. The genie had been let out of the bottle and thereafter de Gaulle's razor-sharp political instincts, which had been awaiting such a crisis since the end of the 1940s, allowed him to play a masterly political game. To the army and settlers he presented himself as the man to save French Algeria, while to the public at large he cast himself as the only bulwark against a military takeover. In such a tense atmosphere all except the communists flocked to de Gaulle and on 29 May he was invited by Coty to form a new government. On 1 June, by 329 votes to 224, de Gaulle was given emergency powers to restore order and draft a new constitution. Just four months later the Fifth Republic constitution was approved by referendum.

The army hardliners and the settlers believed that the establishment of the Fifth Republic was a statement about the integration of Algeria into France, but de Gaulle always had a wider perspective. At the age of sixty-seven de Gaulle was still a tall and imposing figure, and he had not returned to power to preside over a quagmire. He was a man in a hurry who wanted to restore French greatness. He had no desire to be boxed in and during the summer of 1958 his stance was constantly evolving as he felt his way towards a policy.

Initially de Gaulle offered the FLN a truce but when this was rebuffed he sought to bring the FLN to its knees through concerted military action led by General Challe. Crucial to the success was the use of Muslim auxiliaries, the *harkis*, whose knowledge of the local terrain allowed the army to locate the guerrilla bands and then hit them again and again until they were broken. By the end of 1959 the FLN's mountain strongholds had been largely pacified but the price of this victory was very high. The brutality of the French methods, including the relocation of two million Algerians into camps in order to isolate the FLN, alienated the population. As Simon Murray, an Englishman who fought with the Foreign Legion, recalled:

> Just before noon we came across some *mechtas* [villages] and this time the men had not had time to flee. Under questioning … they refused to admit that they had had any dealings with the fell [*fellagha* – a perjorative term for FLN soldiers] and in fact they had very little to say at all. This all changed when they were put inside one of the huts and it was set ablaze. They started to scream blue murder and when we let them out we couldn't stop them talking.[61]

Whatever the success of the Challe offensive, de Gaulle knew that ultimately the way ahead over Algeria was to be found in a political solution and this led to the final phase of the war, the endgame, which began with de Gaulle's nationwide radio and television address on 16 September 1959. Within it he outlined three possible solutions, the first of which was secession, which he warned would open the door to chaos and communist dictatorship, the second full integration, whereby Algerians would become part and parcel of the French people, whilst the third, implicitly de Gaulle's preferred choice, was self-government by Algerians in close association with France.

This speech, the longest he devoted to the Algerian issue, was a major turning point in the war because de Gaulle now recognized the right of Algerians to self-determination, even acknowledging that those taking part in the rebellion would not be excluded from playing a part in a future Algeria. Such an offer, conceding as it did the principle of sovereignty, was the death knell of French Algeria. A succession of rebellions from the army and settlers ensued, culminating in the establishment of the Organisation de l'Armée Secrète (OAS) in May 1961 which tried to assassinate de Gaulle on a number of occasions.

The negotiations between the FLN and de Gaulle were not smooth as de Gaulle dragged his heels over the question of the Sahara, in his view an internal 'sea' that belonged to France and that had become strategically very important with the recent discovery of oil. Eventually the talking ended with a ceasefire agreement on 18 March 1962, signed at Evian, a French spa town on Lake Geneva. The agreement was subsequently approved by 91 per cent of French voters in a referendum on 8 April and by almost 100 per cent of Algerians on 1 July. On 3 July Algeria became formally independent.

■   ■   ■

What is striking about this overview is the contrast between the French and Algerian policies. Whilst French aims were constantly shifting, especially in the final phase of the war, the FLN had one objective, national independence, and this simplicity was to be a major strength. In comparison with the French, increasingly riven by divisions and contradictions, the FLN had an apparent sense of unity and purpose. But behind this façade nothing could be further from the truth. In reality the FLN was a fissiparous phenomenon, and, because of the needs of the armed struggle, deeply secretive. This means that the politics of the FLN was difficult to decode at the time and only now are we arriving at some understanding of the tensions which straddled the organization, in particular the power struggles which set the founders of the FLN against the new wave of leaders, the imprisoned against the free, the internal against the external, and the military against the civil.[62]

The FLN was not a tightly organized vanguard party. It was an umbrella for a number of fiefdoms which became known in popular Algerian parlance as clans. The six administrative areas, the *wilayas*, operated independently and fratricidal conflict plagued FLN strategy from start to finish because everybody knew that as well as fighting the French they were also involved in a merciless fight for power. In effect these clans were clientelist networks whose affinities to a particular chief were based upon family, tribe, region and common experience. This was to be the driving force behind the FLN, carried over into independence to become a fundamental aspect of Algerian politics. Despite its populist rhetoric the FLN was the antithesis of the mass-based party. Although they were lauded at every opportunity – 'for the people by the people', 'one sole hero: the people' – the masses always remained abstract, a fig leaf for the monopoly of power. Indeed if anything the FLN distrusted the people. They were looked down upon as an entity that had to be liberated through violence by a vanguard of dedicated revolutionaries. Significantly too, such thinking was infused with a deep-seated anti-intellectualism. From its inception the whole ethos of the FLN was predicated on the belief that action, not words or thinking, would decide.

The FLN was never an independent organ. Although it and the Armée de Libération Nationale (ALN) were seen to be complementary, the former representing the political leadership and the latter the armed struggle, from the beginning there was a blurring of civil-military relations. The intensity of the French repression meant that by spring 1955 all the historic leaders apart from Larbi Ben M'Hidi and Krim Belkacem were either in exile, dead or captured. New leaders emerged such as Abane Ramdane, who strove to give the FLN unity and purpose. Abane was the moving force behind the first con-gress of the FLN on 24 August 1956 in the valley of the Soummam. Taking place right under the noses of the French army, this was a major propaganda coup, a statement about the power of the FLN.

The key aspect of the Soummam congress was the assertion of the civil over the political. Its intention was to endow the FLN with formal structures and a clear chain of political command. The thirty-four-member Conseil National de la Révolution Algérienne was enshrined as the ruling body of the FLN, a parliament in the making, although it was made clear that ultimate authority resided in the hands of the Comité de Coordination et d'Exécution made up of Abane Ramdane, Krim Belkacem, Ben M'Hidi, all ex-OS, and two centralists, Benyoucef Ben Khedda and Saad Dahlab.

Soummam was the high point of Abane Ramdane's leadership, although his decisions were vehemently opposed by Ben Bella, who was not present.[63] But with defeat in the Battle of Algiers, launched on the initiative of the Soummam congress, Abane Ramdane rapidly became isolated. At the Cairo meeting of the Conseil National de la Révolution Algérienne from 20 to 28 August 1957, the decisions of the Soummam congress were overturned, the primacy of military action reasserted and a new Comité de Coordination et d'Exécution (CCE) was elected, now dominated by Krim Belkacem,

Abdelhafid Boussouf and Lakhdar Tobbal. In practical terms this led to the establishment of a Comité d'Organisation Militaire which would oversee the internal resistance from the Tunisian and Moroccan borders. The command of the eastern front was given over to Mohammed Saidi, and on the Moroccan front to Houari Boumediène.

The Cairo meeting, therefore, established the outlines of a functioning government which succeeded the CCE to become the Provisional Government of the Algerian Republic on 19 September 1958, based in Tunis. It was a defining moment in the future history of Algeria. The way was now open for the so-called 'army of the frontiers', recruited from Algerian refugees in Tunisia and Morocco, to become the dominant force in Algerian politics, a harbinger of the balance of power in the coming Algerian Republic. The marginalization of Abane Ramdane, and the attempt to assert the independence of the FLN, was completed with his murder on 27 December 1957.[64]

The eclipse of Abane Ramdane was mirrored by the rise of Houari Boumediène. A native of Guelma with a secretive personality, he was one of seven children born in 1927 into an impoverished background. His father, who eked out a living growing wheat, was a strict Muslim fiercely proud of his Arab identity who, significantly, spoke no French. Politicized by Sétif, Boumediène studied in Constantine under religious clerics before going to Cairo to the al-Azhar university. Emerging during the early years of the war of independence to command *wilaya* five, he was promoted to command the whole of the western front after the Cairo meeting. The completion of two electrified fences along the borders, the Morice line and the Challe line, cut off the internal resistance from the external ALN, a major schism that facilitated the formation of a large standing army, the 'army of the frontiers'.

Thereafter the army of the frontiers would be united in January 1960 under the single command of Boumediène and transformed into the Armée Nationale Populaire (ANP). In doing so Boumediène reorganized the army. Henceforth, there would be no more attacks on the Morice line to support the internal resistance fighters. Such a strategy was too predictable and was costing too many lives and although Boumediène's caution stirred up opposition, not least amongst the internal resistance who accused the army of abandoning them to bear the brunt of the war, he had the foresight to see that the conflict would be won not militarily but politically, through the diplomatic isolation of the French. The task of the army, now 35,000 strong, was to sit tight and wait, which allowed Boumediène, through his high command at Oujda just across the border in Morocco, to carefully build up his power base. The army became a mini-state apparatus which imposed an iron discipline through purges and torture carried out by the shadowy secret police headed by Abdelhafid Boussouf, in effect prefiguring the state of affairs after independence.

By 1961 the contours of the other various power bases had become clear. In addition to Boumediène's Oujda clan there were the six *wilaya*s of the internal resistance, the Provisional Government in Tunis, the Fédération de France organizing the FLN struggle amongst Algerians in France and the five founder members imprisoned in France. However, at this point the tensions within the FLN were dominated by the opposition between the general staff led by Boumediène and the Provisional Government, which precipitated the gravest leadership crisis to date. Essentially the struggle was about two issues – control of the army and negotiations with the French – and in a bitter war of words the Provisional Government accused the army of selling out the interior, even demanding that it launch an attack on Algeria by 31 March 1961. In return the army attacked the Provisional Government as corrupt and giving too many concessions to the French.

Muddying matters still further was a power struggle within Tunis. Between 1958 and 1960 former middle-class liberals, notably Ferhat Abbas who became president of the government, assumed a dominant position in the Provisional Government and it was they who led the initial negotiations with the French. This stirred up discontent amongst younger activists who doubted Abbas's revolutionary credentials. They accused him of being soft with the French and as a result in August 1961 Abbas was ousted as president by Benyoucef Ben Khedda, the forty-one-year-old former general secretary of the Mouvement pour le Triomphe des Libertés Démocratiques who had come over to the FLN shortly after November 1954. But just because Ben Khedda disliked the old-style reformists did not mean that he was any less suspicious of the army, and he attempted to curtail the army's power by chopping the command structure in two. In the tense standoff that ensued the army of the frontiers displayed unconditional loyalty to Boumediène. Even more decisively Boumediène received the support of three of the historic leaders still imprisoned in France: Mohammed Khider, Rabah Bitat and – most important of all – Ahmed Ben Bella. This legitimacy was crucial and in the face of the Boumediène and Ben Bella alliance Ben Khedda backed down. But henceforth nobody in the liberation struggle had any illusions about the FLN. The cracks might have been papered over but the battle lines for the civil war that would follow independence had been drawn up.

CHAPTER THREE

Darling of the Non-Aligned Movement, 1962–78

For Europe, for ourselves and for humanity, comrades, we must turn over a new leaf, we must work out new concepts, and try to set afoot a new man.

FRANTZ FANON, *The Wretched of the Earth* (1961)

IN THE EYES of many on the radical left during the 1960s, Frantz Fanon was the prophet of the Algerian revolution.[1] Born in 1925 in Fort-de-France in Martinique, and like Ben Bella a veteran of the Free French campaign in Italy, Fanon was a student in psychology at Lyon university in the late 1940s. His first book, *Black Skins White Masks* (1952), denounced French racism. For all the rhetoric of equality, Fanon argued, French Caribbeans like himself would never be considered true citizens; the colour of their skin meant that assimilation was a sham. In October 1953 Fanon began working as a psychiatrist in a hospital in Blida just south of Algiers, where he witnessed the impact of colonialism at first hand. Struck by the number of Algerian patients suffering from mental-health problems Fanon came to interpret this as the psychological effect of French rule. If so many Algerians felt morbid and insecure, this was because colonialism had made them feel unworthy and inferior. Their symptoms pointed towards the connection between economic and psychological domination, between racism and the French 'civilizing mission', all filaments, Fanon concluded, in the subtle web of colonial oppression.

In 1956 Fanon resigned from his post and escaped to join the FLN in Tunis.[2] It was a dramatic gesture and his letter of resignation to the Governor

General, Robert Lacoste, was a stinging attack on the ethics of French medical practice. By failing to see that the root cause of Algerian mental health problems was their experience of day-to-day racism, he argued, psychiatric hospitals were just props for the system. Such anger became the hallmark of Fanon's style and, as a journalist for the FLN paper *El Moudjahid*, he became a tireless champion of the Algerian struggle. In *L'An Cinq de la Révolution Algérienne*, published in Paris in 1959 by the radical publisher Maspero and immediately banned, Fanon uncompromisingly portrayed the liberation struggle as a revolution. The FLN, Fanon argued, was not aiming to restore Algeria to some pre-1830 ideal. Instead, the needs of the struggle were creating a different society, notably in the young women who, because they had to carry weapons and plant bombs, were breaking free from the traditional confines of Algerian society. Through such action Fanon saw the seeds of a new independent female identity.

Fanon died in 1961 of leukaemia shortly after the publication of his most militant work, *The Wretched of the Earth*.[3] Extrapolating from the Algerian experience, Fanon saw the peasantry and lumpenproletariat as the vanguard of the Third World revolution, encapsulating a new beginning untainted by the European ideologies of imperialism and fascism. Even more controversially, Fanon believed in the cathartic necessity of violence. If torture was about sadism and racism and ultimately colonial power then in his eyes anti-colonial insurrection was the necessary riposte, the mirror violence through which Africans and Asians purged themselves of any inferiority complex.

From the Black Panthers in America to the Paris students of May 1968, *The Wretched of the Earth* became an iconic text for the new radical movements of the 1960s. Fanon became the prism through which many radicals abroad understood Algeria and one of the reasons the country became synonymous with Third World revolution.[4] This optimism in the unbounded potential of the Algerian revolution was also present in the writings of Mohammed Dib, Kateb Yacine and Assia Djebar, all of whom conjured up an image of a youthful nation rejecting the jaded compromises of the European world.[5] Encouraging signs included the foundation of the review *La Révolution Africaine*; the strong links with Fidel Castro's Cuba; the arrival of young European revolutionaries such as the Belgian Gérard Chaliand who saw Algerian socialism as an alternative to Stalinism; and the fact that the country was a beacon for the liberation movements of Africa, all of which opened offices in Algiers. Fanon's influence is also plain to see in Pontecorvo's 1966 film *The Battle of Algiers*, especially the stunning scene of Algerian women disguising themselves as French in order to plant bombs in the European quarter.

The wide impact of Fanon and Pontecorvo explain why Algeria came to be seen as the torch-bearer of Third World revolution during the 1960s and 1970s. The post-independence regime encapsulated the aspirations of the 'wretched of the earth', an image that was projected first by Ben Bella and then by Boumediène, who was to overthrow his erstwhile ally in a carefully planned coup in June 1965.

■ ■ ■

The summer of 1962 witnessed a pitiless spiral of reprisals and counter-reprisals as the eight-year war reached a grisly dénouement. Hardline settlers and army renegades opposed to what they saw as de Gaulle's treachery had formed the Organisation de l'Armée Secrète (OAS) during the previous year. Intoxicated with violence, the OAS hit squads, many of them just teenagers, went on indiscriminate killing sprees, usually in the early evening after a day relaxing on the beach. Muslim corpses became a daily sight on the main streets of the capital as the OAS murdered 230 Muslims in Algiers during the first week of May 1962 alone. By June the violence became truly mind-boggling as the OAS also struck out at liberals seeking compromise, settlers who were leaving and the French army. Then, bowing to the inevitable, the OAS resorted to a scorched-earth policy, razing the University of Algiers library, setting oil refineries alight and dynamiting the Oran town hall.

OAS outrages inevitably led to FLN reprisals and on 14 May the FLN attacked known OAS bars in Algiers, leaving seventeen dead. As the familiar cycle of violence and counter-violence intensified few Algerians felt in a mood for reconciliation and by the time of the OAS-FLN ceasefire on 17 June euphoria at imminent independence was mixed with a basic desire for revenge. The FLN leadership had very little control over the grassroots fighters or the thousands who now flooded into the coastal towns lured by the prospect of seizing vacated properties, and during the spring and summer some 3,080 settlers disappeared. Much of the violence was led by the Marsiens, so-called because they had joined the national liberation struggle at the eleventh hour after the signing of peace accords on 19 March. Many of them were deserters from the *harki* units, the Muslim auxiliaries raised by the French army, who now organized the purge of pro-colonial Algerians as a way of demonstrating their allegiance to the new regime. Perhaps this explains the strong ritualistic aspect of the massacres, as those *harki* who had remained loyal to the French army, perceived as the ultimate traitors to their religion and nationality, were subjected to every conceivable form of abuse. Spat at, tortured and killed, some men were castrated and buried alive, whilst others were dressed up as women and paraded in the streets.[6] These grassroots purges started in earnest with independence in July but had petered out by September, at which point the arrival of the army of the frontiers, impatient to assert its authority, led to renewed violence. How many were killed? At the time the *Le Monde* journalist Jean Lacouture put the numbers killed at ten thousand but the figure has since been revised upwards to at least seventy thousand.[7]

The descent into chaos at independence was inevitable. The FLN had at their disposal very few disciplined fighters on the ground and the national liberation struggle, itself an act of violence, encouraged such action. This made looting and violence an integral element of the transfer of power, although much of the local population quickly came to resent the way in which the FLN left them vulnerable by letting the whole situation slip into anarchy.

This violence was particularly tragic since the FLN had talked about a multicultural society. How sincere their commitment was may be open to question but certainly numerous FLN tracts had reached out to Jews and settlers claiming that they had a place in the new Algeria.[8] During the final months, however, the violence reached new dimensions and by this point too much blood had been spilt to make reconciliation a feasible option. Already by April 1962 a hundred thousand settlers had left and by August this exodus had risen to over one million, virtually the whole settler population.[9] With them went the Jewish population, some of whose ancestors had been living in Algeria for thousands of years, and they made a miserable sight as they huddled on the quayside with their suitcases in what was one of the largest forced migrations of the twentieth century.

Only a brave few remained to face the uncertainties of independence, such as the Chaulet family, whose commitment to the FLN meant that they saw themselves as Algerian and no longer French, and the former mayor of Algiers Jacques Chevallier who wanted to smooth the path to independence. The attitude of the Archbishop of Algiers, Cardinal Duval, was symptomatic of just how far the Roman Catholic Church had evolved since the time of Lavigerie. Duval's denunciation of torture and support for independence, which had earned him the nickname 'Mohammed Duval' within the settler press, was nurtured by the dream of a lasting reconciliation between Arabs, Berbers, Jews and settlers. He upheld the idea of a multi-faith society, a vision symbolized by the continued presence of worker priests like Abbé Scotto and the monks who lived austerely in the Tibhirine monastry high in the Atlas Mountains to the south of Algiers.

■   ■   ■

The death throes of French Algeria obscured the divisions within the FLN, which spilt out into civil war in the summer of 1962. On the one side there was Boumediène backed by *wilaya*s Aurès, North Constantine, Oran and Sahara and by Ferhat Abbas and his supporters, still piqued at the way in which they had been sidelined by Ben Khedda. Heading this faction was Ben Bella along with two other FLN founder members, Mohammed Khider and Rabah Bitat. On the other side was the Provisional Government led by President Benyoucef Ben Khedda, Lakhdar Tobbal and Krim Belkacem, along with *wilaya*s Kabylia and Algiers, the Fédération de France and the historic leaders Hocine Aït Ahmed and Mohammed Boudiaf. The contours of the crisis came out into the open with the Congress held at Tripoli between 25 May and 7 June 1962. There Ben Bella's supporters used the Evian agreements as a stick to beat the Provisional Government, which, they argued, had given too much away and become infected with a neo-colonialist mentality. To renew the FLN, what was needed was a popular revolution led by the peasant masses which would combine Islam and socialism. In the bitter war of words that ensued any semblance of unity came to an end as Algerian politics became dominated by a ruthless struggle for power.

The divisions of post-independence politics were plain for all to see. Now, in the rush to fill the vacuum vacated by French rule, a bewildering spectrum of groupings, ranging from Nasserists through to communists and pan-Arabists, entered the fray, each asserting opposing visions of what Algeria could and should be like. Fanon's vision was one amongst many. At the opposite side of the spectrum was the Association of the Algerian Ulema, who intervened with a public declaration on 21 August 1962. Underlining the need to defend Islam and the Arabic language, they called on the FLN to condemn the Fédération de France's blueprint for a secular constitution as anti-Muslim.

These struggles were not just about ideology but also prestige; the mad dash for power motivated by greed, ambition and ego. It was an unseemly sight, which bred in ordinary Algerians a cynicism about leaders hungry for what was popularly referred to as the *kursi* (throne) and its attendant network of influence and profitable relationships, a pattern of court politics that was a hangover from the Ottoman period.

As the Tripoli Congress imploded without any agreement on post-independence institutions, the race to be first into Algeria began. Ben Khedda scuttled away without warning to Tunis, where the Provisional Government of the Algerian Republic (GPRA) issued a tersely worded communiqué calling on the internal resistance to hold firm, while dissolving the general staff and dismissing Boumediène. In response the general staff attacked the GPRA's decision as illegal and prepared the army of the frontiers to enter Algeria.

Ben Khedda and the GPRA arrived by plane in Algiers on 3 July to a triumphant welcome. In the wake of the 1 July referendum de Gaulle proclaimed the independence of Algeria at 10.30 a.m. and in the capital a carnival atmosphere prevailed. The world had been turned upside down as cheering Muslims transformed the streets into a sea of white and green flags with their red crescent and star. Two days later official celebrations marked the end of colonial rule, exactly 132 years to the day after the fall of Algiers to the French. Even so, despite the jubilant atmosphere, there were murmurings of disquiet. The crowds did not understand the absence of Ben Bella, who in their eyes was the face of the liberation struggle. Moreover, they were taken aback by Ben Khedda's warning, delivered from the balcony of the former governor general's office, about an army coup:

> The popular will constitutes the most solid defence against the military dictatorship that some are dreaming of, against personal power, the ambitious, the adventurers, the demagogues, and fascists of all stripes.[10]

When Ben Bella entered the country on 11 July from the Moroccan border and established a power base in Tlemcen, Ben Khedda and the GPRA immediately decamped from Algiers to Tizi-Ouzou in Kabylia. A tense stand-off followed and when negotiations between the two factions broke down Ben Bella established a political bureau with five members on 22 July, accusing the GPRA of hijacking the original FLN.

The scene was set for an armed clash because although the political bureau managed to buy off *wilaya* two, *wilaya*s three (Kabylia) and four (Algiers) remained intransigent. As the incarnation of the internal resistance they had no desire to be absorbed into the army of the frontiers, which, in their opinion, had deliberately left them to bear the brunt of the fighting. In response the political bureau accused the two *wilaya*s of factionalism and separatism and on 30 August Mohammed Khider called on the Algerian Army to eradicate their resistance. Thousands were killed in fighting in Boghari and El-Asnam, a rude shock to many ordinary Algerians who were ignorant of the power struggles within the FLN. In Algiers fighting in the casbah between the two factions led to a demonstration of over twenty thousand civilians who shouted, 'Seven years, that's enough', in the hope of bringing the combatants to their sense and averting an all-out civil war.

Physically and emotionally exhausted by the long struggle against the

French, the internal resistance was no match for the well-equipped army of the frontiers and on 5 September the dissident *wilayas* caved in. Four days later, like a latter-day praetorian guard, Boumediène's tightly disciplined units marched triumphantly into Algiers, their proud body language and smart uniforms marking them out as the heroes of the hour.

Although the liberation struggle was now at an end, the experience of the war would continue to define the fundamental aspects of post-independence Algeria. Mohammed Harbi has drawn attention to the mirage and reality of the FLN, the gap between what the war of liberation claimed to be and what it actually was.[11] For all the talk of popular participation, the army, using Ben Bella as a figurehead to take power, was authoritarian and anti-democratic.

The practice of the war carried over into peacetime in other ways too. Most obviously, the veterans of the anti-colonial struggle argued that they should enjoy a position of power and privilege in the new regime. Many ex-combatants were psychologically unable to make the transition from an underground fighting organization, and as a result much of Algerian politics since has been conducted in terms of cabals and inner circles by militants well versed in the techniques of smoke and mirrors. Indeed, the defining trait of Algerian politics post-1962 can be seen as this lack of transparency, the sense that nothing is what it seems.

FLN nationalism could only conceive of itself in terms of its opposition to French nationalism, with the result that Algerians were automatically defined as for or against the FLN. There was no room for hesitation or error, no place for compromise or ambiguous behaviour because the choices were simple. The corollary of this was that to wittingly or unwittingly play into French hands, to defend the French interests or the *hizb fransa* (the pro-French lobby), was the worse insult in the political lexicon.

The question of *hizb fransa* raises the wider issue of the impact of French rule and the place of French language and culture in post-colonial Algeria. Post-independence nationalism saw colonialism as wholly negative: between 1830 and 1954 Algerians were seen as in a state of permanent insurrection until the FLN assumed the mantle of leadership and recovered national sovereignty. Such a black-and-white view ignored the legacy of ideas, whether about rights, citizenship and democracy or types of political organization, that had become part of Algerian culture. The FLN refused to recognize that colonization had created a hybrid culture from which there could be no going back, especially given that very few Algerians spoke classical Arabic, while French ideas and culture continued to have an enormous influence due to large-scale emigration to the former colonial power. This was the crux of

Algeria's dilemma post-1962: could a pre-colonial ideal, drawing as it did upon myth and invention, be used to govern a post-colonial reality?

The Ben Bella Regime: 1962–65

On 20 September 1962 elections to the National Assembly saw the single list of official candidates receive 99 per cent of the vote. Five days later the Algerian republic was proclaimed and Ahmed Ben Bella became head of the government, with Mohammed Khider as secretary general of the political bureau and Ferhat Abbas as the president of the new National Assembly. The first Ben Bella government contained nobody from the GPRA and all the significant portfolios went to the military. Thus were the spoils of victory divided up amongst the winning coalition. But the nature of the ballot meant that the new regime enjoyed no electoral legitimacy; instead, legitimacy was derived from the war of liberation and the figure of Ben Bella as one of the historic leaders of the FLN.

There is no doubt that Ben Bella was deeply ambitious. Handsome, energetic, at forty-five relatively young to be a world statesman, he saw the leadership as his destiny. But the size of his ambition meant that he quickly alienated his allies. On 16 April 1963 Mohammed Khider resigned as secretary general of the FLN's political bureau, closely followed by Ferhat Abbas who stood down as president of the National Assembly on 14 August. Both men were dismayed by Ben Bella's dictatorial tendencies. Abbas in particular was incensed by the proposed constitution, which enshrined a one-party state and rejected political pluralism. However, this monopoly of power posed no problems to large numbers of Algerians. After all, had not party divisions prolonged colonialism? Only with the FLN had Algerians found the unity to defeat the French and it seemed logical that this unity should be maintained to face up to the challenges of independence. So the constitution was approved by a plebiscite and on 15 September 1963 Ben Bella was elected the first president of the Algerian republic with 5,085,103 votes.

From the outset Ben Bella's style of government was egalitarian. He lived modestly, refusing to take up the former governor general's palace and walking in the street without an armed guard. His door was always open and stories about his personal charisma are legion, whether it be getting up to dance on stage with a Cuban dance troupe or stopping the government train to play an impromptu game of football with his ministers. At the ceremonies to mark the first anniversary of independence on 5 July 1963 war leaders and ordinary people marched together, reflecting the long tradition of social levelling which had been present within Algerian nationalism ever since Messali Hadj. The liberation struggle had been a plebeian war on wealth and privilege as much as a war on colonialism and in this way equality became a badge of pride.

Such egalitarianism was also a reflection of the regime's militant socialism. For Ben Bella the Algerian struggle was nothing less than the invention of a new type of society, a protean event unleashing the dynamic revolutionary potential of the peasantry, and for inspiration he looked not only to Nasser's Egypt but also to China and Cuba. Indeed, in April 1963, as the regime nationalized vacant settler properties – a breach of the independence agreement with France – Ben Bella talked openly about 'Castro-style socialism in Algeria', which immediately raised fears in the West of a hostile regime on the southern shores of the Mediterranean.

The heady idealism of the Ben Bella regime was encapsulated in the Algiers Charter of April 1964, a fusion of socialism and Islam where the rising influence of Marxism was plain to see. Whereas the Soummam congress and the declarations of 1 November 1954 had stressed independence, the Algiers Charter underlined the need for the FLN to transform itself into a vanguard party and called for agricultural reform, self-management, socialization of the economy, Arabization, and the promotion of Algerians to all levels of the administration. The leftward turn of the regime was also reinforced by the support of the Algerian Communist Party whose six thousand members, who had continued to circulate freely despite the party's banning on 29 November 1962, warmed to his pro-Cuba sentiments, which were constantly played up by the party newspaper *Alger Républicain*, run by Henri Alleg.

The Algiers Charter also enshrined a commitment to fight imperialism, and Ben Bella became a tireless champion of liberation struggles throughout the Third World. Unsurprisingly Algeria felt particular affinity with the plight of the Palestinians; anti-Zionism became a cornerstone of foreign policy and in August 1963 Ben Bella accused Israel of trying to destabilize the regime. Such radicalism was further reinforced by hostility to Habib Bourguiba's Tunisia and King Hassan's Morocco, both denounced as too bourgeois, too reformist and too pro-French. Bourguiba was unsurprisingly incensed by Algerian support for plotters against his regime and in January 1963 he recalled his ambassador as a sign of protest. Such posturing underlined Ben Bella's revolutionary credentials and was symptomatic of his desire to promote Algeria as the leader of the Third World.

But beyond the rhetoric of Third World revolution Ben Bella was faced with the fundamental challenges of how to ensure basic services after such a destructive conflict. Edward Behr had been the correspondent for *Time* magazine throughout the war of liberation, and returning one year after independence he painted a grim picture.[12] Algerians were thankful that the war was over but with one in five unemployed many talked of a bitter peace. Plagued by crime and poverty, the country was bankrupt because the settlers had fled without paying their telephone, gas or electricity bills, let alone their income tax, since 1961, while scores of vacant houses, shops and apartments had been taken over by squatters, hardly any of whom were paying rent. By July 1962 the Algerian Municipal Council, which, in the money of the day, used to have 34 million francs of reserves for public works but now had only 55,000 in the coffers, could not pay the monthly wages of its office clerks. The magnitude of the problem obliged the government to resort to emergency measures. Ben Bella established the National Solidarity Fund and called upon his compatriots to contribute everything from jewellery to bank notes and deeds of land. In the same vein he nationalized just over 1 million hectares of land formerly owned by the settlers and handed them over to local workers' committees. However, few Algerians had any experience in accounting or long-term planning – the huge illiteracy rate meant that for the elections candidates had had to wear numbers instead of names. The ensuing chaos frightened off foreign investment.

One measure of the economic crisis was the surge of emigration to France. By 1964 there were 450,000 Algerians in France, a huge embarrassment for the new regime which was explained away as a necessary evil because it alleviated poverty in Algeria. Such statistics underlined the hollow aspect of Ben Bella's bravura. For all the talk of a revolutionary break the reality was economic dependence and in 1963 Ben Bella had to go cap in hand to France to borrow 1.3 billion francs.

As Ben Bella grappled with these seemingly intractable social problems, he was confronted with a range of political opponents from the former FLN leadership who were alienated by his dictatorial leadership. Khider, Boudiaf and Abbas approached Aït Ahmed with the view of creating a united front against Ben Bella. Aït Ahmed had founded the Front des Forces Socialistes (FFS) in September 1963 which, despite drawing significant support from the Kabyles, saw itself as a party for all Algerians opposed to Ben Bella's authoritarianism. A few weeks later the FFS led an armed revolt against the regime with backing and arms from the army commander in Kabylia and those fighters within the FLN who had lost out in the summer of 1962. But although Aït Ahmed hoped to rally the whole of the country, the reality was that the rebellion was restricted to Kabylia and part of the Algiers region. Repression was swift and by the summer of 1964 resistance had been crushed and Abbas, Ben Khedda and Aït Ahmed arrested.

The other historic leader to oppose Ben Bella was Mohammed Boudiaf. In prison Boudiaf had not only played long bouts of table tennis, he had also read widely, sharpening his political instincts through Sartre, Mao and Lenin. A belief in revolutionary socialism led him to found the Parti de la Révolution Socialiste (PRS) in September 1962. In July 1964 Boudiaf attempted to unite the opposition through the creation of the Comité National pour la Défense de la Révolution, which also included the FFS. But an attempted coup in the same month failed and this alliance fell apart. At this point, Boudiaf went into semi-retirement in Morocco, to re-emerge in dramatic circumstances in January 1992.

Outside FLN circles Ben Bella was also faced with religious opposition. Many of the adherents of the Association of the Algerian Ulema refused to work within the confines of the Ministry of Religious Affairs. For their leader Bachir Ibrahami, Ben Bella's 'state Islam' was about the creation of a compliant population rather than the application of true Muslim values and he called for a government based on the Islamic notion of *shura* (consultation). In a letter to Ben Bella of 16 April 1964 he condemned the regime's choices:

> Our rulers do not seem to understand that our people aspire foremost to unity, peace and prosperity and that the theoretical foundations guiding [the rulers'] work should reflect our Arab and Islamic roots and should not be drawn from foreign doctrines.[13]

However, as already discussed the most militant group was al-Qiyam ('Values'), a religious association established in 1964 by a group of clerics, including Abassi Madani, Ahmed Sahnoun and Abdelatif Soltani, which called for the country to be cleansed of anti-Islamic practices. The roots of al-Qiyam go back to 1953, when Soltani was instrumental in establishing an affiliated group with the Muslim Brotherhood in Egypt, founded by Hassan al-Banna in 1928 and dedicated to a renewal of Islamic society through a return to the orginal practices of the Prophet. In the cross-fertilization of ideas that followed, Algerian clerics were particularly struck by the ideas of Sayyid Qutb, whose book *Milestones on the Road* (1964) can be seen as the Islamist equivalent of Lenin's *What Is To Be Done?*[14]

Militant and uncompromising, Qutb observed that under colonial rule Muslims had been forced to face up to the challenge of the West and the corruption of local elites. Now, however, they were confronted by a new and even more treacherous enemy: Arab nationalism. For Qutb leaders such as Colonel Nasser in Egypt – closely identified with the Ben Bella regime –

might talk about defending Islam, but in practice they were leading the Arab masses into a new *jahiliya*, the state of ignorance that existed before the coming of Islam. Muslims, therefore, had a sacred duty to overthrow their Godless rulers and Qutb called for the creation of a young vanguard who would fight the new *jahiliya* as the Prophet had fought the old.

Although suspicious of the political leadership, Soltani felt that the FLN had to be supported in order to Islamicize society from within. However, given the tactical nature of this alliance, it is not surprising that once independence had been achieved in July 1962 he quickly fell out with the FLN regime. For Soltani, Ben Bella was too socialist, too secularist, too Western and had deviated from the true path of Islam.

Presided over by El Hachemi Tidjani, al-Qiyam was not a mass organization but a circle for reflection which organized lectures and meetings, as well as the publication of a journal, *al-Tahdhib al-Islam* ('Review of Muslim Education'), which addressed social, moral and educational issues. Specifically, the association called for the observation of Islamic practices, such as the closing of shops at the hours of prayer, and resistance to the infiltration of ideas seen as anti-Muslim, notably communism and liberalism. For them Ben Bella was deviating from the true meaning of November 1954: the creation of a theocratic state committed to the application of the sharia. Moreover, by falling under the influence of foreign ideologies Ben Bella was ignoring the all-encompassing nature of the Qur'an, which laid down all the rules necessary for life. Al-Qiyam's supporters were especially appalled by the dress of many young women, the new women that Fanon had talked so much about, who had fought in the FLN ranks and now refused to wear the veil. In particular they were shocked by what they saw as the immodest behaviour of Djamila Bouhired, one of the heroines of the Battle of Algiers and an icon for the new regime. During an official visit to Kuwait, she had descended from the plane with her hair uncovered, thereby embarrassing the waiting Minister of Education into telling the welcoming party of veiled teachers, 'Quick, take off your *hijab*', a story widely reported in Islamist circles. For the supporters of al-Qiyam this amounted to an overt display of sexuality, provocative and flirtatious in intent, which demonstrated how women like Bouhired were still infected by French values. It was symptomatic of the continued onslaught of Western culture – fashion, pop music, consumer goods – which was trying to make everything Muslims cherished as sacred irrelevant.

Al-Qiyam's stridency underlined the fractured contours of post-independence politics which was made up of Islamists, opposition parties, Marxists (some in the Algerian Communist Party, others part of the coterie of

Trotskyist intellectuals that made up Ben Bella's inner circle), and then finally Boumediène's army, which was increasingly dismayed by Ben Bella's high-handed leadership. The mass of Algerians were indifferent to these power struggles. Grappling with continuing economic hardship and the aftermath of so many years of violence and war, they were trying to piece their lives together.

Ben Bella's legitimacy was further sapped by a brief war with Morocco in October 1963, caused by the running dispute over the frontiers. Morocco had always been unhappy with the border south of Figuig, which in its view had been imposed by France back in 1856. In July 1961 the GPRA had signed an agreement which Hassan II believed laid the basis for a revision of the Saharan frontiers. At a meeting to resolve the situation peacefully on 5 October 1963 at Oujda, border skirmishes degenerated into open conflict, the so-called 'sands war', as Algeria launched an offensive, decreeing a general mobilization of war veterans. Despite the mediation of Ethiopia, which brokered a ceasefire on 2 November, fighting continued for another three days before petering out. But although the war had temporarily united the country – anti-Ben Bella guerrillas were even willing to put down their arms in order to rejoin the Armée de Libération Nationale – defeat at the hands of Morocco was still seen as a humiliation for the regime in the eyes of the populace.

■ ■ ■

Social crisis, political opposition, military defeat: Ben Bella's three years in power between 1962 and 1965 were overwhelmed almost continuously by a sense of crisis, and as the country slid into chaos he faced opposition from within the army. The fact that the army received half the proceeds of the Saharan oil royalties being paid to the Algerian government underlines the extent to which the military was the arbiter of choices of the regime. It saw the FLN's new role as a revolutionary vanguard as a challenge to its predominance and many officers disliked the Marxist language of the Algiers Charter, which had been written by a small clique of advisers, led by the Greek Trotskyist intellectual Michel Raptis, with no widespread discussion. Conversely, Ben Bella's supporters attacked the army as dominated by petit-bourgeois types, anti-revolutionary opportunists who joined the ALN towards the end of the liberation struggle when Algerian victory was unstoppable.

As tensions increased Ben Bella knew that he had to build up a personal power base. As soon as he had been elected president in September 1963, he set out to purge Boumediène's Oujda clan within the army general staff. He wanted to install people who could be relied upon to do his bidding and his first act was to appoint Tahar Zbiri as chief of the general staff in October 1963 while Boumediène was in Moscow seeking arms. Since Zbiri was not from the Oujda clan but a former *wilaya* chief, the significance of this move was not lost on the army, especially when it was followed up by the dismissal of three pro-Boumediène ministers – Ahmed Medeghri, the interior minister, Ahmed Kaid at tourism and Cherif Belkacem at education. By 1965 the only people remaining from the Oujda clan were Boumediène himself at defence and Abdelaziz Bouteflika at the foreign ministry.

Ben Bella also tried to shore up his vulnerable position by reaching out to erstwhile opponents. Aït Ahmed, who had been condemned to death, was amnestied, although on 30 April he escaped to Switzerland; Abbas was freed and on 16 June Ben Bella officially announced the reconciliation between the FLN and FFS. He then set about creating a popular militia as a way of ending his reliance on the army, while preparing the way for the Afro-Asian conference in Algiers which, by marking the tenth anniversary of the Bandung conference, would legitimize himself as *the* leader of the Third World.

His attempted creation of a popular militia was the final straw and in the early hours of 19 June 1965, just five days before the Afro-Asian conference which would have secured Ben Bella's international standing, Boumediène stepped in to carry out a carefully planned coup. The official radio played classical music and just after midday Boumediène announced the creation of a revolutionary council that would assume all powers. Ben Bella was imprisoned, the reasons for his deposition listed as his promotion of a 'cult of personality' as well as susceptibility to communist influence which was anti-Islamic and a betrayal of the true meaning of the revolution. He would not be freed until 30 October 1980. The figleaf was gone and the confirmation of the army as the power broker was now plain to see. A partner in 1962, the army was now the arbiter of Algerian politics.

There was strikingly little opposition to the coup. Ordinary Algerians were unmoved. The only significant popular demonstration was in Annaba. In Algiers many assumed that the tanks on the streets were taking part in the filming of Pontecorvo's *The Battle of Algiers*. The expulsion of foreigners such as Michel Raptis, Ben Bella's adviser and speech writer, stirred up little reaction, whilst the Algerian Communist Party's attempt to organize armed resistance was quickly broken as the secretary general Hadj Ali was imprisoned and *Alger Républicain* banned. Abroad Ben Bella's demise was denounced in far left circles, but for the most part was greeted with indifference.

BOUMEDIÈNE IN POWER

From the beginning Boumediène presented 19 June as a return to the roots of Algerian nationalism, in short Islamo-populism with the accent on egalitarianism, social justice and Muslim values. Socialism, along with support for anti-imperial struggles, was reaffirmed as the fundamental choice of the regime whilst Boumediène was particularly solicitous towards the Association of the Algerian Ulema, who warmed to his reassertion of Muslim values. Out of this synthesis Boumediène fashioned one of the hardest dictatorships on the African continent.

Initially, there was not much popular enthusiasm for Boumediène, largely because in terms of character he was shy, retiring, even secretive. Famously taciturn, he radiated none of Ben Bella's edgy energy. Yet, although at first ill at ease in front of the crowd, he quickly made this distance into a virtue as he set about bringing an end to Ben Bella's cavalier politics. In place of hysteria and frenzy he wanted to instil the military values of discipline and hierarchy. It was these hard qualities which Boumediène believed would make Algeria strong and they were immediately reflected in the new lustre given to independence celebrations, which now took the form of a military parade with a very clear delineation between the people and the leadership.

To bolster his position Boumediène sought legitimacy from allies abroad, and the support he received from Egypt, China and the USSR was crucial to the survival of his fledgling regime. From the beginning he was utterly ruthless in eliminating all opposition. The backbone of his regime was the shadowy Sécurité Militaire (SM) whose tentacles reached into every part of the system. Boumediène's eyes and ears, the SM saw off any threat to his power, imprisoning Ben Bella and his key supporters, driving Messali Hadj, Boudiaf and Aït Ahmed into exile and quashing the attempted coup led by Tahar Zbiri on 15 December 1967. The key to the SM's fearsome reputation was the belief that nobody was beyond its reach and that it could strike whenever and wherever it wanted. When Mohammed Khider was assassinated in Madrid on 4 January 1967 and Krim Belkacem was found strangled in his hotel room in Frankfurt on 20 October, nobody was in any doubt that these acts had been planned and executed by SM agents as a warning to political opponents both within and without Algeria. The SM, many of whose agents were trained in dirty tricks by the Stasi in East Germany and by the KGB in the Soviet Union, became the spine of the political system, with networks of spies everywhere. It vetted all appointments within the government and bureaucracy, becoming an omnipresent institution which Algerians learned to fear.

But Boumediène knew that he could not rule by fear alone. He was a pragmatist instinctively attuned to the factionalism of Algerian politics. He understood that if he wanted to survive and grow strong compromise was the key. Of course, he had to know when force was necessary but this was tempered by the knowledge that he had to find space for everybody. Unlike Ben Bella he was careful to reach an accommodation with rival groups, incorporating all the old *wilaya* leaders into the system in order to neutralize opposition. In the same way he adopted a conciliatory stance to those associated with the losing coalition of the summer of 1962, going out of his way to make sure some were involved in drafting the new constitution in 1976. Boumediène used positions, whether it be as ambassadors or in the state civil service, to buy people off. The trick was to distribute rewards so that the inevitably aggrieved few would always be outnumbered by the preferred many and the distribution of the huge material resources at Boumediène's disposal became a key element of the game. The economy underpinned the system since allegiance depended on the expectation of the various factions that they were part of an ever expanding enterprise that would always keep them rewarded.

The old 1963 constitution, along with the National Assembly, was abolished, and replaced by a highly personalized style of government in which all the key decisions were taken by Boumediène in tandem with a group of army officers. Algeria became a state within a state whereby power was not institutionalized but controlled by an unaccountable *nomenklatura* which comprised bureaucrats and technocrats alongside the all-powerful military. Boumediène never forgot that Ben Bella, and earlier Messali, had fallen foul of their opponents because each had projected himself as the great leader – in Arabic *el-Za'im* – a conception of leadership which ran counter to long-standing traditions, notably the village assembly meeting where the elders came together to find a consensus. As Hugh Roberts has perceptively underlined, this latter was the model for Boumediène's style of rule and in large part explains why he endured and grew steadily stronger.[15] Boumediène himself was initially too nervous even to speak in public. He never allowed himself to become the focus of a personality cult. With nothing of the ornamental excess of Saddam Hussein's Iraq, he lived a very modest lifestyle which Algerians came to respect him for and this incorruptibility became one of the pillars of his personal legitimacy.

What transformed Boumediène's relationship with the people was the Arab–Israeli Six-Day War in June 1967. In contrast to Nasser, for whom defeat was an unbearable humiliation which produced a disillusionment with pan-Arabism throughout the region, Boumediène won enormous internal support by identifying himself with the Palestinian cause. Sending Algerian units to the Middle East and breaking off diplomatic relations with the United States were very popular measures and for the first time Boumediène was acclaimed in public. In a society which placed so much store on male dignity Boumediène's policies, infused with what Algerians call *redjla* (masculine toughness), struck a deep chord. Algerians responded to Boumediène's message that there would be no more toadying to the West and *redjla*, symbolizing Algeria's new-found power in the world, became the cornerstone of his foreign policy.

For Boumediène the army personified the revolution and under him the old ALN was transformed into a modern professional fighting force. From now on there was to be none of the crisis management that had defined Ben Bella's rule. Military values were to be the basis of his long-term goal, namely a strong nation state, and Boumediène vigorously reorganized the army's various elements. He purged most of the headstrong former guerrilla commanders while retaining professionals of the external army, as well as about 250 officers and non-commissioned officers with experience in the French army. Indeed he came to see their expertise as an advantage, stating in July 1964:

> The revolution having entrusted me with the task of building an army, I do this with those who are the most capable. I prefer to work with Algerians, however late they may have joined our revolution, rather than with foreign experts.[16]

This policy, a calculated slight to Ben Bella's foreign advisors, brought to the fore a class of French-educated officers, Khaled Nezzar, Larbi Belkheir, Mohammed Touati and Bennabes Gheziel, all of whom had been trained in the French army and had only defected to the FLN comparatively late in the day, having spent the war of independence outside Algeria. This group of officers, known as the Déserteurs de l'Armée Française (quickly abbreviated to the acronym DAF), now formed the basis of the army general staff. Immersed in French military culture, their concept of society was a militarized one where a docile population would unquestioningly obey orders from on high.

Most of these officers had been promoted by the Governor General Robert Lacoste in 1956 in an effort to combat discrimination in the French army. Ever sensitive to status, upon defecting they had exploited this promotion as a lever to enjoy a higher command than they would ever have dreamed of in the French force. The Lacoste reforms became the butt of many jokes within military circles because in effect they had turned corporals and sergeants into generals, and the role of the DAFs in the post-independence state has been controversial ever since. Writing in 2002 the journalist Hichem Aboud, himself a former army officer, saw a straight line between the DAF and the violence of the 1990s. For him the DAF were little short of a mafia, who slowly but surely infiltrated the state during the 1960s and 1970s until they had won a position of pre-eminence by the mid-1980s. Thus secure, he continued, they would stop at nothing to hold on to power, which is why they were willing to plunge the country into such violence during the 1990s in the war against Islamism.[17]

Following the 1965 coup, the army exercised its influence through the country's supreme governing body, the Council of the Revolution. Of the council's twenty-six original members, twenty-two were military men with wartime or post-war service. At the end of 1967 Zbiri attempted a coup, following which Boumediène dissolved the general staff and tightened his control over what was now known as the Armée Nationale Populaire ANP by assuming personally many staff responsibilities. The army was central to the running of the country, undertaking local civic action and economic development projects. This role gave regional military commanders powers of patronage that further boosted their political influence as they became more influential in local affairs than the governors of *wilaya*s, who served under the Ministry of the Interior.

In this way the Algerian army became the embodiment of the regime and the custodian of the revolution. This was reflected in a cycle of remembering where, in the quest for an uncomplicated national memory, much of the historical truth was lost. Controversial individuals, such as Ben Bella, as well as rival political groupings, were airbrushed out. Likewise, the dark side of the liberation struggle and the *harki* massacres were never talked about. For the official memory, 1954–62 was the war of one million martyrs which pitted colonizer against colonized and where all Algerians were killed by the French. Consciously or unconsciously, Boumediène borrowed much of this language from French republicanism. Like the French with Bastille Day and the tomb of the unknown soldier, the Algerians needed their own monuments and martyrs from which to fashion a collective identity. They adopted a state religion which, by creating a cult of the dead and reiterating that the army had led a war 'by the people and for the people', inculcated reverence for the military. Algerians were not called upon to develop a critical historical consciousness, merely to gaze on the images of heroes and anti-heroes in respectful silence.

This mythology became a vital weapon of the Boumediène regime, with its constant demands on the Algerian people to display the same heroic spirit, the same discipline and self-sacrifice. The government's language, with its constant talk of campaigns, battles and vanguards, was emblematic of the militarization of Algerian society. In the meantime the idea of the FLN as a vanguard party was quickly abandoned. Many commentators see the role of the FLN as analogous to that of the Communist Party in the Soviet Union. Nothing could be further from the truth. Boumediène had a low opinion of the FLN and under him it became an empty shell. The FLN political bureau was dissolved and there were no congresses as the reins of power were taken over by the Council of the Revolution. The end result was a dictatorship where ordinary Algerians, even if their power was invoked in a vague way, were excluded from decision-making and not considered citizens.

Fundamentally, all of Boumediène's policies were directed to one goal: the rapid transformation of Algerian society into a modern industrialized nation. The war of liberation had created Algeria: now Boumediène had to create Algerians, and his model was the nation state as developed in Europe during the nineteenth century. The path to a uniform national identity was to be found through education, religion, history and military service. Through these mechanisms of social engineering peasants would be transformed into Algerians.

The key to this process was the creation of a centralized state and Boumediène envisaged the authority of the plains asserting itself over a socially diverse country with a long tradition of suspicion of state authority. Boumediène knew that for large numbers of Algerians state rule, of whatever hue, was seen as foreign and that they had developed all sorts of intricate strategies to resist it. Boumediène knew too that even the FLN's argument that an Algerian state had already existed in 1830 was quite flimsy. Historically, central power had always been weak and this meant that Boumediène was arguably creating the first-ever Algerian state. In doing so, he wanted to overcome the tradition of self-governing tribes, as well as the legacy of tension between Berber and Arab, in order to create a uniform national community that would correspond to the state.

What were to be the pillars of the nation state? In first place was Islam. Boumediène had a practical attitude towards religion. Like Napoleon, he saw it as cement which would bind the country together and legitimize the regime. Drawing upon Ben Badis's dictum that Islam and Arabic were the foundation stones of Algerian identity, Boumediène was careful to establish the state control of religion which drew in the followers of the Association of the Algerian Ulema with the creation of a Ministry of Religious Affairs. Through such an alliance Boumediène wanted an Islam that was compliant, whereby preachers and scholars were transformed into civil servants of the state, whilst any activity outside the ministry's control was subjected to surveillance and repression.

The assertion that Algerians were an Arab-Islamic people was at the heart of the Boumediène revolution. It was a monolithic conception of historical identity which tolerated no light, shade or distortion, and it won over the followers of the Association of the Algerian Ulema, giving them a free hand to ban gambling and the sale of alcohol to Muslims in 1967 and eventually to introduce Friday as the day of rest. However, those associated with al-Qiyam, such as Abdelatif Soltani, refused to work for the state, disliking the way Boumediène was trying to appropriate Islam. In 1966 they protested directly to Boumediène over the plight of the leading Muslim scholar Sayyid Qutb, who was shortly to be executed by Nasser. Unmoved, the regime used this opportunity to suspend the work of al-Qiyam before finally banning the association for four years on 17 March 1970.

However, repression went hand in hand with a concerted drive to incorporate al-Qiyam's key ideas. The Minister of Religious Affairs, the notorious conservative Mouloud Kassim, launched a campaign against the degradation of morals which led to a tripling in the price of beer and whisky and calls for women to be put back into the home. He was incensed that Algerians had not learnt to act and think like Muslims. Instead they were still mesmerized by French fashion, ideas and language, particularly young men with their tight jeans and long hair.

At the same time, graduates from the Ulama gained an important presence in the education system. The Minister of Culture, Ahmed Taleb-Ibrahimi, believed strongly that France had tried to systematically rob Algerians of their culture, language and history.[18] So, unlike Habib Bourguiba in Tunisia and Léopold Senghor in Senegal, Ibrahami rejected the Francophone movement. In Ibrahimi's view, speaking about a global French culture which the former empire could make their own was dangerous nonsense. To continue in awe of France ignored the extent to which colonialism had been just as much about cultural and linguistic domination as it had about economic exploitation. It was indicative of a neo-colonial mentality and this was why Arabization had to go hand in hand with Islam. By trying to phase out French as the language of government and education and replacing it with Modern Standard Arabic, Algerians saw themselves as reclaiming the identity that had been stolen from them by colonialism and rekindling their link with the Middle East.

However, the majority of the Algerian teachers, speaking as they did French or colloquial Arabic, did not have the necessary linguistic skills to teach complex subjects in Modern Standard Arabic. The policy, therefore, became dependent upon recruits from the Middle East, many of whom had been trained by the Muslim Brotherhood, and this became a conduit for Islamist ideas. Their beards and baggy dress marked them out as instantly recognizable and amongst Algerian schoolchildren and students they were popularly referred to as the *frérots* (little brothers).

Nowhere was the politicization of culture more obvious than in respect to the Berber language. Ibrahimi rejected the idea that Berber must be put on equal terms with Arabic, on the grounds that it would encourage Kabyle separatism and play into the hands of France. He took the line that the Berbers were descended from the Arabs and that their various dialects should be confined to the home. Then, when attempts were made to give a written form to Tamazight, an oral language with over 500,000 words, the government was adamant that this should be in Arabic script rather than Latin because the latter had clear neo-colonial overtones. In the face of such repression, Berber activists – such as the Mouvement Culturel Berbère (MCB) which emerged during the student unrest of 1968 – operated in a clandestine way, distributing underground tracts supporting pluralism and calling for recognition of the cultural and linguistic rights of the Berbers. Frustration at the lack of headway made by the MCB led some younger members to turn to terrorism and in 1976 one group attacked the headquarters of the FLN paper *El Moudjahid*. Likewise, a clumsy attempt to restrict the air time of Kabyle Radio provoked protests in 1976 which carried on for two years.

Such suppression underlined just how far Algerian politics was defined by fears of French influence; any sign of Berber assertiveness was immediately denounced as the work of the neo-colonial fifth column. Yet, for all the regime's obsession with Arabization the plain fact was that it was impossible to eradicate French language and culture. Huge numbers of emigrants were still making their way to France and French was used by a large part of the press and key writers like Mohammed Dib and Kateb Yacine, even if the arabophone movement was gaining ground. Even in the early 1970s two Algerians meeting in the street were still most likely to greet each other in French.[19]

The lynchpin of the Boumediène revolution was an ambitious programme of industrialization. His aim was to overcome the cycle of underdevelopment and produce a self-contained economy where independence would be a badge of honour. Consequently between 1966 and 1971 the regime took control of the country's minerals, banking, insurance and manufacturing sectors. The climax of this process was the nationalization of the oil and gas industries on 24 February 1971 – one of the first successful nationalizations of oil to be carried out in the Arab world – and thereafter Algeria played a leading role in the Organization of Petroleum Exporting Countries (OPEC), which had been established in 1960 by Iran, Iraq, Kuwait, Saudi Arabia and Venezuela. Algeria joined in 1969 and was instrumental in the oil embargo by Arab OPEC members which was retaliation for the West's pro-Israeli stance during the 1973 Arab-Israeli war. Such bullishness, allied to the seizing of French oil company assets, was a statement about the end of neo-colonialism and although this caused a serious rift between France and Algeria it proved very popular with ordinary Algerians. For them it was another example of Boumediène's much vaunted *redjla*: his willingness to stand face to face with the former colonial master and win.

The architect of industrialization was Belaid Abdessalam, the industry minister, whose policy was predicated on the notion that heavy industry must be privileged over agricultural production because the potential of the land was limited. This thinking drew upon the theories of the French economic advisor Gérard Destanne de Bernis, who argued that for Third World countries like Algeria the hydrocarbon sector should be the motor of the economy.[20] It was influenced too by the examples of Nasser's Egypt, which had set out to fuse Islam with science and technology, and the Soviet Union, where the use of five-year plans geared towards heavy industry had, from the vantage point of the late 1960s, transformed a backward peasant nation into a superpower. 'Study', 'work', 'development', 'progress': these were the watch-words of the Boumediène era as the coastline from Algiers to Arzew became one huge building site. Through rational planning he wanted Algerians to embrace the twentieth century and construct a brave new world that would obliterate 132 years of colonial dependency. Consumer goods would be sacrificed and, unlike his counterparts in Morocco and Tunisia, Boumediène shunned the idea of a tourist industry to attract wealthy Westerners.

Large numbers of Algerians were genuinely inspired by Boumediène's vision and by the mid-1970s Algeria had become a pace-setter within the Third World. The average annual growth of the economy between 1967 and 1978 was an impressive 7.2 per cent, whilst during 1970–73 Algeria was alone among African countries in exceeding the level of investment envisaged in its four-year plan. Likewise, with education taking up 11 per cent of the GNP by the mid-1970s – an enormous proportion for any country – Boumediène could rightfully claim that Algeria was well on the way to his avowed objective: the transformation of the country into a modern Mediterranean state with an educated population.

In large part, though, these impressive figures were the result of the petrol boom. Policy was increasingly based on the premise that the flow of petrol revenues would finance industrialization. The petrol dividend would buy social peace by making sure that basic goods were always in the shops; creating jobs, estimated at some 175,000 a year; and by providing investment, in Kabylia and the Aurès, as a way of calming potentially explosive regions.

In the midst of this industrial revolution Algeria was visited by the Cuban leader, Fidel Castro, who, on 16 May 1972, dressed in his trademark military fatigues, gave an impassioned speech to an audience of tens of thousands packed into the centre of Algiers:

> Between the Algerians and us, that is between the Algerians and the Cubans, meetings have been easy. Understanding has been easy. *[applause]* Unity has been easy. *[applause]* Simply because we are two revolutionary peoples, because we are two peoples who won liberty with weapons in our hands, because we are two peoples who have fought for more than a century to achieve our independence. This is why we understand each other well.[21]

Relayed live on national radio, Castro spoke in Spanish with a sentence-by-sentence French translation, as the crowds, regularly shouting 'Fidel' and 'Boumediène', waved Cuban and Algerian flags alongside huge banners reading 'long live the Cuban revolution' and 'long live Che Guevara'. The speech was the climax of an eight-day visit, and everywhere Castro and Boumediène were being greeted by cheers of '*Yahia Fidel wa yahia Cuba*' ('Long live Fidel and Cuba') and '*Jaish, sha'ab, thawra zara'iya*' ('Army, people, agricultural revolution'). During this time the Cuban delegation had visited hospitals, schools, universities, socialist villages, factories and oil refineries and in each case, Castro told his audience, he had been deeply impressed by the achievements of the Algerian revolution. The French, he proclaimed, had scoffed at the idea that petroleum could flow without them, but now production had increased, new gas pipelines were being constructed and Algeria was a great power in the making:

> Algeria has not only given an example of how to defend the fatherland, how to conquer freedom, how to carry out the revolution with weapons in their hands. *[applause]* This example is there and will always be there for other peoples still suffering under colonialism, oppression and exploitation of all kinds.
>
> But also, after winning its independence, Algeria is now showing the peoples of the Third World what must be done with their natural resources. *[applause]* Other peoples of Africa, Asia and Latin America also possess great natural

resources, mineral resources and hydrocarbon resources, oil and gas. *[cheers and prolonged shouts of 'Long live Castro']* The other countries of the Third World, what have they done with their natural resources? They have handed them over to the imperialists. They have put them into the hands of the imperialist monopolies. And what is happening to these countries? Have the imperialists ensured their development? No. *[cheers]* They take away the natural resources and encourage the people to adopt the consumer habits of developed countries.[22]

In this way Castro underlined the symmetry of the Algerian and Cuban revolutions. Having won their independence from France and America, both were now united in a common struggle against imperialism, poverty and underdevelopment.

The popular enthusiasm for Castro was not choreographed.[23] The Cuban leader's visit encapsulated a moment of intense euphoria and optimism, taking place as it did during Algeria's agrarian revolution, launched on 8 November 1971, which marked a decisive turn to the left for the Boumediène regime. In the run-up to this period Boumediène's language had become more and more radical, as he conjured up the spectre of an Algerian bourgeoisie which was far worse than the settlers and had to be met head-on. According to the 1972 census, just 3 per cent of all farmers, 16,500 landowners in all, owned a quarter of the cultivable land.

For Boumediène such statistics were an affront to the egalitarian sentiments of the Algerian revolution and justified an all-out assault on private property. Until then public property had been expanded through the expropriation of foreign capital alone. Now private property was targeted and large Muslim estates were nationalized. Between January 1972 and June 1973, 640,000 hectares were expropriated from private hands and given to the poorer peasants, many of whom were organized into self-contained socialist villages. Such villages, the pride and joy of the Boumediène regime, reflected the strong millenarian aspect of the agrarian revolution, their purpose the realization of a truly Islamic society based upon social justice and peasant values. The desire to overcome tribal and kinship structures was another important factor in Boumediène's policy-making; he aimed to destroy the traditional centres of power in the countryside and bring rural society under central control.

In announcing the agrarian revolution Boumediène called upon the FLN to lead the transition to socialism. Yet, despite such heady rhetoric Boumediène knew that the FLN, largely because of his own actions, was an empty shell and for this reason he looked to the Algerian Communist Party, which had renamed itself the Parti de l'Avant-Garde Socialiste (PAGS) in

1966. On the face of it this might seem difficult to understand since the Algerian Commmunist Party had opposed the June 1965 coup, but this hostility mellowed following Boumediène's official visit to the Soviet Union in December 1965. At this point the party had revised its analysis of the Boumediène regime, taking the line that the regime was made up of 'conservatives' and 'progressives'. Its aim was to ally itself with the progressives and make sure that Algeria aligned itself with the pro-Soviet block, and it therefore staunchly opposed Kaid Ahmed, a member of the Oujda clan who replaced Cherif Belkacem as the FLN party head in December 1967. A large landowner, former Abbas supporter and staunch anti-communist, Ahmed was very much on the conservative wing of the FLN, cracking down on leftist students and banning the National Union of Algerian Students outright on 15 January 1971.

Not surprisingly, Ahmed was horrified by Boumediène's agrarian revolution. He was also alarmed by the upsurge in pro-Castro sentiments and in the ensuing power conflict he was dismissed as party head in 1972. For the communists Ahmed's ousting signalled that progressives in the regime had the upper hand and, though still in theory illegal, communist militants began to operate out in the open with Boumediène's tacit approval. Infiltrating the trade union and youth organizations, communists organized brigades of secondary and university students who volunteered to work on the newly created socialist villages. These brigades became the eyes and ears of the revolution, seeking out wreckers and saboteurs who were dragging their feet or obstructing the redistribution of land. There was a strong whiff of Mao's cultural revolution about the whole enterprise as Boumediène actively encouraged a spirit of criticism against his opponents in the regime. By calling upon young Algerians to attack capitalism and bureaucracy he wanted to purge those parts of the regime which were hostile to his socialist vision.

In the face of official vilification rich landowners sought to sabotage the agrarian revolution by doctoring records, dividing land up amongst family members and killing animals so that they would not be seized by the state. Some landowners couched their opposition in religious terms, denouncing Boumediène's attack on private property as anti-Muslim and looking towards dissident Islamist clerics such as Abdelatif Soltani for religious legitimacy. The agrarian revolution, therefore, along with the Castro visit, stirred up a revival of Islamist agitation which the regime had so successfully muffled at the end of the 1960s.

Since the banning of al-Qiyam in 1970 Soltani had become a folkloric figure continually hounded by the authorities. His inflammatory rhetoric and ceaseless activism cost him several dismissals from his job as a preacher and at periodic intervals he was placed under house arrest. Through cassettes and pamphlets he developed a strident critique of the FLN interpretation of the past. In particular he viewed the war of liberation in a new light. For Soltani, November 1954 was inspired by Islamic principles; it was about cleansing Algeria of French influences and returning to a society based on religion. In this way he posited a stark contrast between the original principles of the FLN and the betrayal of independence. Controversially, Soltani argued that 1962 was the continuation of the West's relentless war on Islam, albeit in a much more subtle form, because at this point pro-French Algerians infiltrated the FLN and exploited their power to impose an alien francophone culture on the Muslim masses. Furthermore, he began to argue that the war against French rule had not been a true jihad but a struggle motivated by greed and personal gain on the part of the FLN leadership. On this basis he introduced a distinction between those who had died for faith and those who had died for nationalism, arguing that the last category could not be considered true martyrs.

Soltani's world view also had a strong anti-socialist and anti-communist dimension. He was horrified by Boumediène's leftward turn and he rejected any link between Islam and socialism.[24] True Muslims, he demanded, should not pray on nationalized land. In his book entitled *Al-Mazdaqiya Hiya Asl al-Ishtiraqiya* ('*Mazdaqism Is the Source of Socialism*') and published in Morocco in 1974 while he was in exile, Soltani launched a stinging attack on FLN socialism, which he saw as inspired by atheism, in contrast to true Islam which sought to create a society based on the word of God. The title of the book refers to the Mazdaq Persians, a sect from the fifth century BC whose ideology many have likened to primitive communism. The FLN's attempt to fuse socialist ideology and Muslim thought, Soltani argued, was thus symptomatic of an age-old threat, namely the insidious contamination of true Islam by foreign ideas, just as in the past others had attempted to reconcile Islam with Greek philosophy.[25]

For Soltani, Boumediène's repudiation of Islam was symbolized not just by socialism, but also by the promotion of women within the regime and the official prestige accorded to the author Kateb Yacine. Although Yacine was without doubt one of the most significant Algerian writers of the twentieth century, Soltani was scandalized by his left-wing anti-Islamic rhetoric.[26] In Soltani's view all these signs revealed the regime's advanced state of decay. Its populist rhetoric was offensive because it was elevating the people to a position above God. Soltani's anti-socialism went hand in hand with his views that the continuing influence of French culture was poisoning Algerian society because it was undermining the bedrock of Muslim society: the Arabic language. Given the scope of Soltani's challenge – he was posing fundamental questions about who is a true Muslim and what is an authentic Islamic society – it is not surprising that his book was banned by the authorities, even though it was impossible for them to prevent the clandestine diffusion of his ideas, through pamphlets and cassettes, in street mosques and markets.

Soltani's all-encompassing critique of Boumediène's socialism also included an attack on those clergy appointed by the state. For him these clerics were fundamentally irreligious; tamed by Boumediène, they had overseen a cheapening of belief and practice. Moreover, their conduct showed just how far Boumediène had strayed from the path by forgetting that the major divide in the world was not between capitalism and socialism but between Muslim and non-Muslim. The original perfection of Allah's message as transmitted to Mohammed was being obscured as Boumediène became a willing stooge of communism. Socialism, Third-Worldism and non-alignment were not the language of Islam but examples of *bida'* (innovation) which, by corrupting the original tenets of Islam, were the source of *fitna* (division), which Mohammed had expressly forbidden.

During the early months of 1973 clandestine Islamist groups called for resistance to the agrarian revolution, circulating underground pamphlets and cassettes denouncing the new orientation of the regime on the grounds that Algerian leaders – smokers, clean-shaven and wearing Western suits – were not following the ways of the Prophet and as such had become apostates. Most provocatively of all they distributed Soltani's fatwa saying that prayers were forbidden on nationalized land. In winter 1974, reflecting the growing self-confidence of these Islamist groupings, tracts began to circulate in the mosques of Algiers calling for a *shura* (consultation).

All of this opposition explains why Boumediène's leftward turn was a crystallizing moment. The roots of the Islamist movement which emerged in the 1980s are to be found in this episode. On the one hand it cemented the alliance with those groups most threatened by the Boumediène regime – large landowners, business interests, conservative elements of the state administration who provided the Islamist movement with important financial support. On the other hand Soltani's arguments wielded enormous influence and came to form the basis of an all-encompassing critique of the Boumediène regime. Anti-socialism and anti-communism, along with the call for government based upon the sharia, became the cornerstones of the Islamist lexicon. Above all, Islamists wanted to combat the influence of the atheist PAGS, and this division – communist versus Islamist – was to be central to Algerian politics throughout the 1970s and 1980s.

The stirrings of political Islam coincided with growing economic and social problems. Dramatic as Algeria's great leap forward had been, by the mid-1970s parts of the central planning system were coming unstuck. Over-rapid industrialization had created an unbalanced economy, and although Boumediène liked to depict Algerians as austere revolutionaries resolutely committed to the goals of socialism, in reality many of his compatriots were growing weary of the emphasis on heavy industry. Instead of constant sacrifices they wanted more consumer goods such as hi-fis, household appliances and cars. The economy was also plagued by low productivity largely because the shortage of managers and skilled workers, itself a legacy of the high illiteracy rates amongst Muslims inherited from the colonial period, meant that it was difficult to realize the planned targets. As the planning system began to founder the government was forced to resort to foreign companies as well as to the import of goods and services. In the short term these stopgap measures saved the industrialization programme, but in the long term they were counter-productive, undermining national control of the economy and plunging the country into growing debt. The agrarian revolution too ran out steam in the face of huge resistance from middle-ranking officials and larger landowners who were angered by the Marxist bent of the legislation. For all Boumediène's rhetoric, very little of the best arable land was redistributed.[27] Moreover, the land in the public sector was highly inefficient in terms of the production of foodstuffs.[28]

In large part the failings of industry and agriculture were the fault of the system as the country was stifled by a technocratic class of trained experts who, like those in the Soviet Union, ran the state industries in their own interests. Increasingly this bureaucratic layer exploited their position to distribute sinecures and privileges, a phenomenon that would accelerate during the 1980s. The 1970s witnessed the beginnings of nepotism and lethargy and although Boumediène kept a tight rein on any excessive corruption ordinary Algerians now began to talk about shadowy fiefdoms, a *nomenklatura* which was living off the fat of the country.

The Boumediène revolution created a modern, urban society along the Mediterranean coastline. However, the frenetic speed of this transformation produced a huge strain on housing and services and, as the authorities found it difficult to cope with the exodus from the countryside, vast shanty towns sprang up around Oran and Algiers. Such slums were a million miles away from Boumediène's promised utopia and this, coupled with the continuing blight of unemployment which in 1977 still stood at 22 per cent, produced a growing feeling of malaise. Worryingly for the regime, two further factors magnified this discontent. First, in 1974 France, feeling the impact of growing unemployment, closed the borders to immigration. In response Boumediène, not wishing to seem at the mercy of the former colonial power, blocked emigration. These two unilateral actions ended a precious safety valve for the economy, although huge numbers of Algerians would escape to France clandestinely because they still saw the former colonial power as their best hope for a better life. Secondly, the country was confronted with colossal demographic growth. In 1977 the Algerian population was almost seventeen million, five million more than in 1966[29] and double what it was in 1954. By 1977 eight million Algerians, that is 48 per cent of the population, were under fifteen, whilst only 700,000 were over sixty-five. For Boumediène such statistics were a source of pride, showing that Algeria, in contrast to France with its ageing population, was a youthful country full of potential. He boasted that if the population swelled to thirty or even fifty million there was room for everybody. But beneath the bombast these figures posed enormous problems. The school system began to buckle under the weight of numbers; in the first twelve years primary school numbers tripled to 2.5 million. Even more worryingly it was becoming self-evident that the system could not create enough jobs to cope with this population explosion.

Beyond this, Algerian society began to fracture along linguistic lines. Within education the use of the French language was progressively phased out in favour of Modern Standard Arabic. In practice, though, a two-tier system continued to operate, creating a basic divide between those Algerians educated in French and those in Arabic. Since industry and much of central government continued to operate in French, Arabic speakers, most of whom were from poorer, rural backgrounds comparatively untouched by French culture or language, were excluded from employment. Furthermore, because Kabyles were much more likely to speak French they were disproportionately represented in the better-paid jobs. This in turn created a huge body of frustrated Arab speakers who felt shunned by society. Resentful at the continued dominance of French speakers within the elite, their predicament was to provide fertile ground for Islamist arguments.

THE NATIONAL CHARTER, 1976

The emergence of Islamist opposition and the rising tide of economic discontent coincided with serious divisions within the regime. There was unrest within the army about the leftward direction of the Algerian revolution, which provoked Boumediène to purge the rest of the Oujda clan: the expulsion of Kaid Ahmed was followed by that of Ahmed Medeghri and Cherif Belkacem in 1974. In the wake of this bloodletting Boumediène stepped in to assume control of the party himself. Painfully aware of just how far the FLN had become a shambles in terms of mass mobilization he appointed Mohammed Cherifa to revamp the party apparatus. The years 1976 and 1977, therefore, were two years of intense activity as Cherifa set about relaunching the FLN as a socialist vanguard party and reconnecting it with the ordinary population.

The renewal of the FLN was prompted by a sudden awareness of a potential crisis of legitimacy. Boumediène knew that the country had been ruled unconstitutionally since 1965. For the most part this state of affairs had been tolerated because there had been a wide consensus in favour of his policies, above all his nationalization of key sectors of the economy. However, one decade after the June 1965 coup it was increasingly difficult to ignore the constitutional vacuum, while the Islamist pressure for a *shura* was making a clear impact. Boumediène knew that it was too dangerous to ignore and in June 1975 he announced the reconvening of the National Assembly, the drawing up of a new constitution, the National Charter, and plans for a single-candidate presidential election. The draft Charter was published in early 1976 and the people were invited to debate it openly. This was a degree of freedom unknown since the first days of independence and in the following months there were extensive public discussions about all aspects of the National Charter, which was officially ratified by 98.5 per cent of voters in a referendum on 27 June 1976. This now formed the framework for a new constitution, the country's second, which was adopted by a further referendum on 22 November and paved the way for strictly controlled presidential elections in December where Boumediène, the only candidate, won 95.2 per cent of the vote.

The National Charter was a personal triumph for Boumediène which strengthened the legitimacy of his power. The final shape of the constitution was very revealing about the political balance of power. Its model was very much the French one based on the idea of rights, where the constitution guaranteed freedom of expression and assembly as well as the sanctity of private property so long as it was not used to exploit others. Significantly, the right of women to participate in every aspect of national life was also affirmed. The secular tendencies of the whole process were further underlined by the fact that although Boumediène did make concessions to the Islamic lobby, principally by the outlawing of gambling and the introduction of the Muslim weekend, no mention was made of Islam in the initial draft of the National

Charter. Then, when it was affirmed as the state religion in the final constitution the reference to faith was a brief one. Indeed it was stated that the only way in which Islam could renew itself was through socialism.

Elsewhere, the constitution endowed huge powers to the president and enshrined socialism as the ideological bedrock of the regime, whilst entrusting the FLN with the continuing leadership of the revolution. The FLN was tasked with drawing up candidate lists for the Popular National Assembly, which was to be elected every five years. In theory, the Assembly had the strength to amend the constitution and adopt foreign-policy resolutions but in practice it was a pliant instrument of the president, who was not only defence minister but also secretary general of the FLN. Not surprisingly the constitution was enthusiastically endorsed by the PAGS, which saw it as strengthening their hand against Islamists. This belief was further reinforced when in October 1977 the conservative Mesaadia was ousted in favour of Mohammad Salah Yahiaoui who was widely regarded as a leftist.

LEADER OF THE THIRD WORLD

Between 21 July and 1 August 1969 Algiers hosted a momentous event: the first-ever Pan-African Cultural Festival organized by the Organization of African Unity. For eight days the Algerian capital echoed to the sounds of music, dance, film, theatre and political debate long into the night as venues in and around the city became a stage for a remarkable display of the new African identity. Those who were present remember it as a remarkable explosion of creative energy where it was possible to rub shoulders with Black Panther leaders on the run from the American police as well as anti-colonial militants from every corner of the Third World.[30] The radical atmosphere is captured in the film-maker Wilhem Klein's documentary on the Black Panthers and the recording of the free-form African-American saxophonist Archie Shepp in concert with a group of Tuareg musicians at El-Biar. This last event was one of the high points of the whole festival as Shepp, in a ferocious and uncompromising set played off the Tuareg musicians, broke away from the constraints of the European-derived harmonic system and reconnected with the African roots of jazz. Never has the intersection of politics and culture been so explicit as Shepp proclaimed that in Algiers 'Mother Africa has found her long-lost children'.

Shepp's set, preserved on CD as *Archie Shepp Live at the Pan-African Festival*, is one of the reasons why the Pan-African Festival has lived on in Algerian folklore.[31] It harks back to an optimistic time when the population felt self-confident about the future because Algeria, as a beacon of African and Third World militancy, was strong and stood for something. The event too was symbolic of Boumediène's personal prestige. As president of the Organization of African Unity he gave the inaugural address to the festival's intellectual highlight: the symposium on African culture. Here he held up the vision of a new pan-African identity which could be forged out of the common experience of colonization, calling for a dynamic synthesis of the modern with the traditional. Yes, Africans had to go back to the sources of their values, but they must not to be trapped by them. The challenge for Africans was the bringing together of African culture, purged of all that was archaic and stultifying, with the modern world of science and technology. It was the application of the tenets of the Algerian revolution to the rest of Africa and it was indicative of Boumediène's new-found standing in Africa and the Third World.

Boumediène's growing stature was also reflected when, following Nasser's death in 1970, he took up the mantle of pan-Arabism, playing a leading role in organizing the 1973 war against Israel which, even though it was inconclusive, went some way to recover the Arab prestige lost by the humiliating defeat in the 1967 Six Day War, and calling for petrol to be used as a weapon against the West. His high point in terms of international diplomacy came when he addressed the United Nations General Assembly in May 1974, calling for reparations for colonialism and the transfer of resources from the North to the South. As he walked to the podium his body language was light years away from the secretive army leader who had taken power in 1965. Confident and self-assured, he projected himself as the torch-bearer for the Third World. The key points of his speech were subsequently adopted by the UN, above the call for a new international economic order based upon sovereign equality between developed and developing countries, again demonstrating that Algeria was a force to be reckoned with on the world stage.

Algerians took pride in their country's standing as a leader in the non-aligned movement and this was a vital factor in legitimizing Boumediène's system. The fact that Boumediène could reasonably claim that Algeria had fashioned an alternative model to Soviet-style socialism and Western capitalism meant that up until the mid-1970s large numbers of Algerians felt proud about the country's achievements in overcoming poverty and underdevelopment. On a day-to-day level Algerians enjoyed rising educational and employment opportunities in combination with relative prosperity, and up until Boumediène's death in 1978 the system was characterized by stability. Political rights may have been limited but they were balanced by a strong sense of social and economic security; in the eyes of the ordinary populace, conditioned as they were by memories of exclusion under colonialism, such security, coupled with a commitment to social justice, counted for a lot.

Furthermore, Algerians respected Boumediène for standing up to the former colonial power, most famously following the crisis sparked off by Salah Bougrine. Bougrine was an Algerian emigrant to Marseille, who suffered from mental-health problems stemming from an attack by *harki*s in 1969 in which his head was split open with an axe.[32] At 2.30 p.m. on 25 August 1973 Bougrine had boarded the 72 trolley bus, which was carrying a load of Marseillais to the beach. When the French bus driver asked for the fare he was met with an uncomprehending stare which led to a heated exchange of words. What was said exactly remains unclear but once the bus was moving Salah Bougrine pulled out a knife and plunged it into the driver's left shoulderblade, killing him outright. In the crash that followed Bougrine was set upon by the other passengers, whose actions put him into a coma.

This episode was part of a long summer of hate in the south of France. Algerians had been killed randomly by shadowy right-wing terror groups linked to the remnants of the OAS. In many cases these vigilante groups were egged on by a hysterical media, as in the case of the Marseille paper *Le Méridional* which, following Salah Bougrine's attack, likened Algerians to a plague:

> We have had enough. Enough of Algerian thieves. Enough of Algerian vandals. Enough of Algerian loudmouths. Enough of Algerian syphilitics. Enough of Algerian rapists. Enough of Algerian pimps. Enough of Algerian madmen. Enough of Algerian killers.[33]

Such inflammatory language fuelled hatred and Algerians suffered from retaliatory attacks throughout France. By the end of the year some thirty-two had been killed. In one incident on 14 December an Algerian consulate was bombed, leaving four dead and twenty-two wounded.

Back in Algeria Boumediène was seething at this violence, and he provocatively announced that if France could not protect immigrants he would bring them back to Algeria regardless of the cost. Of course, as he well knew, this was posturing. Given the unemployment situation, to have reintegrated huge numbers of immigrants would have stretched the economy to breaking point. Nonetheless such a display of Boumediène's *redjla* was very popular amongst Algerians. As when French oil interests had been nationalized in 1971, hostility to the former colonial power produced a wave of support for the Boumediène regime.

This stand-off underlined the complexities of the Franco-Algerian relationship. On the one hand immigration was regarded by Algeria as a necessary evil. Yet immigrants were increasingly viewed with suspicion by the home country. Large numbers were Kabyle and they were seen as acting, wittingly or unwittingly, as a vehicle for French ideas and anti-Algerian propaganda. Furthermore, since their sons and daughters born in France had the right to take French nationality there was a wider issue about just who these people belonged to. Were they French or Algerian? Inevitably such discussions were shot through with the cry of *hizb fransa*. For the Boumediène regime this became a reflex action as the notion of a neo-colonial fifth column was used to attack Berberists, feminists and Westernized Algerians. To write in French, to have French friends, to drink alcohol and cook French cuisine, to frequent the French cultural centre or meet the French ambassador: these were controversial actions which could lay anybody open to the ultimate political stigma, the accusation of being pro-French. But, paradoxically, for Algerians France continued to be a beacon because of the promise of much higher living standards. For this reason, despite France and Algeria stopping all immigration in 1974, the late 1970s witnessed an upsurge in clandestine workers crossing the Mediterranean.

In an effort to put relations onto a normal footing the French President Valéry Giscard d'Estaing made an official visit in spring 1975, the first by a French president since independence. Both sides were acutely aware of the historic importance of this event. For Boumediène in particular, symbolism was everything. Still basking in the glory of his UN speech, he wanted to show that the page was turned and that Algeria was the equal of the former colonial master. In this respect, Giscard was very obliging and over the three-day visit underlined his hope that France and Algeria could form the basis of an Arab–European dialogue. All the same, beneath the warm words Algeria was still heavily dependent on France economically.

Moreover, this thaw in relations was soon poisoned by Giscard's support for Moroccan action over the Western Sahara. The Moroccan king, Hassan II, had seized upon Spain's withdrawal from the colony to occupy the northern part of the Western Sahara in late 1975, while Mauritania took control of the south. Boumediène was incensed and reacted by expelling a large number of Moroccans from the country. When he went on to recognize the independence of the Saharan Arab Democratic Republic, Hassan II broke off diplomatic relations and closed the border. Algerian–Moroccan relations now plummeted to an all-time low as Boumediène actively supported the Saharan Arab resistance movement, the Polisario (Popular Front for the Liberation of Saguia el-Hamra and Rió de Oro), thus leading to a war by proxy which, in light of Giscard's pro-Hassan stance, provoked a sharp downturn in Franco-Algerian relations, a deterioration that was compounded still further by a fresh wave of anti-Algerian violence across France during 1976.

During 1978 rumours began to circulate about Boumediène's health. Although the press remained silent it became increasingly obvious that his trips abroad were a convenient cover for medical treatment and in October he left for Moscow. When he returned on 14 November, in a coma and suffering from a rare blood disease, the government still kept up the lie, claiming that he was conducting the affairs of state. The agony went on for six weeks as a procession of medical specialists tried and failed to find a cure. Eventually Boumediène died on 27 December 1978. He was fifty-three.

Boumediène's funeral witnessed an enormous outpouring of emotion. Huge, grief-stricken crowds packed the streets as his coffin, placed on a gun carriage, made its way slowly through Algiers. It was a national trauma, which partly explains why the Boumediène era has come to be seen in the popular imagination as the golden years of post-independence. With memories conditioned by the subsequent experiences of the economic hardship of the 'black years' of the 1980s and the violence of the 'red years' of the 1990s, the 1970s are remembered as a time when Algeria was still a young country. As yet less scarred by mistakes, Algerians felt united and enthusiastic about the promises of post-independence. There was no mass alienation. The anger of the dispossessed was being channelled into eradicating the vestiges of colonialism and the result was a close identification between the people and the regime.

Significantly too, Boumediène is characterized as the necessary hardman – unlike subsequent presidents there are few jokes about him – who maintained a system of social equality. Inspiring a mixture of respect and fear, he was a wise helmsman who protected ordinary people. Under him, it is popularly claimed, there was no corruption; anyone considering engaging in such activity knew that they would be instantly punished. Indeed, since 1978 there has been a growing tide of conspiracy theories. Was the president not killed by insiders who saw him as a barrier to their own greedy ambitions? For this reason, for countless Algerians Boumediène's premature death was a tragedy.

Inevitably, though, there is a strong element of selective memory in this idealization. Those nostalgic for Boumediène forget that by 1978 the centrally planned economy was already coming unstuck. They forget too the repression and the lack of political freedom; it was under his rule that the system of the Sécurité Militaire was fine-tuned into an art form. It is just too simplistic to say that if Boumediène had lived then Algeria would have been saved from the economic catastrophe and bloodshed which has followed.

CHAPTER FOUR

Black October

ON WEDNESDAY 5 October 1988 thousands of youths, for the most part secondary school students and the unemployed, ransacked central Algiers. People were fearful of mass redundancies, frustrated by the lack of a regular water supply, resentful at the absence of many basic foodstuffs in the shops, angry at the sharp rise in the price of school materials. The atmosphere on the streets of the capital had been tense for several weeks. The violence was the release of pent-up anger against a system which many people, but particularly the young, felt was humiliating them.

Shouting 'Rise up, Youth' and 'Chadli assassin' and carrying banners proclaiming 'We are men' and 'We want our rights', the rioters targeted the symbols of authority and wealth with relentless determination. Beginning with the boutiques lining the Rue Mourad Didouche – the main street that winds down past the university on the way to the central post office – the crowds attacked department stores, cafés, restaurants, discotheques such as the notorious Blue Note nightclub and others frequented by the *chi-chis*, the sons and daughters of the privileged elite, along with government offices and the property of the ruling National Liberation Front. On one public building the national flag was symbolically torn down and replaced by an empty couscous sack. Cars and lorries were overturned and set alight, and the commercial centre on the heights overlooking the capital at Riadh el-Feth (Victory Gardens) looted, with the result that by the early evening much of central Algiers was devastated. It was the worst day of violence in the capital since independence in 1962.[1]

Inspired by the young Palestinians fighting against the Israeli armed forces since 1987, a struggle given nightly coverage on Algerian television, the movement spread to the rest of the country over the next two days. For the rioters who baited the police as little better than Zionist oppressors, this was their very own intifada. In Blida, south-west of Algiers, the law courts were torched and the town centre occupied by protesters; in Oran two hotels, one of which had previously belonged to President Chadli, were ransacked; while Tiaret experienced the worst violence after Algiers. In each case the riots were essentially male events, as groups of young men, some only twelve, dressed in jeans and trainers, prowled the streets with machetes and clubs.

Throughout, there was a strong sense of carnival as local authority figures were ritualistically humiliated. In the popular Algiers neighbourhood of Belcourt, the police chief was made to strip down to his underwear and the crowd was encouraged to taunt and slap him; in Bab el-Oued policemen were forced to parade the streets shouting 'I am a braggart, I am a betrayer'; while mock trials were staged satirizing the Algerian justice system where 'defendants', accused of abuses of power, were all acquitted.[2] October 1988 represented a world turned upside down, a moment of inversion which, no matter how transitory, no matter how fleeting, allowed the young male rioters to recover a sense of honour, dignity and manhood.

This wish to recover their lost manhood was also expressed by massive popular hostility to President Chadli, Boumediène's successor, who was apparently picked out by the military and endorsed by the party machine as a compromise candidate. Slogans, taking the form of rhyming couplets in colloquial Arabic, ridiculed Chadli as a eunuch. He was a laughing stock, they claimed, and dominated by his wife Halima, the real power behind the throne. By reiteration of the widespread belief that the President's son had exploited his family connections to line his pockets on a massive scale, Chadli was denigrated as a dishonourable, dishonest and unjust leader. He was seen as the personification of the system, a privileged and self-serving elite which had heaped humiliation onto ordinary people and robbed them of any self-worth:

We don't want butter or pepper
We want a leader we can respect

Boumediène, come back to us
Halima has come to dominate us

Chadli, that's enough vice
Tell your son to return the money.[3]

In the minds of the young men behind the violence, the contrast between Chadli – weak and effete – and Boumediène – tough and upright – was ever present. For this reason, as Hugh Roberts has rightly argued, October 1988 must be understood not as a bread riot, still less a mindless act of vandalism, however much the regime tried to portray it as such. Instead, the rioters' actions were structured by a sense of moral and political economy, a desire to return to the certainties of the 1970s when Algerians felt that they could stand tall because their country counted for something on the world stage and they felt protected by a strong ruler who kept corruption in check.[4]

As the rioting continued into a second day, with youths hurling stones and Molotov cocktails in central Algiers, the country was sliding into chaos. At this point General Khaled Nezzar stepped in and on the afternoon of 6 October he declared a state of siege, placing all civilian authorities under military command, banning all demonstrations, imposing a curfew on the Algiers region and deploying tanks at strategic points throughout the capital. The regime's hard man had arrived and for him the issue was simple: this was a direct challenge to the government's authority which had to be met head-on. There could be no question of dialogue; the rioters were hooligans and looters who had to be brought to heel. Consequently the army was given a free rein to shoot into the crowds and to torture arrested protesters.

A climate of panic and violence now pervaded Algiers as the army's repression intensified and thousands of rioters were rounded up and interned in makeshift prison cells. Wild rumours spread about army death squads circulating in unmarked vehicles operating a shoot-to-kill policy, stories that seemed to be substantiated when two young brothers were strafed and killed at El-Biar, whilst army units opened fire near a mosque in Kouba causing fifty deaths. Such brutality produced a rising tide of popular anger that was assuaged neither by the mysterious appearance in the shops of foodstuffs like butter, semolina, flour and cooking oil that had been absent before, nor the televised appeal for calm of Interior Minister Hedi Khediri, the first member of the government to address the rioters.

The following day the violence took on a new dimension when, after Friday prayers, eight thousand Islamist sympathisers fought a pitched battle with the police in the Belcourt neighbourhood, shouting 'Allahu Akbar' and 'Islamic republic' along with 'Chadli murderer'. It was the first appearance of Islamists on the street, and they now tried to take control of the protest movement. With this end in mind, on Monday 10 October the fiery Islamist preacher Ali Belhadj organized a demonstration of twenty thousand people which marched down Hassiba ben Bouali Street before continuing along Boulevard Zighout Youcef on the sea front, until the demonstrators were stopped in their tracks by a military barricade. A tense confrontation lasting half an hour ensued, following which the precise train of events becomes unclear. Some eyewitnesses claimed that a demonstrator fired on the army; others that the gunshots heard were the work of *agents provocateurs*. Whatever the truth, the army reacted by firing indiscriminately into the crowd, killing fifty people. With the air thick with tear gas, fleeing rioters shouted out to foreign journalists on the spot, 'It is worse than South Africa, it is worse than Chile!', and 'They are worse than the Zionists! Zionists do not fire on mosques, you must write this down.'[5]

By this point some five hundred Algerians, mostly young men, had been killed, and the country was on the edge of an abyss. Until then President Chadli had been curiously absent from the political scene but that night he at last went on television to deliver a twenty-minute address. Stern-faced, he knew that he had to reassert his authority before an expectant nation reeling from a week of unprecedented violence. Recognizing that nothing could be the same again, he made clear his intention to introduce far-reaching reforms, while promising lower retail prices and more subsidized goods:

> My conviction is that it is time to introduce necessary reforms in the political field, and to revise some institutional structures and constitutional foundations in order to adapt them to the next stage ... On this matter, a project is being prepared which will be subject to the decision of the People ... We will eliminate the current monopoly of responsibility and will permit the official institutions of the State, the Parliament or others, to play their part in the control and monitoring of the State.[6]

Although many were suspicious – after all, the address contained no concrete proposals – Chadli's intervention made an impact. That night rioting subsided and the following day saw signs of a return to normality, with shops reopening. Twenty-four hours later the state of siege was lifted and on the following Saturday schools nationwide reopened. The October crisis was at an end, dissipating as abruptly as it had started, but in an effort to maintain the momentum plans for political reform were published on 23 October, the central premise of which was the separation of the state and the FLN. The way was now open for a multi-party system and this was overwhelmingly approved in a national referendum on 3 November by 92.3 per cent of the vote.

The speed and direction of Chadli's reforms underline the gravity of October 1988. It is no exaggeration to say that these riots – known popularly as 'Black October' – were the most significant historical event in Algeria since the eight-year war against the French. Algerians themselves talk of before and after. It was their intifada and henceforth nothing could be the same again. The status quo was simply untenable because the army, which saw itself as the guardian of the revolution, had fired on the people. 'Black October', the climax of a rupture between state and society that had opened up during the previous ten years, encapsulated a dramatic fall from grace from the heights of the Boumediène period. For this reason the descent into violence during the 1990s was not the result solely of the rise of the Islamist movement post-1989. The breakdown had already happened. How, therefore, did the heady optimism of the 1970s give way to cynicism, despair and ultimately revolt?

GENERATIONAL DIVIDE: THE NEW ALGERIA OF RAI AND FOOTBALL

The starting point for October 1988 was the worldwide economic crisis, which gathered pace during the 1980s and hit Algeria very hard. The second oil crisis in 1979 caused a dramatic increase in oil prices, and the Algerian government hoped that this windfall would continue to finance the economy. Unfortunately the outbreak of war between Iran and Iraq in 1980 destroyed this strategy as both sides, desperate to finance their own war efforts, flooded the oil market. In March 1986 the price of Algerian crude fell to $12 a barrel, an unmitigated disaster which was made all the worse by the parallel collapse of gas prices. During 1986 alone hydrocarbon revenues dropped 40 per cent, forcing the leadership to keep the country afloat by borrowing massively on the international finance markets, whilst introducing a policy of austerity, restricting imports to essential foodstuffs only. At the fifth FLN congress in December 1983 these policies were justified to the people as temporary expedients, to be done away with once the government had made up for lost oil and gas revenue and was in a position to bring the country's burgeoning foreign debt under control. In reality, though, they were completely ineffective and led to a downward spiral in the economy. The more gas and petrol prices fell, the more the government resorted to extreme measures, producing a vicious circle that brought widespread hardship and social polarization, especially within the big cities. Food queues, water shortages, galloping unemployment: for the average Algerian the degradation of everyday life during the 1980s became only too obvious.

Demography exacerbated these social tensions to breaking point. Algeria had one of the highest birth rates in the whole world, a phenomenon that had been encouraged by Boumediène as a sign of national strength. Between 1966 and 1987 the population nearly doubled to 23 million, two-thirds of whom were under twenty-five, and it was this post-independence generation that bore the brunt of the 1980s crisis. Not surprisingly, society began to fracture along generational lines as youth became the spectre which stalked Algeria, revolutionizing the political landscape.

Nowhere was the clash between old and young more apparent than in terms of the relationship with the colonial past. This new generation had no memory of French rule; no sense of the contrast between pre-1962 and post-1962. For the most part their knowledge of the past was derived from the image of the glorious war of liberation trundled out via the cycle of official commemorations, which bore the dominant message that young people had to be deferential to those in power because of the huge sacrifices the older generation had made in liberating Algerians from the colonial yoke. Confronted with the ever-increasing hardships of daily life, young Algerians saw this official memory as more and more remote until eventually it became associated with the perpetuation of the status quo; a cynical veneer which, by continually blaming any problems on the legacy of colonialism, became a way of confusing issues and escaping responsibilities. As Rabah Bouaziz, a wartime veteran of the FLN, explained, by the late 1980s his own children in their early twenties were indifferent to the regime's version of the past because they were sick of having it rammed down their throats ad nauseam.[7] What concerned them was the present, not the past. Bouaziz's children were symptomatic of the general attitude which perceived the official history as a millstone which, by keeping a discredited elite in place, was dragging the country ever further downwards. Indeed, in some cases people born during the colonial period began to think the unthinkable and contemplate how to reapply for French nationality. Theirs was a cruel dilemma which gave rise to much soul searching, with the practicalities of day-to-day survival weighed against feelings of guilt or disloyalty. Of course, at a fundamental level the young remained profoundly Algerian but the sheer magnitude of political mismanagement during the 1980s meant that their formal bonds of attachment to the state had been tested to breaking point. For them becoming a French citizen was not the rejection of everything their parents had fought against but a means of escape to a better future.

If history was one aspect of the generational conflict, the other was unemployment. By 1985, 72 per cent of those looking for work were under twenty-five. It was a staggering statistic which in human terms took the form of groups of adolescents who, with nothing to do, gathered together on street corners in the major towns and cities. Commonly referred to as the *hittistes*, derived from the Arabic word *heta* meaning walls and a comment on how they congregated around the walls of their local neighbourhoods, these unemployed young men defined 1980s Algeria. Their lives were hard. In the absence of work most days were dull, boring and monotonous, devoid of hope or expectation. To cope, large numbers lived on their wits, grinding out an

A page from *Pour Que Vive l'Algérie*, a popular comic book lionizing the war of independence that was produced by the Algerian government in 1989. By this time many young people were increasingly cynical about the sanctified official version of events.

existence through petty theft or black-market trading. Inevitably this brought many into conflict with the police which only served to accentuate the mood of generational alienation. Every assertion of police authority, whether it be an arrest or an identity check, was experienced as a tiny pinprick designed to keep young people down, and the result was an undercurrent of latent male aggression, a tinderbox atmosphere which by the mid-1980s was ever present on the street.

Mass unemployment also created a deep-seated psychological malaise. In the teeming slums of the casbah and Bab el-Oued, where families frequently slept fifteen to a room, or in the hastily constructed shanty towns made from cardboard and corrugated iron, whose inhabitants had to pick their way through rubbish-strewn neighbourhoods with no electricity and lakes of open sewage, huge numbers of young people felt that they were living in limbo. Too old for school, yet too young for military service, too poor to think of marriage, with nowhere to meet apart from the mosque, young people were left feeling that it was impossible to become a fully grown adult.[8] Abandoned by the regime, with no means of support, they felt trapped, in effect forced to live a kind of prolonged adolescence. Unsurprisingly huge numbers found it difficult to imagine a future in Algeria and as depression became endemic so too did the desire to escape. In October 1989, when stories began to abound about a passenger ship destined for Australia anchored close to the Algerian shore, large parts of the population became seized with the hope of a better life on the other side of the world. The sheer implausibility of this scenario did not deter huge numbers from queuing for days outside the Australian embassy gates, a rush that continued even when the rumour was proved baseless. This whole episode, which later became the basis of a famous stand-up act by the Algerian comic Fellag, said something profound about the state of the country at the end of the 1980s. The sheer scale of desperation had made the country prone to all kinds of myth-making, big and small.

The plight of this young generation was magnified even more by the fact that this was just at the point that the West in general, and France in particular, turned its back on Algeria. In the 1980s French politics were dominated by the rise of the National Front, led by the bullish Jean-Marie Le Pen, a paratrooper veteran of the Battle of Algiers and erstwhile supporter of French Algeria.[9] With his talk of closed cultures and separate races; his crude correlation between unemployment, crime and North Africans; and his contention that the galloping immigrant birth rate would make France into an Islamic republic within a hundred years, Le Pen depicted the Algerian community as a mortal threat to Gallic national identity. Fears of this nature secured him 10 per cent of the vote on a regular basis at major elections from 1984 onwards, creating a climate of racism and intolerance which pulled French politics to the right even though he himself did not secure power. Consequently, although France had closed the borders to immigration in 1974, the new right-wing government turned the screw still further in 1986 with the introduction of visas.[10] This desire to stem the flow of immigration from the poor South was not unique to France. It was symptomatic of a general global crisis and the more the richer countries went into recession, the tighter became their border controls. Entry visas were introduced for Algerians wanting to travel to America and Western Europe, meaning that legal immigration was no longer an option: Algerians were being told to keep out. Ironically this came just when the spread of satellite television was intensifying the lure of the rich North still further.[11] French channels, with their provocative commercials, underlined just how much Algerians, their own economy in tatters, were missing out on consumer society, and this in turn fuelled the desire for clandestine immigration, which became a growth industry for the Algerian criminal underworld.[12]

This sense of being hemmed in on all sides was central to the *hittiste* street culture. Theirs was a blocked society but this obligation to inhabit a world with no future led the young unemployed to develop their own codes, signs and language. Wonderfully inventive, consciously subversive, mingling French and spoken Arabic, this street slang was bitter, proud and angry: the raw emotions of a new generation deliberately expressing its disaffection in a way that older people could not understand. First and foremost, their language was directed against those in power, commonly referred to as *le pouvoir*, on the assumption that any wealth and influence could only derive from ill-gotten gains. Money was equated with dishonesty and exploitation, and *hittiste* humour was laced from beginning to end with archetypal hate figures – the lazy bureaucrat, the corrupt politician, the grasping capitalist, the vindictive police officer – all part of the same system leeching off the people. The greatest venom, though, was reserved for the *chi-chis*, the sons and daughters of the elite, whose displays of wealth, whether it be flashy cars, the latest Parisian clothes or the fact that they had been educated abroad in private schools in France, America and Switzerland, were particularly nauseating. So-called because of their accent – '*Tcha pas vu Djamel?*' – the *chi-chis* led a lifestyle that revolved around shopping at the new mall at Riadh el-Feth, sunning themselves at specially reserved beaches in skimpy costumes and dancing to Michael Jackson at open-air discos. It deeply affronted the *hittistes*, who saw it as financed by the millions their parents had siphoned off from the country.

The *hittistes*' view of the world was marked by a strong strain of misogyny; they knew that in sexual and emotional terms *chi-chi* women were beyond their reach and this sense of rejection made them angry and resentful. Favourite *hittiste* pastimes included baiting the *chi-chis* by picking their pockets, stealing their cars or, in the case of women, harassing them with lewd gestures and remarks.

Hostility to the *chi-chis* underlined how for the young *hittistes* 1980s Algeria was made up of two types of people: insiders well connected to the powers-that-be and outsiders, the majority, with no entry into the inner corridors of the system. The outsiders had to find a way to survive and in doing so they developed a gallows humour whose lexicon of disaffection went hand in hand with the lexicon of complaint. One favourite topic of conversation was endless anecdotes about the lack of essential goods, whilst another centred around the word *zaguet*, meaning 'nothing works any more', which was applied to all aspects of daily life as well as the political situation.[13] *Hittistes* liked continually listing what was forbidden (*la yadyouz*) as a way of conveying just how far the system was stifling any sense of enjoyment, a perspective that was encapsulated in the popular joke about the fall of the Berlin Wall in November 1989: 'Instead of tearing down their wall, the Germans would have done better to send it to us in Algeria.'[14]

To make ends meet most resorted to the black market, known popularly by the word *trabendo*, dealing in everything from food to spare parts for cars and household goods. Otherwise the young unemployed found solace in drugs and alcohol, temporary highs which usually took the form of hashish or *zombreto* (a potent mix of lemonade and industrial alcohol) and music. The 1980s witnessed the explosion of a new musical phenomenon, raï music. Raï, meaning opinion or point of view in Arabic, originated from Oran, the seaport in western Algeria and the country's second largest city. Known as the 'little Paris' of North Africa, Oran is steeped in cosmopolitan musical traditions, whether it be classical Andalusian music with the *oudh* (Arab lute), *darbuka* (drum) and *rababa* (rebec), or Jewish forms – until independence the city was home to Jews expelled from Spain in 1492 – or the elaborate form of sung religious poetry recited by *sheikh*s, or *sheikha*s, women singers who performed in the brothels and cabaret bars of colonial Algeria. Raï is steeped in these varying idioms which it then mixes with French and Spanish influences, as well as Western pop, jazz, reggae, disco and even rap through the use of guitars and synthesizers.[15] In essence it is a hybrid form based around a frenetic three-beat rhythm and the resultant sound is raw, edgy and abrasive.

Lyrically speaking raï expressed itself in the language of the Algerian street. Assertive, rebellious and proud, raï singers sang about life as it really was, creating a sharp disjuncture between the upbeat tone, inviting people onto the dance floor, and the mordant, melancholic message of sadness, boredom and frustration. In their eyes raï music held up a mirror to Algerian society much as Bob Marley's reggae had done to Jamaica in the 1960s and 1970s. It was the 'word of the people' encapsulating a truth and honesty which was so lacking in the country's leaders. Thus, when Cheb Hasni, who by 1991 was selling some four hundred thousand cassettes a year, sang, 'My country is a flower which they have devoured', nobody was in any doubt about who he was referring to. In the same way the song '*El Habra wine*' ('Flee, but where to?'), later recorded by Khaled, became the song of the October uprising, a poignant lament for all that had gone wrong with Chadli's Algeria:

> Egotism has replaced solidarity
> In this organized chaos,
> Where are the men of yesteryear?
> All that remains is to flee. But where to?[16]

Raï had really taken off after 1974 when cheap cassette recorders became readily available. Sensing a new market for music, makeshift studios started producing cheaply made tapes to sell on the street and, although rough and ready in quality, they were selling by the hundreds of thousands by the 1980s. Raï was the product of a do-it-yourself culture, much like punk and new wave in Britain in the late 1970s, which was beyond the control of the state. The stars of the new scene were Cheb Khaled, Cheb Hasni and Cheb Mami. Donning the title *cheb*, meaning 'young man', was a way of demarcating themselves from the older generation and underlining the spirit of youth rebellion. Modelling themselves on Elvis Presley, Mick Jagger and Joe Strummer, their showy individualism, celebrating a lifestyle of sex, drugs and wine, was shocking to both Islamists and the stalwarts of socialist orthodoxy as raï singers confronted difficult subjects head-on, most famously in the case of Cheb Hasni's daring 1987 duet with the female singer Chaba Zahouania, '*Beraka*' ('The Shack'), which was a graphic celebration of illicit sex, a notoriously taboo subject in Algerian society.[17] Although the regime eventually tried to appropriate raï through a series of officially sponsored concerts it was never comfortable with its message of hedonism and rebellion. But the government could do nothing to stem the huge appeal of raï in Algeria and beyond. Indeed Cheb Khaled, the self-styled king of raï, has gone on to become a global superstar with his 1992 single '*Didi*' selling over a million copies worldwide.

■ ■ ■

Alongside music, football was another fundamental aspect of the generational divide. Its popularity among the young was made obvious in June 1982 when Algeria beat West Germany by two goals to one in an opening game of the World Cup in Spain. It was a thrilling match, broadcast live in Algeria, and in the aftermath of victory thousands went delirious, flooding into the streets, brandishing flags and hooting car horns until the early hours of the morning in a scene that briefly recalled the euphoria at independence. Unfortunately jubilation was matched by despair a few days later when West Germany, in a boring, lacklustre game, beat Austria one nil meaning that the Germans and not Algeria reached the next stage. Collectively the whole country felt cheated. The Austrian team was accused of deliberately letting West Germany win and the press began to talk about dark plots, accusing FIFA of racism.

The passion aroused by the 1982 World Cup revealed just how far football had become an integral part of the new urban culture. Post-1962 the government had devised a new league system where each town and city had their own team and soon football was being played on every street corner as it became a national obsession followed daily in the national press, radio and television. With one team in Oran and three in Algiers, football began to articulate rivalries between towns, regions, even local *quartiers*. Just as, for the Catalans, supporting Barcelona under General Franco was a statement of Catalan nationalism and a rejection of fascism under conditions of severe political repression, for young Algerians supporting Jeunesse Sportive de Kabylie, known locally as the 'canaries of the Djurdjura' because of their yellow jerseys, and chanting on the terraces in Berber, 'We are free men,' was one of the few public ways they could make an explicit challenge to the domination of Arab-Islamic values.

Football also became an expression of youthful male aggression. The football terraces were for men only, a male space that was also reflected in the wider vogue for bodybuilding, judo and boxing. With nothing else to do, having a well-toned body and being able to defend oneself in a fight became a badge of pride for many young men. Physical prowess became equated with political assertiveness and the terraces became a meeting place for the 'dangerous classes' because here at least young men felt strong enough to voice their discontent without fear of reprisal. At football matches they were the many and the police the few, and chanting anti-government slogans and songs became a well-established tradition during the 1980s; in fact at national games President Chadli was so heavily jeered that it became a political embarrassment. The football terraces, encapsulating as they did the huge chasm of unforgiving contempt between the rulers and the ruled, were the harbinger of October 1988.

THE CAULIFLOWER PRESIDENT: THE REGIME OF CHADLI BENDJEDID

The party leadership and presidency of the republic was contested at the fourth FLN congress held on 27–31 January 1979 – just one month after Boumediène's death – by two ALN veterans, Mohammad Salah Yahiaoui and Abdelaziz Bouteflika. As we have already seen, Yahiaoui had closely allied himself with the communists, allowing the Parti de l'Avant-Garde Socialiste (PAGS) to gain a hold over the mass trade union and youth organizations. Bouteflika, meanwhile, had been a permanent fixture as foreign secretary for some sixteen years. Always well-dressed – at the UN he was known as the 'dandy diplomat' – he was a leading member of the Oujda clan and widely perceived at home and abroad as something of a pro-Western liberal. Deadlock between the two factions meant that the leadership went to the compromise candidate Colonel Chadli Bendjedid.

A veteran of the French army – he fought in Indo-China and was a non-commissioned officer when the rebellion there erupted in November 1954 – Chadli was an unknown quantity, although he had been a senior figure in the Revolutionary Council. Born on 14 April 1929 in Bouteldja, near Annaba, he had joined the Armée de Libération Nationale in 1955, whereupon he became a protégé of Boumediène who backed his rapid rise up the hierarchy. In the summer of 1962 he stood shoulder to shoulder with Boumediène against the Provisional Government and as a reward in 1964 he was given the military command of the Oran region, Oranie, which over the next fifteen years became his personal fiefdom. His unexpected succession came largely because in the opaque game of bargain and counter-bargain conducted in the backrooms and corridors he was supported by Kasdi Merbah, the head of the shadowy Sécurité Militaire (SM), known popularly as 'Boumediène's executioner'. The SM became Chadli's power base, along with a large number of senior leaders from the eastern part of the country, the so-called Biskra–Tabessa–Skikda triangle. The succession crisis confirmed once again that in Algeria power was the preserve of the elite – the ordinary populace was neither involved nor consulted – and that the army was the determining force. The army's hold on the inner circle of decision-makers was strengthened still further in November 1984 when colonels Abdallah Belhoucet and Mustapha Benloucif were promoted to the rank of major general. Together they formed the nucleus of the army general staff within which Khaled Nezzar was the pivotal figure, in effect a caste apart which enjoyed access to levels of subsidized housing, schooling and welfare provision unobtainable for most Algerians.[18]

Algerians saw Chadli as a faceless apparatchik, conjured out of the hat by the power brokers because he was weak and unthreatening and could be manipulated at will. He soon became the butt of a huge number of popular jokes, which painted him as a stupid and uncultured character dominated by an overbearing wife. How, Algerians asked themselves, could they take their new leader seriously? Not only was he henpecked, he sported a shock of bouffant white hair which made him resemble a cauliflower.[19] Such caustic humour made it clear that, initially at least, Chadli was not seen as a credible force. Rather he was seen as a caretaker figure who would be replaced in the near future once he had outlived his usefulness.

In fact Chadli proved himself to be a wily operator who neatly outwitted his opponents. He built up his power base carefully, slowly but surely purging the close political allies of Boumediène. At the next party congress, held on 15–19 June 1979, he skilfully manoeuvred out Yahiaoui in favour of Mohammed Cherif Messaadia, who then expelled Yahiaoui's supporters and communists from the trade union and youth organizations. It was a major turning point, a sea change that marked the receding influence of the communists and FLN leftists. Further signs that times were changing came with the release of Ben Bella in October 1980, the abolition of exit visas to leave the country and a new economic policy by which, in a bid to win over the middle classes and business interests who had felt so threatened by socialism, greater emphasis was placed upon free-market enterprise.

The move away from the Boumediène era was also apparent in Chadli's attempt to revitalize the FLN. By introducing strict legislation to ensure that all officials in the mass organizations were FLN members – the so-called article 120 of the party statute – he made a conscious effort to transform the party from the empty shell of the 1970s into a force that could win over the population. In doing so, however, Chadli was not motivated by democratic instincts. On the contrary; candidates for local councils were vetted by the secret police and the party leadership alone appointed members to the Political Bureau and the Central Committee. Likewise Chadli made no attempt to bring in new blood that could renew the party. If anything, joining the party became well-nigh impossible as the war generation, determined not to share any privileges, made the FLN into a closed shop.

■ ■ ■

Although Chadli did introduce some timid reforms, shifting the emphasis away from heavy industry in 1981, he did not yet feel strong enough to take on the Boumediène old guard in the economic realm. Instead he preferred to preside over a creeping retreat from socialism, a process that was accelerated after the fifth FLN congress on 19–22 December 1983 when Chadli won approval from the delegates for a second term. Boosted by this victory, Chadli became more strident in his criticisms of the socialist economy. For him the tenets of the 1976 National Charter were too rigid, too doctrinaire; by stifling individual initiatives they were now aggravating the economic crisis. However, he was careful not to suggest a full-scale assault on the planned economy. Instead, he focused on pragmatically adapting the present system to a new context, hoping to strengthen the case for reform by presenting himself as an arbiter above ideology and faction fighting.

However, by 1985, frustrated by the fierce resistance of the old guard, Chadli dropped all pretence to impartiality and explicitly identified himself with reform. More and more outspoken, he scored a significant political victory at the FLN congress on 24–25 December 1985 when, by talking about the need to 'enrich' and 'modify' the National Charter, he got through further measures of economic liberalization. In embracing free-market economics Chadli hoped to appeal to a younger generation of technocrats who now saw capitalism as the only way to deliver better living standards. By the same token he wanted to win over the private sector by giving them greater freedom to make money. On the international scene, keen to ingratiate himself with the International Monetary Fund and the World Bank, he talked himself up as an Algerian Gorbachev. As a result many commentators in the West saw Algerian politics through the prism of the Soviet Union – a reforming leader they could do business with pitted against a hard-line *nomenklatura* who were blocking liberalization for doctrinaire reasons.

Despite Chadli's measures, the economic situation grew worse. Reeling from the collapse of oil and gas prices, the state of the Algerian economy made grim reading by 1987. At this point the national debt was an estimated $87 billion in the US equivalent of the time. Servicing the foreign debt alone accounted for half of all export earnings; whilst the collapse in agricultural productivity meant that nearly two-thirds of the grain needed had to come from imports. Confronted with its own self-evident failure, the Algerian government had no alternative but to go cap in hand to the International Monetary Fund. It was a humiliating moment, a historical watershed because, by abdicating to IMF diktat, the government was accepting that Algeria could no longer strike an independent economic course.

Henceforth the IMF would have a determining role in Algerian politics and economics and from the outset it made clear that the precondition for help was the break-up of the socialist economy and the opening up of the economy to the rigours of the international market. In return for a rescheduling of its debt repayments, the Algerian government implemented the economic equivalent of a shock treatment as all obstacles to the functioning of the free market were dismantled. The command economy was disbanded, collective farms, the showcase of the Boumediène revolution, were split up into individual holdings and the principle of subsidies for basic foodstuffs severely eroded. Thereafter the IMF became, in effect, a stick with which to beat the old guard and the IMF restructuring became a codeword for the imposition of a Western model of capitalism. In the long term the government justified these measures on the grounds that they unleashed the creative forces in Algerian society long stifled by bureaucracy and socialism and opened up the country to foreign investment and greater prosperity. In the short term, though, the gains were difficult to discern, and the losses only too evident as unemployment mushroomed to over 25 per cent and basic commodities became virtually impossible to find, making daily life – already hard – intolerable.

Of course there had been resentments during the Boumediène years but it was not until Chadli that mass cynicism became endemic in Algerian society. Rumours about the elite siphoning off vast sums of money began to take root in the popular imagination as the baronial system, already in place, really took off. In large part this was a direct consequence of Chadli's reforms of the FLN, which saw the party balloon into a bureaucratic apparatus with an annual budget of over $100 million and thirty thousand paid workers. Chadli might have hoped to revitalize the FLN by reconnecting it with the people, but in practice the party became an apparatus for distributing favours as the FLN was colonized by a network of clans whose raison d'être was personal enrichment on a vast scale. In turn this meant that these clans were perfectly placed to exploit the transition process, using inside information to bleed the country dry. So as the movement towards the free market gained momentum and the new system of state monopolies was allowed greater autonomy in the establishment of import and export arrangements, a shadowy political-economic mafia emerged which expected foreign companies to pay a bribe of 10 to 15 per cent on any deals concluded. This practice meant they had a vested interest in keeping the country in a permanent state of underdevelopment since to reduce any reliance on imports would weaken the system of corruption.

The economy now became saturated with a culture of corruption, nepotism and kickbacks. The battle between Chadli and the old guard was not just about ideology. It was also a struggle between clans who did not want to lose their position within the system, a battle for the power to procure resources and favours. The sums involved were truly mind-boggling – in 1991 prime minister Ghozali talked about a figure of $27 billion being creamed off. The most visible expression of this illegitimate wealth was the establishment of shopping complexes within the major cities, restricted zones of rich villas with swimming pools (dubbed 'Dallas' and 'Dynasty' by the populace after the American soaps screened on television), and in restaurants businessmen making a play of their brash, brick-like mobile phones and huge cigars.

Such ostentation went against the egalitarian instincts of ordinary Algerians and was encapsulated in the popular phrase 'Villa, Honda, Blonda', a bitter swipe at officials who had no sense of public interest and were just fixated with the acquisition of villas, Hondas (the state-supplied cars of the 1980s), and loose female company. In the eyes of the populace the growth of the new rich was a break with the Islamo-populist orthodoxy at the base of the original FLN ideology and, as the contradiction between the slogan 'by the people for the people' and the grubby reality of social fracture became more and more evident, any lingering idealism seeped away. Ordinary people were particularly incensed by food traffickers, whose activities caused permanent but unnecessary shortages of staples such as semolina, flour and cooking oil. Occasionally official noises were made about the need for a clean-up campaign, but the examples made were mostly small fry, lower-level bureaucrats and managers, only increasing general cynicism. For poorer Algerians the failure to confront corruption – Bouteflika, for example, was never brought to trial despite a plethora of charges against him – was damning. Any graph of Algerian society during the 1980s would reveal a rising tide of violent anger, beginning in Oran in 1982, continuing with Constantine in 1986 and peaking with Algiers in 1988. In each case the rioting crowds were defending customary rights which they felt were being uprooted by Chadli's liberalism, thereby underlining how notions of egalitarianism and social justice, derived for the most part from Messali Hadj's ideology of Islamo-populism, were still deeply embedded within Algerian society.[20]

■ ■ ■

Foreign policy had been a very important pillar of legitimization for Boumediène. He knew that the image of the revolutionary Third World leader who stood up to the West and strode the world stage played very well to the domestic gallery and won him widespread support. In contrast Chadli was much less confrontational and much more accommodating. The stress was now put on moderation as Chadli developed a low-key approach which sought to realign Algeria with Europe and America. The new orientation first became apparent with the involvement of Algerian diplomats in behind-the-scenes attempts to resolve the Tehran embassy crisis from November 1979 to January 1981 when Americans were held hostage by the new Shia regime in Iran. However, these overtures became even more explicit from 1985 onwards as Chadli came to the conclusion that he needed the World Bank and the International Monetary Fund to force through his economic reforms.

Chadli's policy was as much about realism and adaptation as it was about ideology or credo. By the later 1980s he could sense the winds of change. Socialism was on the wane and free-market liberalism in the ascendant and with the end of Eastern Europe and the USSR between 1989 and 1991 there came a new international context that had a far-reaching impact upon Algeria. With the demise of the Soviet Union Algeria lost a vital political, economic and military ally. Although never as significant as that between the Soviet Union and Castro's Cuba, Algeria's link with the Soviets had always been a prominent feature of the country's foreign policy. Boumediène sought the support of the USSR after the June 1965 coup while the Soviet premier Aleksei Kosygin made an official visit in October 1971 and Soviet advisers trained the Algerian army in the use of Soviet military hardware. Even in 1991, the final year of the USSR's existence, four thousand Soviet citizens were living in Algeria. In an instant this support evaporated and the Algerian regime had to re-evaluate who were friends and who were enemies, particularly as the successor to the USSR, the Russian Federation, became embroiled in negotiations to recover loans estimated at $4 billion. The failure of the Soviet system also rebounded badly on the Algerian variant of socialism because, for all the talk of a grassroots alternative, central planning had undoubtedly influenced Boumediène's economic thinking. Like so many leaders in Africa and Asia, Boumediène had been impressed by the way in which communist economics had transformed the USSR from a backward peasant country into a superpower by the 1950s. From the vantage point of 1989, though, such a model was a relic from a bygone age. The future belonged to capitalism and if Algeria wanted to survive in the new world order the last vestiges of the Boumediène experiment had to be discarded, in effect bringing about the death of Algerian socialism, a term – all-pervasive in official discourse since 1962 – that disappeared overnight.

The end of socialism went hand in hand with the end of non-alignment because globalization made Third-Worldism meaningless. With the Cold War the non-aligned movement had been able to carve out an alternative political space, in part by playing one side off against the other. In this manner Boumediène, like Nehru in India, Nasser in Egypt and Tito in Yugoslavia, had punched above his weight on the international scene, as witnessed by his greatest foreign policy triumph, his 1974 address to the United Nations. But if in the 1950s, 1960s and 1970s the non-aligned movement had been vibrant, vital and alive, by the 1980s it seemed sad and defeated. Gone was any sense of common purpose or idealism and with the end of the Cold War it finally lost all possibility for leverage. The harsh reality was that Algeria, as with the rest of the non-aligned movement, had no alternative but to sign up to the free-market system, thereby losing any sense of international leadership. If under Boumediène Algeria had stood tall amongst Third World leaders, under Chadli Algeria became in the eyes of many just another country, prostrate before the machinations of the global economy, and this fact gnawed away at the legitimacy of the system.

Other developments underlined Algeria's international marginalization. In the case of the Arab League Algeria was overshadowed by an increasingly strident Saudi Arabia whilst attempts to foster North African unity with the proposed Maghreb Union in 1989 were a double-edged sword. Yes, on the one hand there was the prospect, however distant, of a union, much like the European Economic Community after 1957 in Western Europe, producing greater prosperity and re-igniting the ideal of political cooperation. But on the other such moves, along with the attempts to resolve the Western Sahara issue, further undermined the system because solidarity with the Polisario and hostility to Morocco had acted as a cement uniting the rulers and the ruled. Moreover, with the relaxation of border controls – an arrangement eagerly anticipated by football crowds who chanted about easy access to hashish – Algerians saw for themselves the relative prosperity of Morocco, another chink in the official armour which for years had derided King Hassan II as bourgeois, capitalist and pro-Western, presiding over a system inherently inferior to Algerian socialism.

Chadli's new realism was perhaps most evident in the relationship with France.[21] The victory of the left in the French elections of May 1981, ushering in the first socialist government for twenty-five years, brought with it much hope of a rapprochement and on 30 November 1981 the new president, the veteran François Mitterrand, visited Algiers. In November 1954, as the interior minister, Mitterrand had loudly proclaimed that Algeria was France and that the only possible response to calls for independence was repression. In public, though, he now struck up a rapport with Chadli, who two years later repaid the compliment with an official visit to Paris. At one point Chadli grasped Mitterrand's hand with his own and held them aloft together at a major press conference, something seen as a sign of new-found unity, and in official circles there was much talk about Algeria becoming a focal point of French foreign policy, symbolic of Mitterrand's desire for a new relationship between the rich North and the poor South.

Yet as the decade went on Franco-Algerian relations became less and less about big political ideas and more and more about practical issues such as controlling borders, stemming illegal immigration and integrating the *beurs*, the second generation who because they were born in France had the right to French citizenship.[22] This was especially true after the victory of the right at parliamentary elections in April 1986 when, with Jacques Chirac as prime minister, there was an uncomfortable two-year 'cohabitation' with the socialist president Mitterrand. From the beginning the spotlight was on the interior minister Charles Pasqua, who cultivated a reputation for 'straight talking'. In an effort to steal Le Pen's thunder, Pasqua underlined that France was not an open door to the Third World by restricting access permits, initiating a 'zero tolerance' of illegal immigration, and a tightening of access to French citizenship whereby children born in France to non-French parents would no longer automatically have French nationality at the age of eighteen.

This domestic agenda defined much of the Franco-Algerian relationship and Chadli came to be seen as a point of stability for a government determined to block any further influx of Algerians. In effect this made the Chirac government into a prop for the Chadli regime, and in 1987 France even colluded in the cover-up of the murder of Ali Mecili, a member of Aït Ahmed's Front des Forces Socialistes and a well-known oppositionist, by quickly extraditing his killer back to Algeria in a bid to hush up the affair and save Chadli's face.[23] It was a clumsy measure which raised howls of protest within the left-wing press. In *Libération* Serge July subsequently likened French policy over Algeria to that of the United States in Latin America. By deliberately turning a blind eye, by following a policy of double standards about human rights and by failing to pose any awkward questions, the French government had become hopelessly entangled with Chadli's discredited regime. The end result, July argued, was an abdication of responsibility that made France partly responsible for October 1988.[24]

THE BERBER SPRING

Just one year after coming to power, when his authority was still fragile, Chadli was faced with his first popular uprising. This was quite different to what had happened under Ben Bella and Boumediène. Then opposition had been about court politics within the system, usually taking the form of underground conspiracies by those disaffected not because they contested the form of the regime but because they had lost out in the struggle for power. Now, however, opposition took on a different hue. It was about mass protest and a challenge to the very nature of post-independence politics.

The first significant event was the 'Berber spring' in May 1980. The immediate trigger for this event was the government ban upon a lecture by the writer Mouloud Mammeri on the use of the Berber language to be delivered at Tizi-Ouzou university on 19 March 1980. In protest, staff and students occupied the university, and in April this opposition widened with the launching of a general strike across the whole of the Kabylia region. Since the Kabyle minority speak Berber as their first language, French as their second and Arabic only as a third, they were protesting against the official notion of the Algerian national identity as being Arab-Muslim. They were vehemently opposed to Arabization, whereby classical Arabic was progressively replacing French as the language of teaching at all levels of education, demanding instead that the latter be retained while Berber language and culture be put upon an equal footing. Although the Berber spring was severely repressed – thirty people were killed and hundreds injured – it gave rise to a movement which, by advocating democracy, human rights and cultural pluralism, continued to challenge the authoritarian nature of the one-party state.

Of course, as Hugh Roberts has underlined, many of these Berberist concepts are laced with historical inaccuracies.[25] Berberism in Algeria is essentially a Kabyle affair and Berberist discourse ignores the fact that the political outlook of the Shawiya Berbers of south-eastern Algeria, who did not support the Berber spring, is significantly different. Furthermore, although singers like the late Lounès Matoub talked about Arab colonization, they conveniently forget the fact that significant aspects of the traditional Kabyle culture are Arab-Islamic in origin. One only has to look at the extent to which the Berber language of politics and honour is borrowed from Arabic, and the village councils which are traditional in both Berber and Arab regions. Consequently it is impossible to talk about a pure, undiluted Berber identity.

Even so, the Berber spring represented the first instance of mass political protest and initially Chadli gave in to the movement's demands, pledging to create a chair in Kabyle Studies at the University of Tizi-Ouzou and, even more controversially, to re-establish the chair of Berber Studies at Algiers university, which had been symbolically abolished at independence. He also promised to review the regime's cultural policy. However, once Chadli felt stronger he began to back-pedal. At the FLN central committee meeting in June and July the new Cultural Charter made no mention of the Berber aspect of national identity, and, although the teaching of Berber was introduced into the higher-education curriculum, the government made it clear that these courses had to be taught in Arabic because Berber did not have the status of a language. In the meantime the government resorted to the usual accusations, denouncing the Berber spring as a carefully orchestrated French plot designed to undermine the Algerian nation.

In response, the Mouvement Culturel Berbère (MCB), which had emerged from the anti-Boumediène unrest of 1968, called for a general strike in the region in September 1981 to protest against the Cultural Charter. The response was relatively weak and the government clamped down, arresting and imprisoning hundreds of activists. Yet despite the ferocity of this repression the Berber movement could not be stifled. Henceforth the Berber spring would be commemorated each year with meetings and protests, an alternative cycle of remembrance that seriously dented the regime's legitimacy, especially when the Berber movement openly contested the official memory, not just through the semi-clandestine press like the journal *Tafsut*, but also through the establishment of grassroots group such as the Comité des Enfants de Chouhada (Committee of the Children of the Martyrs) which aimed to preserve the memory of their parents' role in the liberation struggle. These groups explicitly set out to reclaim the memory of the war of liberation for themselves, proclaiming a Berber perspective not just on the war of independence but on Algerian history as a whole. They cast 1962 as a defining moment because it was then that the army of the frontiers, which had cynically abandoned the internal resistance, swept into Algeria and used the Arab-Islamic idea of the one and indivisible nation as a way of forging a false national identity and seizing power. As Saïd Sadi, one of the leaders of the Berber spring, later explained, the post-independence regime was a mirror image of the former colonial power, a centralized state modelled on the French Republican tradition which, by denying the Berber component, cultivated a climate of self-hatred that would have dire consequences. Alienated from their real history by the frenetic rush into socialism, Third-Worldism and pan-Arabism, the post-1962 generation were destined to become rootless. Is it little wonder, Sadi asked, that so many were seduced by Islamism?[26]

The language used by Berber dissidents, particularly anti-establishment musicians such as Lounès Matoub, Idir and Djamel Allam, was inevitably highly emotive. The groups talked about cultural and political genocide and totalitarianism, arguing that the desire to eradicate Berber identity was symptomatic of a unitary political culture founded on censorship and authoritarianism. In the eyes of Berber activists history and culture were synonymous with human rights, a point that was underlined even further in July 1985 when the veteran human rights lawyer Abdennour Ali Yahia founded the Ligue Algérienne pour la Défense des Droits de l'Homme (LADDH) to defend twenty members of the Comité des Enfants de Chouhada who had been arrested. From the beginning, Ali Yahia, a veteran of the war of liberation, was a canny and resourceful fighter.[27] By affiliating to the International Human Rights Federation and linking up with Amnesty International, he ensured some measure of protection from the worst excesses of the regime. Even so, by putting anti-Berberism and the abuse of human rights in the international spotlight he incurred the wrath of the regime, which declared his organization illegal and imprisoned him for eleven months in July 1985. Such measures were counter-productive, making him an international cause célèbre and tarnishing the regime's image abroad precisely at the moment when Chadli wanted to build links with the West. Thereafter the regime resorted to more subtle approaches, trying to procure a split with the LADDH before eventually forcing Ali Yahia into exile in Paris in 1987, whence he continued his criticism of the regime.

The Berber spring was a major turning point. For the first time since independence a popular movement had challenged the historical legitimacy of the regime. Political and cultural pluralism, along with the language of human rights, was now a fact of life and for Ali Yahia this was the real victory of the 1980s. The Berber spring was a fracturing moment and in this sense there is a straight line between April 1980 and October 1988.

■ ■ ■

Confronted with the spectre of Berberism, as well as continued communist influence, Chadli set out to court the Islamist movement as a political counterbalance. Elsewhere in the Arab world, disillusionment with pan-Arabism's failure to defeat Israel meant that Islamism had been steadily gaining ground in the 1970s. This was the case in Algeria too and from 1980 onwards Chadli began to tacitly encourage the Islamists on the ground, quietly instructing the police to back off as gangs of bearded men intimidated communists, Berberists and women who were thought to be immodestly dressed. Through such action Chadli hoped to control the movement for his own ends, using it as a battering ram to eradicate the left. It was a delicate balancing act by a man who was careful to position himself as above the fray, but Chadli reasoned that if the situation got out of hand he could send in the forces of law and order, thereby underlining the need for strong leadership.

The dangers of this strategy soon became apparent in the universities. There Arabization had produced a hybrid system: the traditional one where students learnt in French, and the Arabizing one where the students were taught entirely in Arabic. During the early 1980s clashes between French-speaking and Arabic-speaking students became frequent at Algiers university where Arabic-speaking students were bitter about the inequality of opportunities, pointing to the fact that the standard of teaching within the Arabic system, particularly in the all-important technical and scientific subjects, was thought inferior to that in the French-speaking system. Thus, they argued, French-speaking students, who in the main were the sons and daughters of the political elite, enjoyed much better employment prospects. Islamist groups exploited these disaffections, transforming the complexities of Algerian society into a crude divide between 'us', the Arabic-speaking majority, and 'them', the French-speaking minority. Frustrated ambitions produced a ready flow of recruits and through the course of 1981 this new-found stridency became more and more manifest. Groups of bearded men occupied a major lecture theatre and turned it into a mosque, whilst on 19 May 1981 the communist-dominated national students' union's 'Day of the Student' – marking the anniversary of the union's strike in May 1956 – was violently attacked by Islamist students brandishing sticks and knives. Then on 2 November 1982 a left-wing student, Kamel Amzel, was beheaded by blows from a sword by Islamists at the Ben Aknoun campus of Algiers university.

The Islamists had gone too far. The police stepped in and arrested four hundred of them but this repression provoked huge uproar and demonstrated the dangers of Chadli's strategy. The genie was out of the bottle and Chadli could no longer control it, as became only too evident on 12 November 1982 when a huge meeting at the central campus of Algiers university was attended by a hundred thousand, many wearing white skullcaps and white robes (*goundouras*). It was an impressive show of public strength as the crowds, straining to hear the dissident clerics Sheikhs Madani, Soltani and Sahnoun, spilled over into the streets and paralysed downtown Algiers. For the three speakers it was the end of a long march to the very centre of Algerian political life and they seized the opportunity to unveil a charter for an Islamic state.

Claiming to embody the ideas and aspirations of the vast majority of Algerians, the charter based itself on the sharia and called for the ending of secondary and higher education for women and the prohibition of alcohol. No less importantly all three used the meeting to attack the enemies of Islam, an unholy alliance of communists, freemasons, Jews and the United States, all of which were engaged in a new crusade against Muslims not just in Algeria but everywhere. It was inflammatory language and not surprisingly Soltani and Sahnoun were placed under house arrest and Madani was imprisoned.

In contrast to the Boumediène years, or neighbouring Morocco and Tunisia where Islamist movements had been brutally repressed, the clampdown was not harsh. Madani and Sahnoun were released without charge, those accused of beheading the leftist student received comparatively light sentences, and the trial of the arrested Islamists was eventually called off. By playing a game of incorporation and accommodation rather than repression, Chadli was very much out of step with the rest of the governments of North Africa and this made the Islamist movement increasingly self-confident. Many felt that they were being given a green light by Chadli, who wanted to harness political Islam as a way of legitimizing his regime.

The rising force of Islamism was symbolized by the reaction to the death of Sheikh Soltani on 12 April 1984 at the age of eighty-two. In spite of no mention in the official media, his burial in the Kouba district of Algiers was a huge event, attended by twenty-five thousand mourners. Such emotion put the regime on the back foot, making clear that Islamism was a force which the government could not ignore, and in the following months Chadli, like Boumediène before him, tried to appropriate religious arguments.

It was in this climate that the Family Code of June 1984, inspired by the sharia, was discussed by the one-party National Assembly and overwhelmingly passed. The Code's most zealous supporter was Abdelaziz Belkhadem, a member of the FLN's political bureau. Rejecting the idea of a modern Islam which could coexist with notions of liberty, equality and fraternity, he pronounced:

> The sincere Muslim is the one who conforms to the sharia in its entirety ... There is no ancient, or mediaeval, or modern, or progressive Islam, there is only one Islam.[28]

In the Code women did not exist as individuals in their own right but only as 'daughters of', 'mothers of', 'sisters of' or 'wives of'. The Code made them dependent on their father, brother or closest male relative for work, marriage, education, divorce and inheritance. Polygamy was authorized, whilst women could not arrange their own marriage contracts or marry a non-Muslim. Women were not allowed to travel without the approval of a male family member. At every level the Code contradicted the Constitution, which gave women the right to vote and the right to work, and was a testament to how far the country had changed since the early 1970s. The Family Code was for the Islamists what the agrarian revolution had been for the leftists and a new atmosphere prevailed throughout Algeria. The state had given men the licence to treat women as minors whose actions were now subjected to constant surveillance.[29]

State Islam went on to the offensive, trying to take over the themes of street Islam in other ways too. This was perhaps clearest in the attack on Sufi practices. Notions of the evil eye, images of saints, the lack of any divisions between the sacred and the profane, religion and magic, now and the here-after, the idea of miracles: for state Islam, taking its cue from the traditionalist clerics, these practices were pagan in origin, long associated with the supposed dominance of women in the countryside, and had to be rooted out, con-demned as the expression of an obscurantist Islam. The drive for conformity was about the assertion of the male over the female, the urban over the rural, the orthodox over the religiously suspect, and went hand in hand with a cam-paign against drugs and alcohol. At schools the influence of Islamists was more and more obvious, not just in terms of teachers warning children that parents who did not obey the sharia would go to hell but also as regards the day-to-day curriculum, with the teaching of Arabic now based upon the Qur'an. Chadli gave further encouragement to Islamists by decreeing that Arabic place names had to be used instead of French, so Algiers officially became el-Djezaïr, Constantine was renamed Qacentina and Blida became el-Boulaïda. The new National Charter in 1986 underlined the centrality of Islam to the Algerian identity:

> Islam brought to the world a noble conception of human dignity that condemns racism and rejects chauvinism and the exploitation of man by man; the equality it champions is in harmony with and adapted to each of the centuries of history.[30]

The regime also sponsored a massive expansion of mosque building. Some six thousand were built during the 1980s, including a major new Islamic univer-sity at Constantine in September 1984 dedicated to the Emir Abd el-Kader. Given that Constantine – the birthplace of the Association of Algerian Ulema – was a bastion of traditionalism, this was a major statement by the regime about Islam. To bolster the religious legitimacy of the whole initiative the regime invited from Egypt two of the most prestigious sheikhs in the Muslim world, Muhammed al-Ghazali and Yusuf al-Qaradawi. Qaradawi in particular was a rising star within Sunni circles but the fact that the authorities had to look abroad betrayed a lack of confidence, and during their period in Constantine the two paid only lip service to the Chadli government regime whilst calling for an Islamic awakening that would weaken the regime from the inside.

From 1981 onwards a three-day Islamic book fair was held annually at Aïn El Bey university in Constantine. This was a huge event with stands displaying the books, reviews and cassettes of Islamist scholars, many of whom were theoretically censored in Algeria. Photographs of alleged Israeli and Soviet atrocities against Muslims were accompanied by loudspeakers calling on Muslims to wake from lethargy and see what was being done to their brothers and sisters throughout the world. The same speakers also called on those attending not to be seduced by the glossy messages contained within Western clothes, music and television soaps like *Dallas*, which they thought would pollute hearts and minds and do untold damage to the Muslim way of life. Particular venom was reserved for Western pop music and in 1985 the fair had a special exhibition devoted to Punks and New Romantics in London drawn from the French music press. Pinpointing Boy George, Marilyn and the Thomson Twins, Arab translations conjured up an image of a debauched lifestyle where men wearing make-up took drugs and committed homosexual acts on a regular basis. Most horror was reserved for Marilyn, whose androgyny and camp sensibility, a staple of Western pop music from David Bowie to Marc Almond, subverted the traditional gender hierarchies essential to the teaching of Islam. Without a reassertion of Muslim values, the exhibition warned, this would be the fate awaiting Algerian youth:

Man-woman. Bloke-chick. Walks like a man, dances like a man, speaks like a man, but looks at himself in the mirror like a woman, knows how to put on blusher and powder.[31]

The image of bearded clerics poring over pictures of Marilyn, with his long blond hair, trying to discern whether he is a man or a woman might have a surreal quality, but it pinpointed the schizophrenia at the heart of the Chadli agenda. On the one hand he encouraged consumerism, on the other he sought to align himself with Islamists who, even if they had no problem with the principle of the free market, were opposed to the cultural values that Western-style modernity brought with it.

These contradictions demonstrate that it is simplistic to think of Algeria in terms of secularists versus Islamists. The Islamists always had allies within the system. Yet despite these attempts at incorporation and accommodation Chadli could not stifle the growth of militant forms of Islamist activism beyond his control, the most spectacular example of which was the Mouvement Islamique Armé (MIA). Made up of three hundred hardliners and led by Mustapha Bouyali, the MIA brooked no compromise as it set out to overthrow the Chadli regime by violent means, foreshadowing the violence of the 1990s.

Born in 1942, Bouyali was a veteran of the war against the French before being expelled from the FLN after participating in the FFS *maquis*. Details about this period of his life are hazy; he drifted from one dead-end job to another until the late 1970s before undergoing a conversion experience upon hearing the preaching of Abdelhadi at the El-Achour mosque in Algiers. Bouyali warmed to his attacks on the corrupt francophone elite to such an extent that he became the imam at the El-Achour mosque in 1980. Styling himself a diehard Islamist he set out to clean up the local neighbourhood, attacking drinking dens and brothels while denouncing the FLN state as corrupt and communist. Such was his stature as a model of Muslim behaviour that when the police came to arrest him in October 1981 he easily went to ground, taking to the mountains just south of Algiers in early 1982 to form a *maquis*.

In calling for a holy war against the regime, Bouyali's first point of reference was the example of the Prophet going into exile, what Malise Ruthven has perceptively termed the 'Mohammedan paradigm'.[32] Specifically, he wanted to replicate the flight from Mecca in AD 622, when Mohammed and his small band of followers, no longer able to practise their religion, withdrew to the city of Medina before returning triumphant to Mecca eight years later to usher in a just and perfect society based on the sanctity of God's word. The image of exile, struggle and victory in the face of overwhelming odds; the notion that Muslims will be tested but, if they remain true to God's will and Mohammed's teachings, will vanquish their foes: both ideas were constantly invoked by Bouyali as he held up Mohammed's story of flight as a model of action. By taking to the mountains his followers were establishing an Islamic refuge which would eventually overcome the apostates of the plains. His second point of reference was November 1954, and because he had fought in the fourth *wilaya*, he was able to emphasize the continuity with the original war of liberation. Then he had had a duty to take up arms and resist colonialism; now he had the self-same duty against a Godless state.

Participation in the war of liberation had given Bouyali a detailed knowledge of the Atlas Mountains that rise dramatically just to the south of Algiers, a knowledge he deployed to deadly effect. Thus, although the authorities intercepted arms that were being smuggled into the country in August 1983 in the Aurès Mountains, they were not able to stop a series of robberies, including the snatch of the payroll of a factory near Algiers on 21 August, and an attack on a police barracks at Souma just 25 miles to the south of the capital. Such reverses were damaging to the government's prestige and a large army force began to sweep the small town of Larba and the surrounding mountain hinterland, an area well known for its Islamist sympathies. But, although some of the MIA were captured on 21 October, Bouyali turned the tables on his pursuers in spectacular fashion and killed five policemen in a gunfight.

The fact that Bouyali was able to escape capture was a measure of the support he and his band enjoyed among sections of the local population to the south of Algiers. In part this was because Bouyali's language and actions tapped into deeply embedded patterns of thought, evoking memories of the bandits of honour in the mountains, paralleling the life of the Prophet and drawing on the original war of liberation. Many ordinary Algerians felt instinctively on his side and, although the government-controlled media did everything to play down the phenomenon, the MIA continued to score spectacular successes against the forces of law and order. The government was, therefore, palpably relieved when Bouyali was killed in a dramatic ambush in the Algiers casbah on 3 January 1987, a shoot-out which also led to the deaths of the commander leading the hunt and an informer. It was followed by a further crackdown that led to a round-up of 202 MIA militants. When they were put on trial in June – the largest ever trial of Algerian Islamists – it seemed that the back of the terrorist movement had been finally broken. Yet many questions dogged the Bouyali affair. Why had he been able to remain at large for so long? Did he have friends in high places? And was he eventually sold out by more moderate Islamists who wanted to curry favour with Chadli?

Although the MIA was spectacular in impact its actions were still those of a minority. Many more Algerians were drawn into the orbit of Islamism through the hundreds of unofficial street mosques that mushroomed all over the country during the late seventies and early eighties. These came to represent an alternative space beyond the control of the state, a portable Islam made up of cassettes, photocopied tracts and dissident journals that interpreted the world as the perpetual war between belief and unbelief. Loudspeakers, moved from neighbourhood to neighbourhood, were used to great effect, creating the image of an unstoppable movement that was wresting control of the religious sphere from the state.

Many of the younger clerics involved in the movement had received their theological training in Saudi Arabia which, encouraged by the United States to use the financial power derived from oil to challenge Iran for leadership of the Muslim world during the 1980s, provided huge sums of money for mosque building and the schooling of imams. The 1980s witnessed the growing ascendancy of Saudi Wahhabism in Africa, Asia and the Middle East through the Saudi-led World Islamic League. Wahhabism is a version of Sunni Islam that stresses the strict observance of outward rules of behaviour (orthopraxy), combined with hostility to non-Islamic religions, including Judaism and Christianity, as well as anti-Sufism, anti-Shiism and a literalist interpretation of the Qur'an: in short a fundamentalist conception of religion that at the time was hardened still further by Saudi Arabia's support for the holy war against communism in Afghanistan.

Wahhabism provided much of the inspiration behind the grassroots movement led by Sahnoun, Soltani and Madani. Presenting itself as a community of believers, committed to the moral and political rebirth of Algeria, the movement was a loose coalition of groups and networks operating throughout the country and was aimed explicitly at the young and the poor. Rebuilding from the bottom up, through welfare and charity work as well as the setting up of schools of boxing and martial arts to combat drink and drugs amongst the young, this was a society within a society, providing not only spiritual guidance, but also practical help and support for those in need. As Malise Ruthven has argued, this phenomenon, which also became widespread in Morocco, Tunisia and Egypt, envisages the construction of a divine society from below:

> Before jahiliya can be overcome, society must be rebuilt 'from below'. To borrow Christian terminology, the solution is 'postmillennial' and world-constructing: before the Messiah comes, we must build a world fit to receive him.[33]

For large sections of the urban poor, attuned to cynicism about the system, such purity and dedication was impressive, and the Islamists quickly built up a large base of popular support. In the face of unending economic hardship, this vision of Islam exerted a powerful pull because, in providing an all-embracing credo, it gave people a sense of new-found purpose and dignity. Young people in particular found the movement hugely empowering. The links, friendships and social welfare provided by the street mosques gave meaning to lost lives because they offered up joy, warmth and human solidarity. Even more importantly, by casting young people as the warriors of God, proud, strong and deserving of respect, the street mosque movement instilled self-belief. Fired up by religious indignation, its followers had nothing to be afraid of. After all, even if it was Shia in inspiration, did not the 1979 Iranian revolution provide an example of a mass Muslim movement triumphing over a political system copied from the West?

The young *hittistes* were especially attracted to the young cleric Ali Belhadj. The son of a martyr in the war against the French, trained in Wahhabi circles in Saudi Arabia, the youthful-looking Belhadj was only thirty-two in 1988 and as an orator he had no rival. Soberly dressed in his long white *kamis* and skullcap, scrupulously orthodox, every Friday, at the Kouba mosque in a rundown district of Algiers he delivered thundering sermons that got the blood racing and the heart pounding. He was direct, funny and violent, effortlessly mixing classical Arabic with Algerian dialect in a manner that was exhilarating, viscerally thrilling and easy to understand. Utterly convinced of his beliefs, he made the crowds – passionate, excited but above all young – hang on his every word. He could make them laugh, he could make them cry and when the questions came he had an answer for everything. This, he told them, was not a frivolous counter-culture. No, it was a movement of the righteous marching inexorably towards a pure society based upon the word of God. For this reason there was only one sense of liberation: submission to the will of God through a complete and unquestioning belief in the Qur'an, the one and eternal source of morality. They were his servants whose lives were already predestined and any doubts, detours and deliberations were nothing but French-influenced frippery, the distractions of infidels, blind to the truth.

For the poor and unemployed such language was very seductive. Converts talked about before and after: once they had heard Belhadj's sermons and let God into their lives they experienced a rush of freedom and self-sufficiency that was akin to being reborn. By giving them a mission and showing them the true path Belhadj had taken them away from the dull monotony of their lives. Belhadj talked about the need for the personal jihad within and the external jihad without; both parts of the same struggle to re-Islamicize Algeria by ridding it of the intoxicating Western evils of communism, socialism, liberalism and feminism. What the regime had forgotten, Belhadj reminded his audiences, is that Islam is self-sufficient. It does not need to borrow, adopt or adapt from the West.

Belhadj particularly attacked the regime's huge memorial to the war of liberation, unveiled at Riadh el-Feth in 1982 to mark the twentieth anniversary of independence. Designed by the Polish architect Andrej Konieczny and made up of three figures from the war, the memorial, which dominated the Algiers skyline, consciously echoed the tombs of the unknown soldier that sprang up in Europe after the First World War. For Belhadj such 'idolatry' was genuinely shocking. By donning the garb of the West the regime was encouraging the people to worship false gods, in effect obscuring the message of Islam by supplanting it with a dangerous human fabrication. In Belhadj's eyes it was symptomatic of the way in which the regime had allowed the message of Islam to become obscured by secular ideologies. Like the monument, these ideologies had to be torn down so that the purity of the Qur'an could be brilliantly revealed and the country's corrupted religious identity reclaimed.[34]

For Belhadj the goal was spiritual purity and to this end he heaped scorn on the elite, the 'new settlers' and francophone intellectuals, 'the French fifth column', even issuing a fatwa condemning the francophone Algerian writer Tahar Djaout in 1987 for reducing Algeria to 'a swamp of spiritual and bodily sloth'. His greatest venom, though, was reserved for women who wore make-up and Western clothes, whom he saw as a mortal threat, a temptation that, by stimulating pornographic desires in young men, would destroy traditional family values at the heart of Islam. This was why Belhadj was so angered by the transmission of the American soap operas *Dallas* and *Dynasty* on Algerian television. By exposing young men to these images of women dominated by sexual lust and material greed, the regime was falling into a carefully laid Western trap, the promotion of promiscuous values that would ensnare men and erode Islam's spiritual and moral cohesiveness from within. Such ideas became common currency within the street mosque movement and were repeated by other preachers throughout Algeria. In the mosque in the Filali quarter of Constantine, loudspeakers proclaimed:

> the women who imitate Marilyn Monroe or Brigitte Bardot will only produce abortions, an effeminate offspring like Clo-Clo, Adamo or Macias. Women must wear the *hijab* ... in such a way that the veil covers the whole body.[35]

Belhadj and his ilk were careful to claim that they were not anti-women. Rather they were showing respect for honourable Muslim women, warning them against the pitfalls of the Western lifestyle and asking them to fulfil their role as guardians of the domestic sphere.

For young men, unsure of their position in society, such an assertion of traditional gender roles, reaffirming their status as guardians and protectors, was empowering. Many male converts transformed their guilt at their previous 'sinful' lifestyles into anger and violence against women. Angry with themselves for being prey to impure impulses which had made them sin against the divine purpose, they strove to make amends by being ever vigilant against the snares of promiscuous women, denounced as the conduits of the West and the Devil. The conduct of women was now closely monitored whilst many male converts made it a rule to walk in the street with downcast eyes, glancing neither left nor right and never behind, their eyes shunning the eyes of women lest they stir lustful desires.

The question of women and Islam demonstrated how receptive urban youth were to Belhadj's interpretation of religious knowledge in a directly political fashion. To talk about politics as the expression of divine will was a revelation to them, a new activist form of religion that combined moral purity and social action with the promise of divine grace; not just redemption of Algeria, but salvation of the troubled soul as well. The need to return to God was a powerful call to a younger generation, for whom the rigorous observance of Islam became a way of rebelling against their secular elders. For many of them, in their eyes socialism was now a failure – exhausted, spiritless and impersonal – and as the regime withered on the vine the prestige of the new religious politics grew inexorably. Among the clearest examples of this sea change were the many young women who made a conscious decision to take up the veil. In 1987 fifteen-year-old Malika, a schoolgirl in Algiers, explained that she was proud to wear the *hijab*. For her it was not a symbol of oppression but a statement about her belief in God.[36]

To many of the older generation such reasoning was difficult to comprehend. As a teacher in a secondary school in Algiers in 1987, Khalida Messaoudi vividly remembers the transformation that took place.[37] In the summer of that year only five out of an average forty-two students wore the *hijab* but by the autumn this had risen to half. This change deeply shocked her, even if she was quick to recognize the multiple reasons for it. For some girls the impetus was the need to be left in peace from the unwanted advances of young men; for others it was the need to hide their poverty; others were yielding to family and social pressure; but for a great many it was about expressing their new-found pride in Islam and rejecting the godless regime.

■ ■ ■

If one thread of the Islamist movement was Bouyali, the second thread the street mosque movement, the final dimension was Afghanistan. The significance of the Soviet invasion of Afghanistan on 25 December 1979 across the Arab and Muslim world cannot be overstated. The fight against godless communism became a beacon, much like the Spanish Civil War for international anti-fascists between 1936 and 1939, and for those who went to fight it was a radicalizing experience that was to have long-term consequences in terms of religious ideas and the practical knowledge of conducting warfare.

When the Red Army went into Afghanistan to shore up an ailing pro-communist regime, the United States saw it as a unique opportunity to inflict a damaging defeat on its superpower rival. Building upon its existing links, the CIA entered into an alliance with the Saudi Arabian and Pakistani secret services to coordinate the recruitment of Sunni volunteers.[38] Members of the Muslim Brotherhood and the Pakistani Islamist Party – *Jamaai-I-Islami*, many of whom were advisors to the Pakistani head of state General Zia between 1977 and 1988 – were also enrolled in the operation and through these networks the American CIA contributed $6 billion to the training, equipping and paying of the Afghan *mujahidin*, a figure matched by $4 billion from the Saudi government. Significantly, too, huge sums were raised from mosques, non-governmental charities and private donors throughout the Muslim world.

The call of the anti-communist jihad brought a flock of Islamist volunteers from all over the Muslim world, including many on the run from their own governments, as Afghanistan became a safety valve for regimes in Egypt and Tunisia desperate to rid themselves of extremists. Early on, the CIA gave Pakistan full control of the allocation of weapons and resources on the ground, and this hands-off approach meant that few questions were asked about the religious and political indoctrination of the volunteers, most of whom passed through the burgeoning religious *madrasas* that sprang up on the Pakistan–Afghanistan border.[39] Given that these religious schools were financed by Saudi Arabia and run by strict local Deobandi clerics, it is not surprising that they offered up a hard-line Wahhabi version of Islam that profoundly coloured the nature of the holy war against the Soviet Union.

Somewhere between 150,000 and 250,000 Afghans were engaged in the war along with a maximum of 25,000 Afghan Arabs who were attached to various *mujahidin* factions. The raising of these foreign fighters was left to Islamic organizations and from the beginning the Saudi millionaire Osama bin Laden played a key role in recruiting thousands to the Afghan cause. A rich man who scorned luxury and claimed to model himself on the Prophet, bin Laden had acquired a legendary status in Afghanistan by the late 1980s not only because of his contribution of millions of dollars to the anti-communist jihad, but also because of his reputed personal courage in combat, which he demonstrated during the battle around the town of Chaprihar, south-east of Jalalabad in early 1989. Bin Laden was brilliant in building a network of recruiting offices throughout the Muslim world which brought fighters from every Islamic nation, including Saudi Arabia, the Yemen, Egypt and of course Algeria.[40]

Once in Pakistan bin Laden's fighters were sent to Peshawar where they were placed under the control of Abdullah Azzam, a Jordanian of Palestinian origin, who had fought against the Israelis in the 1967 war and then pursued doctoral studies at al-Azhar in Cairo in the early seventies, where he struck up a close friendship not only with the family of the executed Sayyid Qutb but also with Sheikh Abdel Omar Rahman, the spiritual leader of *al-Gamaa al-Islamiyya*, which was violently opposed to the rule of President Anwar Sadat. In 1978 Azzam settled in Saudi Arabia to become a teacher and, after meeting Afghan leaders there in 1980, he became a convert to the anti-Soviet jihad.

In Peshawar Azzam, charged with the training of the growing numbers of volunteers from North Africa and the Middle East, rose to become the leading hard-line religious ideologue. As the war against the Soviet Union intensified so too did Azzam's language as he distilled the complex ideas found in the tradition of the Muslim Brotherhood of al-Banna and Qutb into a simplistic brew of good against evil, faith against unbelief, God against Satan. For him the Afghan struggle was nothing less than the sixth pillar of faith, a moral obligation for all Muslims, and he conjured up the anti-communist jihad as an epic narrative, akin to the struggles of the Prophet in the seventh century. Azzam eventually died in murky circumstances from a car bomb in November 1989 but not before he and his training camps had exerted a huge influence on a generation of foreign fighters, including Algerians such as Saïd Makhloufi, Kamareddin Kherbane and Abdallah Anas, each of whom would become pivotal in Islamist violence during the 1990s. Estimates vary as to how many Algerians travelled to Afghanistan, with numbers ranging from 300 to 2,800, but what is not in doubt is the impact this experience had upon their conception of the world. Henceforth nothing would be same again.

The Algerians particularly warmed to Azzam and bin Laden's argument that the defeat of the Soviet Union in Afghanistan was a divine act that had led directly to the fall of the Berlin Wall and the end of communism. Whereas pan-Arabism had failed to defeat Israel, the foreign fighters, armed with Wahhabi doctrines, had been central in humbling the Red Army, underlining the fact that a return to basic Islamic values was the prerequisite to a general Muslim renaissance. Therefore, Azzam and bin Laden continued, jihad did not end with victory in Afghanistan. Empowered by the defeat of the Soviet

Union the foreign legion had a duty to go back to their own countries and take the war to their own godless elites, a view that was appreciated by the Algerian contingent given Algeria's close ties with the Soviet Union and Cuba. Unlike much of the street mosque movement, Azzam and bin Laden believed that power must be seized from above through direct action. For them the Chadli regime, like so many other Muslim governments, was a rotting edifice mired in unbelief and waiting to collapse. Inspired by these arguments the returning veterans were to have a huge impact in 1989 as they appeared at the head of demonstrations in combat fatigues, beards and *pakols*, the round woollen hats donned by the *mujahidin*. These veterans, lithe and muscular, were God's own warriors; a stark contrast to the government where there were no more heroes, only grey, faceless bureaucrats devoid of any higher purpose. Unsurprisingly the Afghan look took off amongst sections of Algerian youth, becoming a statement about their rejection of the Chadli regime.

The disappearance of a clear social project under Chadli did away with the rationale for dictatorial rule and led to concerted challenges from Islamists, Berberists and human rights activists. But these were not the only groups to contest the regime's legitimacy. The 1980s witnessed the emergence of a feminist movement as well as intellectual dissent in novels and films. No less importantly the issue of official history, one of the foundation stones of the post-1962 regime, was lain open to increasing scrutiny as Algerians posed the question of who controls the past and for what purpose.

During the 1980s a small group of women mobilized around the issue of women's rights. The trigger for this militancy was a ministerial decree at the beginning of 1980 prohibiting women from leaving Algeria without a male chaperon.[41] This was immediately challenged by female postgraduate students studying in France who, knowing that they would be prevented from travelling to see their supervisors, invoked the 1976 Constitution which had enshrined equality of the sexes and freedom of movement. Other female students at Algiers university organized a petition supported by the PAGS followed by a large demonstration on 8 March 1980, International Women's Day, and in the face of this protest the decree was rescinded.

Even so the decree pointed to the growing influence of religious conservatives and, as talk grew about the new Family Code being secretly prepared by the government, hundreds of young women occupied the offices of the National Union of Algerian Women, an FLN organization. Led by Khalida Messaoudi, the demonstrators formed a collective, Collectif Femmes, to defend women's rights against conservatives. Modelling themselves on civil rights movements the collective put pressure on the regime through high-profile action culminating with five hundred gathering before the National Assembly on 16 November whilst the Code was being debated. Confronted with this direct action the regime made some late concessions, which split the feminist movement between those prepared to make a deal and those who were not. Messaoudi was in the latter camp and participated in a further demonstration in front of the main post office of Algiers on 23 December, at which the young women were joined by thirty female veterans of the war of liberation including Djamila Bouhired, the heroine of the Battle of Algiers. Brandishing banners which said 'No to the Family Code' and 'No to the Betrayal of the Ideals of 1 November 1954', the women made this a hugely symbolic moment and in an open letter to Chadli, couched in the language of freedom and citizenship, they called for the recognition of sexual equality in work, marriage and divorce. On top of this they told the government in no uncertain terms that polygamy should be abolished, family inheritance divided equally and, perhaps most controversially, women should reach the age of legal majority at the same time as men. Given the veterans' legitimacy Chadli was forced to back down and shelve the Code. As Messaoudi remembers:

> the revolt of the 'history makers' put him into a difficult situation. He could not claim that this was a revolt led by women of the extreme left who sought to take revenge on the bourgeois government, or by feminists who were fighting a misogynous state. The *moujahidat* [female veterans] are the most legitimate women in the eyes of the people. So Chadli withdrew the bill for the Code. For us it was a great victory – but, unfortunately, a temporary one.[42]

Building on this victory, the collective planned to produce a manifesto of women's rights setting out in clear and authoritative terms how the proposed Code contravened not just the Constitution but also United Nations legislation which Algeria had signed up to. However, their work was increasingly disrupted by government repression. They were denied access to the media and a number were arrested in December 1983 which made it very difficult to oppose the renewed Family Code, rushed through with great haste in May and June 1984. Even so, Khalida Messaoudi and her fellow feminists remained unbowed; the abolition of the Code became the focus of militant activity and the Association for Legal Equality Between Women and Men was formed in May 1985.

Although its members were a small minority of the population, the spirit of dissent encapsulated in Collectif Femmes had a strong influence on

Algerian literature. There was a shift in themes and subject matter from the late 1970s onwards, among not just well-established writers like Assia Djebar and Mohammed Dib but also a younger generation of talented authors such as Rachid Boudjedra, Nabile Farès, Rachid Mimouni and Tahar Djaout.[43] Rather than continually harking back to the war of liberation these writers, for the most part writing in French, were anxious to reflect the subtle complexities of the new Algeria. However, publication was a long and arduous process with authors being forced to run a gauntlet of censorship and bureaucratic inertia. Controversial manuscripts would often be left to gather dust on some forgotten shelf in the backrooms of the state-owned National Publishing and Distribution Company. Not surprisingly, those unwilling to become mouthpieces for either Boumèdiene's socialism or Chadli's liberalism were obliged to look abroad. Assia Djebar and Fettouma Touati, both of whom wanted to expose the powers-that-be by putting the spotlight on the brutal plight of women in post-independence Algeria, had little choice but to publish in France.[44] There was equal frustration in the ranks of arabophone writers such as Abdelhamid Ben Hadouga and Tahar Ouettar. At the core of their work was the issue of Arab identity and they felt that the regime was not doing enough to hasten the whole Arabization process, preferring instead to indulge a narrow francophone intelligentsia.

In the Algerian cinema world, too, there were subversive voices, the most famous example being the remarkable corpus produced by the director Merzac Allouache. Born in 1944 Allouache, unlike many of his contemporaries, consciously eschewed making films about the war of liberation to focus on the hopes and aspirations of the post-independence generation. Beginning with *Omar Gatlato* in 1976, the first of a trilogy of films about life in the Bab el-Oued neighbourhood of Algiers which continued with *Bab el-Oued City* in 1993 and *Bab el-Web* in 2004, he has always dealt with the daily pre-occupations of ordinary Algerians, deploying irony and humour to deadly effect. A recurring target was those who had inflated or even invented their roles during the war of liberation to the detriment of the real fighters, but although his caustic wit won him many international accolades it also brought him into conflict with the authorities. Nervous about images which did not conform to an heroic ethos, the government closely scrutinized Allouache's output, reflecting a climate of repression which also explains why the government banned Okacha Touita's 1982 *Les Sacrifiés* on the grounds that, in portraying the violence and intensity of the civil war between the MNA and the FLN, it was undermining the image of a glorious nation at one in the war of liberation against colonialism.

Touita's film demonstrates how history was increasingly contested on all sides during the 1980s. The government was not immune to this new mood of questioning and on the official side there was a loosening up of the straitjacket. Krim Belkacem was rehabilitated in the run-up to the thirtieth anniversary of the November insurrection in 1984 and an international conference of historians brought together researchers from all over the world, including Alistair Horne and Benjamin Stora, and seemed to pave the way to a more detached analysis of Algerian history.[45] That said, there were limits to this openness. Mohammed Harbi's work, despite being recognized as seminal by other specialists, was still censored; in July 1985 a special issue of the weekly review *Algérie-Actualité* was seized and destroyed because in assessing the role of the Organisation Spéciale, the forerunner of the FLN, it dared to mention Aït Ahmed, Ben Bella and Boudiaf; whilst Ali Haroun's history of the FLN in France, *La Septième Wilaya*, was banned because the book's subtext, that the workings of the Fédération de France represented a blueprint in democracy quashed in 1962, was unpalatable.[46] The authorities hoped to shore up the old mythologies but this was no longer possible.[47] By the late 1980s the official memory was a fragile edifice waiting to be kicked over.

■ ■ ■

October 1988, therefore, was the climax of a legitimacy problem that had been gathering pace throughout the 1980s, known popularly as the 'Black Years'. The economic and social dislocation throughout the country explains the anger and intensity of the violence which engulfed the country. Young men in particular felt that they had been robbed of their self-esteem and during those five days in October they gave vent to this frustration.

The short-term causes were to be found in a conflict that set the old guard, an alliance of FLN leftists, communists and pan-Arabists who feared liberalization, against a coalition of reformers, led by President Chadli, determined to push through more reforms. As both camps vied for control of the state, the infighting became ever more bitter and polarized before finally spilling out into the open during the summer of 1988. The first evidence of this mounting tension was a package of proposals put together by a team of advisers to the president, under the direction of Mouloud Hamrouche, which met immediate resistance from hard-line conservatives. Upping the pressure still further was the fact that, with the FLN congress in the autumn, Chadli was obliged to canvass support for his nomination as presidential candidate for the December elections. With this obstacle looming large the anti-reform faction sharpened their knives, using communist trade unionists to launch a series of damaging strikes within key sectors of the economy at the beginning of September 1988.

Tapping into fears about rising prices and mass redundancies, this was a potentially fatal scenario for the reformers, and as the strikers dug in Chadli knew that he was fighting for his political life. On 19 September he publicly turned on his critics. In the most strident speech of his career, he declared his intention to take on his opponents and win. In response to the strikers' demands, he painted an unflattering portrait of the Algerian people, condemning them as lazy and work-shy. Then he attacked the hardliners within the political elite. Depicting them as motivated by narrow self-interest, incompetent and irresponsible in the extreme, Chadli warned that unless they adapted they would be swept aside by the pressure of events.[48]

From that point on the relationship between elite infighting and the subsequent events of October becomes difficult to decipher. Some Algerians feel that frustration at continued resistance led Chadli to adopt a high-risk strategy whereby he engineered a confrontation between the army and the ordinary populace in the hope that the anti-reform faction would be fatally discredited. Without any hard historical evidence such a hypothesis must remain in the realm of conjecture, but there is no doubt that in the first week of October wild rumours began to circulate within the poorer districts of Algiers, telling the populace that something violent was going to happen, whilst on 5 October itself there was a strange atmosphere on the Algiers streets, with a minimal police presence, almost as if it was designed to encourage an outbreak of popular violence. Similarly it is irrefutable that following Black October Chadli held the upper hand, not only ushering in a new constitution but winning the nomination for a third presidential term at the FLN party congress six weeks later, a position of dominance then reinforced on 22 December, when he was elected by 81 per cent on a turnout of 88 per cent. In terms of court politics Chadli was now stronger than ever. He had ridden the crisis and turned events to his advantage.

But beyond the court elite Black October represented an historic shift. Nothing could be the same again because the repression shattered one of the pillars of the post-1962 regime. By shooting on unarmed civilians, the army had broken a bond between itself and the people. As Khalida Messaoudi put it:

At school … I'd been taught in great detail that the army serves the people, not repression. So, when I saw the tanks, the armoured cars, and the uniformed soldiers on the street, I was immediately reminded of Bigeard and Massu … I realized that the army of my country was just like the one it had fought, the colonial army ... I couldn't accept that they would strip us so suddenly of our remaining source of pride in being Algerians. The war of liberation was the only thing that held us together as a nation, and during those days, these criminals killed us twice.[49]

Black October came to be seen as a cathartic act by the younger generation, altering their relationship to Algeria's history. At one point, for example, rioters were ransacking Omar Boudaoud's furniture shop at the top of the Rue Mourad Didouche in central Algiers. Angrily Boudaoud, a former leader of the FLN in France, intervened, brandishing his veteran's card and shouting at them to stop. Unmoved, the young men ignored him and carried on trashing the shop. For Salim Guendouz, a young basketball teacher whose mother was a veteran of the war of liberation, such disrespect explains why the rioting liberated the young from an inferiority complex.[50] Suddenly they were no longer intimidated by their parents' history because they had unquestionably done something of historic proportions themselves. They had their own heroes and their own dead, a fact that was chanted by the young crowds on the football terraces who quickly composed their own hymn to the martyrs of October 1988, 'Bab El-Oued El-Chouhada'.

Such goading reflected an incendiary anger that refused to go away. For the families of the dead and wounded psychological closure was difficult because nobody in power was brought to account or prosecuted. This fact was underlined on the first anniversary when a public meeting at Algiers university organized by the National Committee against Torture, a pressure group established by journalists, academics and trade unionists, published a comprehensive account of human rights abuses during October 1988 by the authorities. Drawing upon eyewitness accounts, the report included graphic details of torture as the army, not for the last time, drew upon the techniques used by the French army between 1954 and 1962. It was in every aspect a damning document, symbolic of the way in which Black October cast in stone the generational conflict of the preceding ten years. If large swathes of young men were drawn into the web of Islamist terrorism during the nineties it was partly because they saw such violence as revenge for the killings of their brothers and sisters in October 1988. Taking up arms was a sacred duty, a logical riposte to a political system that was a mockery of freedom and a mockery of justice.

CHAPTER FIVE

Political Islam

The most dangerous moment for a bad government is usually when it begins to reform itself.

ALEXIS DE TOCQUEVILLE, The Old Regime and the Revolution (1856)

A LEXIS DE TOCQUEVILLE'S famous dictum is as true today as it was in the nineteenth century. An insecure political system becomes highly vulnerable when it embarks on change and this was the case in Algeria in 1989, just as it had been in Absolutist France in 1789 and the Czarist Russia in 1917. Many in the Algerian political elite were painfully aware of this balancing act, looking around nervously at parallels elsewhere across the globe. They saw how in the USSR Mikhail Gorbachev's experiment in openness and economic restructuring was already running out of control by 1989, burying the system rather than resurrecting it. They observed, too, how in China communists chose a different route, saying yes to the free market but a bloody no to political reform when they massacred pro-reform students in Tiananmen Square in June 1989.

Given the train of events in China and the Soviet Union, as well as the fall of communist regimes in Eastern Europe, nobody was under any illusions about the scale of the task ahead. In October 1989 Ali Haroun, a lawyer and one of the former FLN leaders in France, admitted in an interview with one of the authors that he was very anxious. Although he was in favour of the introduction of multi-party democracy in principle, he was very aware that it was a process bedevilled by pitfalls on all sides. Without a better material future, he feared, the regime was running huge risks, opening up a Pandora's box where the young generation would be drawn towards extreme solutions. For this reason he was under no doubt about the short-term future, stating emphatically: 'The country is about to enter the most difficult period since independence.'[1]

Chadli's policy was based upon the belief that preservation implied transformation. By controlling the nature and direction of change, he hoped to produce a system by which the FLN would still predominate. His first and most significant target was the army which, under the new constitution overwhelmingly approved by voters in February 1989, was now limited, in theory, to a purely military role. Not only did the constitution curtail the influence of the army, which withdrew all serving officers from the governing Central Committee in March 1989, it also guaranteed freedom of expression, association and meeting, thereby ending years of censorship; and it formalized the separation of party and state and recognized the right of Algerians to form their own political organizations, thus opening the way to multi-party politics. Unlike its predecessors, it contained no reference to socialism.

Chadli's reforms were a bold experiment and in the months following February 1989 Algerians became accustomed to a new political vocabulary which stressed the values of debate, openness and democracy. Visiting Algeria in 1989 and 1990, we were struck by the way in which people, particularly students, academics and journalists of the post-independence generation, were genuinely excited by this new type of politics, even though they understood its adoption to be a long process. They saw Algeria as poised at the beginning of a steep learning curve whereby Algerians could break free of authoritarianism and embrace democracy.

The ascendancy of liberal values was reinforced by the revolutions in Eastern Europe in autumn 1989. Now, with communism out and the transition to democracy in, Algeria was seen as part of a global process that was seemingly unstoppable and was now spreading to the Arab world. The question was, however, where would this experiment lead? Did it have an obvious end point? Would it really secure Algeria's democratic future? The transition process was closely controlled by the government. Article 40 of the constitution, for example, which was subsequently enshrined in the law on political parties passed by the National Assembly in July 1989, gave the authorities wide powers to frame the conditions of political life; parties had to be officially registered with the Ministry of the Interior before they could operate legally. Equally, parties had to use classical Arabic for their official proceedings, a calculated snub to the Berber parties and an attempt to limit the use of French. Likewise, no organization would be permitted that acted contrary to 'Islamic behaviour or to the Revolution of 1 November 1954', a date still enshrined as the foundation stone of Algerian history; on this basis Messali Hadj's old party was banned. Furthermore no party could operate on an 'exclusively confessional, linguistic, regional … or professional basis', a qualification that although aimed at Berber parties also raised the question about what the government would do about religious parties.

Finally parties had to rely on state aid for funding, in effect limiting their independence.

The introduction of a multi-party system went hand in hand with the liberalization of the media, and during 1989 there was a mushrooming of newspapers and journals without precedent in the Arab world.[2] In all, 150 new news publications appeared, including *El Watan*, *Le Matin* and *Le Nouvel Hebdo*, many of them in French, ensuring that French remained a primary medium for political debate.

For journalists like Omar Belhouchet, the editor of the daily *El Watan*, who revelled in the new atmosphere of investigative freedom, one issue mattered above all others: the recovery of their country's history. From now on there could be no more taboos, no more mysteries, no more fabrications. History had to be objective, a litmus test of the transition to democracy, as journalists, much like their counterparts under Gorbachev scratching away at the Stalinist past, asked searching questions about how Algeria had got here, transforming the past into a remembered horizon of alternative narratives, hidden possibilities and counter-factual scenarios. The years 1989 and 1990 witnessed a spate of provocative articles on the subject. One headline pondered whether Messali Hadj, the founding figure of modern Algerian nationalism, should be posthumously rehabilitated; others examined the roles of Ben Bella and Aït Ahmed, both historic leaders who had been largely airbrushed out of official accounts.

Yet despite this new openness many Algerians wondered how committed the government really was to its proclaimed policies. Might the new approach be little more than an elaborate façade, a game of smoke and mirrors, to protect the powerful economic mafia that had emerged during the 1980s? Such speculation was fuelled when on 9 September 1989 Mouloud Hamrouche replaced Kasdi Merbah as prime minister.[3] Hamrouche, a well-known champion of economic liberalization, immediately unveiled an ambitious programme in an effort to impress the International Monetary Fund and the World Bank. Measures that would have been unthinkable under Boumediène were introduced overnight as the country witnessed an abrupt transition to a free-market economy, with the liberalization of exchange rates, credit, customs, foreign trade and foreign investment as well as the establishment of a Central Bank that was independent of the government.[4]

However, throughout this reform process General Khaled Nezzar remained omnipresent, an indication of the power struggles within the regime and the way in which Chadli's experiment was being closely surveyed by the army leadership. A tireless watchman, Nezzar's finely tuned political antennae ensured his appointment as head of the army general staff on 16 November 1988, followed by his elevation to Minister of Defence on 25 July 1990. In this last post he oversaw the comprehensive reorganization of the Sécurité Militaire into the Département de Renseignement et de Sécurité (DRS), giving key posts to members of his close military clique. Mohammed Médiène became head of the new organization, which was subdivided into three branches: counter-espionage headed by General Smaïn Lamari, external security headed by General Saïdi Fodhil and army security led by General Kamel Abderrahmane. Nezzar justified these changes in terms of greater military efficiency but few were in doubt about their true meaning. The constitution might have separated civilian and military power but these reforms represented a tightening of the grip of the power behind the throne. In allowing the democratic transition to take place, Nezzar reasoned, the guiding principle was flexibility. Survival required cunning; an adroit manipulation of the façade which recognized that for everything to remain the same everything must have the appearance of change.[5]

There were thus clear limits to the democratic experiment and the establishment of the DRS was a coded warning to Hamrouche and his entourage: whatever reforms were introduced, nothing must be done to harm the networks of corruption based upon imports and exports. This was a fundamental rule of Algerian politics that people ignore at their peril.

■ ■ ■

The political liberalization of 1989 led to a proliferation of political parties in Algeria – sixty by the end of 1991. Most of these had a tiny membership and no popular base. Some were simply bogus official concoctions. Recruitment and the development of a party structure were immensely difficult in the face of a large number of practical and financial obstacles. Access to the state-controlled television was denied to genuine expressions of opposition to the military, and obtaining expensive office space in Algiers was hard without state support. So most of the new party leaders stopped short of criticizing Chadli.

Some of the parties were totally new organizations, whilst others had operated clandestinely or in exile. Each now suggested an alternative blueprint for change. Comparing the various political programmes, it quickly became clear how much Islam now dominated Algerian political discourse. All the major parties, including Ahmed Ben Bella's Mouvement pour la Démocratie en Algérie (MDA), the reorganized FLN and the Berber-led Front des Forces

Socialistes (FFS), openly acknowledged the central significance of Islam within Algerian society. However, the clearest expression of the dominance of Islam in political life was the dramatic rise of the Front Islamique du Salut (FIS) led by Abassi Madani and his number two, Ali Belhadj. As the FIS's two leaders, they were a compelling double act, the gnomic-looking Madani appealing to the pious businessmen whilst the finger-wagging Belhadj remained the spokesman of dispossessed youth. As the FIS gathered momentum and swept all before it, the other parties found themselves reacting to the Front's aggressive and increasingly popular campaign for an Islamic state based on sharia law.

Chadli's decision to grant official recognition to the FIS after its foundation on 10 March 1989 was controversial. Quite apart from the party's evidently subversive ideology, the FIS did not meet the requirement, under electoral law, that a party should not refer to race, religion, language or region in its political platform or name. Chadli's strategy of incorporating Islamism, one that he had begun in the 1980s and that was very different from the repressive path being followed by Morocco and Tunisia where Islamists were regularly imprisoned, caused considerable alarm in army circles and in the West. In particular France, Spain and Italy felt threatened, fearing a mass influx of immigrants and loss of economic and political influence if an Iranian-style revolution erupted in the Mediterranean. In fact, Chadli and his circle of advisers intended to use the FIS to break the political hegemony of the FLN and allow the president himself to act as arbiter in the new pluralistic arena. At the same time they sought to dilute the strength of the FIS by recognizing rival Islamist parties, notably the an-Nahda party under Sheikh Djaballah and Hamas under Sheikh Mahfoud Nahnah, both of which were hostile to the FIS. It was a classic divide-and-rule tactic, but one that engendered suspicion within the Nezzar camp, which became convinced that Chadli was seeking out a pact with the FIS in order to hang on to the presidency.

Ironically, given that multi-party politics had allowed the FIS to emerge, the Islamist party's distrust of pluralism struck a deep chord with many ordinary Algerians. They warmed to Madani and Belhadj's denunciation of parliamentary democracy as a French concept designed to sow hatred and division amongst Muslims. Furthermore, by choosing to call itself a Front, the FIS evoked the unity of the liberation struggle, looting key tenets of the FLN's old ideology, while investing them with an uncompromising opposition. By conjuring up the heady spirit of the war of independence, according to which all Algerians were brothers together fighting for Islam, this sense of solidarity fed into the bitter resentment towards Chadli's economic liberalism that had done so little to help the poor.

The foundation of the FIS was proclaimed by preachers from different parts of the country outside the El-Sunna mosque in Algiers on 18 February 1989. Some Islamist radicals, such as Ahmed Sahnoun and Mohammed Said, were unsure whether the time was yet ripe for a unified front, but after discussions that lasted for eighteen hours the various groupings found common ground. The resulting platform was a landmark in the new era of multi-party democracy. Drawing on language and ideas that had been fashioned by Soltani in the 1960s and 1970s, this programme represented the long march of the Islamist movement from the margins to the centre of Algerian politics. As Madani argued to delegates:

> ... the birth of the FIS is an event that has its roots in the history of the country. How? The FLN was after 1954 ... the Front of a historic phase that began with the war against colonialism to end with freedom and independence ... What remains to be realized since then is the construction of a free and independent state on the basis of Islamic principles as well as those of November. The Front (FLN) has been deviated from its historic project by a political project linked to the *pouvoir* [those in power] itself.[6]

Looking back in anger, Madani claimed that the Islamic essence of November 1954 had been betrayed by the subsequent Charters of Tripoli and Algiers as well as those Charters subscribed to by Boumediène and Chadli Bendjedid. He continued:

> These documents have no credibility in relation to the ideals of November which constitute the most brilliant pages in the history of this nation ... It is this denial of history and principles that has led us to fall into the trap of the personality cult ... the Islamic Salvation Front [FIS] wants to save the acquisitions of November that have been lost.[7]

People, Madani argued, must understand that their society was cursed because there was too little belief. They had allowed themselves to become mired in filth and pollution. The FIS's special mission was to rescue a country that had forgotten the enduring principles of a meaningful religious existence. Divinely inspired, the movement had to cleanse Algeria of depravity, reasserting the basic message of Islamic doctrine. Weighing in to support Madani during the inaugural meeting, Sheikh Benazouz, an imam from Algiers and vice-president of the FIS, warned:

We have seen moral calamities that have no link to religion, nor to the Algerian people's traditions. The consumption of wine has become legal, and mixed classes in schools, *lycées* and universities has had as a consequence a proliferation of bastards.

Depravity has spread, we see women no longer hiding themselves but flaunting their naked and made-up bodies before everyone … Where is the Algerian people's dignity after their honour has been publicly besmirched, after the land whose soil has been sprinkled with the blood of martyrs takes part in competitions for wine production and wins the golden medal? … The battle of our Front is the struggle against delinquency and evils as well as the search for an Islamic society that won't barter its fundamental principles nor its material or spiritual interests.[8]

A preparatory committee, under the aegis of Sheikh Sahnoun, was set up to create a constitution and the FIS was officially launched during Friday prayers on 10 March 1989 at the Ben Badis mosque in the Kouba neighbourhood of Algiers. There, Othman Amokrane read out a seven-point programme that aimed to 'substitute Islam for imported ideologies'.[9] The FIS would opt for 'the middle way' and 'moderation', Amokrane claimed on behalf of the leadership, which included Saharaoui Abdelbaki, Benazouz Abda and El-Hachemi Sahnouni as well as Belhadj.

Within the regime there was much agonizing about the consequences of legalizing the FIS. Conscious of this threat, on 22 August 1989 Abassi Madani warned of popular revolution if the FIS was not recognized.[10] From the beginning the FIS brandished the spectre of violence, as the party set out to articulate the anger of the urban dispossessed, a fact that was underlined by its Arabic-language paper *El-Mounquid* ('The Saviour') on 5 October 1989, the first anniversary of Black October. November 1954 and October 1988, both examples of popular revolt against unjust rulers, were constantly invoked as the language of the FIS leadership became more and more strident. Algerians, Madani warned, must be ready to repulse the onslaught of 'Western crusaders' and their 'Zionist allies', cunning foes who were ready to use all kinds of manipulative chicanery to spread doubt in the Muslim world.

The FIS leadership constantly claimed that the senior echelons of the military were not only ready to use fraud in elections (as had the French administration before independence), but were effectively in the pay of France, on the grounds that most had served in French forces until relatively shortly before independence. Such conspiracy theories struck a chord with many Algerians, who supported the FIS argument that in effect two Algerias now confronted one another: the people and their religion on one side, and colonialism and its lackeys on the other.

The FIS claimed to encapsulate the right of the Arabic-speaking majority to rebel against their pro-French minority rulers, the 'new settlers', with the result that by March 1990 Madani was dropping any pretence to moderation, declaring in an interview: 'This is a front, because it confronts …'[11] Confident of final victory, he asserted, chillingly, that once the FIS were in power there would be no more elections.

At the FIS's apex was the sovereign Consultative Council (Majlis al-Shura) made up initially of thirteen members and the National Executive Bureau.[12] The composition of both bodies was highly secretive as the party operated in a rigid top-down manner in which the base was expected to implement the decisions of the leadership. At the grassroots the FIS was a fusion of the street mosques with other charitable and religious associations that had come to the fore in October 1988 under the title League of the Call (*Rabitat Dawa*). By uniting most of the Islamist groups into one movement, the FIS already had an impressive organizational network in place, a fact that was displayed dramatically at the end of 1989 when the party's activists mobilized four hundred thousand demonstrators on to the streets of Algiers. By any measure this was a highly intimidating expression of pro-Islamic, anti-government fervour that showed doubters that the FIS was not a pale imitation of Iran or Sudan but an Algerian phenomenon with Algerian roots.

This tidal wave of religious fervour, the visual index of which was the increase in the numbers of veiled women on the street, underlined the extent to which the FIS was not really a political party in the traditional sense. In truth it was an umbrella movement that brought together a variety of ideological and religious currents ranging from Bouyali supporters and Afghan veterans through to former FLN members and street mosque activists. Inevitably, although united by their opposition to the regime, these groups were riddled with conflict, contradictions and clashes. The most obvious point of tension was between the Salafists and the faction known as the Algerianists (*djez'aristes*). The Salafists saw democracy as anti-Islamic and aimed to overthrow the regime, through violence if need be. They had a global vision of the oppressed *umma* and sought to link Algeria to the wider struggle against corrupt Muslim regimes. In contrast the Algerianists were more pragmatic and nationalist, willing to work within parliamentary democracy if it respected Islamic identity.

Who was attracted to the FIS? The urban middle classes, particularly small traders who had been attracted to Islamism since the early 1970s, had always disliked the socialist language of the FLN and wanted a more business-friendly economy.[13] Arabophone students, specifically science graduates, warmed to the FIS's ceaseless denunciation of francophone Algerians. However, the bedrock of the FIS support was unemployed youth, who saw the party as the natural expression of their anti-establishment feeling. After a decade of edgy submissiveness, FIS rhetoric appealed to disaffected youth, eager for fresh rhetoric and a renewed image of themselves. Above all the FIS had an answer to the unanswered questions that plagued their existence. Why were there shortages when the country was so rich in oil and gas? Why were there so many oranges in the countryside but so often none in the shops? Why did people live in shanty towns? By embracing the FIS's religious credo the young unemployed were no longer trapped by the same gangrenous resentments, the same modes of inactivity. Theirs was a higher form of political identity. Based upon the will of God, their activism pitted the new order against the old, the future against the past, virtue against vice.

Armed with this aggressive message, pumped out via a well-organized FIS press, Islamist militants began to assert themselves at all levels of society.[14] The party gained further supporters among the urban poor in the wake of the earthquake in the Tipaza region in November 1989, which killed thirty people and injured four hundred others. As the state haphazardly organized the relief effort, FIS militants arrived with their own teams of rescue workers, nurses and ambulances bearing the party insignia. By delivering clothing, food and blankets collected by the party's network of mosques from around the country, the party's organizational capabilities provided a telling counterpoint to the failings of the regime, announcing to Algerians that the FIS was a government in waiting. Their activists had already taken control from below, building a new society based upon the ethic of religious solidarity.

Two weeks after the earthquake, the fiery Belhadj preached vehemently against the authorities' incompetence at the El-Sunna mosque:

Our so-called leaders speak of socialism and equality ... of being 'by the people' and 'for the people', but they are rich and you are poor. We believe in God and his Apostle, but not their fairy tales and nonsense. Our governors have governed so long with lies and deception, they no longer know where the sun rises, their children's names or the colour of the sky. They are so lost in the vomit of their deception they think they have fooled us ... The *Jihad* of 1954 must continue. Those who died for Islam thirty years ago were betrayed.[15]

Spurred on by this fierce rhetoric, some FIS activists between 1989 and 1991 angrily desecrated monuments to the fallen of the war of liberation. By aping the West's military rituals, the FIS argued, the army generals were inviting Algerians to worship craven images that obscured God's message. Not surprisingly this incendiary behaviour genuinely appalled the inner circles of the army's higher command led by Nezzar, who in turn believed that the sacred tenets of the war of liberation were under attack from barbarism.

Islamist activists also poured scorn on Kateb Yacine, making strident protests against a major international conference about the writer held in Algiers in October 1990.[16] The conference held up Kateb, who had died in France the previous year, as the country's greatest-ever writer – the Algerian James Joyce in his subtle and provocative use of the French language to express an anti-colonial perspective – but for the Islamists he had been a long-time hate figure. For them he was the example par excellence of the communist infiltration that had been indulged by the regime and had inspired other leftist writers like Taha Djaout. The fact that the conference was organized by four female academics only intensified the hostility and the whole event was conducted in an uneasy atmosphere.

Opposition to the conference underlined what the FIS saw as its central mission: to combat the spread of French culture. Again and again France was accused of orchestrating a merciless crusade against Islam. Madani was outraged by the take-off of French satellite television in the major cities during 1989, as whole apartment blocks clubbed together to receive the major French television channels.[17] The fact that Western game shows and soft pornography could be beamed into millions of Algerian homes was the devil incarnate in Madani's eyes and FIS militants denounced the satellite dishes as *paraboliques diaboliques*. As one indignant FIS supporter in his mid-sixties put it: 'Disney cartoons … If this is allowed to continue it will lead to the end of Islam.'[18]

When interviewed in 1990, Belhadj explained, in characteristically violent and colourful language, how the FIS planned to deal with French culture and francophone Algerians:

> with arms and faith, [we will] ban [French oppression] intellectually and ideologically and finish with its partisans who have suckled its poisonous milk.[19]

In particular the FIS singled out women's groups who were calling for the abolition of the Family Code. For the FIS they were nothing short of pro-French fifth columnists and on 22 March 1990 Madani took on the women's movement luminary Khalida Messaoudi in a televised debate watched by millions.[20] In preparation for the encounter Messaoudi defied five of the bans imposed on women by the Islamists. She went to the hairdresser, curled her red hair, applied lipstick and make-up, wore trousers and wore her hair loose on her shoulders. During the debate she defied two further bans, glaring directly at Madani rather than lowering her eyes, and questioning him in French and Algerian Arabic. Madani refused to reply, commenting acerbically in classical Arabic that she 'did not represent Algerian women'.

Madani's comments reflected the FIS's targeting of women who refused to adhere to Muslim codes of dress, accusing them of demonstrating a neo-colonial subservience to France's popular culture. Women who wore make-up or trousers were jeered at and threatened physically as groups of FIS militants, young men for the most part, patrolled streets and beaches, searching out women who were dressed in ways they considered immodest. The FIS also mounted a violent campaign against two planned concerts in Algiers by the renowned Portuguese singer, Linda de Souza, in December 1989.[21] Posters, deemed too sexually provocative by the FIS, were defaced en masse, whilst the FIS press denounced the singer as a 'Jew' and a 'Zionist'. The strength of feeling stirred up by the FIS left the authorities running scared and, in an effort to appease Islamist feelings, they cancelled the concerts.

This was a spectacular victory for the FIS. In the eyes of many ordinary Algerians such a retreat was a shape of the things to come, showing that even the authorities were convinced that the FIS's forward march to power was unstoppable.

■ ■ ■

The rise of the FIS was mirrored by the sudden collapse of the FLN, which failed to transform itself into a genuine political party in the Western sense. Discredited by failure and corruption, its leadership feared the reformed system would end their extensive privileges since the FLN was, of course, still intimately connected to the state. In analysing the FLN's transformation Hugh Roberts has cautioned against drawing straightforward parallels with the contemporaneous changes in the Soviet Union.[22] According to Roberts it is simplistic to regard the FLN's old guard as analogous to Marxist hardliners in the Soviet Union opposed to perestroika. Unlike Marxism-Leninism in Eastern Europe, the nationalist ideology that spawned the FLN had not been discredited. In the wake of the October 1988 riots, therefore, the arguments within the political elite revolved around one overriding issue: how to reinvigorate the system and give it a new lease of life. Many hoped to usher in a new era for the FLN, reshaping it into the natural party of government within the new multi-party system. Unlike the Communist Party in the Soviet Union, the FLN had never been the true centre of power, which meant that after the army's ostensible retreat from government the party had the potential to disentangle itself from the state and operate as an independent political force. The party congress held in November 1989 saw vigorous debates as delegates outlined strategies on how the FLN could continue to dominate in the new environment.

Yet, despite these signs of revitalization and redirection, it soon became clear that the FLN would find it difficult to survive within the new political landscape. The crux of the problem was generational. The acronym FLN might still have an allure for wartime veterans but to the young it was mired in the failures of post-independence. Instinctively they were drawn to the FIS who, in taking up the mantle of November 1954, accused the FLN of betraying its original ideology at every turn. Given the dearth of younger recruits on the ground, the FLN was no match for the FIS, a fact that was humiliatingly revealed by an FLN march in Algiers in May 1990. In the absence of FLN supporters eager to demonstrate their allegiance, the demonstration was entirely organized by the Ministry of the Interior.

Alongside the FLN were the Front des Forces Socialistes (FFS) and the Rassemblement pour la Culture et la Démocratie (RCD), both effectively Berberist parties, although they rejected this label and saw themselves as parties appealing to all Algerians. Together they positioned themselves as democrats who were not afraid of looking towards Western political models. They rejected Arabism and were much more secular in outlook, even if they recognized the centrality of Islam within Algerian life. Cultural pluralism, seen as inseparable from political pluralism, was a key aspect of their platforms. But both parties failed to break out sufficiently from Berber strongholds, gaining only limited support elsewhere in the country.

Significantly, these Berber-led parties were bedevilled by personal antagonisms. Their two leaders – Hocine Aït Ahmed and Saïd Sadi respectively – detested each other, making cooperation virtually impossible. Although there were no deep ideological differences between them, the FFS and RCD became political rivals, with some observers claiming that Saïd Sadi obtained tacit government support in order to weaken the potentially stronger challenge of the FFS.

Aït Ahmed returned to Algeria on 15 December 1989. As one of the historic FLN leaders, untainted by the mistakes made following independence, he had enormous personal legitimacy and from the beginning he based his politics on trenchant opposition to the regime. For this reason he refused to accept government subsidies to fund his party, accusing the regime of systematically trying to discredit the FFS whilst arguing that the multi-party system was an illusion created to maintain the status quo. He was particularly vehement in his denunciation of the role of the secret services in Algerian politics. Refusing all talk of alliances, he boycotted the June 1990 local elections on the grounds that they would be rigged. In terms of doctrine the FFS modelled its programme on a Western social democratic party, stressing the need for human rights, democracy, sexual equality, the market economy and the separation of religion from state. It also called for the Berber language Tamazight to be accorded the same status as Arabic in all spheres, including education.

Kabylia quickly became a bastion of FFS support, with Kabyles pouring into Algiers for two huge demonstrations in 1990. As many as three-quarters of the electorate in Kabylia followed Aït Ahmed's call to boycott the 1990 local polls. The FFS drew most of its support from ordinary Kabyles in their homeland and Kabyles in Algiers who wanted to defend their cultural and linguistic heritage. The personal legitimacy they gave Aït Ahmed and his *marabout* family was clear at the party's first congress in March 1990, which also underlined its social democratic position. The problem, however, was that beyond Kabylia the Berber question, even if it was linked to democracy and human rights, failed to make an impact on the population.

The FFS faced competition from the RCD, which was officially registered as a political party on 16 August 1989. Many of the key RCD members were veterans of the Mouvement Culturel Berbère and the Berber spring. The party's inaugural conference took place at the Berber capital city of Tizi-Ouzou on 9–10 February 1989 and within six months it claimed some 32,000 members. Many were drawn from the younger professional, Westernized middle classes – lawyers, doctors, teachers – and a high percentage were women who were not afraid to describe themselves as feminist. In fact at its first congress, held in December 1989, a tenth of the 950 delegates were women, a high percentage by the standards of the Arab and North African worlds, as the party presented itself as a champion of sexual equality. There the leader Saïd Sadi unveiled his programme for a mixed economy, respect for the rule of law, democracy, the official recognition of Tamazight as a national language, and cultural pluralism. Presenting itself as a national party that was open to all, the RCD called on Algerians to recognize that their future lay with closer ties with Europe. With this aim in mind the RCD called for French to be restored to the education system, arguing that French was not foreign but an essential asset that opened the country to Europe. To underline this belief the party eschewed Arabic in official proceedings and whenever he appeared on television Sadi spoke in French, therefore reinforcing his image as a champion of secularism.

Although the RCD publicly attacked the regime, it did offer support for Mouloud Hamrouche's reforms of the government, a willingness to compromise with the *pouvoir* that differentiated the RCD from the FFS. This led some observers to speculate that the RCD was at least partly sponsored by the regime in order to neutralize the FFS, just as rival 'moderate' Islamists were encouraged to draw votes away from the FIS. Not surprisingly both parties were despised by the FIS as agents of France who were trying to splinter the unity of the nation through Berberism. The RCD in particular was singled out as being elitist, francophone and feminist, and FIS activists denounced its initials as standing for 'Rassemblement Contre Dieu' ('Rally against God').

Perhaps the most obvious casualty of the new multi-party system was the Parti de l'Avant-Garde Socialiste (PAGS). Until this point the PAGS had enjoyed a weight in politics out of all proportion to its actual support in society, being arguably the second most influential party during the 1960s and 1970s. Inevitably, though, it was hit hard by the Soviet invasion of Afghanistan followed by the collapse of communism in Eastern Europe. Furthermore, given the surge in Islamic feeling, the party's atheism was a major handicap to obtaining mass support. However, at its first congress held in December 1990 the old guard of pro-Soviets, Benzine and Hadjeres, were ousted by the 'young Turks' led by El Hachemi Cherif, who was determined to adapt to the new political context. But despite embracing democracy and setting out to form an anti-Islamic alliance, the PAGS made little headway. When compared to the FIS its support was minuscule largely because, beyond nostalgia for the leftward turn under Boumediène in the 1970s, the party was bereft of a larger vision for society.

If the marginalization of communism was one measure of the transformed political landscape, another was the reception accorded to Ahmed Ben Bella on his return. He remained a name to conjure with even though the younger generation knew little about him, and he nourished hopes of becoming a saviour figure, an Algerian de Gaulle. Openly critical of the system that had 'confiscated' his revolution in 1965, he had gone in exile upon being freed by Chadli, first to France and then to Switzerland. He had briefly supported the Khomeini revolution in Iran before forming the Mouvement pour la Démocratie en Algerie (MDA) in May 1984. Officially legalized in 1989, the MDA unceremoniously ditched Marxism and Third-Worldism in favour of championing Islam.

Ben Bella returned dramatically with his supporters by boat to Algeria on 27 September 1990, following which he undertook a large-scale tour of the country. Obviously he hoped to whip up a bandwagon effect and make a big impact upon the political firmament but apart from in his native Oran, where he did receive a rousing welcome, his reception was lukewarm. People were respectful but he was not mobbed and there was no mass adulation. In general he was seen as yesterday's man, an exile who no longer understood the pulse of the country. Yes, he could point to his role as one of the historic leaders of the original war of liberation but for huge numbers of Algerians Ben Bella was no longer a genuine man of the people but just a distant memory who no longer lived and breathed their struggles. For this reason he could not hope to compete in popularity with the likes of Belhadj.

■ ■ ■

The status of the FIS as the main opposition party was confirmed emphatically by the local elections held on 12 June 1990, the first free elections since independence. In an exciting and ebullient contest over 13,600 candidates from a dozen parties campaigned for office in the communes and *wilaya*s. At mass meetings the FIS used lasers to project religious slogans, including the name of Allah, into the night sky, thereby reinforcing the idea that the party enjoyed heavenly support.[23]

With the FFS and MDA boycotting those polls, turnout was only 65 per cent and the FIS garnered an extraordinary 54 per cent of the votes cast. In contrast the FLN managed only 28 per cent, the independents 12 per cent, the RCD a mere 2.1 per cent and the PAGS a derisory 0.3 under the proportional representation system. This gave the FIS control of 856 out of the 1,541 Assemblées Populaires Communales (APCs), whilst for the Assemblées Populaires de Wilaya (APWs) the FIS won an absolute majority in 31 out of 48 and took control of 45 in all.

The FIS made a good showing across the whole country with the exception of Kabylia, the Berber power base where Islamism was shunned. In Algiers, Oran and Constantine the FIS chalked up a stunning 70 per cent of the vote. It attracted not only the miserable slum-dwellers of Bab el-Oued and the shanty towns on the outskirts of Algiers but also won the biggest number of the smaller, rural communes with ten to twenty thousand inhabitants. Many voters were undoubtedly attracted by the FIS's fusion of politics and religion, and by the movement's perceived purity; unlike the FLN it did not feel tired or compromised. Many, however, saw their vote as the best way to register their disgust with the status quo. By voting FIS they were signalling their dismay with a system which had failed to prevent the social and economic dislocation of the 1980s.

Speaking three days after the victory, at the Ben Badis mosque in Kouba, Belhadj was triumphant. He was in no doubt about the message of the elections. They were a sign from God:

> The elections were won by the grace of God and the people. Your vote has given a slap in the face to those who betrayed the FLN. The road ahead will be hard. Those who have made so many mistakes themselves will not pardon ours. The elections were not a victory for democracy, but for Islam.[24]

The sheer magnitude of the victory stunned the *pouvoir*, which had consistently underestimated the FIS's electoral potential. Once the implications sank in of the apparent inevitability of another FIS landslide in a legislative election, the inner circle of the army leadership became gripped by one question: how to prevent an FIS regime taking power through the ballot box.

After the municipal elections, Algerian society began to polarize. Berber culture was pitted against Arab culture, secular society against the Islamist movement, Arabist sentiment against the francophone tradition. Civilian rebelliousness and frustration came into conflict with military authoritarianism. The growing atmosphere of confrontation was discernible to everyone as voices of compromise became drowned out by those calling for all-out conflict. As Salim Guendouz, a basketball teacher, explained, 'It is impossible to have a dialogue with Madani.'[25] In particular the francophone middle classes – regular hate figures for FIS supporters – began to fear for the future and in 1989 two thousand lawyers and doctors left for France. In October 1990 a group of university academics were quite clear in their reasoning.[26] For them the FIS were just like the Nazis in 1933, cynically exploiting parliamentary democracy to come to power; once there they would use the state's levers to impose their will on the rest of society. Consequently the pro-Western middle classes had no option but to consider fleeing the country.

Subsequently commentators such as Gilles Kepel would identify the alienation of the secular, francophone middle class as the FIS's cardinal error. This mistake prevented Madani and Belhadj from successfully emulating the Iranian revolution, seen by Kepel as the yardstick of radical Islamist triumph. In its heady early days the FIS relied too much on its natural support base of *hittistes*, the pious petite bourgeoisie and Islamist intellectuals.

In Iran the secularized bourgeoisie had backed Khomeini because he professed openness and the inclusion of every element of society in his revolutionary project. In Algeria, by contrast, as soon as the FIS was in control of local power ... [it] took issue not only with the regime but with a whole sector of society for its 'francization'. This imprecise notion, with which the FIS exposed a substantial sector of the urban middle classes to the wrath of the *hittistes*, was – not unreasonably – construed as a threat.[27]

Among those trying to make sense of the turmoil was Nesroulah Yous, owner of a small business, who had lived since 1984 in Baraki, a surburb just south of Algiers close to the village of Bentalha. A member of the Front des Forces Socialistes since 1990, Yous and his fellow activists could make little headway because their whole neighbourhood had already been won over to the ideas of the FIS. Consequently he was not surprised by the FIS successes in the June polls, which for him came to represent a turning point:

The local and regional elections took place in euphoria, with exuberant but unclear expectations of change. The FIS garnered more than 50 per cent of the communes, a score that nobody expected and which gave wings to the sympathizers of this party. But the military, for their part, felt the danger approaching, and I think from that moment on they worked together to avoid FIS victory in future polls. Already many professional people I knew were getting ready to leave the country.[28]

Yous rightly surmised that the FIS municipal elections had alarmed the army; a conclusion that was also reached by Habib Souaïdia, a special-forces officer whose eyewitness account, published in France, would provide a rare close-up look at the mood inside the Algerian armed forces during the 1990s.[29]

Souaïdia recounted how, as a native of the farming region of Tébessa, he nourished ambitions of a military career from an early age, the only alternative in the poor region to a life of crime in the smugglers' underworld. Souaïdia became a cadet at the elite Koléa military academy, set up in 1962 principally for the children of the martyrs who died during the independence war. He went on to attend, in 1989, the prestigious Cherchell joint services academy. Students at Cherchell, which prided itself on training elite soldiers from around Africa, held political opinions from across the spectrum. Pro-Islamists, pro-Berberists or even those who wanted to continue with the one-party system, faced off in virulent debates. But the majority, Souaïdia remembers, including himself, took no interest in politics. For them the army was there to protect the people and the nation, not to re-establish order or intervene in internal problems.

After the FIS municipal victory, however, he perceived a change of attitude in the army command:

> Citizens were happy to have jettisoned the single-party system, but uncertainty set in. One thing was sure, the Islamists decided to pursue their logic to the end. For many citizens, especially women, this meant restrictions of individual and collective freedoms: women were not to work, study or think about their emancipation. Men also had to change their habits – no more cigarettes or alcohol. The rise of the FIS seemed unstoppable.[30]

He feels that this was the point when the army began to prepare for confrontation. In the barracks officers talked about the threats made by Ali Belhadj against the army. There were rumours too about weapons being stockpiled by the FIS on the fringes of the mosques. Souaïdia recalls that unit commanders were discreetly instructed to 'laissez faire', in the hope that the FIS would push the country to the brink by overestimating its own strength and underestimating that of the army.

Within the FIS-controlled municipalities decision making was handed over to a local Islamic council which replaced the APCs and met in secret. Daubing Islamic slogans on town halls, the FIS leaders demanded the application of the *sharia* at a local level, although in reality there was much variation from commune to commune. Some continued to tolerate discotheques and the selling of alcohol while others were much more hard line. The FIS council in Sidi-Bel-Abbès, for example, quickly became notorious. Keen to quash the town's reputation as the country's equivalent to 1960s Liverpool, derived from the bustling music scene led by Lotfi Attar's internationally famous group Rainer Raï, the FIS council refused to hire out halls to raï bands. It also closed a school teaching traditional music; condemned the *gaisba* – a traditional Algerian flute – as an instrument of the devil; and forbade a well-known troupe of women singers from performing publicly.

As regards its promise to supply better housing and jobs the FIS was soon pointing the finger at the government, which turned off the flow of funds to FIS-controlled councils in an effort to undermine Islamist popularity. Angered by the government's strategy and keen to deflect criticism, Madani delivered an ultimatum to the regime. Speaking on 1 November 1990, he told supporters to prepare for imminent victory:

By dialogue, we will change the regime. If it hangs back, then it will be jihad ...
Algerians, your position is crucial ... This year will see the establishment of a
Divine Republic.[31]

It was by any token inflammatory language. In inciting Algerians to prepare
for a jihad he was explicitly raising the political tension that in turn was
exacerbated by the parlous state of the economy. At the same time Hamrouche
sought to bring down the sky-high budget deficit through economic reforms,
especially privatization. Inevitably this shock therapy increased the already
explosive level of unemployment as labour was shed from unproductive or
inefficient state-run industries. Trade unionists, old-style socialists and Third-
Worldists were outraged. For them the dire consequences suffered by the less
well-off members of society meant that Hamrouche's reforms were not solving
the country's economic problems but ratcheting up the crisis to breaking
point.

The FIS was not necessarily at odds with Chadli and Hamrouche over these
reforms. FIS business supporters were sympathetic to liberalization and many
observers saw every possibility of some sort of accommodation with the FIS,
especially after a law of December 1990 that aimed at the complete Arabization
of the official administration by 5 July 1992 and of higher education by 1997.
However, the first Gulf War changed the entire political situation.

Algeria was one of the first Arab states to condemn Iraq's invasion of
Kuwait on 2 August 1990 and this initial position was largely supported by
Algerian public opinion. However, the situation was rapidly transformed by
the huge Western military presence deployed on Arab and Muslim soil. Soon
Algerian opinion swung in favour of Saddam Hussein, who was seen as a hero
for ostensibly standing up to America and Israel; a popularity that was
strengthened by the fact that there was little sympathy for Kuwait, considered
a Western protectorate established to safeguard the flow of petroleum.

Chadli adopted a cautious path, carefully ensuring that his call for an Arab
solution did not antagonize the West. At this stage, Ben Bella was the person
most in tune with opinion. Ever the populist, he called for Algerian volunteers
to fight in Iraq. He also attacked France's 'crusading mentality', reflecting the
way in which French support for the American-led coalition was unpopular in
Algeria.[32] The FIS itself was initially caught off guard by the depth of support
for Saddam. FIS leaders were well known for their hatred of Baath secularism
and Arab socialism. The FIS had also received crucial financial support from
Saudi Arabia, which supported Kuwait and opposed Saddam. At first,
therefore, Madani and Belhadj condemned both the invasion and Saddam –

Belhadj referred to Saddam as 'Haddam' ('destroyer') and 'Khaddam' ('lackey') – while attacking the Kuwaitis for accumulating riches 'against God's will' and criticizing Saudi management of Mecca and Medina.

The country, however, was gripped by a pro-Saddam fever. Car stickers portrayed Saddam as Superman, riding a missile with sabre brandished above a winning smile, whilst in market kiosks postcards depicting Saddam's head superimposed on to Arnold Schwarzenegger's torso sold in their thousands. Mothers called their newborn sons after the Iraqi leader and on 14 March 1991, shortly after the end of hostilities, Algerian television staged a twenty-four-hour fund-raising event to help Iraqis rebuild Baghdad, purportedly raising the equivalent of $2 million. Such feelings obliged the FIS leadership to trim their sails, and they sacrificed the party's links with Saudi Arabia and some traditional aspects of its Islamist doctrine in order to maintain its popular base. An anti-war demonstration on 18 January mobilized several hundred thousand people, uniting all shades of the Algerian political spectrum from Islamist to Third-Worldist, socialist and pan-Arabist, in their opposition to Western imperialism. But it was the FIS, now adopting the most radical posture, calling for volunteers to fight in Iraq and support the Iraqi people, that captured the militant mood. Taunting the army as militarily impotent and cowardly kowtowing to imperialism, Belhadj called for training camps to be set up for volunteers, before leading a group of volunteers to Jordan. The FIS then organized a further show of force on 31 January, bringing sixty thousand on to the streets and fusing international and national issues by calling at the same time for the National Assembly elections to go ahead.

The stridency of the FIS's support for Iraq shows how far the Gulf crisis radicalized Algerian politics.[33] Indeed, as Hugh Roberts rightly argues, it was the crucial dimension in the ever deepening domestic crisis because the destabilizing effect of the run up to the Gulf War forced the government to postpone national elections twice – at the end of 1990 and in the first quarter of 1991. In the meantime Algerians had to put up with a makeshift government which had no popular legitimacy. This meant that the Hamrouche government had no mandate to push through the transition to the free market. The result was an all-pervasive sense of drift as the social crisis continued unabated, making any rapprochement between the FIS and the regime increasingly unlikely. Moreover, the enormous anti-Western sentiment whipped up by the first Gulf War made the situation impossible for the Hamrouche government. Not only did it improve the FIS's electoral chances, it also made the prime minister's economic reforms seem more than ever an imposition from the West.

In the short term the Iraqi defeat reflected badly on the FIS, something that promoted a dangerous excess of self-confidence in Chadli and Hamrouche. Suddenly they began to believe in the corresponding recovery of the FLN's electoral prospects and on 1 April Hamrouche set national elections for 27 June and 18 July. Even more significantly he announced the introduction of a new electoral system under which constituencies would return a single member only. Under this formula only the two parties with the most votes in the first round would go through to the second ballot. Hamrouche wanted to squeeze voters into a stark choice between the FLN and the FIS in the belief that this would bring the FLN victory because enough Algerians would vote against the prospect of an Islamist regime. The electoral boundaries also were changed to damage FIS election prospects, giving more weight to those rural districts where the FLN vote had held up in June 1990. The regime also tried to reassert control over the mosques, decreeing in early April that they could not be used for political purposes. On top of this the FIS was attacked virulently in the official media as puritanical and extremist.

Yet, in believing that the Gulf War had fatally wounded the FIS, Chadli and Hamrouche badly misjudged the situation. Their intention to manipulate the system to deny the FIS victory was plain to everybody, precipitating a summer of confrontation that was to have fatal long-term consequences.

THE LONG HOT SUMMER OF 1991

The FIS was quick to react to Hamrouche. On 2 April Madani conjured up the spectre of a general strike. Three days later, in a typically histrionic sermon at Koléa in Tipaza, Belhadj went further, telling his audience that the FIS had a 'warrior vocation':

> I respect neither laws or parties that do not have the Qur'an or the Sunna. I crush them under my feet. These parties must leave the country, they must be repressed.[34]

Upping the rhetorical stakes, Belhadj derided the *pouvoir* as not so much a regime, more a network of corruption and licensed violence, a mental disease, an array of laughable, improbable lies. Chillingly, Belhadj decreed that it was forbidden to resign from the FIS, an act that would amount to apostasy, for which the punishment would be death. Belhadj also evoked the violence that would rack the country if the regime tried to rob the FIS of its divine mission:

> We do not underestimate the value of arms ... the impious *pouvoir* and the miscreants do not deserve to be killed with bullets, for during the war of liberation one cut the throats of the traitors, one did not shoot them.[35]

From then on Belhadj made much play of his father's background as one of the 'martyrs' who died fighting the French, dramatically holding up his father's portrait during a press conference that received wide television coverage. As the true inheritors of the independence struggle, Belhadj argued, the FIS had to be ready to renew November 1954 through force if necessary. To this end tracts calling for civil disobedience and violence had been circulating in FIS ranks since January, and FIS training camps for martial arts and hand-to-hand combat were open secrets amongst the population.

In the face of continued government pressure, and after some debate, the FIS leadership called a general strike to begin on 25 May. At first it failed to attract wide support but the anger amongst unemployed youth, the typical foot soldiers of the FIS, was very clear. The scene was set for confrontation, as the FIS organized another demonstration, bringing a hundred thousand people on to the streets of Algiers on 27 May. Calling for immediate transition to an Islamic republic, the crowd held up banners proclaiming 'Chadli out', 'Islamic State', 'No Charter No Constitution' and 'Down with Democracy'. At the end, in a continuation of the protest, thousands camped out on the streets, erecting barricades and setting up loudspeakers that poured forth FIS rhetoric.

Initially the army did not intervene, though units were in position lest the situation deteriorate into a repeat of the 1988 riots. Before long, however, the FIS strike was seen as a direct challenge to government authority that could not be tolerated. On the night of 3–4 June riot police started to clear the streets, firing tear gas to disperse bearded Islamist militants brandishing the Qur'an and Algerian flags proclaiming 'God is Great'. As in October 1988, wild rumours spread of agents provocateurs firing on the police and FIS in order to stoke up the atmosphere.

With the police losing control General Nezzar had the pretext for intervention he had been looking for. Under his orders the army units descended on Algiers and in fierce street fighting a number of people were killed. The official casualty toll was thirteen dead and sixty injured, while thousands more were arrested and interned in camps in the Sahara. The following day Chadli declared a state of siege for four months, introducing a curfew in Algiers, Blida, Tipaza and Boumerdès. The national elections were postponed until further notice and the Hamrouche government was dismissed since the prime minister had opposed the use of force. On 7 June the new government – led by prime minister Sid Ahmed Ghozali, director of the public-sector oil and gas concern SONATRACH during the Boumediène period, promised new elections before the end of the year, and Madani and Belhadj called off the strike.

By now the FLN was in complete disarray. It was the end of the political line for Hamrouche, who had hoped to renew the FLN on a platform of free-market liberalism and a country firmly oriented toward the West. Furthermore, Chadli now resigned as president of the FLN in a bid to distance himself from a political organization that seemed fundamentally moribund. He also announced that he would not seek a fourth term as President of the Republic.

For the army hardliners the lessons were obvious. The FLN was too damaged to be a credible bulwark against a FIS victory and was incapable of yielding a credible presidential candidate to challenge Madani. So the military leadership took it upon themselves to reassert what they saw as the fundamental values of the national war of liberation. On 25 June the army ordered the removal of Islamic slogans from FIS-controlled town halls, to be replaced by banners carrying the motto of the national liberation struggle: 'By the people and for the people'. The banner removal led to more street battles in the Bab el-Oued district of Algiers and other FIS strongholds. Then on 30 June the authorities arrested Benhadj and Madani, accusing both of them of preparing a full-frontal military assault on the state.

With the leadership decapitated the nerve fibres of the FIS began to fragment. Younger men, no longer willing to be reined in by the moderate elements within the FIS, took to the mountains. Their minds charged by the events of June, they were now won over by the Salafist wing of the movement. Soon the first armed groups were established in the mountains of Zbarbar near Bouira to the south-east of Algiers, already known locally as 'Zbarbaristan'. Led by Abdelkader Chebouti and Mansour Meliani, both of whom had fought with Bouyali and the MIA, Kamerdine Kherbane, an Afghan veteran, and Saïd Makhloufi, a former air-force captain, they met in secret in July to discuss the implementation of a 'jihad' that all were impatient to bring into being, even if they maintained links with varying factions in the remaining FIS leadership. There the rules of their actions were fixed in general terms. These *maquis* groups were loose and autonomous but all were committed to the ideal of an Islamic state. Motivated by a doctrine of violent jihad, they believed in a simple law of religious credit, whereby those in power must pay whilst those who take up arms will find their reward in heaven.

June 1991 took the country beyond the brink. The general strike ended any hope of a peaceful transition from one-party state to democracy or of any alliance between the FLN and the FIS. Moreover, the crisis had bolstered the strength of General Nezzar's inner circle who, itching as they were to take on the FIS, had successfully splintered the Islamist movement. No less importantly, Nezzar's supporters exploited the strike as a smokescreen to get rid of Hamrouche since his liberal economic agenda was threatening the well-oiled machine of corruption. To underline this point, one of the hardliners, General Larbi Belkheir, was promoted to the rank of major general on 5 July.

National Elections

If there was one word that described Algeria in autumn 1991, it was 'febrile'. The country was awash with rumours: rumours about coups, rumours about deals between Chadli and the Islamists, rumours about impending Islamist insurrection. Chadli himself had little breathing space as he desperately tried to fashion a moderate Islamist movement that would be willing to play the political game.

The embattled president knew that he could not ignore public opinion and had to listen to the parties and people without apparently being high-handed or authoritarian. However, a conference of government members and leaders of political parties, held in July and August 1991, was an abject failure because it was boycotted by the Islamists and the FLN. Any Islamist leader who participated knew that he would lose all credibility, while Hamrouche, now the dominant voice on the FLN central committee, wanted to discredit his successor. In response, Ghozali sought to undermine the FFS and the FLN by supporting independents and the smaller parties. He also cast himself as the last bastion against the FIS, which he conjured up, playing to the Western gallery, as obscurantist, mediaeval and barbaric.

Within the FIS, with Madani and Belhadj imprisoned, an emergency conference was convened at Batna on 25–26 July in an effort to restore a sense of direction and cohesion. Under intense pressure, the remaining leaders became embroiled in bitter discussions about the way ahead. The crucial issue was whether the FIS was trying to achieve power by legal or revolutionary means and at this point internal divisions came out into the open. It became clear that a number of figures on the Majlis al-Shura had opposed Madani's general strike as much too confrontational. During the discussions there was much dissent – five prominent figures were suspended whilst Saïd Guechi left the conference before the close – but the end result was that the Algerianist *djez'ariste* reformist wing led by Abdelkader Hachani, a petroleum engineer born in 1957 and previously unknown to the public, took control. Hachani made clear his willingness to engage with the electoral process, mapping out the legal road to power whereupon the FIS, once in possession of the levers of power, could Islamicize from within. Hachani was under no illusions about the difficult circumstances in which the FIS had to operate, and he put in place clandestine structures in case the party was dissolved. He was also painfully aware of the *maquis* groups in the mountains around Algiers preparing to bypass the electoral process. Indeed, fearful about loss of control over the Salafists, Hachani created his own armed group, the Front Islamique pour le Djihad en Algérie (FIDA).

Belhadj, even in captivity, was still highly influential. On 3 September a tract written by him was smuggled out of prison and some twenty thousand copies circulated on the street.[36] For him the failure of the strike was a test of faith by God, part of an ongoing trial where the decisive factor would be unbroken religious conviction. So, he warned that anyone weak did not belong in the party's ranks; anyone spreading an atmosphere of panic played into the enemies' hands. His language couched in violent absolutes, Belhadj divided society into a virtuous majority versus a tyrannical minority.

Belhadj's courage strengthened the resolve of ordinary militants as, much to the astonishment of their opponents, the FIS proved to be remarkably resilient. Quickly recovering from the hammerblows of June, it organized a huge demonstration on 1 November at the Martyrs Square in central Algiers, the timing underlining the fact that the party continued to see itself as the true embodiment of the war of liberation. A Qur'an on a chair was held aloft to show that only Allah's word should occupy the presidency as demonstrators called for the freeing of FIS prisoners as well as the liberation of Jerusalem and the end of sanctions against Iraq. In a political masterstroke, Belhadj's five-year-old son took the microphone calling for the release of his father. Once the crowd knew who he was there was a wave of emotion, with murmurs of 'God is Great' growing ever louder to create a crescendo of religious fervour.

During this period the armed groups in the mountains, at least those still in close contact with the FIS leadership, chose to wait on events, unwilling to harm FIS electoral chances by precipitous action. The relationship between the FIS and the *maquis* was extremely porous as militants moved freely between the mountains and the plains. Consequently Hachani was still able to put a temporary brake on armed action although the most hardened group, calling themselves Takfir wa-l-Hijra ('Excommunication and Exile'; the name is commonly used by Islamists throughout the Muslim world), had already run out of patience. They did not believe in the electoral game and began the jihad against the regime on 29 November with an attack on a military post at Guemmar near the Tunisian frontier.

In this tense atmosphere the interior ministry announced on 15 October that the two rounds of elections would be held on 26 December 1991 and 16 January 1992. At the same time Ghozali introduced a revised set of electoral laws and re-drew the constituency boundaries. Ostensibly these changes were justified by the need to give the electoral process credibility in the eyes of the international community. Few, however, doubted that this was a desperate attempt to favour independent candidates who Ghozali hoped would support his government as a last bastion against the Islamist movement. Even more significantly Chadli approved legislation allowing civilian authorities to appeal to the military to maintain order if necessary, thus reminding Algerians, if they needed reminding, that the army was overseeing the electoral process. ·

After deliberation, the FIS leadership announced on 28 November that the party would participate in the elections. From that point on the FIS had the edge in the campaigning process. Voters were told that to vote against the FIS was to vote against God, and FIS activists sought to scare away their opponents through intimidating behaviour. Fatima Kartout, a doctor in her thirties who was standing for the FFS, was subjected to physical and verbal abuse. She told a British reporter:

> There are threats against my children and myself ... When I drive around, people gesture to me as if they are going to cut my throat. But I will not let them intimidate me.[37]

In comparison, the other political parties, apart from the FFS in Kabylia, had very little presence on the ground. The FLN in particular led a lacklustre campaign, leaving a void that made an FIS victory a near certainty.

In the run-up to the first round the FIS had all the momentum, a point that was painfully clear to Algerian immigrants returning to vote from all around the world. Talk on an Air Algérie flight from Paris to Algiers, for example, centred on how life was changing at home. One young woman, a university student in Paris who was going to vote against the Islamists, told a Western reporter that her mother, an education officer, was one of only two women among thirteen in her office not to wear a veil. Three years earlier all had worn Western clothes.[38]

The complex and contested symbolism of covering female hair was self-evident on polling day as Western reporters in the teeming suburb of Bab el-Oued, an FIS stronghold, watched women wearing the latest French fashions queue at voting stations alongside others in *chador* and the full head-to-toe *hijab*. Once the ballot papers had been counted there were accusations of fraud and intimidation on all sides: anti-FIS parties claimed that Islamist activists had got fully veiled women to vote several times, while FIS-supporting husbands were accused of forcing their wives to vote for the FIS. In response the FIS dismissed these allegations as lies and trickery, a hysterical response from pro-French lackeys doing everything to de-legitimize the FIS vote.

During the night the announcement of the results was repeatedly delayed. Eventually, at around 2.30 a.m., after the European newspapers had closed, the interior minister shuffled in and sheepishly admitted that the FIS appeared to have won by a landslide. Under the single-member constituency – which the regime had hoped would favour the FLN – the FIS gained 188 of the 231 seats won outright during the first round. Against this the FLN took a paltry 15 seats, whilst the FFS did only marginally better, securing 25 seats, mainly in Kabylia. Elsewhere the independents and the moderate Islamists, two groupings Chadli and Ghozali had placed great hopes in, obtained derisory results. With 199 seats still to be decided in the second round, few doubted that the FIS was now poised to win a two-thirds majority of the 430-seat National Assembly.

It was a stunning victory, even if commentators such as the left-wing journalist Mina Kaci have sought subsequently to qualify the results.[39] Given that only 59 per cent of the electorate voted, the FIS landslide was based upon 24.5 per cent of those eligible to vote. By this measure the largest vote was abstention, although, as Kaci readily admits, it is difficult to know what this abstention meant in political terms. Was it a question of apathy, indifference, or a conscious rejection of the political choices on offer?

The days that followed the first round had a feverish quality as Algerians absorbed the implications of imminent FIS victory. Everywhere people debated, in intense and emotional terms, the arguments for and against continuing with the democratic process. Both the PAGS and the RCD, despite their lack of electoral legitimacy, called for the cancellation of the second round and both too were instrumental in the establishment on 30 December of the National Committee for the Safeguard of Algeria (CSNA) under the leadership of Abdelhak Benhamouda, the leader of the Algerian Workers' Union (Union Générale des Travailleurs Algériens, UGTA).[40] Bringing together a range of bodies, including business organizations, feminist groups and anti-Islamist intellectuals, the CSNA immediately called for military intervention to prevent an FIS government, although this was not universally supported by the UGTA rank and file.

In contrast the FLN secretary-general Abdelhamid Mehri declared that his party was ready to work with the FIS in a government of national reconciliation. The FFS, meanwhile, organized a rally in Algiers that brought three hundred thousand on to the streets on 3 January 1992, chanting 'neither police state, nor Islamic state, but a democratic state'. Through such action Aït Ahmed wanted to demonstrate that Algerian politics was not just a stark choice of Islamist or military. Addressing the crowd, he was adamant that the electoral process must be followed to the end and called for vigilance against any possible military coup.

Six days later thousands of women took to the streets of Algiers to demonstrate against the FIS and the prospect of a hard-line Islamic state. During the elections the FIS had campaigned against Hassiba Boulmerka, the popular 1,500 metres champion, 'for running with naked legs in front of thousands of men'. But, despite a stream of threats, the twenty-three-year-old athlete, the first Algerian woman to capture a world title (at the world athletics championships in Tokyo the previous summer), denied reports that she intended to flee to Italy: 'Like 25 million other Algerians, I have no other country. I will continue to stay in Algeria no matter who the rulers are.'[41]

Boulmerka's case underlined just how much of the conflict was mediated through what women do or do not wear, especially after Mohamed Said, a prominent FIS imam, told Algerians the day after the first round that everybody must be ready to change their daily customs regarding clothes and food. As Chafia Aitmenguellt, a twenty-two-year-old medical student, put it: 'It's already an attack on our freedom, even before they're in parliament. We're afraid now. It's worse for us than others because we're girls.'[42] At the demonstration women, their fists clenched in the air, listened to Khalida Messaoudi warning them that they must fight to prevent an Islamic state.

On the opposite side, Hachani's electoral strategy seemed to have paid off handsomely. Chadli was ready to arrive at some sort of pact, whilst discreet contacts were initiated with Western governments and multinational companies, the latter of which were assured that their investments were not in danger. Of course there was the suspicion that the military establishment might still act but Hachani was reassured by Ghozali's televised address on 5 January. Calling on Algerians to vote massively in the second round, particularly those who had abstained, Ghozali's statement seemed to indicate that the authorities were ready to abide by the democratic experiment. If so the FIS were poised to take control with Hachani as the next prime minister.

Coup d'État

On 11 January Chadli Bendjedid announced on television that he was stepping down from office with immediate effect. Hesitant and ill at ease, the president read out a prepared statement declaring that he had taken his decision because the democratic process he had set in motion could no longer guarantee law and order. Initially most people were perplexed by this turn of events. This incomprehension was intensified when it was announced that the National Assembly had already been dissolved by the president one week earlier. However, matters became clearer once Ghozali declared that, in the light of these new circumstances, he had asked the military to deploy units on the streets as a preventative measure. At this point some newspapers called Chadli's demise a 'sofa coup d'état', referring wryly to the divan on which Chadli sat, evidently livid, during his final televised adieu.

With the president jettisoned the Supreme Court stepped in, claiming that, since this was a situation without precedent, power had to be handed over temporarily to the High Security Council (Haut Conseil de Sécurité, HCS), a hastily convened body made up of Ghozali, along with Benhabiles, president of the supreme court, Benkhelil, the justice minister, Brahimi, the foreign affairs minister, and three senior military officers: Nezzar, the defence minister, Belkheir, the interior minister, and Guenaizia, the chief of staff. To nobody's surprise the HCS immediately declared that in light of Chadli's resignation it was impossible to continue with the elections.

On 14 January presidential power was transferred to a newly created institution, the State High Committee (Haut Comité d'Etat, HCE), which was to act as a provisional government until new presidential and parliamentary elections to be held at a later, unspecified, date. The head of the HCE was Mohammed Boudiaf, one of the historic leaders of the November 1954 uprising, who had been offered the presidency after much discussion within the army high command. At a secluded seaside villa just outside Algiers many names had been bandied around, even Ben Bella at one point, before eventually the gathering alighted on the seventy-two-year-old Boudiaf. Sounded out by Ali Haroun, on 16 January he returned from exile in Morocco where he had been running a brick business, determined, he claimed, to save the country from crisis. The other four HCE members were Ali Haroun, minister for human rights, Ali Kafi, president of the war veterans' association, Sheikh Tedjini Haddam, rector of the Paris mosque, and, inevitably, Nezzar.

In this flurry of activity most of the legal subtleties were lost on Algerians. Clearly it was a putsch, however much Nezzar and his ilk might try to dress it up as otherwise, and this made large numbers of people very angry. FIS supporters in particular felt cheated of victory. Aït Ahmed was one of the first political leaders to grasp the import of these murky manoeuvres by the authorities. When asked by reporters whether this was a takeover situation he immediately replied, 'Yes, even though it has been done without apparent violence.' By forcing Chadli to resign, he argued, the army had manufactured a constitutional crisis in order to stop the second round. Indeed, as the seasoned *Libération* journalist José Garçon noted, the coup allowed the army to achieve three objectives simultaneously:

> It is both true and false to say that the legislative elections were cancelled 'to prevent the FIS from taking power'. The operation also aimed to sack President Chadli and at the same time torpedo Hocine Aït Ahmed, the long-standing opposition leader, who the regime wanted to prevent becoming a rallying point for the opposition after a poll in which his party was the only one apart from the FIS to emerge as a winner.[43]

The FIS, the FLN and the FFS all denounced the events as illegal. The FIS in particular was fearful about the immediate consequences. Bracing itself for a clampdown by the security forces, the leadership moved from its Algiers headquarters, issuing a statement calling on the people to stand up to the military:

> We call on veteran fighters, religious leaders, army officers and soldiers, sons of the martyrs and all who love Algeria to take a stand against this giant of power ... no individual can remain neutral when there is a war between the people and their religion on the one hand and the agents of colonization on the other.[44]

On the bustling streets of Kouba, one of the main fiefdoms of the FIS in Algiers, a Western reporter met Muslim militants patiently awaiting instructions on how to foil the coup, insisting their orders would come directly from the movement's jailed hard-line leaders. Standing in his battered shop, a hole in the wall that specialized in selling both children's toys and Islamist tracts, a bearded man called Hosein was adamant:

> If circumstances dictate it we will go underground to continue the struggle clandestinely ... This is a coup d'état in disguise ... People say that the FIS is a totalitarian organization but it is the party in power that is totalitarian. All we want is an Islamic state.[45]

His assistant, Lyes, was just as uncompromising:

> I don't see democracy at work … What happens now depends on our leaders in prison in Blida, Ali Belhadj and Sheikh Madani. If they ask us to take to the streets and demonstrate against the army we will do so.[46]

As the call to afternoon prayers rang out over the unmade streets of Kouba, the atmosphere was tense but calm, testifying to the militants' strict discipline. Displayed between Disney games in Hosein's shop were books and tracts with titles such as 'Whose turn is it after Iraq?', 'Islam faced with a new world order' and 'The West's pretensions to dominate the planetary destiny', whilst on the road out of town slogans had been freshly daubed on walls proclaiming 'FIS is the only solution' and '*Vive* FIS, we will die for the FIS'.

The main loser out of all of this was Hachani. The legal road to power had failed and on 22 January he was arrested for inciting desertion. With the older leadership imprisoned much younger militants now surged forth to take their place and on Friday 8 February violent clashes with the army broke out around mosques in the major towns and cities across the country. Tanks were deployed on the streets and the following day the HCE declared a state of emergency across the nation as a prelude to suspending basic freedoms. From this moment on the FIS was subjected to blanket repression. More than eight thousand FIS members or suspected members were incarcerated in detention camps in the Sahara desert where there was little shelter and temperatures rose to 56°C. Then, on 4 March, an Algiers administrative court officially dissolved the FIS, by which time casualties in clashes between Islamists and security sources stood at an estimated 103 dead and several hundred wounded.

Abroad, many African and Arab leaders breathed sighs of relief. They had been fearful of the domino effect of an Islamist victory in Algeria, which might have been a beacon for Islamist movements throughout North Africa and the Middle East. The Tunisian daily *Al-Sabah* characterized the military intervention as 'a last-minute change of direction by a train heading toward the abyss',[47] and both Ben Ali, the Tunisian president, and Colonel Qaddafi, the Libyan leader, expressed their support for the new regime, while President Mubarak in Egypt warned the international community not to intervene.

In France the official language was very cautious, nervous about the way in which any French statement would affect the Algerian situation. Although President Mitterrand described the events as 'abnormal' and called upon Algerians to take up the 'threads of democratic life' at the earliest possible

moment he hung back from a blanket condemnation of the coup.[48] The
American response was similarly guarded. American military experts had
visited Morocco to assess the kingdom's defence needs in the light of the FIS
victory, even delivering twelve F-16 fighter jet aircraft to Rabat earlier than
planned, but in public officials chose to talk in subdued tones. This, the
official line ran, was an internal Algerian affair, although as *Time* magazine
commented such a muted response raised questions about the ethics of foreign
policy. By making no pronouncement was the West tacitly supporting an anti-
democratic act for its own selfish interests?

> For a Western world grown accustomed to drawing facile distinctions between
> villains and heroes as it witnesses one political convulsion after another, Algeria's
> crisis posed a jarring dilemma: which takes precedence – democratic principles or
> geopolitical self-interest?[49]

Amidst all this strife one question was predominant: who was Boudiaf and
what would he do to resolve the crisis? Two Western reporters watched from
the edge of the runway as hundreds, many of them pounding drums or
playing flutes and brandishing his photograph on high, welcomed Boudiaf at
Algiers International Airport on 16 January. Among the welcoming crowd,
Lamara Abdelwhed, a veteran of the war of independence from Boudiaf's
native town of M'sila, had high hopes of his hero as he was greeted by Ghozali
and Nezzar. He told a British newsman: 'Boudiaf will save Algeria from the
anarchy of the fundamentalist party and from corruption. He is a unifier. He
will be Algeria's de Gaulle.'[50]

Yet in making such a claim Lamara Abdelwhed was forgetting one crucial
dimension. Veterans might know Boudiaf as one of the 'historic chiefs' of
November 1954 who, by rejecting the army's seizure of power in 1962, was a
completely clean pair of hands, unsoiled by the mistakes of independence.
Similarly they might like to compare him with de Gaulle in May 1958. But
when de Gaulle had returned to power every French person knew who he was
and what he represented. For the new post-independence generation, given
the deliberate historical ignorance cultivated by the regime, Boudiaf meant
nothing. Ignorant of the nuances of 1962, all they saw was a cynical ploy to
drape the coup in the legitimacy of 1954.[51]

Boudiaf knew that in trying to win over the population he faced a huge
challenge and during his first press conference he outlined his priorities as
being corruption, justice, and the economy. Although he was clear that the
HCE had saved Algeria – after all, he was adamant that November 1954 had

not been about the creation of a theocratic state – he wanted first and fore-most to restore faith in good governance by tackling profiteers within the regime itself. In fact, appearing on television on 9 February hours after the state of emergency was imposed, he made clear that 'nepotism' was the root cause of the crisis. It was courageous language that won him support amongst ordinary Algerians.

Conscious of the HCE's lack of legitimacy Boudiaf established a sixty-member council in April, the Conseil Consultatif National (CNN), and a new political party, the Rassemblement Patriotique National (RPN) in May. By taking these initiatives he wanted to heal divisions and unite Algerians, a theme which he addressed in a major speech to the nation one hundred days after his appointment. Speaking with brutal frankness, Boudiaf warned against the exploitation of Islam for political aims, although he recognized that the FIS had found a ready audience amongst the very poor. For Boudiaf the crux of Algeria's predicament was the question of a common identity:

What are the pains that this country is suffering from … In reality Algeria is suf-fering from three crises – a moral crisis, a spiritual crisis and an identity crisis. For thirty years our people have been torn between socialism and capitalism … between East and West, between the French and Arabic languages, between Arab and Berber, between tradition and modernity.[52]

These divisions had torn the country apart. The challenge, therefore, was to find common ground amongst Algerians, who must stop looking elsewhere and look to themselves:

The Algerian must stop imitating. We must break out from all complexes and be ourselves … That is the principal meaning of 1 November: first be Algerian.[53]

To avert an economic catastrophe Boudiaf asked France for financial aid and on 4 March the French government was instrumental in rescheduling Algeria's $25 billion debt, in effect keeping the HCE afloat. However, such a respite was only temporary. The money received was siphoned off by the well-established networks and within two months the regime had no option but to cut subsidies on basic goods. In response, Boudiaf, outraged at the way recovery was being sabotaged from the inside, announced a high-profile drive to root out corruption within the regime.

The first person arrested in this anti-corruption drive was General Mustapha Belloucif, charged by Boudiaf's investigators of embezzling 60 million French francs which went into Swiss bank accounts and property in France. The fact that Belloucif was a senior army officer won over large numbers of ordinary Algerians. Here at last, they concluded, was a strong man willing to face down the shadowy mafia bleeding the country dry. Inevitably, such language also earned Boudiaf enemies from within. Powerful figures were increasingly nervous at Boudiaf's stance. Where, they asked, was his anti-corruption campaign going to stop?

The final straw was Boudiaf's decision to liberalize the oil and gas sector. As major Western companies queued up to sign contracts with SONATRACH, many in the higher echelons of the military became worried at the implications for the well-greased machine of corruption. It was all right to throw some individuals to the wolves, powerful men began to mutter, but the system of venality as a whole must not be threatened. Boudiaf was going too far. What they wanted was a figurehead for the battle against Islamism, not someone turning the spotlight on nepotism.

1 Delacroix's 1834 *Women of Algiers*, painted four years after the French invasion. The portrayal of Algerian women as sexually submissive was a recurrent theme in French painting and photography.

2 The 'wretched of the earth': a concluding scene from Pontecorvo's 1966 film *The Battle of Algiers*, which depicted the anger and violence of the war of liberation.

3 Third World leaders: Ahmed Ben Bella and Houari Boumediène at independence in July 1962. Boumediène overthrew Ben Bella in June 1965.

4 Women celebrating independence and the new socialist regime in 1962. The prominence given to women in these public parades caused controversy in Islamist circles.

5 Chadli Bendjedid receiving a rifle from French president François Mitterrand in 1981. Chadli Bendjedid became president after Boumediène's death in 1978 and adopted a more pro-Western policy.

6 Anger of the post-colonial dispossessed: the widespread violence in October 1988 is the pivotal event in post-independence Algeria.

7 Government repression in January 1992, after the cancellation of elections which the FIS was poised to win.

8 Abassi Madani, the leader of the Islamist Front Islamique du Salut (FIS). Between 1989 and 1992 the FIS channelled much of the anger against the system.

9 Ali Belhadj, the FIS number two and firebrand spokesman for Algeria's disaffected youth.

10 A crowd at Algiers airport on 16 January 1992 welcomes the return of Mohammed Boudiaf to head the government. Boudiaf was one of the historic leaders of the war of liberation.

11 A rare shot of the generals at the funeral of Boudiaf, who was assassinated in suspicious circumstances on 29 June 1992.

12 The funeral service for the monks of Tibhirine on 2 June 1996 at the Basilique de Notre Dame d'Afrique overlooking Algiers. Their murders caused major tensions in Franco-Algerian relations.

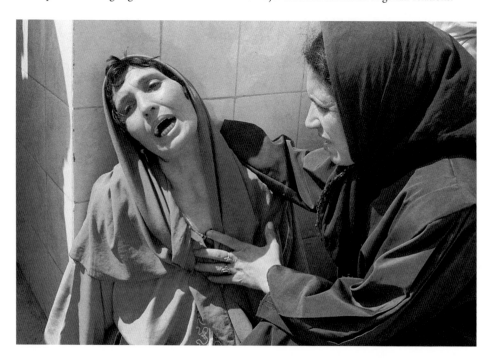

13 Oum Saad breaking down upon hearing that her eight children had been massacred at Bentalha in September 1997. This photograph by Hocine, encapsulating the Algerian trauma, was World Press Photo of the Year 1997.

14 Elections poster for Abdelaziz Bouteflika, who was elected president despite widespread fraud in April 1999. He was re-elected in April 2004.

15 A mother of one of the disappeared protesting. Bouteflika's transition process has ignored the pleas of the families of the disappeared for truth and justice.

16 Mass protests in Kabylia in spring 2001. The violence was symptomatic of a general disaffection with the political system.

17 Bouteflika with Tony Blair during an official visit to Britain on 11 July 2006. Bouteflika has been seen as a vital ally by Britain and the United States in the 'war on terror'.

CHAPTER SIX

Algeria's Agony

We live in terror, told that we must choose between being a victim or an executioner. But that choice is no choice at all. We can and must be neither.

ALBERT CAMUS, quoted in *Camus at Combat: Writing 1944–1947* (2006)

A T 9.30 A.M. on 29 June 1992 President Boudiaf strode into the hall in the eastern port city of Annaba to address a meeting of young Algerians. Gaunt, tall, outwardly serene, he had barely begun his speech when there was an explosion from behind a curtain, followed by a series of shots. In the confusion minor functionaries on the stage dived for cover while Boudiaf, struck by bullets in the head, slumped over the green-baize table on the podium. Rushed by ambulance to the local hospital, he died shortly afterwards.

By any standards it was a shocking event; a presidential assassination caught live on television that was beamed across the world, making the lead story on the BBC Nine O'Clock News that evening. The authorities immediately arrested one of Boudiaf's security agents, Second Lieutenant Lembarek Boumaarafi, who was hauled up in front of the cameras to confess to the murder. According to the official line, Boumaarafi was acting on his own, inspired by his Islamist sympathies.

Yet such an account posed many awkward questions. Why, given the train of events in Algeria, was the protection afforded Boudiaf on that day so lax and uncoordinated? At least three security agents left their posts beside Boudiaf just before the attack happened, and differing branches of the security services were operating on the scene apparently oblivious of each other's presence.[1] Commander Hadjeres and Captain Sadek, charged with Boudiaf's close protection, subsequently claimed to be ignorant of the presence of a unit of the specialist Groupe d'Intervention Spéciale (GIS) standing just behind Boudiaf. But it was as a member of this GIS detachment, included at the very last minute, that Boumaarafi was given such close proximity to Boudiaf.

Moreover, when the shooting began, Hadjeres and his two adjutants Captains Zaidi and Sadek were conveniently outside the hall, while none of the GIS agents reacted to the gunshots. In fact one of them, Driham Ali, went so far as to shoot and wound Hamadi Nacer, the only police officer who pursued Boumaarafi.

Where too were the other ministers? In the normal course of events the prime minister, interior minister or minister for sports and youth might have been expected to accompany Boudiaf to such a high-profile meeting designed to re-establish bridges with the nation's youth. But all were conspicuous by their absence, giving rise to the suspicion that they stayed away because they had an inkling of Boudiaf's fate.

Finally, why was there no autopsy on Boudiaf's body? Why too did the pistol supposedly used by Boumaarafi disappear? For Boudiaf's son Nacer these were deliberate oversights because the results of any investigation would not tally with the official account of the lone gunman. Speaking in June 2001, Nacer claimed that the pattern of bullet wounds suggested a second gunman. In the face of official silence he declared his willingness to go to the International Tribunal at the Hague to expose his father's killers.[2]

During the days following Boudiaf's death the assassination became the Algerian equivalent of the killing of President Kennedy, mired in theory and counter-theory. Boumaarafi's swift conviction for murder had all the hallmarks of a show trial, and no attempt was made to look for evidence of a wider conspiracy.[3] Instead everything was done to substantiate the thesis of the lone assassin, and General Belkheir insisted publicly that the interior ministry could not be accused of involvement in Boudiaf's killing. However, six years later the president's widow, Fatiha Boudiaf, asked for the suspension of the death sentence against Boumaarafi, then languishing in prison in Algiers. Speaking at length to the Spanish newspaper *El Pais* in June 1998, Madame Boudiaf described her first reaction to the murder: 'I thought immediately – some of them made him return from exile and the others have killed him.'[4] She was absolutely certain that Islamists were not responsible; instead, responsibility lay with hardliners in the regime who had quickly realized that he was not going to be a puppet. She recalled:

My memories of the attack start on the night before, when, unexpectedly, my husband changed his mind. He asked me not to accompany him to Annaba and to go and stay with my family in Oran. That night he spent more time getting washed than usual and when I went into the bathroom he covered himself up. I thought, amused, that he had become more modest after becoming head of state.

Today I think, instead, that as a good Muslim he wanted to be pure when he went into the other world. It was as if he had a premonition or someone had tipped him off that there was the risk of an attack, but he was determined to make the journey.[5]

A subsequent inquiry led by Ahmed Bouchaib, a friend of Boudiaf and one of the FLN founders during the liberation war, tried to ask more searching questions. But this immediately raised the hackles of the military inner circle who clearly wanted to bring the case to a speedy close. Acting beyond its brief, the inquiry concluded that Boumaarafi did not act alone, although it stopped short of naming the instigators. Suspiciously, Youcef Fethallah, a member of the Algerian League of Human Rights and the prime mover in preventing the inquiry from being a whitewash, was assassinated eighteen months later.

Seven years later a group of dissident officers, the Algerian Movement of Free Officers (MAOL), would claim that Boudiaf was killed because he courageously challenged the army barons. Based in Madrid but with links to the higher echelons in the military, the MAOL posted their conclusions on the internet, describing how Boudiaf appointed a senior officer of the Département de Renseignement et de Sécurité, Colonel Mourad, with a top-secret brief to investigate corruption at the very highest level. By the end of June Boudiaf had a list of prominent figures whom he wanted to put on trial in an effort to restore the lost trust between the people and their rulers. These included Mohammed Lamari and Mohammed Médiène, who were going to be retired by presidential decree on 5 July, the thirtieth anniversary of independence.[6] Boudiaf's murder, therefore, just one week before these announcements, was a last-ditch attempt to head off this purge. For this reason, the MAOL continued, Colonel Mourad was found shortly afterwards in the east of Algiers, with three bullets in the neck, supposedly murdered by 'terrorists'.[7] In addition the MAOL accused one of the commissioners, Rezag Bara, of being a long-standing DRS agent who tried to whitewash the final report and was implicated in Fethallah's murder.[8]

These revelations were given further credence by the former DRS number two, Samraoui, who sought political asylum in Germany in 1992. Speaking on Al-Jazeera television in August 2001, he explained that the murder was part of a sophisticated plot: 'If he had not been executed at the Maison de la Culture at Annaba, a bomb was to explode at El Hadjar, where he was going to go, and if that also failed, he was to eat a plate of poisoned couscous at the military hotel.'[9]

By the time of the funeral at Al-Elia most ordinary Algerians had come to the conclusion that Boudiaf had been killed by insiders within the regime worried about his anti-corruption campaign.[10] Tens of thousands lined the streets to pay their last respects to the head of state as his cortège wound its way to the Martyrs' cemetery. Shouting and chanting, many carried a photograph of Boudiaf aloft with the headline 'They killed him' as others mobbed the car carrying the coffin. One reporter for *La Nation* chronicled how 'a sense of deep anxiety could be felt moving among the crowd in sad disarray, undone by their mourning. There was a premonition of a descent into hell.'

The procession was diverted from its original route to avoid a pro-FIS demonstration outside a mosque. Near the cemetery a few hundred fundamentalists congregated, shouting slogans. Security forces fired into the air to disperse them. Yasser Arafat and Roland Dumas, the French foreign minister, were among the few foreign leaders attending the funeral. Around the burial scene ordinary people in the throng muttered 'they killed him' and, as the coffin was lowered into the grave, a voice shouted out 'Ghozali – assassin'. For most Algerians Boudiaf's murder was a chilling example of the machinations of *le pouvoir*, an octopus whose tentacles spread through every walk of life.

At the funeral the Swiss photographer Michael von Graffenried immortalized a rare public scene of the generals together, many corpulent in outsize uniforms, some wearing dark glasses, others smoking. With their puffed-out chests there was a clear whiff of the Mafia or a South American junta, a cabal that will do anything to protect its lucrative system of sinecures and backhanders. In the following weeks investigations into state corruption were quietly shelved, while the figure of $26 billion creamed off by the oligarchs and invested abroad now entered folklore. Thereafter, the generals retreated into the 'corridors of power', that shadowy place out of the public gaze where the real decisions are made. They were reluctant to put themselves forwards as figureheads, some because they had fought on the side of the French army for much of the war of liberation and only changed sides late in the conflict, but ordinary Algerians knew that they were omnipresent.

Among those affected by Boudiaf's death were a group of French Roman Catholic monks living at the monastery of Tibhirine, near Médéa, south of Algiers. Christian de Chergé, the prior of the monastery of Our Lady of Atlas, remarked in the annual community bulletin how Boudiaf's straightforward way of talking had made people trust him: 'He talked of building a new sense of national unity through honest work and the participation of all classes in opportunities. Again the youth are at a loss.'[11]

Also depressed was Nesroulah Yous, the entrepreneur living in the poor district of Bentalha, south of Algiers. He saw the event as a turning point and felt that a lifesaver had been drowned, although in the pro-FIS area where he lived, his was a minority viewpoint:

> One has to say that Boudiaf was not at all liked by the people in our neigh-bourhoods ... He was in fact the symbol of the ban on the FIS and the opening of concentration camps ... One has already heard about the use of torture ... little by little, I learn about victims, some young people I know, who died under torture and were buried anonymously.
>
> As far as my neighbours at Bentalha and Baraki were concerned, the *taghout* ['false idol', a word used to describe the inner circle of the regime] had used Boudiaf, who allowed himself to be manipulated in legitimizing the putsch and repression.[12]

Yous's pessimism was further echoed by Habib Souaïdia, then a young officer cadet at the prestigious Cherchell academy:

> ... with the death of Boudiaf, the population which had begun to believe again was disappointed anew. The president had dared to attack the taboo subject of the politico-military Mafia. He had all the files. The people for years wanted heads to roll and Boudiaf offered some to them. Like many Algerians, I am convinced that this is what caused his death.[13]

In the wake of Boudiaf's murder Algeria was a country cut adrift. Scared, vulnerable and unprotected, the people now began to feel that events could only spiral downwards. If the regime was willing to kill Boudiaf, what would it do to ordinary Algerians?

As the atmosphere grew tenser by the day, Algeria began to feel like a country preparing for war. In April the radical cleric Ikhlef Cherati produced a sermon on cassette saying that Muslims must kill all those not opposed to the junta: effectively, a fatwa. This was followed by another cassette in the summer calling for insurrection, on which he stated:

> The regimes which hold sway are secular regimes imported from the materialist West ... Our leaders want to submit to the new world order imposed by the Americans and behind them the Jews, in order to bring about at last the World Jewish Order which the children of monkeys and pigs have dreamed of for ages. With the help of God, this will not happen. We will eradicate the roots of the evil just as the God the All Powerful promised, but after we have destroyed the off-spring of colonialism, issued from out own blood.[14]

Written fatwas were also posted up at pro-FIS mosques calling for a jihad to overthrow a regime that was nothing more than a lapdog of 'Jews and crusaders', along with a hit list of a thousand magistrates, army officers and policemen, specifying names and addresses. All over the country the streets were full of angry young men ready to respond to these calls. Angry with the regime for cheating them of victory; angry with the intellectuals who had supported the coup; they were angry with the West too. The fact that Western countries had not intervened against the coup showed the hypocrisy of the so-called democracies – 'one law for them and one law for Muslims' – and they became consumed with a self-righteous anger that had one deadly aim: to destroy the regime through all-out violence.

With the older, more middle-class FIS leadership imprisoned or exiled, these angry young men – many of whom shaved off their beards to escape detection – now rose to the fore. Unlike Madani, the standard-bearer of the pious middle classes, and the university-educated Hachani, these young men came from the limitless reservoir of urban unemployed. Pumped up and bristling with aggression, religious certainty flowing through their veins, they plotted revenge in the dark basements of deserted buildings in rundown neighbourhoods. Abdenour Alia Yahia, the veteran human-rights lawyer who was defending Madani, could sense polarization all around him. With thousands of young men preparing for war it would take just one trigger for the situation to spill over into uncontrollable violence. He warned, 'The present government has committed a grave error by forcing the FIS to go underground. This is lethal for the Algerian nation.'[15]

Many of these young men looked to the armed groups that had been organizing themselves since the summer of 1991 in the mountains around Algiers. The most important of these was the reformulated Mouvement Islamique Armé (MIA) led by Abdelkader Chebouti, the former army officer and right-hand man of Bouyali who had been condemned to death in 1987. His stronghold was the town of Larba, fifteen miles south-east of Algiers at the foot of the Atlas. Other prominent leaders included Saïd Makloufi, Mansouri Meliani, Hocine Abderahim and two former members of the FIS ruling council, Hachemi Sahnouni and Benazzouz Zeba. By June 1991 each Larba commune had small groups under an emir (or 'prince', as the local leaders styled themselves) and vice-emir and in the wake of the coup support for the MIA was largely drawn from greater Algiers' grimy urban slums, the suburbs of El Harrach, Les Eucalyptes, Baraki, and Bachdjarah, as well as from students at the Bab Ezzouar and Ben Aknoun universities.

The most significant new recruits to the MIA in terms of military expertise were the fierce Afghan veterans led by Aïssa Massaoudi and Tayeb El-Afghani. It was this sixty-strong group that had attacked Guemmar police station, near to El-Oued and close to the Tunisian frontier, on 28 November 1991, killing three young reservists and getting away with a formidable arsenal that included 21 rifles, 25 Kalashnikovs, 2,000 rounds of ammunition and several rocket launchers. This in turn provoked a huge counter-insurgency operation and, although twenty-five insurgents were killed and a further dozen captured, the rest, including El-Afghani, escaped.[16] El-Afghani's group was marked out by a strong sense of the collective struggle of the transnational Muslim *umma* against 'crusader imperialism', a struggle in which he saw Algeria as a major front alongside Palestine, Chechnya and Kashmir.

Within Algeria, as on an international level, there was never one unified Islamist structure. Rather there was a huge number of different groups and cells, each with their own localities, leaders, even their own imams willing to issue fatwas. Indeed, their bewildering number of organizations was a deliberate tactic, intended to create confusion amongst the authorities. Often these groups had little knowledge of what action the others were engaged in, and sometimes they were at odds with one another. Takfir wa-l-Hijra, operating out of the Belcourt mosque, known locally as Kabul mosque, had clashes during 1991 with FIS supporters, whom they did not consider sufficiently Islamic. Overall numbers were difficult to quantify precisely but by 1993 they had grown in strength to about 22,000 armed men across the country.[17]

The mountains of Meftah and Chrea became no-go areas. There the Islamist guerrillas established safe havens from which to launch a war on the irreligious, consciously imitating the Prophet, who had withdrawn from society as a necessary prelude to his final glorious victory. It was the familiar theme of the pure mountains versus the decadent plains, as groups of armed young men, inspired not just by Mohammed but also by the war against the French, Bouyali and Afghanistan, prepared themselves for jihad. Living off the land and dependent upon local people for food and care, these groups now set up the infrastructures of supply and communications. With little artillery, no tanks and no planes at their disposal they were laying the basis for a classic guerrilla war.

For this reason there was no attempt at a mass insurrection against the regime. Surrendering the towns and cities to the army, Chebouti's followers shied away from mass action even though the regime was highly vulnerable. This was because the MIA believed in the virtues of guerrilla warfare where a dedicated vanguard would draw the army on to their own terrain in the mountains. In 1992, therefore, there was a series of small-scale attacks on

military installations and personnel. Moreover, there was the basic considera-
tion of security. The armed groups were suspicious of accepting large numbers
of volunteers from the cities for fear of being infiltrated by the secret police.

The armed groups' effectiveness was further undermined by personal dis-
agreements over tactics. Mansouri Meliani, for instance, was at loggerheads
with Chebouti, rejecting any control from the old FIS leadership. Attempts
were made to unite the various groups but these initiatives were dealt a
hammer blow when a meeting of *maquis* leaders on 31 August was broken up
by the specialist troops. Acting on a tip-off they surrounded the area with
helicopters, capturing Meliani and killing a number of others. Since the army
was clearly acting on inside information, his arrest, a major propaganda coup
for the regime, made trust between the guerrilla groups impossible and
produced further splintering and faction fighting. By the autumn the armed
groups were clearly losing momentum, to such an extent that, in an effort to
boost flagging morale, Ali Belhadj, now sentenced along with Madani to
twelve years' imprisonment for armed conspiracy, proclaimed his support for
violent insurrection in an inflammatory letter smuggled from his prison: 'If I
was outside the walls of this prison, I would be a fighter in the ranks of my
brother Abdelkader Chebouti.'[18]

Belhadj's letter was a testament to the success of the army, which throughout 1992 did not flinch at repression. Again and again throughout the
summer Nezzar, the de-facto head of state, made it clear that the army was
digging in for a long battle in which they would be the only victor, no matter
what the cost to Algeria and Algerians. It was to all intents and purposes a
declaration of war on those who were preparing for terrorism.

Boudiaf was replaced as head of the Haut Comité d'Etat by Ali Kafi, the
uncharismatic secretary of the war veterans' association. The army saw him as
a safe choice and by supporting Arabization he sought to take the wind out
of the Islamists' sails. Furthermore, he installed as prime minister Belaid
Abdesselam, who had presided over the nationalization of gas and oil
production, playing on nostalgia for the Boumediène years.

The new government made no attempt at dialogue with the Islamist guerrillas, demonizing them as a fanatical minority in the pay of outside forces,
especially Sudan and Iran.[19] Instead, it followed a policy of repression, taking
the view that even if terrorism could not be eradicated then it could at least be
reduced to levels that the state could tolerate. In particular, the regime sought
to take back control of the mosques. Thus, all prayers, but specifically those
given by known Islamists, were conducted under the watchful gaze of the riot
police. Imams were vetted and those suspected of FIS sympathies were put

under twenty-four-hour surveillance with their phones tapped and mail opened. There was also a clampdown on the press as freedom of expression came to be seen as a costly luxury. New laws gave the Ministry of the Interior the right to have any journalist arrested or paper suspended for security reasons. In tandem with these draconian moves the government dissolved the FIS-dominated local councils and replaced them with new administrative bodies known as Délégations Executives Communales (DECs) in a bid to re-establish the authority of the central government at the local level.

The short-term success of these repressive measures made the regime over-confident. Drawing up a balance sheet at the end of 1992, many in the regime argued that the casualty figures – below six hundred police and soldiers killed – were acceptable rates and this bolstered the belief that the armed threat could be contained or even exploited to frighten the population over to their side.[20] In the longer term, however, this policy just produced a breeding ground for radical Islam. When added to October 1988 and the cancellation of the elections, Nezzar's bellicose stance was the final insult, a spur to action for hundreds of young men who felt that they had no choice but to embrace violence.

The first example of this violence was the bomb at Algiers international airport on 26 August 1992 that killed 10 people and wounded 128 others. Algerians were shocked by this act of indiscriminate terrorism, the first of its kind since independence, but there was also widespread bitterness about the failings of intelligence agents, who were tipped off in advance but made no effort to evacuate the airport. Algerians were sceptical about the authorities' subsequent claim that there had not been time to clear travellers and staff, noting how the government used the atmosphere of insecurity to push through further repressive measures: on 5 December 1992 the authorities imposed a night-time curfew in Algiers and the provincial capitals of Blida, Tipaza, Boumerdès, Ain-Delfa and Bouira.[21]

INTO THE ABYSS

The year 1993 saw Algeria finally tip over into the abyss. Journalists and commentators had been using this language for the past three years, to such an extent that the image of a country on the brink of uncontrollable bloodshed had become a journalistic cliché. Now, however, really was the moment when the slowly lit fuse finally exploded; the point when toxic hatreds that had been festering for years spilt into violence and all-out war.

The genesis of this violence came from dissident groups from the MIA, many of them Afghan veterans, who broke away and returned to the towns and cities in a disciplined fashion at the end of 1992. The nucleus has been linked with the captured Meliani who had become disenchanted with the MIA's strategy of rural guerrilla warfare. Following Meliani's lead they were determined to adopt a new and more daring campaign of urban terrorism which, by unleashing a maelstrom of violence, would bring the regime to its knees.

Drawing in a raft of new recruits from the young and the poor living in Baraki, Les Eucalyptes, Bachdjarah, and El Harrach and incensed by the army repression, each group was led by a series of local commanders, the most notorious of whom were Djaffar El-Afghani, Mohand Levelley and Omar el-Eulumi, who operated autonomously within their own fiefdoms. Collectively these groups became known by the French acronym GIA, standing for Groupe Islamique Armé, but in practice these three neat initials stood for a nebulous, many-headed entity.[22] Operating from the bottom up through small grassroots cells, the GIA honed their techniques to deadly effect with one stream specializing in murdering intellectuals, another in car bombs, and another still in the assassination of government officials.

Numerically these various urban groups were made up of two to three thousand fighters, and through the well-aimed use of terrorism they were able to wreak havoc far in excess of their numbers.[23] Their first major success was in March 1993 when the GIA attacked the Boughezoul army barracks, killing forty-one people including eighteen soldiers. From that moment on, the intensity of the violence was truly bewildering. Barely had the government recovered from one attack when it was confronted with another. Soon whole areas were slipping out of government control, forcing the army to extend the curfew beyond the Algiers region to the neighbouring districts of Chelif, M'Sila and Djelfa in May 1993.

The regime's inability to halt the daily attacks gave the GIA a religious aura in the eyes of the poor and the young. This mystique was derived from the fact that the GIA cells seemed to be able to hit at any time and anywhere. With each attack more audacious than the last – one car bomb narrowly missed Nezzar whilst another wounded the employment minister Tahar Hamdi – their credo was propaganda by deed, every success reinforcing the conviction that they were God's own soldiers. This seeming invincibility came from their intimate knowledge of the neighbourhoods. The young men, many from a criminal background, knew every nook and cranny and they deployed their sense of locality to deadly effect.

Death at the hands of the GIA came in many forms. One was beheading, another slitting throats, whilst another still involved cutting the throat and severing the tongue which was then draped over the dead body.[24] This latter was the favourite technique of the cocaine cartels of Latin America, so became known locally as the 'Colombian necktie'. Heads were also arranged on poles, and intestines used to decorate trees. Nesroulah Yous described the scenes of horror at Bentalha when armed groups encircled the district and selected people to decapitate.

> The operation started at 8 p.m. and lasted until three in the morning ... that night I could not sleep. At dawn I left to go to work ... a woman and her two sons were coming toward me in tears. It was the family of the retired sergeant major of the Republican guard ... at the main boulevard I saw something large covered with a white sheet stained with blood. Some newly arrived people lifted the sheet. I had to make an effort not to vomit at the sight of three bodies piled on top of each other; the first cadaver had no head.
>
> ... some metres away, behind a nursery, a satellite television dish was lying on the ground. In the plate was an orange box on which a head had been placed. It belonged to the retired sergeant major. This spectacle was so monstrous that it became nearly surreal ... thirteen people had been killed, among them some soldiers ... Was this a double warning? For the soldiers and for those who owned a satellite dish or a television?[25]

Alongside this mayhem the GIA carried out a scorched-earth policy. Spurred on by a raging nihilism, in March 1994 one group stopped a passenger train outside Algiers, ordering the three hundred passengers to disembark before setting the carriages on fire. In early July forest fires in the eastern and central part of the country destroyed more than thirty thousand acres of forest (although this might have been security forces destroying cover for the insurgents), and in September over five hundred schools were set alight in the run-up to the new term.

Within Algiers GIA groups roamed freely, carving out enclaves where the rigour of their puritanical prohibitions became ever more intensive. In Blida, for example, residents were ordered to disconnect satellite dishes that broadcast Western films; women were forbidden to consult male physicians; and shops selling alcohol, videos and raï music were forced to shut down. Women-only hammams (bathhouses) and hair-dressing salons were also closed, whilst butchers who overcharged during the month of Ramadan were threatened with execution.

By the summer of 1993 one blue-uniformed police officer was being assassinated every few hours and as many as ten a night. Maps tabulating GIA activity came to resemble a smallpox outbreak and morale amongst the forces of law and order plummeted, weakening chains of command and account- ability. Many did not go home but slept in the office with a gun on their laps, wearing the same clothes for days.

Sensing that they were losing the war on the ground, the regime created a specialist anti-terrorist force of fifteen thousand men in April 1993. Using fast landcruisers these units were highly mobile and trained to deal with confused, intense bouts of fighting whether they were raids, ambushes or sudden counter-attacks. Their task: to restore law and order in the Mitidja, the 'triangle of death' between Algiers, Blida and Médéa, and areas where the people had voted FIS and were sympathetic to the Islamist insurgency. Garbed in black balaclavas to protect them against recognition and reprisal, they became known as the 'ninjas' because of their uncanny resemblance to the popular children's cartoon Ninja turtles. Operating outside the law they quickly gained a fearsome reputation, cordoning off neighbourhoods, using hooded informers to search homes and arrest suspects and leaving bodies in the street to rot as a warning to others, thereby breaking all the injunctions of Islam which demands immediate burial. In the war against the GIA, savagery was seen as a source of strength as the 'ninjas' became infamous for a whole host of torture techniques including electric shocks, sexual abuse with bottles, beatings with sticks, especially on the genitals, and, an Algerian speciality, the *chiffon* (cloth), in which prisoners were tied down and partially suffocated with a cloth soaked in dirty water.

Although Amnesty International continually drew attention to these human-rights abuses, Western governments turned a blind eye.[26] Little was said about the special military courts, established under the anti-terrorist decree of September 1992, even though they violated many of the inter- national fair trial standards. Under this system more than fifty went on trial, including several high-ranking FIS officials, for terrorist offences including alleged involvement in the bombing of Algiers international airport. Thirty- eight were sentenced to death and the others were given prison sentences ranging from one to twenty years. In the dock Mansouri Meliani, still lame in his left leg after being wounded in the gun battle during his capture, mouthed defiance right to the end, telling his accusers that if released he would continue his jihad against the regime. Others of the condemned took their sentences calmly, mouthing verses from the Qur'an.

Much to the regime's embarrassment, the trial shone the spotlight on their own practices as many of the accused protested their innocence. Hocine Abderrahim, who ran the office of the jailed Abassi Madani, claimed that his own confession, shown on television, was extracted under torture. The death penalty, therefore, meant martyrdom because God knew that he was not implicated in the airport bombing he was convicted of. Such appeals, however, were brushed aside by the authorities, who wanted to show what fate awaited the insurgents as the country descended into a pitiless cycle of violence and counter-violence.

What was the meaning of this violence? At a fundamental level it was about the assertion of power. Each armed group was a male brotherhood and the realization by its members that they had the capacity to invert traditional relationships and inspire fear in the regime was liberating. Through bloodshed these young men felt a surge of energy. By killing they were telling the regime that they, the dispossessed, could no longer be kept in a state of subjugation. The product of rage, rejection and injustice, theirs was mirror violence, a reply to a regime that had lied, swindled and bullied. It was also a transformative violence. They were standing up and giving vent to their pent-up frustration.

For all these reasons there was a curiously strong echo of Frantz Fanon about the violence. For Fanon anti-colonial insurrection was the way in which the colonized peoples purged themselves of an inferiority complex. In the same way, this new 'wretched of the earth' looked to violence to cast off their sense of oppression. This, as Martinez has demonstrated, is why so much of the early violence was directed against local police officers.[27] In explicitly targeting the men who had hitherto humiliated them on a day-to-day basis they were enjoying the satisfaction of revenge. The violence was cathartic, which explains why so much of the bloodshed had a strong ritualistic aspect. By kidnapping, gagging and verbally abusing police officers in broad daylight before finally killing them, the armed groups were displaying their manhood.[28]

The very intensity of the violence was framed by the preceding years of non-existence. Dispensing with boredom and emptiness, these young men were now furiously alive. Through bloodshed they were telling the world that they were no longer outsiders. Their souls ignited by action, they were moving from the margins to the centre in a bid to impose themselves on the rest of society. Empowered by the belief that in doing God's work they would enjoy paradise in the afterlife, their purpose was to cleanse the country of heresy. By destroying the regime, dubbed the great Satan (*Al-Taghout*), they were allowing all Algerians to reclaim the beauty and glory of their faith. Of course, their actions were based upon a highly selective reading of the Qur'an. By forgetting those parts that condemned murder or reminded believers that there must be no compulsion in religion, they became locked into a frenzied logic of competitive extremism. Each action had to be more outrageous than the last, as the GIA groups continually widened the range of the enemies of God.

Inevitably, given the social background of so many in the GIA, their religious motivations blended easily into warlordism and criminality. Styling themselves as 'emirs' who had the right to impose their will on their neighbourhoods, they became in effect local godfathers carrying out extortion and racketeering on local businesses in the name of the holy war. Soon it became possible to talk of 'terror chic' as many of the young GIA emirs paraded around in their neighbourhoods, Kalashnikov in hand, in an open act of defiance. Undeniably this image fed off the long tradition of the honourable outlaw encapsulating the true values of the community, but it also reflected the powerful influence of superhero figures such as Batman and Superman, as well as the impact of martial arts films, and the films of Arnold Schwarzenegger and Sylvester Stallone, all of which they would have seen on pirate videos.[29] Wishing to emulate Bruce Lee, Jackie Chan or Rambo, they conceived of themselves as righteous avengers.

This twilight world between criminality and armed Islamism is brilliantly captured in the novels of Yasmina Khadra and Aziz Chouaki, as well as the sociological research of Luis Martinez.[30] Through violence the GIA emirs became cult figures, the terror equivalent of the 1982 World Cup team or Cheb Khaled. Usually dressed in Levi 501s and Italian shoes, with their hair gelled back, their macho swagger made them into folkloric heroes with nicknames like Yacine 'Napoli', Lyes 'L'égorgeur' (throat-cutter) and Hocine 'Flicha' (arrow – a reference to the speed at which he could kill a policeman and run away). Indeed, such was the notoriety of 'Flicha', captured and executed in 1998, that he was lionized in a football terrace song directed against the police where the chant 'Flicha's coming after you' built up into a deafening crescendo intermingled with doglike baying.[31]

The more extreme the GIA groups became the more they accused the FIS of selling out, an accusation fuelled by rumours about secret negotiations with the regime. Conversely, the remnants of the FIS were worried by the GIA. At one level they were fearful of being left behind by the GIA, especially when Mohammed Said and Abderrezak Redjam, two members of the FIS executive, defected to the GIA in February 1994. On another they were perturbed by the impact of the GIA tactics as it became increasingly obvious that indiscriminate violence was alienating large parts of the population. To counter the GIA, increasingly seen as dangerously out of control and infiltrated by the secret services, Chebouti supporters (Chebouti himself was killed in action in autumn 1993), formed the Islamic Salvation Army (AIS) in July 1994, a group which was styled as the 'official' wing of the FIS and subject to its political control.

At the core of the militants' anger was the ulcer of colonialism. From end to end their language was laced with talk of latter-day 'crusaders' and 'colonialists' who were bleeding the country dry in a grand 'anti-Muslim plot'. In large part this fury was derived from Belhadj, who had railed continuously against France's poisonous legacy – secularists, liberals, communists, feminists – whose ungodly influence had to be purged from Muslim minds. Armed with such religious justification, the GIA groups now unleashed a war against those francophone intellectuals who had supported the coup. Academics, teachers, writers, journalists and lawyers: all had to be silenced by a campaign of assassination and here the young emirs took great pleasure in instilling fear and panic. Many intellectuals received death threats by fax or an envelope pushed under their front door with a Kalashnikov bullet inside. Others found little knives wrapped in cloth in their post.

By intimidation and murder the GIA groups wanted to underline the minority status of the francophone middle classes. Living in relative luxury these intellectuals, the argument ran, were cut off from the Arabic-speaking majority and represented nobody. They might claim to speak on behalf of civil society, but in reality they were apologists for the military and, by writing in the 'language of the Devil', mouthpieces for colonialism. Killing them, therefore, gave these disenfranchised young men a feeling of absolute righteousness and allowed them to express their most basic feelings of class hatred.

On 17 May Omar Belhouchet, editor of the Algiers daily *El Watan*, had just dropped his two children off at school. He looked back to be sure they were safely through the door. Then he saw two gunmen with pistols running forward and firing at his tyres. Lying almost flat on the front seat, he floored the accelerator and survived. Faced with this type of violence, more than five hundred journalists left the country, while those who remained, like Belhouchet, lived in a specially guarded residence west of Algiers, the Club des Pins. He sent his two children to stay with a relative in France, although his wife, riven with terror, died of a heart ailment. As he coped with this tragedy, Belhouchet remained determined to defeat not only terrorism but government repression and censorship:

> Only democracy can save this country. That is why I publish. So that we can have a real debate. Of course the government tries to shut us down every time we publish something they don't like. They can do what they want to us. We are ready for them and we are not afraid. Without a debate, there is only darkness here.[32]

This campaign of murder had taken off with a vengeance in the middle of March 1993. On three successive days first Djilali Lyabes, a former higher-education minister, then Ladi Flici and Hafid Senhadri, both members of the Conseil Consultatif National (CCN), were assassinated in broad daylight. El-Hashemi Sherif, head of the communist PAGS – now renamed as the avowedly anti-Islamist Ettahaddi ('Defiance') party – was hurt in an attack on his car in April. On 22 June Mohammed Boukhobza, a respected sociologist, was killed in his apartment by intruders who slit his throat in front of his daughter.

Another victim was the internationally acclaimed Kabyle writer Tahar Djaout, editor of the left-orientated weekly *Ruptures* and winner of the 1991 Prix Méditerranée for his novel *Vigiles*. His was a unique voice, finely tuned to the dilemmas of Algeria – one bleak poem described the stark choices for women in a country where they could be killed for accepting the veil and killed for rejecting it. He had long been an Islamist bête noire; in 1987 Ali Belhadj had issued a fatwa against him and he had received numerous death threats. Now, on the morning of 26 May 1993, Djaout had just got into his car when someone tapped on the windscreen. He looked up to see a man pointing a gun. Two shots rang out and Djaout slumped against the steering wheel. A second man helped drag him from the car and then both leapt in the car and drove off. Rushed to hospital in a coma, Djaout died a week later. His murder was keenly felt in his native Kabylia where the burial, in the village of Oulkhou, was highly emotional.

If journalists and writers were major targets, so too were women deemed to be too French in their manners and style of dress. Why precisely these women were singled out had complex psychological and cultural roots. The motivations were as much about class envy, romantic rejection and sexual frustration as they were religious convictions. Killing women, but particularly economically successful women who were high-profile teachers or magistrates, affirmed the murderers' manhood and became a benchmark of their struggle to purify society. The two principal hate figures were Khalida Messaoudi and Leïla Aslaoui, both of whom had been at the forefront of feminist opposition to the Family Code in the 1980s, had supported the cancellation of elections, and had public careers in politics on an anti-FIS platform, one as a member of Boudiaf's CCN and the other as Minister for Sport.[33] On 12 June 1993 Messaoudi was condemned to death by fatwa and forced to leave her teaching job and go into hiding. The fatwa, signed by Saïd Makhloufi, warned:

The men of the Islamic Jihad therefore say to those unbelieving collaborators of the Despot, that the striking force and the length of the Islamic military arm is growing every day – with God's help – and that it is able, now more than ever, to pursue all these traitors, renegades, and criminals, wherever they may be.[34]

During 1994 Messaoudi survived two assassination attempts, which led an Islamist newssheet, published in London in April, to reiterate that her death was only a matter of time. Equally, on 2 September 1993 Leïla Aslaoui received an anonymous phone call at 2 a.m. in which a young man's voice recounted to her the opening passage of Sura 36 of the Qur'an, entitled *Ya sin* – the extract traditionally used by the armed groups to justify the elimination of apostates:

For most of them the Word has been decreed, because they are unbelievers.

We have bound their necks with chains of iron reaching up to their chins, so they cannot bow their heads. We have put barriers before them and behind them and covered them over, so that they cannot see.

It is the same whether or not you forewarn them: they will never have faith.[35]

Miraculously, both survived but the list of women killed was soon long. Running into hundreds between 1993 and 1995, it included women journalists like Rashida Hammadi and Malika Sabeur, and Karima Belhadj, who worked as a secretary at the Algiers police welfare organization. Just twenty, she had become engaged to a local bus driver. Walking home one evening she encountered men lying in wait who grabbed her hair, threw her to the ground and fired a bullet into her abdomen. Sportswomen too came under intense pressure, notably the 1,500-metre runner Hassiba Boulmerka, gold medallist at the Barcelona Olympics in 1992, who was repeatedly threatened and at one point forced to train overseas.

Pop singers, too, were targeted on the grounds that their music, demonized as pornographic and anti-Islamic, represented the invasion of Western culture. This hostility led Cheb Khaled to speak out against the FIS. He had left Algeria for Paris in the mid-1980s and now felt unable to return. Interviewed by *Melody Maker* in September 1992, shortly before his first major release in Britain, the self-styled 'King of Raï' was very clear about why he was a marked man:

The FIS call me 'The Devil' … They want to pass laws forbidding singers like me. They don't like it because I sing about sex, alcohol and drugs and I use the language of the street. They want to forbid women to play sport, they want to forbid everything. Young people are afraid; they only leave their houses at night, like rats ... The FIS want to destroy the people and the culture of Algeria. And a country without culture is a dead country.[36]

Others too, like the young folk singer Souad Massi, were driven into exile, while those who remained ran huge risks. Lounès Matoub, the Kabyle bard and champion of Berber rights, was kidnapped by an armed group on 25 September 1994. Two weeks later he was released but in the meantime Cheb Hasni was assassinated in Oran on 29 September in broad daylight in front of his house, killed by a young man whom Hasni mistook to be a fan wanting an autograph. Nobody had done more than Hasni to give voice to the frustrations, hopes and needs of his generation.

As the killings continued intellectuals elsewhere voiced their solidarity. Speaking to the International Parliament of Writers in London on 5 November 1994, Salman Rushdie saw parallels with his own experience after the publication of *The Satanic Verses* in 1989. He argued that, like him, Algerians were the victims of religious intolerance and bigotry, and he called on France to grant political asylum to those threatened by terrorism. In the same way the pro-government press, backed up by intellectuals like Rachid Mimoumi and Rachid Boudjedra, did not hang back. They deployed a vocabulary of horror, talking in apocalyptic terms about 'the beards' as the Muslim equivalent of the Khmer Rouge who were determined to transform Algeria into one huge killing field.[37]

Some, however, were worried by the way in which official accounts of these murders frequently did not add up. In the case of Djaout's death, for example, days later a young man confessed on the television evening news. Belebassi Abdellah, the alleged getaway driver, said a GIA commander, Abdelha Layada, had ordered Djaout's death on the grounds that he was a communist and his way with words influenced Muslims. Shortly after, the other two alleged assassins were killed by security forces in a shoot-out, news which Said Mekbel, author of a famously acerbic column 'the rusty nail' in the daily *Le Matin*, greeted as a farcical joke. Given that the police neither conducted a ballistic analysis nor interviewed neighbours, why were the authorities so ready to pin the crime on these four culprits?

After the funeral a group of thinkers created the Tahar Djaout Truth Committee with the psychiatrist Mahfoud Boucebsi, known popularly as 'the friend of the poor', as president and Mekbel as coordinator. Both were determined to establish the truth and unearth who exactly was behind the killing.

However, on 27 August 1993 Boucebsi was knifed to death as he arrived at hospital for work. Then, on 3 December 1994, Mekbel was killed in broad daylight when assassins walked into a pizzeria and shot him twice in the head as he ate lunch.

The Tahar Djaout Truth Committee raised some of the first questions about the exact nature of the violence as journalists such as Séverine Labat pondered whether the regime was letting the murder of high-profile intellectuals happen as a deliberate tactic to get the international community on their side.[38] After all, they did little to protect them and their deaths allowed the army regime to portray themselves to the West as the last rampart against barbarism.

By autumn 1993 news from Algeria had become depressingly familiar. With the violence endemic, individual murders did not rate more than a paragraph in the international press. Fearing that their struggle was falling off the international agenda, the GIA groups, knowing full well that in terms of the 'oxygen of publicity' a foreign death was worth much more than an Algerian one, looked to widen the conflict. They wanted to keep the regime isolated and put pressure on what were seen as the generals' Western backers. Dramatically, therefore, the GIA conferred a death sentence on all Jews, Christians and non-believers still living in the country on 30 October. Signed 'Abu Mariam', the declaration stated: 'Foreigners have thirty days to leave the country. If they do not, they are responsible for their own death.'[39]

The murder of foreigners had already begun on 1 September with the deaths of two French surveyors, François Bartellet and Emmanuel Didion, at a fake checkpoint near Sidi-Bel-Abbès, former headquarters of the French Foreign Legion. Now, however, the killings really intensified, with the victims including Raymond Louzoum, a fair-haired Tunisian Jew well known for playing bit parts as a torturing French officer in films about the war of independence; Vincent the well-known Jewish bookseller on the Rue Mourad Didouche; Father Henri Vergès and Sister Paule Raymonde, two librarians in the Algiers casbah working for a Roman Catholic foundation; and Roger-Michel Drouaier, a French businessman who was killed along with his twenty-four-year-old son at their suburban Algiers villa. Malcolm Vincent, a British employee of Pullman Kellogg, was shot and killed while filling his car at a petrol station in Arzew, the big petrochemical complex at Oran. Olivier Quemener, a highly experienced French cameraman on assignment for ABC News, was gunned down in the Algiers casbah on 1 February 1994.

The worst single incident came in December 1993, when twelve Croats working at a dam were found with their throats cut. The attackers on that occasion were reported to be as young as fifteen years old. On 7 July 1994 seven Italian seamen were found with their throats cut on board their ship, the *Luciana*, at the port of Djendjen,[40] and on 11 July two Belarusians, a Russian, a Ukrainian and a Romanian, all engineers working for SONATRACH, were shot dead in an ambush whilst travelling through Oued Ouchayeh, a suburb of Algiers. Five men disguised as police officers stopped their bus, then separated the foreigners from the Algerians and ordered them out of the bus and shot them with machine guns.

The level of violence was undeniable, but the Algerian Movement of Free Officers (MAOL) would subsequently ask questions about why and in what precise circumstances the campaign began. The GIA Declaration, for example, was given to three French consular officials, Jean-Claude and Michèle Thévenot and Alain Fressier, who were taken hostage but subsequently released near the diocesan residence of Henri Teissier, the Archbishop of Algiers, in October 1993. The MAOL argued that the whole drama was mounted by Algerian and French intelligence to discredit Islamists. As evidence they pointed to the fact that the three consular officials, unusually for Western hostages who have been released in such situations, shunned the media entirely after their ordeal, and were all subsequently transferred to obscure postings in the Indian Ocean.

By July 1994 fifty-one foreigners had been murdered with the result that the remainder led tightly circumscribed lives. Diplomats rarely left their embassy grounds and foreign companies either cut their staff to a minimum or pulled out. On 1 April 1994 France had declared that it would be closing all schools and cultural centres except one. The ambassador also told the remaining two thousand expatriates to leave. Armed guards were deployed to protect the Catholic cathedral, Notre Dame D'Afrique, while priests and their small congregations, often too frightened to go to their churches, held midweek mass in privacy.

In a move to distance itself from the GIA, the AIS condemned the killing of foreigners. In a communiqué released in Bonn on 25 July 1994 and signed by the two AIS leaders, Madani Mezraq and Ahmed Benaïcha, it called on all factions to unite around the imprisoned leadership. Moreover, the communiqué was openly critical of the brutality of the GIA, which through needless excess was turning the population against the Islamist cause. In response the GIA groups accused the AIS of selling out and reiterated the slogan 'No negotiations, no truce, no dialogue'.

This rivalry between the AIS and GIA groups led to a blurring and con- fusion about the bloodshed.[41] Often it was unclear which particular group controlled which particular area. Making sense of these boundaries was complicated still further by power struggles within the regime as opposing clans exploited the generalized violence as a smokescreen to settle accounts. Kasdi Merbah, former head of the secret services and prime minister from 5 November 1988 to 10 September 1990, was killed in a car ambush close to his home on 21 August 1993. As he returned to his home in Bordj el-Bahri, 28 miles to the east of Algiers, five attackers, wearing civilian clothes and carrying their weapons in large shoulder bags, were lying in wait. Positioned ahead of and behind the cortège, they left no escape route, raking the cars with machine-gun fire which killed not only Merbah but his brother, son, driver and bodyguard. Reportedly Merbah's dying words were: 'I was betrayed.'

Algiers radio immediately pinned the blame on 'terrorists', but Merbah had powerful enemies within *le pouvoir*. He had been one of the key figures behind Boudiaf's anti-corruption drive, providing a catalogue of precise details and information. Undeterred by Boudiaf's death, he had continued to express reservations about the cancellation of elections and had urged the authorities to enter into negotiations with the FIS. On 13 July 1993 he had published an open letter calling on insurgents to lay down their weapons. Moreover, Merbah was behind the creation of the Hakim, a secret cell of high-ranking army officers who were not only determined to root out high-level corruption, but were also opposed to the strategy of repression and chaos favoured by hardliners such as Mohammed Lamari.[42] H stood for 'honneur' (honour), A for 'armée' (army) and K for 'Kasdi Merbah', and this allegiance, more than anything else, was why Merbah was liquidated. In 1997 Hakim became the underground Algerian Movement of Free Officers (MAOL) which, as mentioned above, continued to expose human-rights abuses and corruption within the regime.

One week after Merbah's death Islamists in political asylum in Germany sent a fax to the Associated Press in Bonn claiming that they had learned from reliable sources that military security agents were behind the killing: 'It is part of a junta plot to liquidate high-level opposition politicians who challenge its savage policies against the people.' On 23 August, two thousand people attended his funeral in Martyrs' Square in the national cemetery of El-Alia. As the funeral cortège set off from the family home, his widow, Fatima, her head covered by a white shawl as a sign of mourning, told the waiting crowd that Chadli Bendjedid was the murderer since it was he who had led Algeria to the present chaos.

Like Boudiaf's assassination, Merbah's death turned the spotlight back on to power struggles within the regime. Rumours began to spread about the existence of a shadowy elite death squad, the so-called 'Unit 192'. Recruited from the army and the gendarmerie, this unit of two hundred men was the praetorian guard of the army inner circle. With the number signifying the month and year of the January 1992 coup d'état, its purpose was to eliminate enemies within and without through 'dirty tricks'.

Questions were also beginning to be asked about who exactly was behind the GIA. From the beginning, the secret services knew that their most precious weapon in the war on terror was intelligence. They were painfully aware that they had little information on the names and identities of the thousands of young men who had taken to the hills after 1992. To remedy this lack of hard intelligence the DRS created a false *maquis* in Ténès to the west of Algiers in order to infiltrate the armed groups from the inside. In the same vein, on 10 March 1994 the secret services engineered a prison break-out from Tazoult in the Aurès Mountains. Thousands escaped but amongst them were many double agents with the brief to sow confusion, prevent any rapprochement between GIA and ex-FIS leaders and ferment civil war.

■ ■ ■

On 10 July 1993 Nezzar, who was known to be suffering from serious vascular problems, stood down as defence minister, although he stayed on as a member of the five-man Haut Comité d'Etat. His replacement was General Liamin Zeroual, who was brought out of early retirement. Born in Batna in 1941, a veteran of the war of liberation, Zeroual had left his post as deputy chief of staff in 1989 because of political differences with Chadli, later serving briefly as ambassador to Romania. He did not have blood on his hands from October 1988 nor was he involved in the anti-FIS repression, and he was thus seen to represent something of a clean break. In terms of policy he was thought to favour some form of dialogue with the armed insurgents, a view which quickly brought him into conflict with the hardliner Mohammed Lamari who was named as army chief of staff.

The political uncertainties were also matched by uncertainties over economic policy. Belaid Abdesselam, a diehard socialist and the brains behind the industrialization programme of the 1970s, had been made prime minister by the military leadership in July 1992 and he immediately reversed the liberal polices followed by the previous Ghozali government. Consciously trying to play on the nostalgia for the Boumediène years, he introduced protectionism, austerity and a war economy. Drastically reducing imports and firmly opposing debt rescheduling, he was also adamant that Boudiaf had been wrong about corruption. The figures had been exaggerated and anyway the real culprits were the liberal reformers not the traditional military establishment.

Officials at the IMF, World Bank and European Commission soon became exasperated by Abdesselam's unwillingness to accept the rigours of the market, especially when he suspended the key articles of the April 1990 law on credit and money which had opened up the country to foreign investment. Just one year into his premiership and the statistics made very grim reading with inflation at 30 per cent, unemployment at 20 per cent and industrial growth in the first quarter of 1993, 7.5 per cent down on the same period in 1992. Faced with howls of protests from political parties, trade unions and business leaders alike, he was forced to stand down in August 1993, his policies an ignominious failure.

His replacement was Redha Malek, born in Batna, who enacted a brutal shift back to economic liberalism. A veteran of the Evian talks in 1962 and well known in international circles as a former ambassador to Paris, London, Moscow and Washington, Malek had been a key intermediary in the release of American diplomats taken hostage in Iran after the 1979 revolution and had formed a lasting relationship with Warren Christopher, then under-secretary of state in the Carter administration and now secretary of state under Bill Clinton. Through these contacts Malek sought to rebuild bridges with the IMF as the new government tried to grasp the nettle of the national debt. Just servicing this sum ate up a staggering $9 billion of the country's $11 billion exports, but the IMF made it clear that it would only help with debt rescheduling if the regime finally opened up the country to the global economy. On these grounds Malek's premiership was a decisive turning point in post-independence Algeria. Despite its brevity – his tenure lasted a mere seven months – this was the moment when Boumediène-style socialism was finally consigned to the dustbin of history. From now on there would be no turning back from the free market, no matter how painful the consequences.

As the government got to grips with the IMF strictures Malek tried to seize the initiative through a major workshop on 14 September 1993, gathering together the country's bankers, business people, trade unionists and repre-sentatives of farming, tourism and building. His aim was to find some sort of consensus and in the opening session all speakers urged an orderly transition to a liberal economy. For example, the desperate need for raw materials and spares for old machinery meant that much industry was operating at only 50 per cent capacity.

But if the government recognized that the best way of defeating terrorism was to give economic hope to the young, it also stressed the need to win militarily. The Haut Conseil de Sécurité met on 15 September, the first time since Chadli had resigned, and as a demonstration of strength the meeting was accompanied by a crackdown. Teachers sympathetic to the armed groups were purged and a hundred magistrates suspended because they had voiced doubts about the special anti-terrorist courts. Riot police also swamped the streets of the major cities.

In tandem with this economic and military strategy Malek sought out help from France. He held talks with French ministers in June 1993 in the first visit to Paris by a member of the Haut Conseil d'Etat (HCE), warning France of the impact of the crisis on its Algerian community. Malek also looked for closer security coordination with Tunisia and Egypt as he stressed that in the war on terror 'fear now had to change sides'.

Despite Malek's initiatives the higher echelons of the regime knew that they lacked legitimacy in the eyes of large numbers of Algerians. They knew too that in theory at least the rule of the HCE was scheduled to be wound up at the end of January 1994. On 25 and 26 January 1994, therefore, a two-day national conference in Algiers, trumpeted as an initiative towards national reconciliation, tried to find a way out of the impasse and usher in a transition process. However, since the proceedings were boycotted by all the major parties, it was an abject failure, leading neither to the establishment of a new regime nor the nomination of a new president.

Rumours abounded that Bouteflika was offered the post – reportedly refusing on the grounds that he would be too constrained by the army elite – but this only served to underline the manner in which Algerian politics had become an eternal merry-go-round, peopled by the same faces and the same alliances jockeying for power and influence. The total failure of the political elite to connect with the populace was one of the root causes of the ongoing crisis. For the vast majority politics was seen as a closed game, restricted to a small set of clans fuelled by self-interest.

So, as in January 1992 when the country was confronted with a constitutional vacuum, the Haut Conseil de Sécurité was trundled out to confer the presidency, this time on to Zeroual, on 31 January 1994. Once again, therefore, the head of state was from the army and from the beginning Zeroual was careful to combine the presidency with the position of minister of defence. Economically his new government, led initially by Malek who was replaced on 11 April by Mokdad Sifi, continued with the IMF austerity reforms, desperate to make the country a willing participant in the global free market, the result being the devaluation of the dinar and mammoth price rises of basic foodstuffs and fuel.

The other major challenge facing Zeroual was the Islamist violence, especially as the armed groups were determined to prove their staying power. In June 1994 dozens of conscripts were killed in clashes all over the country: at Telgah, fifty miles south of Oran; in Ténès, on the coast seventy-five miles west of Algiers; and around the port of Jijel, nearly two hundred miles to the east.

As the bloodshed continued the regime became dominated by two lines of thinking: those who supported some form of dialogue, led by Zeroual, and those who supported military eradication, led by Mohammed Lamari. Of course, between the two poles there were considerable points of common interest. Both men wanted to maintain their privileges. Both were fearful of reprisals if they lost their grip on power. Nonetheless the two men became involved in a struggle for power that was inextricably linked to the course of the war against the Islamist guerrillas. However, deciphering the relative strengths of the two camps was never easy as the regime was dominated by a series of complex and shifting clan networks determined by family, region and personal friendship. The army, for example, was riven with divisions, especially during the period 1995 to 1997 as the regional commanders – mostly veterans from the war of liberation – were replaced by younger officers. This made the contest for promotion into a trial of strength as both Zeroual and Mohammed Lamari built up their bases of patronage, support and influence. In the same fashion the FLN, which was trying to assert itself as an independent political force, was composed of divergent currents with one group much closer to the army and another much more sympathetic to the FIS. Then finally there were the bureaucrats and technocrats within the government and industry, some of whom supported conciliation whilst others favoured all-out war.

Within these power struggles any sign of movement in terms of contacts between the regime and the FIS fuelled rumour and speculation. When in September 1994 Madani and Belhadj were moved from prison and put under house arrest, this was interpreted as a significant move, signalling that Zeroual was in the ascendancy and the way was open for dialogue. But when these talks finally broke down in November 1994 the hardliners seemingly regained the upper hand. The minister of the interior, Abderrahmane Mezziane Cherif, called for the elimination of the insurgents and set about arming civilian groups on the ground to resist terrorism.

■ ■ ■

A man is stopped by a roadblock. The hooded men ask him if he supports the government or the GIA. He replies 'the government' so they cut his right ear off.

Shortly after, he is stopped by another roadblock of hooded men. They ask him the same question. When he replies 'the GIA' they cut his left ear off. The following day he goes to the doctor, who asks him which part of his face he wants sewn up first. 'My mouth, so I cannot speak,' he replies.

Q. What is the difference between the GIA and the AIS?
A. The GIA will cut your throat whilst the AIS will give you a choice between a knife and a bullet.

(Two Algerian jokes circa 1994)

Like the macabre observation that the average assassination takes 2.7 seconds, such gallows humour peppered conversation as everyday life became a nerve-wracking experience. Tension was everywhere. People knew that even the most innocuous activity could have fatal consequences. Survival might depend on how you greeted people. Was it in French, Arabic or Berber? Did it include any religious references? It might depend too on wearing the veil or a beard, going to the mosque, and not listening to Western pop music or watching French satellite television. In Chlef, east of Algiers, the local population took down their satellite dishes after graffiti appeared threatening death to anybody caught watching pornographic French films. Equally, some Westernized women chose to wear the veil as a form of protection against attacks on the street.

Memoirs, letters, personal accounts, Merzak Allouache's remarkable 1993 *Bab el-Oued City* filmed on location in Algiers: all testify to the edgy atmos-phere that now invaded every aspect of daily life.[43] As the environment around them became dangerous and unpredictable, nervous exhaustion became etched into people's faces. They did not feel safe. Each day was filled with trepidation. Constantly alert – their eyes would dart furtively from side to side to assess any suspicious behaviour – people became taut, tensed and watchful. They avoided public places. Parks became deserted and at school pick-up times children were hurried away. Remembering that 'routine is the friend of the terrorist', people began to follow basic precautions. Police officers, civil servants and politicians now checked for bombs under their cars, varied the times they left for and returned from work and continually checked in the rear-view mirror to see if they were being followed.

The psychological impact of this fear was enormous. Huge numbers took tranquillizers to cope with the stress, and the weeks and months slipped by without memory as people were absorbed by the rigour of simple survival. To hang on to life was a feat in itself, the single organizing principle of existence. The nights were the worst. Again and again people talked about the constant dread brought on by dusk. Lying awake, counting away the hours, they felt a rising terror about what horrors possibly lay in store. As Mourad, a fifty-six-year-old veteran of the war of liberation, living in retirement in the suburbs of Algiers, wrote to a friend in 1994:

> I am afraid, afraid of dying with my throat slit ... I am fearful for my sons, for my daughter, for my wife, for myself, for my brothers and their children. I am afraid of my shadow, of a stranger's look ... of the telephone ringing, of a knock at the door, of roadblocks, of cars that follow me or cross in front of me, of the market, the tobacco seller, the street. And at night! It is a circus. Insomnia! At the slightest noise, we jump up.[44]

In large part this fear was derived from the fact that the violence had an elusive, intangible, unknowable quality about it. It had no moral compass, no rules, no boundaries. It could happen anywhere and at any time. Moreover, it was a violence that became normal very quickly. So it was normal to walk past dead bodies on the street. It was normal to hear gunfire at night or to see walking wounded, blood mixed with bone splinters bubbling out of their mouths. And it was normal to see children looking for bloodstains on the street or playing games of 'cops against terrorists'.

As these scenes became commonplace during 1993 everyday life was militarized. Daily routines were punctuated by the sight of the police, flanked by sniffer dogs, automatic arms at the ready, conducting routine security checks. Invariably stopping any car with young men aboard, particularly those with short hair and a beard, they frisked each passenger, checking identity papers and carefully inspecting each vehicle. The landscape too was transformed. Trees by roads were cut back and a security fence erected alongside the Algiers to Oran railway line to prevent ambushes.

The grisly reality of day-to-day survival gave rise to a mordant humour that was powerfully expressed in visual form through the work of Slim, Karim Mahfouf and Ali Dilem. Slim, with his cartoon character Bouzid, was already well established by the 1980s but Mahfouf and Dilem were a new generation of caricaturists. Both born in 1967, both deeply marked by October 1988, their first cartoons appeared in the press in 1990 and thereafter their drawings – savage, biting, unforgiving – formed a visual commentary on the unfolding violence. Mahfouf went under the pseudonym Gyps and within a series of political comic books – *FIS and Love, Algé-Rien* and *L'Algérie, c'est comme ça* – he presented an unsparing portrait of contemporary Algeria, a world of horrors where ordinary people struggled to survive cruel generals, bomb-wielding bearded terrorists and bloated bureaucrats, all intent on inflicting misery, misery and more misery. In one cartoon, for example, a well-dressed older man tells an adolescent that 'young people have all their lives in front of them'. To which the youth replies: 'Exactly, that is our problem.'[45]

Mahfouf was forced into exile in France in 1995, but these cartoons have since become the basis of a provocative stand-up act charting contemporary Algerian history. Likewise, Dilem produced a series of satirical images that set out to denounce both the army regime and the armed Islamists. Condemned to death by one of the GIA groups, he was also ceaselessly harassed by the authorities, who understood the power of his images to articulate ordinary anger. But despite these threats Dilem carried on regardless. For him the ability to attack the regime and the armed groups through political cartoons was essential in the battle for human rights and freedom of expression. He had to bear witness even if this meant death or prison.

'The Position of the Press in Algeria', by Gyps. The cartoon is a comment on the way in which basic press freedoms have been threatened by both armed Islamist groups and the regime.

'Algeria: Hope Remains', by Slim, an ironic comment on the savagery of the violence in Algeria in the mid-1990s.

If these cartoons testified to the reality of war, the regime itself remained in a state of denial. No official casualty statistics were published for fear of panicking the population. However, by July 1994 French intelligence put the estimate as high as fifteen people a day.[46] The Algerian press tried to downplay talk of such figures, with *Le Matin* producing an official balance sheet for 1994 on 4 March 1995. Yet, even taking into account the deliberate under-estimation, it was still a chilling portrait of a country falling to pieces, with 6,388 civilians killed, including 122 FLN veterans, 101 teachers and 76 mayors, and 2,289 wounded, as well as more than 200 hold-ups and 13,000 armed robberies. Alongside this there was the huge material cost as bomb attacks and arson seriously damaged 915 primary schools, 7 research institutes, 3 universities and 224 town halls.

As the bloodshed worsened, civil society groups and parties tried to mobilize against the violence. On 22 March 1994 women in Algiers marched to defend their rights against Islamist attacks. Similarly, on 9 May 1994, the anniversary of the 1945 Sétif uprising, thirty thousand FLN and Hamas supporters, many carrying roses aloft, demonstrated in favour of peace and dialogue. Such protests were testament to the stoicism of the Algerian people, their capacity for physical and mental resilience, which was also being tested by the impact of the IMF reforms. Cooking oil, meat, semolina and basic medicines were almost unobtainable for ordinary people, who came to feel abandoned on all sides by the government. Some neighbourhoods began to resemble ghost towns and people realized that they could only rely on themselves to survive.

In all this mayhem one place of relative calm was Tizi-Ouzou in Kabylia, fifty miles to the east of Algiers. On the streets the bars were full and young women walked down the main street wearing skirts. Alcohol was sold in restaurants and shops, although visitors wrapped their bottles in newspapers just to be on the safe side. At weekends hotels and discotheques turned away customers fed up with the empty streets in the rest of the country. Property prices doubled from 1993 to 1994 as people sought to escape from the violence elsewhere. Of course, beneath the surface there was an atmosphere of anger and suspicion. Most Kabyles mistrusted both the armed groups and the regime, wishing a plague on both their houses, as they closely followed the unfolding conflict.

By the autumn of 1994 the GIA had suffered significant reverses. As the security forces became more skilled in dealing with the threat on the ground, Al-Afghani's successor Sherif Gousmi was killed on 26 September. After much internal fighting, the new national GIA emir was Djamel Zitouni, a thirty-year-old son of a chicken farmer. How he had risen to prominence was shrouded in mystery. Furthermore, he had little knowledge of the Qur'an, and on these grounds his legitimacy was contested. However, Zitouni was ruthless in liquidating his opponents as he vowed to move the holy war on to another stage. To this end he issued two communiqués on 30 and 31 October announcing his intention to attack France.

■   ■   ■

At 5.15 p.m. on 26 December 1994 at Marseille airport, French elite forces stormed an Air France A300 airbus that had been hijacked by a four-man GIA cell fifty-four hours earlier in Algiers. The men, aged between twenty and twenty-five, were trapped in a pincer movement as two masked policemen entered the cockpit. As the four Algerians rushed towards them firing their Kalashnikovs and automatic pistols, fifteen commandoes blasted open the rear door before throwing down flash grenades. All four Algerians were killed whilst the 170 passengers slid down the emergency chute. The whole operation lasted ten minutes.

It was a spectacular end to a series of events that had begun at Houari Boumediène airport in Algiers on Christmas Eve. There the four men, disguised as Air Algérie cleaners and with the obvious complicity of ground staff, had slipped on to flight 8969 shortly before it was due to depart for Paris Orly at 11.15 a.m. More than 240 people, including 40 French citizens, were on the plane as the hijackers, calm and collected, began asking for their passports. An Algerian policeman was taken to the front door and shot as he begged: 'Don't kill me! I'm married, I have a child.' A Vietnamese diplomat, Bui Giang To, was also killed. The following day Yannick Beugnet, the French embassy cook, was executed after the deadline for a decision to allow the plane to leave passed. All three bodies were thrown from the plane to show that the hijackers meant business. In the meantime the men, who called each other by numbers, kept reciting Muslim prayers and passed round scarves so that women could cover their heads. They also reassured the Algerian passengers that they only wanted to terrorize the foreigners. The hijackers insisted on the immediate release of Madani and Belhadj from house arrest and more fuel to fly on to France.

As the negotiations dragged on into Christmas Day, the French prime minister, Edouard Balladur, was worried that the Algerians were not making a serious attempt to end the crisis and, in a move to hurry events on, he offered help in the form of commandos on stand-by in Majorca. However, the Algerian authorities were reticent. Acceptance of aid from the former colonial power would be humiliating and they did not drop their refusal until midnight on Sunday.[47] Coaxed on to French soil, the plane arrived at Marseille at 3.33 a.m., whereupon the French took control of negotiations and their special forces fine-tuned their plan for a rescue operation.

On 27 December the Algerian interior ministry claimed that the GIA cell leader was Abdallah Yahia.[48] From Les Eucalyptes, Algiers' most rundown neighbourhood and an infamous GIA fiefdom, Yahia was not an emir but a trusted lieutenant with a ruthless reputation. His group, known as El-Mouakioune Bi Eddima ('Those Who Sign with Blood'), had taken the lead in killing foreigners, including five Frenchmen. Ferhat Mehenni, a Kabyle singer and one of the founders of the Rassemblement pour la Culture et la Démocratie (RCD), had been one of the hostages. In an interview with *Libération* he was adamant that all talk of the release of Madani and Belhadj was a ruse; the hijackers' real aim was to explode the aircraft over Paris or crash it into the Eiffel Tower.[49] Twenty-four hours later five Roman Catholic missionaries from the Pères Blancs (White Fathers), four French and one Belgian, were assassinated in Tizi-Ouzou in a revenge attack.

As the war came to France, the violence began to have an eerie echo of the original war of liberation, an irony recognized by Ben Bella on French television in 1994:

> When they speak about *ratissages* [counter-terrorist operations involving combing terrain for insurgents], about terrorists ... that brings back droll memories, those who knew this situation thirty years ago, to hear the vocabulary of General Massu or General Salan reproduced.[50]

The trauma and dynamics of the war of liberation were at the nerve centre of the violence of the 1990s. As the French had, the authorities tried to sanitize the conflict by talking a law and order problem. Like the FLN in the 1950s, the insurgents were criminalized and their strength continually downplayed. And like the French the official communiqués talked about final pockets of resistance about to be mopped up. Beyond this, the authorities, in a bid to take the moral high ground, produced dossiers of Islamist violence for journalists, just as the French had done with FLN terrorism.

The counter-insurgency tactics too were modelled on those of the French. During the original Battle of Algiers, Paul Léger, a French officer specializing in counter-terrorist strategy, used FLN prisoners converted to the French cause. By sending them back into the FLN he successfully infiltrated the liberation struggle and turned Algerians against themselves, leading to large-scale purges amongst the internal resistance.[51] Now the DRS adopted exactly the same strategy. As with Léger and the FLN, their aim was to manipulate the GIA groups from the inside. Equally, in the same way as the French between 1954 and 1962, the authorities authorized the formation of self-defence militias to protect villages from sun-down to sun-up, many of them war of liberation veterans who, in their ragged trousers and tattered boots, were armed with old French service rifles.

At the core of these tactics was an argument about the meaning of November 1954. The regime claimed to be defending the true values of the war of liberation against traitors and hence stigmatized the armed groups in terms of the ultimate betrayers, arguing that they were led by the sons of *harkis*.[52] Leïla Aslaoui, for example, maintained that Soltani's Islamist doctrine, by making a distinction between those who died for faith and those who died as a consequence of personal greed, liberated *harkis* from a guilt complex. Free to cast off feelings of culpability, their sons had now launched a war of revenge on the post-colonial state.[53]

Conversely, the armed groups attacked the army regime as the new colonialists. Taking the line that the regime was fatally infected by communism and idolatry, they spoke in contemptuous terms of the army leadership as 'Lacoste's corporals', those who had benefited from promotion under Robert Lacoste as governor general before joining up with the liberation struggle at the very last minute. As one AIS pamphlet stated in April 1995:

> The bombing has returned. The destruction is going on now. Firing is everywhere. The SAS are back. The massacres have restarted. Ill treatment of citizens is a daily routine. In short, all the elements of the colonialist scenario have returned, updated, through the actions of 'Lacoste's corporals'.[54]

The groups also threw words like 'terrorist' back in the regime's face. As one piece of graffiti in the GIA fiefdom Les Eucalyptes proclaimed: 'If we are terrorists then jihad is terrorism.' Significantly too, they made it clear that it was the men with the guns in Algeria and not FIS politicians in exile who had political and religious legitimacy. They did not want to repeat the mistake of the original war of liberation when the army of the frontiers won out over the internal resistance.

As this battle of memories and words was played out, the war on the ground became invisible. Huge human-rights abuses were being carried out by insurgents and the government but it was usually impossible for Amnesty International and Human Rights Watch to collect the evidence on the ground because the Algerian authorities declined to cooperate.[55] Given this lack of images and hard facts, the award-winning BBC documentary *Algeria's Hidden War*, produced by Phil Rees and broadcast on BBC2 on 19 November 1994, was enormously important.[56] Shot in the battle zone, it was the first to penetrate the world of the armed groups. Indeed, with the GIA and AIS working together in this area, it was clear that whole swathes of the countryside had been abandoned by the army, as the armed groups set up their own roadblocks, occasionally disturbed by the overflight of a helicopter.

The key to the documentary's success was the researcher Abdelhamid Aoun. He obtained the names of contacts in Algiers from FIS representatives in London. Then, after strict vetting, these contacts organized the trip to Chlef, a large town 125 miles west of Algiers. There, after following a car another fifty miles to the heart of the Islamist insurgency, the 'liberated areas' high in the mountains that stretch between Ténès and Mostaganem, Aoun was given a unique view of the war from the Islamist side:

> We saw a bomb factory full of explosive powder, detonators, batteries and timers.

The bombs produced are deadly, programmed to cause maximum damage. The bomb maker fills them with pellets in canisters. The material he uses is either stolen or bought in local shops. The fighters pride themselves on their self-sufficiency.[57]

The final documentary contained remarkable footage of the AIS near Blida not only making bombs, but also manning a makeshift hospital and faxing death threats to opponents in the beleaguered cities. Computers stored information on their military strength and the enemies they planned to murder. From these mountain camps, the hundred or so fighters, armed with shotguns, knives and some automatic weapons, maintained direct contact with the leadership in Algiers, insisting that no decisions could be made without consulting them. Importantly the documentary also explored the clash of ideas at the heart of the conflict, containing interviews with Islamists and government supporters. By any measure it was a remarkable achievement, getting inside the conflict and escaping the tight controls of the Algerian media. Predictably, however, the authorities were incandescent. Aoun's Algiers office was trashed and he was forced to seek political asylum in Britain, in fear for his life.

■   ■   ■

How to stop the cycle of violence? The internationally respected Sant'Egidio community in Rome, a Catholic liberal movement that emerged from the fringes of Europe's 1968 protests, was dedicated to promoting cooperation among religions and resolving conflict. It already had an impressive record in Mozambique, rebuilding dialogue where it had been lost. In this spirit the community invited all the political parties and the government to a peace conference on 21 and 22 November 1994 aimed at finding a way out of the crisis. The government and the RCD and Ettahadi (formerly PAGS) parties refused, but Aït Ahmed for the FFS, Ben Bella for the MDA, Abdelhamid Mehri for the FLN, Louisa Hanoune of the Trotskyist Parti des Travailleurs, Abdallah Djaballah of Ennadha, Ali Yahia Abdenour of the Algerian League of Human Rights and, perhaps most significantly, Anwar Haddam for the FIS all agreed.

What followed was a set of long and arduous negotiations. In large part this was because the FIS representatives wanted to make a distinction between what they saw as legitimate violence and terrorist violence by the state. However, eventually all found a measure of consensus and 13 January 1995 saw the announcement of a common platform, the so-called Rome Platform. Within it the signatories reaffirmed their belief in the message of November 1954, namely the restoration of an Algerian state, sovereign, democratic and based on the principles of Islam. Thereafter, they underlined their rejection of violence; respect for human rights as outlined by the United Nations; belief in freedom of worship; and support for the removal of the army from politics. Berberity was also recognized as a constituent element of the national identity along with Islam and Arabness. Finally, all called for new parliamentary elections and re-legalization of the FIS, thus getting the FIS to recognize the principle of political pluralism for the first time.

Unsurprisingly, the regime immediately rejected the document on the grounds that the other parties had allied themselves with the FIS and that any negotiations held under non-Algerian auspices were illegitimate.[58] The GIA groups too were vehemently opposed, arguing that it was a sell-out. In France President Mitterrand was initially sympathetic, but his right-wing government, led by Balladur, was hostile. This failure to take a strong line meant that the initiative quickly became a dead letter in the European Union. By the summer it took on the allure of a huge lost opportunity, especially once the violence spilt over again into France on an even grander scale.

This violence began on 11 July 1995 when Abdelbaki Sahraoui, the local imam, was shot dead outside his brightly painted mosque in a former garage on the otherwise grubby Rue Myhra in the 18th arrondissement of Paris. One of the founders of the FIS, Sahraoui had attacked the GIA groups as deviating from the true principles of Islam through racketeering and trafficking. The finger of suspicion, therefore, was immediately pointed at the GIA.

Whoever was behind it, his murder was a body blow for French policy. During the previous two years Sahraoui had become a vital bridgehead for the French authorities who were prepared to allow pro-FIS networks to organize openly, so long as they did not stoke up the religious demands of the French Muslims. Such a strategy kept the social peace but also made it easier to track Islamists by keeping their activities above ground. However, 1994 witnessed a radicalization of attitudes amongst a small minority. French citizens of Moroccan and Algerian origin were behind an attack on tourists in Marrakech in August, and French, Italian and German police forces dismantled a series of networks supplying weapons to the armed groups in Algeria. Meanwhile the GIA emir Zitouni, seething with anger at the hijacking, vowed revenge with one underground pro-GIA paper, *Al-Ansar*, portraying an exploding Eiffel Tower superimposed on to a map of Paris. Worryingly for the French secret services, he sought recruits amongst young French citizens of North

African origin with some going to Afghanistan along a well-oiled transnational network.

On 25 July a bomb at the busy Saint-Michel Métro station on the left bank in the heart of the Latin Quarter of Paris killed ten and left a further fifty-seven wounded. Following the attack Paris was gripped by panic. Everywhere on the underground the fear was tangible. Schools, railway stations, museums and popular tourist spots were all put on high alert. When further devices were found, including a pressure cooker packed with explosives and metal debris placed in a dustbin bag on the TGV railway line north of Lyon, troops were brought on to the Parisian streets. Throughout August and September not a week went by without the police recording the number of people they had stopped, searched and detained.

The terror campaign lasted three months, ending with the death of Khaled Kelkal, a boyish-looking twenty-four-year-old French-educated Algerian who left his fingerprints on the bomb near Lyon. Shot dead by police – footage caught officers finishing him off on the ground – Kelkal's story, much like those of the 7 July bombers in Britain ten years later, led to much soul-searching in France. Why had he done this? What had transformed him into a person at war with French society? Unsurprisingly the story was one of a lack of opportunities. Born in Algeria in 1971 but raised in France from the age of two, Kelkal had grown up in a poor suburb of Vaulx-en-Vélin near Lyon, where he had found it difficult to integrate socially and economically. For him the French Republic might proclaim liberty, equality and fraternity but the reality was very different. In a remarkable inter-view, given to a German sociologist three years before the bombing, Kelkal explained:

> I had the capacity to succeed but there was no place for me because I said to myself: total integration is impossible; I can't forget my culture and eat pork. They [his classmates] had never seen an Arab in their class. As they said when they got to know me: 'You're the exception.' At secondary school, in my class, there were only rich students.[59]

After school he had drifted into petty crime. In jail, however, he rediscovered his religion. On his release he went back to Algeria where he contacted the GIA and underwent military training. Back in France he recruited a small group of like-minded Muslims, sons of North African immigrants, who wanted to strike back at the former colonizer.

Unlike Kelkal, most citizens of Algerian origin resisted the pull of GIA-style terrorism. Even so, for Areski Dahmani, president of *France-Plus*, an organization committed to promoting the integration of French people of immigrant descent, the example of Kelkal made him pessimistic about the future. He feared that a small minority would see him as a martyr, believing that the lesson of the Kelkal affair was that 'French society is not working. More and more people are excluded from participation. Unless there is dramatic change, we could fall into the abyss of civil war within a few years.'[60]

Kelkal's story also pointed to an underground world of Islamist networks which ran from France through Bosnia to Afghanistan. The equipment for the Paris bombing was bought in Brussels, whilst Rachid Ramda, an Algerian originally granted asylum in London and linked with the Finsbury Park mosque, was accused of controlling the GIA cells in France. For this reason the French authorities became involved in a long battle to have Ramada extradited to France to stand trial.

Yet, as always, nothing was as obvious as it seemed. Two years later, a former agent in the DRS, known as Joseph, told the London *Observer* that the bombs were partly the handiwork of the Algerian secret services.[61] By manipulating the GIA, it wanted to galvanize French public opinion against the Islamists and turn the regime of the new president, Jacques Chirac, away from the Rome Accords. If so, it was a spectacular success. A poll published on 23 October showed that 91 per cent of the French supported the government crackdown.[62]

■ ■ ■

With the violence spilling over into France, Western governments greeted the prospect of presidential elections, already promised by Zeroual in November 1994, with trepidation lest they led to a further escalation of bloodshed. However, Zeroual knew that he had a fundamental problem of legitimacy. He had to re-launch some sort of democratic process in the hope that it would yield the mandate necessary to efface the memory of the 1992 putsch.

The elections, dubbed by the government media the 'elections of hope', were set for 16 November 1995. Amongst the few participants were the 'moderate Islamic' party Hamas led by Mahfoud Nahnah and the RCD of Saïd Sadi. Both opposed the Rome platform. Both saw the elections too as an opportunity to establish themselves in the absence of the FIS, FLN and FFS as the main Islamic and secularist parties. The fourth candidate was the Islamic liberal Nourredine Boukrouh of the Party of Algerian Renewal.

Tens of thousands of reservists guarded polling booths as the GIA promised to disrupt the campaign with attacks. The foreign media were allowed to cover the election but only in Algiers. From the outset it was clear that there was only going to be one winner: Zeroual. Yet his campaign struck a genuine chord with Algerians who wanted an end to the violence. Pledging to be a president 'of dialogue and openness', he promised to ensure that 'no Algerian will be excluded' from the political process; he would be 'the president of all Algerians'. Moreover, Algerians concluded that in all likelihood the only way out would be through an insider who understood the regime and might reform it from inside.

Officially the turnout was nearly 75 per cent (unofficial sources estimated 50 per cent) and Zeroual was declared the winner with 60 per cent of votes. Nahnah was credited with 25 per cent and Sadi 10 per cent. Boukrouh got a tiny 3.8 per cent. Despite evidence of vote-tampering, Zeroual's opponents conceded that the result was a significant glimmer of light, suggesting that ordinary people were yearning for a return to some sort of normality. Rabah Kebir, the exiled FIS leader, might claim that 'nothing had changed' with the ballot but the Sant'Egidio mediators disagreed, stating: 'The wish for peace was visible. It is a fact that all parties, winners, defeated and partisans of abstention, must take into account.'[63]

On 27–28 November Zeroual received a further boost when Algeria signed the Barcelona Declaration between the EU and twelve southern and eastern Mediterranean states. The initiative was intended to foster political, economic and social ties between the EU and the southern Mediterranean. While recognizing the need to respect human rights and the rule of law and democracy, the final Declaration underlined the security aspects of the agreement and the need to fight against drugs, organized crime and terrorism. The accord thus gave the regime a measure of much-needed support on the grounds that Islamist terrorism had replaced the Cold War as the main threat to regional security.[64]

The question now was what Zeroual would do with his new-found legitimacy. The outpouring of emotion on the streets was genuine enough. The people saw Zeroual as a figure of hope. They saw him as the new strong man. They wanted to believe that Zeroual could bring a full stop to the violence. Tragically, however, there would be no full stops in Algeria.

CHAPTER SEVEN

The Algerian Question

If you did not study during Boumediène's time then you will never study.
If you did not make money during Chadli's time then you will never
* make money.*
If you did not die during Zeroual's time then you will never die.

(ALGERIAN JOKE CIRCA 1998)

IN 1958 THE Paris-based Editions de Minuit published *La Question*, Henri Alleg's harrowing account of the cruelties suffered at the hands of the French army during the Battle of Algiers. Jewish, a member of the Algerian Communist Party (PCA) and a journalist on the left-leaning daily *Alger Républicain*, Alleg was exactly the type of subversive intellectual the paratroopers of General Massu's 10th Division detested.[1] Accused of aiding the FLN, Alleg was picked up in June 1957 along with his friend and party comrade Maurice Audin, a PhD student at Algiers university.[2] Both were taken to El-Biar, one of the infamous detention centres, but although Audin would never be seen again – one of the many thousands of disappeared still not accounted for even today – Alleg himself survived. Displaying great physical courage, he withstood electric shocks to the hands and mouth, injections with truth drugs and various forms of water torture, including one instance where his head was repeatedly ducked until he was half drowned.[3]

His story was a savage indictment of the French methods, principally because he showed that torture was not an isolated incident but an integral part of the counter-terrorist strategy. The fact that Alleg's account was published by Editions de Minuit, founded during the Nazi occupation and an icon of Resistance values, emphasized that the war in Algeria was perverting

French democracy. In cataloguing in detail the full horror of human rights abuses Alleg was disentangling truth from lies, highlighting the discrepancy between the Fourth Republic's high ideals and base practice. What made Alleg's words so horrific and so emotional was his explicit parallel between France's violation of Algeria and Nazi Germany's violation of France.[4]

The book provoked a major international scandal. Selling some 65,000 copies before being banned by the government, *La Question*, translated into numerous languages, brought the issue of French abuses to the attention of the world. Through the power of his eyewitness account Alleg argued that although the French might win via torture in the short term, in the long term such methods brought only a pyrrhic victory because the French were losing Muslim hearts and minds. Alleg confronted French people with a basic question: were they prepared to stand aside and allow torture to be carried out in their name?

By 1996 the Algerian regime was bogged down in a post-colonial conflict every inch as bitter and violent as the original colonial war. But, as evidence about the massive human rights violations grew by the day, through organizations such as Amnesty International as well as a series of eyewitness accounts published in France and on the internet, the parallel with the French paratroopers' actions was no deterrent to the Algerian perpetrators.[5] On the contrary they used exactly the same justifications: torture was the only way to defeat an invisible enemy. Like the French thirty-eight years before, Algerians were obliged to grapple with their own questions: What were the moral limitations of the battle against terrorism? Was it being fought at the cost of fundamental human rights?

In the aftermath of the 1995 elections some Algerians likened the moustachioed Zeroual to the cartoon character Zorro: a strong man whose sense of justice, allied to his inside knowledge of the Algerian system, would lead him to reach out and bring an honourable end to the violence. Others, as with Boudiaf, made the parallel with de Gaulle and certainly his campaign posters had portrayed him as a benevolent figure, motivated by the search for national unity. For a time all the talk was of the need to pull together in order to extract the country from its pitiless morass. So the new government included the FLN as well as Hamas.

For all this optimism, Zeroual's political capital quickly began to evaporate. On the one hand the economy continued to spiral downwards. April to June 1996 saw a rescheduling of debt to France, Italy and a number of private banks as well as a significant reduction in French aid.[6] For the ordinary population life just got harder and harder, with more water shortages and the absence of basic foodstuffs. Around the country the detritus of war was all too evident. The roads were scarred and rutted, whole factories were left burned out while countless towns and villages degenerated into hopeless thoroughfares of rubble and broken concrete. From whatever vantage point you chose, Zeroual's Algeria continued to be a desolate landscape.

At the same time the GIA Islamist groups wanted to demonstrate their power by making Algeria into a bloodbath. To this end the violence became highly concentrated in the *wilaya* of Relizane and in the Mitidja plain. The former was a mountainous region thirty miles to the east of Oran, made up of remote impoverished villages such as Kherarba, Meknassa and Had Chekala, with no electricity or running water, whilst the latter, composed of lush orange groves and rolling wheat fields encircled by mountains, lay between the towns of Médéa, Blida and Boufarik in the rural hinterland forty miles south of Algiers. These two areas bore the brunt of a violence that was blunt, brutal and unsophisticated as hooded groups terrorized the population.[7]

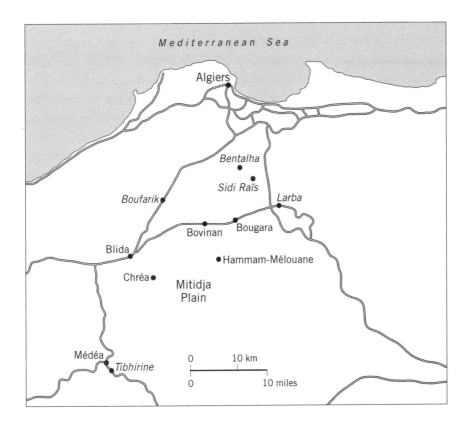

The centre of the violence; place names in italics are the location of massacres.

Ironically, the geographical spread of the killings was a direct result of the success of the counter-insurgency forces on the ground. In 1993 the army and the police had been complacent and vulnerable. They had not grasped how the GIA's local knowledge would transform the rundown streets and alleyways of Algeria's cities into death traps. Three years later the regime had learnt the hard lessons of the guerrilla war.[8] A willingness to deploy a counter-terror offensive every bit as ruthless as the GIA; greater skill in counter-insurgency tactics; the use of former GIA operatives in order to gain vital inside information; the employment of better weapons and technology: all of these factors meant that the infamous ninjas, well paid and well trained, were able to claw back control, pushing back the GIA from its urban fiefdoms into the countryside.[9] They scored a number of significant victories and, although opponents questioned how much this was just propaganda, it was difficult to deny that cumulatively these defeats hit the GIA hard. The regime began to regain the initiative as the GIA's strength was further undermined by the establishment of rural militias in the countryside and the political and military rivalry of the AIS.

At this point, in 1996 and 1997, the focus of the violence moved to the Mitidja plain. This was the jugular vein of the conflict, linking the various GIA groups' mountainous bases in Hamma, Meloua, Bougara, Bouinan and Chréa with what remained of their financial and logistical infrastructures in Algiers. To control Mitidja was to control the GIA's ability to attack the capital.

With hindsight we can see that the GIA threat peaked in 1993. This was the moment when the GIA groups were at their most powerful. Enjoying widespread support, their each successful attack was a moment of supreme exhilaration, a stepping stone on the path to a general victory. In the words of Nesroulah Yous, who lived in the Mitidja throughout the 1990s, at the beginning of the conflict the GIA groups were like fish in water, drawing upon a wide infrastructure of support.[10] There was a strong sense of local identification, proprietal claim even, as the armed young men, 'our men out there', were seen to embody collective and community resistance to the illegal army regime. Three years on and the context was very different. Many of their leaders had been killed. The pulsating energy was gone. No longer were the rebels pushing at an open door. Stasis had set in and each reversal was a sign of the regime's tenacity, its capacity not just for survival but revival. Furthermore, in the eyes of ordinary people the GIA had become tarnished with brutality and gross excess. Although the GIA could still draw recruits from the most dispossessed, the moral and political legitimacy it had enjoyed in 1993 was gone.

The question for the GIA leadership, of course, was how to break out of this impasse. Djamel Zitouni's only answer was violence, violence and more violence but by 1996 this strategy was exhausted. The will to fight was still sustained by raw anger, but beyond these primal emotions it was difficult to see a coordinated plan, a clear political alternative. There was no intelligible strategy beyond the notional one of imposing the caliphate by force, which by 1996 many ordinary Algerians viewed with horror.

As support for the GIA groups diminished, their list of enemies increased in inverse proportion. At the beginning of 1996 a steady stream of communiqués expanded those condemned to death to include families of police and army officers, wives of apostates, conscripts and all those working in the hydrocarbon sectors.[11] The logic of this approach was ultimately one of extermination: all who did not support the GIA were apostates, enemies of God, and had to be liquidated. For this reason the bloodshed that blighted Algeria from 1996 all the way through to spring 1998 was one borne of frustration not euphoria, of weakness not strength. Thwarted, the GIA groups lashed out in all directions. Calling for one last surge to defeat the regime, they pushed the young men around them to action that was ever more extreme. Desperate for victory, the GIA groups unleashed mass murder on civilians.

The upsurge in violence also reflected the deteriorating conditions in the *maquis*. Pinned back in the mountains, life for those in the makeshift camps became very hard. Confronted with the strain of being constantly pursued, bedevilled by problems of communication and arms shortages, suffering from cold and hunger, the GIA groups were under great psychological stress. There was now a steady flow of deserters, taking up the government's offer of clemency in place since February 1995, despite Zitouni's warnings that all deserters would suffer terrible reprisals both to them and their families.

Staving off this defeatist mood became a primary dynamic in *maquis* life. The armed groups, as male societies based upon the cult of the strong, were under constant pressure to assert themselves as fighting men. Fearing that their failure to overthrow the regime would be perceived as weakness, they had to show that they had not capitulated. This led to the search for other ways of expressing their masculinity and the end result was that women and young girls, some as young as fifteen, were kidnapped and raped or forced into temporary marriages, known as *zaouedj el moutaa*.[12] For the young men this was a way of playing out their pent-up frustrations and asserting their power and sexual domination. Women became objects, trophies of war, to be exploited at will. Some were subjected to multiple rape and in many cases then killed; others were forced to cook and clean in the *maquis* camps, in effect becoming bargaining counters to blackmail the local population.

On 10 April 1998 Algerian television broached this subject through a documentary based on harrowing eyewitness accounts. Some claimed this was government propaganda, cynically using these women to blacken the Islamist cause as a whole, but it seemed impossible to deny the basic truth of their accounts or their courage in telling them to the camera. For example, one women, Horra, a mother of eight children, recounted how she was bundled away by three men and then kept hostage for three weeks where she was subjected to repeated sexual and psychological abuse. Another, Djamila, described how she was forced to march for hours before being raped by eight men. We will never know the real number of women who suffered like this because most of the survivors do not want to talk about their ordeal, owing to the shame attached to being raped in Algerian society, particularly in the more conservative rural regions. But it was widespread between 1996 and 1998 and in 2003 an Amnesty International report put the figure as running into the hundreds.[13]

One of the few women who came forward to be interviewed by the Amnesty investigators was twenty-year-old Chérifa Bouteiba. Married and pregnant, she was kidnapped by seven men on the morning of 2 June 2001 while visiting family in Douaïdia in the *wilaya* of Chlef, midway between Algiers and Oran.[14] She was taken on a forced march into the mountains and gang raped over two days before managing to escape on the third day. This ordeal brought on a miscarriage. In hospital she received medical care but no counselling to deal with the psychological aspects of her trauma. Then her husband divorced her on the grounds that she had dishonoured him. Homeless and suffering from terrible nightmares and sleeplessness, she was forced to live with her parents, who were terrified that her presence would expose them to reprisals from the armed groups. Thereafter, marked by the stigma of rape, she could not find work, which made it impossible for her to afford her prescribed medicine. Her story provided a unique insight into the full consequences of her ordeal, one that must be multiplied countless times across Algeria.

The GIA emirs also became enmeshed in smuggling, extortion and racketeering, a continuation of the parallel economy of survival that so many of the recruits had grown up in.[15] At the outset local traders had been willing to accept this as a logical consequence of the GIA's existence. But by 1996 huge resentments had built up against the GIA taxes, which in the eyes of many were an abuse of religion, a front for armed young men who simply wanted to line their own pockets. Like the practice of kidnapping, rape and temporary marriages, such criminal activity turned ordinary Algerians away from the GIA in droves.

How did people join these groups? They were not a political party. There were no membership lists, although the press put the numbers at just over eight thousand whilst Martinez cited the figure of ten thousand in 1996.[16] They were clandestine, drawing adherents from the ranks of young unemployed men, some as young as sixteen or seventeen. Invariably little educated and with a rudimentary knowledge of religion, many were attracted by the lure of racketeering as much as hatred of the regime. Violence was a rite of passage: men were recruited only if they had already put themselves beyond the law through an attack on the armed forces or police. From then on promotion to leadership was based upon further violence; numbers murdered were badges of honour, the only possible way to be accepted and taken seriously.

But if the period 1996 to 1998 was defined by a violence of frustration it was also marked by ever more intensive infighting as the armed groups descended into a patchwork of fiefdoms. Fragmentation had always been one of the defining characteristics of Islamist revolt and now this phenomenon intensified. Zitouni declared war on the AIS on 2 January 1996, heightening the suspicion that he was a pawn of the secret services since civil war between the GIA and the AIS played directly into the hands of the regime by setting the armed groups at each others' throats. The AIS leaders, Madani Mezraq and Ahmed Benaïcha, who together commanded 4,500 men, certainly believed that the GIA's violence was controlled by the secret services, desperate to turn the population against Islamism and they, like the FIS in exile, went to great lengths to criticize the idiocies and stupidities of the GIA's tactics.[17] In contrast the AIS emphasized the political logic to their own violence, which was neither senseless nor uncontrolled. Their armed resistance was based upon the premise that the more conciliatory elements within the regime would eventually realize the error of January 1992 and readmit the FIS into the political game. On these grounds, they argued, the GIA now represented the gravest danger to the prospect of an Islamist state since it allowed the regime's hardliners to win support both at home and abroad by lumping all Islamists together into one diabolical plot against Algerian society.

On 5 January 1996 a GIA communiqué attributed to Zitouni called on GIA groups to cleanse its ranks of the Algerianist tendency, in other words those within the FIS who saw politics from a national rather than an international jihadist perspective.[18] The executions of these men, who were accused of deviating from Salafist precepts, had begun the previous year with Mohammed Saïd and Abderrezak Redjam, two former members of the FIS executive committee who had publicly defected to the GIA in 1994 but were becoming increasingly critical of GIA tactics.

However, the killings created huge misgivings among many of the GIA groups. People wanted proof of Mohammed Saïd's guilt. When this was not immediately forthcoming they distanced themselves from Zitouni, who was accused of being a spy in the pay of the secret services.[19] After all, were not these murderous tactics just doing the dirty work of the regime? In western Algeria Kadi Benchichi, a thirty-three-year-old former hairdresser, refused to share arms and ammunition stolen from Sebbou and De Talegh barracks and formed his own groups opposed to the GIA. He in turn was then sentenced to death by Zitouni. In the east, one local preacher, Al Abani, produced a cassette, widely circulated, which disavowed the GIA, condemning civilian massacres and indiscriminate terrorism.

The upshot of all these divisions was a bewildering period of bloodletting and purges. Throughout the armed groups there was a chain reaction of suspicion that produced fresh rifts. Many groups now disavowed Zitouni, who was killed in mysterious circumstances in infighting some time between early May and mid-July. A pitiless struggle for his crown ensued, the eventual winner being Antar Zouabri, a twenty-six-year-old from the Blida region with a reputation for wanton cruelty even by GIA standards. Vowing to continue with Zitouni's strategy, he enlisted the theological support of Abu Hamza, a preacher based in the Finsbury Park mosque in North London, whose right hand had been replaced by a hook, supposedly as a result of a wound sustained in Afghanistan whilst fighting the Red Army. Tall and imposing, Hamza was already an iconic figure in international Islamist circles and his mosque now started producing a paper, *Al Ansar* ('The Victor'), which supported GIA actions in Algeria. GIA recruiting videos, glorifying the GIA violence in explicit detail, were also sold openly at the Finsbury Park mosque.[20]

Hamza's influence explains why London became known as 'Londonistan' amongst French and Algerian secret services. His relentless and all-consuming hatred for the West was notorious and this rhetoric now fuelled Zouabri's paranoia as he saw treachery, infiltration and cowardice everywhere.[21] The Rome platform based on the logic of negotiation and compromise; the 1995 elections where the population rejected violence; the FIS condemnation of civilian massacres: confronted by all these threats, Zouabri was seized by a kind of madness. Reiterating the slogan 'no truce, no compromise, no negotiations', he threatened with execution any who dissented. Under no condition, Zouabri thundered, would his men lay down their arms, and on

13 June 1997 a GIA declaration divided the population into those who supported the GIA and those who did not, and therefore deserved to be killed as apostates.

By this time the GIA was a headless monster, inflicting senseless murder and violence on all sides. Theirs was a directionless anger that the secret services found easy to infiltrate and manipulate as they established a network of counter-insurgency centres throughout the country at Ben-Aknoun, Châteauneuf, Centre Antar, Blida, Oran and Constantine, each of which became a byword for inhumanity in the eyes of the ordinary population.[22] Of these the most important centre, as a result of its proximity to the GIA mountain bases, was at Blida, commanded by Colonel Mehenna Djebbar under the direct orders of Smaïn Lamari. There the DRS developed a reputation for unparalleled cruelty. All prisoners were greeted with the 'welcome' that 'here we do not know God or Amnesty International: you talk or you die', and the camp became notorious for torture techniques that stripped prisoners naked and then suspended them from the ceiling by their genitals.[23] There too the DRS honed its stock trade of lies, deception and extreme cunning. Deploying a web of spies and double agents, the DRS became embroiled in a Machiavellian game whose aim was to sow division and confusion in the Islamist ranks.

■ ■ ■

Increasingly aware of the DRS's ghastly strategy, journalists, such as José Garçon of the French daily *Libération*, started to become sceptical about the GIA. Like others she wondered where the GIA communiqués were coming from and whether they were genuine, and in her reportage she was always careful to refer to the 'GIA' in inverted commas. By 1997 the extremist language of these communiqués, just calling for massacres, massacres and more massacres, had reached the point of caricature. They were also written in classical Arabic, displaying a detailed knowledge of the finer nuances of the Qur'an that the uneducated Zouani seemed unlikely to possess. Here fingers were pointed at either Abu Hamza or the hidden hand of the DRS.

FIS leaders in exile believed that the GIA paper, *Al Ansar*, faxed mysteriously to the European media at intermittent intervals, was a fabrication by the Algerian secret services.[24] They argued too that the DRS, in a masterstroke of cynicism, was letting the GIA groups attack the former FIS strongholds in the Mitidja. By leaving these villages dangerously exposed, they knew that the population, however reluctantly, would have no alternative but to turn to the army for protection. The DRS, therefore, had a vested interest in encouraging a poisonous atmosphere that was submerged in fetid intrigue and confusion on all sides.

The charge that the GIA was a creature of the regime became a standard accusation which was given further credence by the subsequent accounts of former DRS officers. Born in 1968, Abdelkader Tigha was an officer in a DRS unit based at the Centre Territorial de Recherche et d'Investigation (CTRI) in Blida between 1993 and 1997. At the end of 1996 he completed an investigation into the death of two pro-GIA teachers that angered his superior officers because it implicated the military judiciary.[25] Worried by rumours linking him with Islamists, Tigha began to fear for his life and fled to Tunisia in December 1999, eventually ending up as an asylum-seeker in Thailand. In exile Tigha gave an inside view of the DRS's full panoply of dirty tricks. Operating undercover in unmarked cars, untroubled by the constraints of the law, their aim was to locate and assassinate suspects. He also provided detailed explanations on how Blida not only manipulated Zitouni but also set up death squads to kill political opponents.[26]

Tigha's claims were also corroborated by a former DRS colonel, Mohammed Samraoui, who in a book, *Chroniques des Années de Sang*, published in France in 2003, and in interviews with Al-Jazeera television, claimed that the DRS invented the GIA in 1991.[27] He also gave an inside view of the hardliners within the DRS, recounting how in a top-secret meeting at Châteauneuf in May 1992 Smaïn Lamari told fellow officers, 'I am ready and prepared to eliminate three million Algerians if it is necessary to maintain the order that the Islamists threaten.'[28]

It was a chilling statement, reflecting a mentality that rejected any talk of dialogue. Within this schema the DRS and the GIA groups represented two extremist fringes that fed off each other and needed each other to survive. For the DRS, keen to deflect any attention away from the mafia economy, the GIA was a necessary scapegoat, keeping the status quo going by justifying Algeria's draconian system. The DRS took every opportunity for extravagant hyperbole, holding up the GIA as a diabolical menace for Algeria and the world, whilst simultaneously infiltrating and manipulating these groups. On the other side the GIA groups wanted to perpetuate the conflict because, in a impoverished society, it became a means to personal enrichment.

Both sides, therefore, had a vested interest in quashing anybody preaching reconciliation. All bridges had to be kept permanently burnt: one of the defining characteristics of the violence was that individuals who broke out of the polarized thinking imposed by the DRS and GIA mindsets were eliminated on a regular basis.

In between these two extremes the Algerian population lay trapped. Ordinary people trying to survive had to negotiate a complicated path between the warring parties as they became increasingly hostile to both the GIA groups and *le pouvoir*. As such the war in Algeria was a unique situation without an obvious precedent. The French president, François Mitterrand, had talked of a 'civil war' on French television during his Bastille Day interview with journalists in 1994, but this was a misnomer.[29] Algeria was not like the Spanish Civil War between 1936 and 1939. There, the two sides had possessed stable continuous territories, but in Algeria this was a war amongst the populations with no clearly defined battle lines, just a permanent sense of terror.

By 1996 Algeria had become a murky place with no dividing line between truth and untruth. With no dates, no battles, no chronology, the dirty war on terror was shapeless, inchoate and never-ending. It became impossible to impose a pattern on the violence beyond the fact that this was a cowards' war where defenceless civilians were massacred at will. In this confused atmosphere Algeria became mired in a series of mysteries – beginning with the killing of seven Cistercian Trappist monks in May 1996 – which, like the Boudiaf assassination four years earlier, raised one key question: who was killing whom and why?

■   ■   ■

Tibhirine is a majestic place. Perched to the south of the bustling market town of Médéa, the spot commands a magnificent view of the Atlas Mountains, dominating the surrounding countryside for miles around. There in 1934 five monks established a Cistercian monastery in a nineteenth-century English colonial farm famous for its gardens. Later these gardens would become a religious motif, recalling Gethsemane, the garden of anguish, when between 1993 and 1996 Tibhirine, located in the 'triangle of death', entered the eye of the Algerian storm.[30]

During the war of independence the monastery was a place of refuge. In 1956 a colony of refugee Muslim children was lodged in the abbey's shadow. Families from the neighbouring massif of Tammesouida, fleeing from fighting, created a small Tibhirine village one and half miles down the road. The religious order was threatened only once between 1954 and 1962, when Brother Luc Dochier was kidnapped by the ALN. However, when he was identified as the local doctor, famous for his devotion to the local Muslim community, Dochier was immediately released.

After independence the Algerian authorities tolerated the remote monastery thanks to skilful negotiations by Archbishop Léon Duval of Algiers. Following the exodus of Algeria's Europeans, Archbishop Duval was dedicated to preserving Algeria's Christian tradition, which had produced St Augustine, St Cyprien and the French soldier and mystic Charles de Foucauld.[31] He wanted to show that this Christian tradition transcended French rule, and he also wanted to demonstrate a different vision of Christianity, one that was neither colonialist nor crusading. For him Tibhirine was the symbol of a multi-faith post-colonial Algeria where Christians and Muslims, along with Jews, could live together in mutual respect and dialogue, and he considered that preserving the monastery there was one of his greatest achievements.

Post-1962 Tibhirine was a reassuring presence rooted in the lives of the local population. Influenced by the teachings of Abbé Pierre, who founded the Emmaus Movement in 1949 dedicated to helping the poor and the homeless, and the Worker Priest Movement, which until it was banned by the Vatican in 1953 sought to immerse itself in the daily struggles of the working class, the monks developed a special relationship with the Muslim poor as life at Tibhirine expressed a commitment to radical poverty and a belief in Christian–Muslim dialogue. Brother Dochier, for example, became a legend, sometimes seeing seventy patients a day in his small dispensary. As the violence intensified after 1993, the monks, none young and some in their sixties or seventies, saw it as their sacred duty to carry on living there whatever the danger. Despite the fact that Médéa was a GIA bastion, despite the pressure from the authorities who were patently unhappy at this outside presence witnessing the reality of the dirty war, and despite the fact that Tibhirine's strategic importance clearly put them in the firing line, they were determined to stay as a mark of solidarity with the suffering population.

By the early 1990s the nine monks still living at Tibhirine were very conscious of living on the seismic fault-lines that mark the world – Islam–the West, North–South, rich–poor – and for these reasons believed that it was vital to maintain a Christian presence committed to peace, love and understanding despite the violence. From 1993 they charted a difficult course through the bloodshed, caught up in cross-fire between the 'brothers of the mountain', as they called the GIA, and the 'brothers of the plain', as they dubbed the soldiers manning a post in a watch tower a few hundred yards from the monastery. They disregarded the GIA's demand in 1993 that all foreigners leave Algeria or face execution, although they knew that they were easy targets since they carried no weapons and refused an offer of army protection. The worse the violence got the more they felt compelled to stay, just like Pierre Claverie, bishop of Oran, who when asked if he should leave always responded by quoting his Muslim friends: 'Do not listen to the "last call" siren. Stay, we need you.'[32]

The sense of encroaching violence worsened at nightfall on 14 December 1993 when twelve Croatian Catholic workers whom the monks knew had their throats cut at Tamesquida, a few miles from the monastery. A week later, on Christmas Eve, six armed 'brothers of the mountain' visited the monastery, led by 'Emir' Sayah Attiya, who had been responsible for murdering the Croats. The son of a harki, Attiya had the macabre distinction of having cut the throats of 145 people. Prior Christian de Chergé, appealing to the Qur'an, told him that the monastery was a place of prayer where no arms had ever entered. When Attiya demanded money, medicines and medical assistance, de Chergé patiently explained that this was not possible.[33]

After this harrowing experience the monks debated whether or not to leave the monastery and, following a series of secret votes, they agreed to stay put unless they were subjected to intolerable ransom demands or posed a danger to the village. Christian de Chergé recalled another night-time visit when an armed group:

> asked to use the telephone. We had to argue with them a lot and when people are armed that is not easy … in the end they were able to use our mobile telephone, but outside the house and we, that is to say Brother Robert and I, were present all the time they telephoned. But, during the time they tried to make their connection, which was difficult because of a storm, many things were said. And so Brother Robert, who was rather tense and a heavy smoker, asked for permission to smoke.
>
> Their chief said, 'It's *haram* [forbidden].' He began to warm to his theme, saying the prophet had forbidden it, etcetera. At the end of his remarks, I said, 'Listen, if you can show me a single text of the Hadith or of the Qur'an that forbids cigarettes I will believe you, but I can assure you that none has been written.'
>
> Silence followed … and then three minutes later, Robert calmly struck a match, lit his cigarette and said, 'What is haram is to kill another person.'

The call, to a number in Sweden, was monitored by Algerian intelligence, heightening irritation with the monks in official circles.

However, as the conflict around them in the 'triangle of death' worsened, the monks felt protected by divine grace, even if the danger they were in was clear to those who have made the journey to Tibhirine. The road from Algiers to Médéa runs along a narrow gorge, known as the chiffa, and the civilian traffic travelling on it formed convoys and drove as fast as possible to reduce the threat of an ambush. Recalling these risks, Father Nicolas, the priest at Médéa and a close friend of the monks, said that it would be wrong to think that Christian de Chergé did not experience fear.

> He had seen the worst with his own eyes. A bus burning in the gorges of the chiffa, for example, while those who set fire to it were still present. He used to go to Blida sometimes to visit the Sisters of Charity, to support their courage and celebrate Mass for them. But he never left without apprehension. He was conscious of the peril.[34]

In 1995, during a final visit to his family's home in south-eastern France, another of the monks, Christophe Lebreton, was pressed by friends to leave Algeria. He replied: 'Why should I have the choice to flee, while the Algerians do not? They are the victims, not us.'[35] Likewise, while visiting his mother at Bonvaux in the wine-growing Chablis area, Paul Favre-Miville told her that his luggage included several shovels 'for digging our graves better'. Meanwhile Michel Fleury prepared his family for the worst, writing:

> Through our windows there is only smoke and fire in the hills and the mountains … If something happens to us, I wish to be in solidarity with the people here. Keep all that I tell you in your prayers. Without a doubt the hardest to live is yet to come.[36]

Each of Fleury's letters ended with '*Inshallah*', 'If God wills it.'

By early 1996 the danger was growing by the day. On 26 March the monks held a meeting of the Lien de la Paix, an organization dedicated to understanding between Christians and Muslims. The following night about twenty armed men surrounded the monastery, smashing a window to gain entry. The monastery was ransacked and the telephone wires cut as seven of the monks were bundled away. Two survivors, Brothers Amédée and Jean-Pierre, were unable to venture out since the curfew was in force and guards in the nearby watchtower could have shot them on sight. As they waited for dawn they prayed, before raising the alarm at exactly 7 a.m.

According to Brothers Amédée and Jean-Pierre the gunmen spoke with an eastern Algerian, not a local accent, and responsibility for the kidnapped was immediately attributed to Djamel Zitouni, who had always underlined the need to cleanse Algeria of Christians and Jews, accusing them of orchestrating a grand plot to destroy Islam. In a communiqué the GIA demanded that the Algerian and French governments release prisoners; both refused.

The drama lasted fifty-six days with intense coming and going between Paris and Algiers. The only apparent proof that the monks were alive was a recording of their voices made on 20 April 1996, delivered to the French embassy; a momentary glimmer of hope which was finally extinguished on 23 May when a terse communiqué announced that the monks had been executed – their throats cut. Seven days later their severed heads were found, the largest massacre of French people since the beginning of the violence in 1992.

The FIS leader in exile, Rabah Kebir, condemned the act as criminal and opposed to the basic tenets of Islam. President Chirac called the monks the embodiment of tolerance and on television millions shed tears as they watched Cardinal Lustiger, the archbishop of Paris, snuff out the seven candles that had been brought from Tibhirine to Notre Dame cathedral as a sign of hope. Bells were tolled in every church in France on Pentecost Sunday whilst political organizations from across the spectrum marched in memory of the dead brothers. By a cruel symmetry Cardinal Duval died within hours of the fate of the seven becoming known and a moving funeral service for all eight men was held on 2 June in the Basilique de Notre Dame d'Afrique, overlooking Bab el-Oued. Thousands went to pay their last respects, filing past the coffins each adorned with flowers and a photograph.

After the kidnapping the Church, desperately trying to secure the release of the monks, had found itself strangely hampered by the French government. In Rome, the Cistercians were told day after day by the French ambassador that there was no new information, which led one senior Cistercian official, angered at this stonewalling, to tell the envoy: 'Either you are stupid or you are lying to us.' The Algerian authorities were equally baffling. When the deputy head of the order, Father Armand Veilleux, arrived in Algiers on 30 May, he was informed that the remains of the monks had been found. Bizarrely the authorities had already ordered coffins from Marseille, in which the remains had been sealed ready for expatriation. Unwilling to be fobbed off, Father Armand insisted on seeing the bodies for himself at the Algiers military hospital morgue and the grisly sight yielded another mystery. The authorities said the heads had been found on a tree near Médéa. But the heads of the men were covered with earth, meaning that they had been buried and then dug up.

A further tussle with the Algiers authorities concerned the future of the monastery. The Algerian officials wanted the monastery cleared of furniture and personal effects but Father Armand was firm, saying 'We want to keep our things here for when we come back.' Like many Christians, Veilleux felt the authorities wanted the monastery to close and that this was part of the mystery of the kidnapping. After more tough negotiations, Father Armand was assured that the monks would be buried at Tibhirine. The Algerian army deployed at least a battalion of soldiers for the burial as if they wanted to make a show of strength. As the coffins were lowered into the ground by Algerian military cadets, one soldier cried out: 'These men loved God and Algeria more than any of us.'

Throughout the drama the Algerian authorities sought to control media coverage of the affair to ensure that the kidnappings were blamed on Islamist guerrillas. For the Church authorities, however, there was a stream of un-answered questions, not just in terms of who was responsible but also of how they were able to keep the monks prisoner for two months without being detected. The Church also wanted to know how, when and where the monks died. Yet when the Church pressed the authorities for the outcome of the official investigation into the kidnapping, no information was forthcoming. Frustrated, the archdiocese approached three Algerian lawyers to ask them to act for the monks' families in a civil case. When none accepted, it was clear that they were coming under pressure from above.

The whole affair produced tension and recrimination between Algiers and Paris. Some in the French secret services suspected the hidden hand of hardline elements in the DRS, keen to embarrass President Zeroual or perhaps worried that the monks knew too much. Meanwhile the FIS in exile suggested that the Algerian secret services let the monks be killed because they were angry that the French had bypassed them and contacted the GIA directly, and that through the monks' murder they wanted to teach Paris not to meddle in Algerian affairs.

In this emotional atmosphere the French foreign minister, Hervé de Charette, arrived for an official visit on 31 July. Fearful that the conflict could spread to the rest of France's backyard in North Africa, he wanted to repair the damage and assess the state of the country. De Charette visited the monks' graves and met with the bishop of Oran, Pierre Claverie, a fourth-generation settler and an outspoken champion of tolerance. In November 1995, revolted by the murder of Sister Odette Prévost in Algiers, he had written an open letter to her assassins.[37] Since he could not say with certainty who had killed her he condemned all proponents of the violence, from the GIA through to shadowy elements in the army. Significantly Claverie was not afraid to talk about agents provocateurs within the system whose aim was to sow confusion and transform the Islamists into a demonic force. He commented, 'Nobody, obviously, is any longer sure of anything or of anyone. And it is in this fog that people kill and are killed.'[38]

Such a statement, clearly intended to make the regime uncomfortable, was a measure of his fierce independence. Claverie was determined to tell the outside world about the complex reality of the violence but, with a horrible inevitability, soon after de Charette's departure Claverie was killed on 1 August by a remote-controlled car bomb, the nineteenth servant of the Roman Catholic Church to die violently in Algeria since 1993.

The outrage was immediately condemned by Zeroual but once again the FIS in exile accused the DRS.[39] After all, they argued, Oran was not noted for the presence of armed groups and this was a meticulously prepared operation where the killers must have had inside information. Moreover, they continued, Claverie's death served a triple purpose for the DRS: not only had it got rid of a notoriously turbulent presence, it had also won over public opinion by discrediting the Islamists and had tied France to the Algerian regime.

The rumours about the DRS's involvement in the mystery continued to surface at regular intervals and were given further dramatic credence in December 2002 when *Libération* published an extremely detailed series of articles on the affair.[40] *Libération*'s scoop hinged upon an interview with Abdelkader Tigha, an ex-officer in the DRS based at Blida, who was involved in infiltrating the armed groups. He recounted how the monks were kidnapped by members of Zitouni's band and taken to his lair of underground caves at Tala Acha. There, Zitouni immediately contacted the DRS in Blida via his number two, Mouloud Azzout. However, a rival GIA group, led by Hocine Besiou, who was not controlled by the DRS and was determined to usurp Zitouni's leadership, forced Zitouni and Azzout to hand over the monks and it was this group that eventually killed them. To recover the initiative the DRS ordered Zitouni to seize back the monks in early May and it was during this mission that he conveniently met his end. As Tigha explained, 'Zitouni was killed in an AIS ambush. His death and the disappearance of Azzout ended all traces incriminating our services. Zitouni would only be declared dead in July.'[41]

Thus the monks were pawns in a deadly situation that by 1996, as the former DRS colonel Mohammed Samraoui explained, had become a mess, because the DRS no longer controlled the groups that they had infiltrated or even set up in the first place.[42] They did not know who belonged to these groups or whom they could deem 'friendly'. The monks' deaths, therefore, could be seen as the consequence of a counter-insurgency game that went disastrously wrong.

■ ■ ■

As the drama of the Trappist monks reached a tragic dénouement, Zeroual was well aware that the legitimacy conferred on him by the presidential elections had run out. With the violence going from bad to worse in the Algiers hinterland he needed to regain the initiative and in April he promised to hold new parliamentary and local elections in 1997. By way of preparing the ground he unveiled a new constitution that would be put to a referendum in November. This made significant changes to the Chadli constitution, above all by enshrining the power of the president, thereby making sure that any transition was carefully controlled.

By stressing the centrality of Islam, the Arabic language and the enduring example of 1 November 1954, Zeroual hoped that the constitution would produce a broad consensus.[43] In fact it provoked huge opposition on all sides because everybody felt aggrieved in one way or another, underlining that the political landscape remained as fractured as ever. The RCD and the former PAGS, reformed as Ettahaddi, were disappointed at the failure to move towards a secular state; Islam was reaffirmed as the country's official religion. On the other hand the proposed constitution explicitly banned any party that exploited Islam for political purposes. By putting religion above politics Zeroual wanted to make Islam a source of unity rather than division but this approach only alienated the two parties Hamas and Ennahda. The RCD and parts of the FFS were also angered by the fact that the constitution did not give the Berber language the same official status as Arabic, even though it acknowledged the Berber dimension of Algerian national identity.[44]

The proposed constitution emphasized the central importance of democratic and republican values and talked about Algerians as citizens enjoying the full range of political and human rights. But in the eyes of the FFS leader Aït Ahmed this was little more than an elaborate façade to disguise the fact that Zeroual's proposal amounted to a constitutional dictatorship. He disliked the way in which enormous power was concentrated in the president's hand at the expense of the elected National Assembly and of the prime minister and the interior and justice ministries.[45] For him this represented a major attack on basic democratic principles. Zeroual's supporters argued that this strengthening of presidential powers was what the country was crying out for. A strong president would ensure stability and the development of a coherent policy from the centres of power, overcoming a major problem that had dogged Algeria since independence: the way the different clans had used the various government posts as fiefdoms for infighting and power struggles. By overcoming paralysis and factional divisions the new constitution would, in theory, create the basis of an accountable government and anyway the presidential powers were limited in key ways. Any president was limited to two terms in office while a High State Court was established to monitor any abuses of government closely.

Predictably, the constitution, which clearly drew upon Western models, was anathema for the GIA groups, who were determined to make the subsequent referendum impossible. Since 1995 the regime had armed tens of thousands of civilians – dubbing them the patriotic militia and village self-defence groups – and by the end of 1996 huge numbers of villages had became small fortresses surrounded by watchtowers, barbed wire and mines.[46] The GIA groups specifically targeted these pro-government villages, declaring them to be full of apostates, as they submerged the country in a fresh wave of violence.

As the countdown to the referendum on 28 November began, death became commonplace. On 10 November at least fifteen were killed, including children, in a car-bomb attack at a bus stop in an Algiers suburb; on 24 November five were killed and fifteen wounded, by a car bomb in Blida; and on the referendum day itself twenty-six were killed. In the rundown villages of the Mitidja the GIA launched a policy of total war on civilians regardless of age and sex. On 12 November thirty-two people, including ten women, had their throats cut. The GIA also began beheading civilians in Islamic trials, using a makeshift guillotine mounted on a truck to speed up the process.

Villagers fled to the main cities where they crowded into shanty towns, the authorities doing little to alleviate their misery, distress and trauma. On 4 December the Algerian air force bombed mountains in the area of Larba, a well-known GIA stronghold, but this did little to quell the violence. On 11 December twenty bus passengers were murdered, bringing to nearly sixty the number killed in Blida province in under a week.

As in 1995 the conflict spilt over into France. On 3 December a bomb at Port Royal métro station in Paris left three dead and a hundred injured. Nobody claimed responsibility but the design, a gas canister filled with nails, had all the hallmarks of the GIA. Then on 24 December a letter from the GIA to President Chirac demanded that France stop all support for the regime, identifying the French as being amongst 'the blasphemers, the most dangerous enemies of Muslims'.

The deterioration in the security situation put the Zeroual government on the defensive. Hauled up before the United Nations Committee against

Torture, the Algerian delegation defended their government on the grounds that few understood the nature of the menace. Explicit in their argument was that in the face of terrorism human rights were a costly luxury. Details of institutionalized torture were also contained within an Amnesty International report, which once again the Algerian government condemned, arguing that the fact that the report was released ten days before the referendum 'was proof of Amnesty's bias'.

On 9 November, in a bid to stop the escalating warfare, a group of politicians headed by the former prime minister Mouloud Hamrouche along with Aït Ahmed, Ben Bella and retired general Rachid Benyelles published an impassioned call for peace. Attacking Zeroual's constitution as an attack on November 1954, this *Appel pour la Paix* called for an end to all violence and the opening up of a genuine dialogue that would heal the country's divisions. Above all they wanted to break down the wall of silence that surrounded the country. The new constitution might trumpet freedom of speech but in reality the opposition were forbidden to hold meetings or to have access to the state-controlled television. This sense of outrage was echoed by foreign journalists who on 29 November protested:

> … in the name of security journalists have been prevented from leaving their hotel without escort, even if it was only to go to the international press centre 200 yards away. These working conditions, amounting to residence under police surveillance for the foreign press, have not allowed normal coverage of the referendum and even less of the situation in Algeria.[47]

As regards the referendum itself only the FLN and the former premier, Redha Malek, called for a yes vote. The FFS called for a no vote, the RCD boycotted the process whilst Hamas and Ennahda told their supporters to vote as they pleased. So, when the government announced that 85.8 per cent of the 12.7 million votes cast were in favour of the constitutional changes, these figures were instantly challenged by opposition leaders as inflated and preposterous. In France *Libération* reported that few Algerians believed the results whilst *El Watan* gave prominent coverage to Aït Ahmed's assertion that the referendum was a fraud.[48]

The referendum did little to enhance Zeroual's legitimacy. On 12 December the European Parliament passed a resolution condemning the lack of democratic reform contained within the referendum and the lack of freedom of the press; at home the gulf between ruler and ruled was wider than ever, while within the regime itself Zeroual seemed weak and isolated.[49]

■ ■ ■

Ramadan began on 10 January 1997 and once again this was the signal for a ghastly upsurge in bloodshed. As with the referendum the protagonists' major aim was to discredit Zeroual, whether they were the various GIA groups or government hardliners determined to maintain their grip on power. In between were caught the ordinary people who were subjected not just to new depths of savagery – whole village populations were hacked apart like animals – but confusion and disinformation on a grand scale. Algeria became a living nightmare in which nobody could say with certainty what was happening. On 5 January an AIS statement reiterated the call for France to end all support to the 'putschist' regime. But it also clearly distanced the AIS from the GIA attacks on civilians, accusing the Algerian secret services of fabricating the letter to Chirac in an effort to make the French stand shoulder to shoulder with the regime.

The armed groups wanted to show that the capital was not secure despite the government's extravagant claims that terrorism had been defeated. They also wanted to relieve their hard-pressed brothers in the mountains south-west of Algiers, who were being subjected to huge sweeps from the army using helicopters and tanks. Two days later twenty were killed and one hundred injured in a car bomb in the main street in central Algiers. Most of the violence, though, was focused in the 'triangle of death' to the south of the capital. On 15 January fourteen were killed and fifty more injured at Boufarik by a bomb packed with nails and pieces of metal and hidden in a shopping bag. On 23 January twenty-two people were found with their throats slit south-west of Algiers. On 31 January thirty-one people were decapitated in Médéa. On 18 February in the outskirts of Algiers at Babi Ali, nineteen people were murdered and their houses looted and pillaged. Relatives could not return because doors and corpses were booby-trapped. One woman, holding her six-month-old nephew whose parents had been killed but who had miraculously survived the bloodbath, cried out in vengeance:

> Give me a gun and let me take revenge for the death of my family. The family of these terrorists are living undisturbed in the middle of the village. My brother and the others have had their throats cut and been mutilated.[50]

On 24 January, in a desperate attempt to reassert his control, Zeroual went on national television.[51] With no alternative but to issue an uncompromising message he promised the 'extermination' of the terrorists who were branded as criminals, traitors and mercenaries in the pay of foreign powers. He also accused the signatories of the *Appel pour la Paix* and the supporters of the Rome platform of orchestrating a huge plot to undermine the Algerian people and destroy the values of November 1954. It was a depressingly familiar line that made little impact and underlined the powerlessness of the regime. Boxed into a corner, Zeroual had little option but to mouth General Lamari's line that Islamist terrorism would be defeated within three months. In the mean-time the violence was accompanied by worsening social conditions. Water was severely rationed whilst on the heights of Algiers dozens of families, fleeing the bloodshed in the Mitidja, were living in tents without water, electricity or sanitation.

Amidst this general carnage infighting within the regime also split out into open violence, most obviously with the assassination of the trade union leader Abdelhak Benhamouda, the thirty-three-year-old secretary general of the Union Générale des Travailleurs Algériens (UGTA), who was killed by a group of five men on the afternoon of 28 January outside the union's office in the centre of Algiers. He had announced his intention to form a new political party to take part in the forthcoming general elections, and had also been mooted as a possible successor to Zeroual as president. Fiercely anti-Islamist, he was opposed to dialogue and in favour of a military solution but was equally critical of the IMF agreements and wanted to put a break on the privatization of state companies. Although the Islamist group Front Islamique pour le Djihad en Algérie (FIDA) allegedly claimed responsibility for his assassination there was widespread speculation that he was killed by the anti-Zeroual faction within the regime who were fearful of his growing influence and wanted to fire a warning shot at Zeroual himself. This conspiracy theory was fuelled by the fact that Benhamouda was murdered in public in broad daylight and that the assassins got away so easily. His dying words were, 'Kamel, brother, they have betrayed us.' And his supposed killer, Rachid Medjahed, died in detention before coming to trial.[52]

As the descent into violence continued into February, with the regime reporting that Zouabri had been killed along with two hundred of his men, Aït Ahmed called for American mediation. In the same vein Amnesty International condemned the massacres of civilians and called for an inquiry to establish who was responsible and to bring them to justice. There was a brief let-up in March but there were more massacres to come. On the night of 21/22 April ninety-three people, half of them women, young girls and children, were killed only fifteen miles south of Algiers, bringing the number of deaths to more than three hundred in two weeks.

The magnitude of the crisis made Algeria one of the first issues confronting Tony Blair's Labour government, newly elected in the landslide of 1 May 1997. The new foreign secretary, Robin Cook, immediately called for an ethical foreign policy whereupon the left-leaning *Observer* seized upon the forthcoming Algerian elections – dubbed 'the blow-torch elections' in reference to the secret police's preferred method of torture – as an example of New Labour hypocrisy. How ethical was the Blair government, the *Observer* asked, when it had no qualms about continuing to supply military hardware to the Zeroual regime?

Back in Algeria Zeroual, worried by the lukewarm support for his constitutional changes from the established parties, launched his own party, Rassemblement National Démocratique (RND), in March. He wanted to seize the initiative and the RND became the unofficial state party although it inspired little confidence amongst the population. Against this Zeroual's one major success was the fact that all the Algerian political parties, with the exception of the still-banned FIS, agreed to participate.

On election day on 5 June the regime mobilized over 300,000 soldiers and policemen to look after the 37,000 polling stations. Their presence was meant to send out a powerful message about the power of the state but in reality this visibility only angered the population, who asked why, with so many soldiers at their disposal, the regime had been unable to stop the massacres. Zeroual, at pains to impress the outside world, invited in UN observers but there were still numerous accusations of fraud – one French television crew even caught election rigging on camera. Likewise the opposition parties found it difficult to monitor the mobile polling booths and were denied access to the count.

When the official results were announced and the RND was declared to have won over 40 per cent of the votes and an absolute majority in the National Assembly, there was widespread outrage, producing the largest public demonstrations since 1992. For the opposition parties the elections were clearly not about democracy: since, as in the presidential elections, the winner was never in doubt, they were intended merely to give the ruling elite the veneer of legitimacy so obviously lacking since January 1992. They were also meant to draw the respectable Islamist parties into the political game. Ordinary voters were just bit part players in a complicated game where Western governments were willing to turn a blind eye to fraud on the grounds that to have elections at all was a remarkable event for an Arab country.

With the elections over violence returned with a vengeance in August and September. On 29 August 300 people were slaughtered in the farming town of Sidi Raïs in the Mitidja. Again survivors asked why the army, despite the screams, did not intervene. Standing by a minibus that had been burnt out by a Molotov cocktail and wary of hovering security agents, Mohammed, an engineer who had lived at Sidi Raïs all his life, told one foreign reporter:

> My wife and I were watching an American movie, *Towering Inferno*, on television when the attack began. We began running to the police station for help when I met one of the terrorists. He tried to kill me with an axe but I wrestled him to the ground and beat him before getting away with my family. Some of the attackers wore masks. Others were barefaced or they wore false beards and wigs. I don't know whether the soldiers intervened or not. I was taken to hospital and that's all I remember.[53]

On 5 September a further fifty were massacred at Béni-Messous just outside Algiers.

The peak of horror, however, was reached at Bentalha, a small township in the Mitidja just twelve miles to the south of Algiers, on the night of 22/23 September. At 11.30 p.m. between fifty and a hundred men launched a well-prepared attack on two specific parts of Bentalha – Boudoumi and Hai Djillali. Cutting the electricity beforehand, the men told residents to open up because they were the military, before beating the doors down with axes or blowing them up with gas cylinders packed with TNT that had been brought to the village by military truck. Armed with lists of names the hooded men went from house to house, slaughtering all occupants regardless of age or sex. As Mohammed Saal, living in a heavily fortified villa on the edge of the village, explained the following day:

> The killers came at 11.30 p.m. and they stayed until about 2.30 a.m. There were about thirty-five to forty of them. Half of them were dressed in military tunics. The others wore civilian clothes. The ones in military tunics had automatic weapons. The others were carrying knives and axes.[54]

Within the smothering darkness space lost all dimensions as the assailants, revelling in their power to produce atavistic fear, declared in bloodcurdling tones, 'We are coming … we are going to cut all your throats, it will happen to everyone, it is our duty.' In the confusion families, vainly hoping for the soldiers stationed in barracks just five hundred yards away to come and save them, fled into the street where they were cornered and dragged away to their deaths. By this point the village was submerged in shouting, screaming and wailing; some residents pleaded to be shot rather than have their throats cut.

During the six hours of killing that followed, scores of women and elderly men were hacked to pieces and, according to some survivors, babies were thrown into ovens and burnt. Even after death bodies were mutilated before being wired with booby traps.

Between 4.00 and 4.30 a.m. the drivers of the trucks began sounding their horns, warning the killers it was time to leave. The assailants used children to carry loot pillaged from the houses into the trucks before murdering them on the spot. The official figure put the number of deaths at ninety-eight killed when in fact it was well over four hundred.[55]

On 23 September journalists visiting the scene were greeted with an appalling sight. Still awash with blood, the village resembled one huge abattoir. Picking their way through the decapitated bodies –feet poking incongruously from beneath tarpaulin covers – the reporters tried to make sense of the bloodshed around them by interviewing residents. Confusion, shock and disbelief registered on the faces of the survivors, many of them carrying ancient hunting guns on their shoulders. In the distance smoke swirled across the road leading through the Mitidja. Self-defence units known as patriotes burned down the pine trees alongside the main road to eliminate cover for members of the GIA roaming the area at night from their bases in the nearby Atlas Mountains.

At the cemetery of Sidi Rizzine, where the bereaved gathered around the freshly dug graves to keen, a matriarch known as Madame Laroussi said the youngest villagers had been subjected to the greatest evil. 'The assassins threw babies in the ovens and turned on the gas,' she wailed, holding the hand of a tiny, newly orphaned granddaughter. 'They killed my son, they killed my son.'[56] Amongst this grief one question began to impose itself: why didn't the army intervene? There were thousands of soldiers stationed within a few miles, some of them less than five hundred yards away. How were fifty to a hundred armed men able to pass by without being spotted and intercepted? How too were they able to carry out the massacres for some six hours before disappearing into the night? One elderly woman who managed to flee said that soldiers approached while the killing was going on but did not intervene. They claimed later that the assailants had sealed off the area with mines or booby traps. 'It is certain that there was complicity,' said the woman, who was too frightened to give her name.[57]

Bentalha marked the first time that the authorities had allowed foreign reporters to speak to survivors. The reporters, who included one of the authors of this book, were taken under escort to Boufarik, Bentalha, Sidi Raïs and other massacre sites in minibuses emblazoned bizarrely with the logo of the

Touring Club d'Algérie. This concession followed pressure from the United Nations, which had been pushing for an international fact-finding mission to investigate the massacres on the spot, but the initiative proved a public relations disaster for the regime. Despite attempts to shackle the foreign journalists, who were obliged to stay at the Soviet-style Aurassi hotel facing the defence ministry and allowed out only on authorized trips under escort, many of the correspondents followed the line of inquiry of the Sunday Times which openly pointed the finger at the army, headlining its report from Bentalha 'Army link to Algeria slaughter', and accompanying the piece with a harrowing photograph of a sixteen-year-old girl who lost nine family members.[58]

Challenging the official script of the 'good army' versus the 'evil terrorists' was a difficult business. Desperate to control the flow of information out of the country, the regime found ways of exerting pressure on the foreign press. Making it clear that those who dissented from the official line would no longer be welcome, the regime became famously parsimonious in issuing visas to correspondents. By 1997 reporting from Algeria, with a regime one of whose defining characteristics was disinformation on a grand scale, was notoriously hazardous. As the Le Monde journalist Thomas Ferenczi recorded, it was almost impossible for journalists to get to the villages where the killings were taking place. Moreover, once there, it was difficult to know the exact circumstances of the murders or to say with certainty who was behind them and what were the motivations.[59]

The extent of the confusion gave succour to a widespread feeling that the army and the DRS were implicated to some degree in the massacres, not least on the grounds of failing in their duty to protect defenceless civilians from attack. Much more, however, was learned with the publication, in October 2000, of Nesroullah Yous' sensational account Qui a Tué à Bentalha? (Who killed at Bentalha?), by the French left-wing publisher La Découverte, excerpts of which were serialized by Le Monde.[60] The book lifted the veil on not just the massacres but the genesis of the conflict, in a dramatic fashion. The detail and specificity of Yous's account, allied to the fact that he was a long-time opponent of the armed groups who had lived in Bentalha until he escaped to Paris in February 1998, meant that his book could not be dismissed as Islamist propaganda.

On the night of the massacre Yous had saved dozens of inhabitants who sought refuge in his house, on which he had built rudimentary fortifications enabling him and a small group of men and women to fight off the assailants for a short time by lobbing Molotov cocktails along with bricks, stones and tiles from his terrace. After the attackers had blasted their way into the building with explosives, he and a handful of neighbours escaped by jumping from the roof and fleeing into market gardens on the edge of Bentalha. As numerous green and red tracer bullets marked the sky Yous briefly caught sight of the attackers:

> Out of the alley coming from the little *oued* [river] in front of me I saw about fifty well-armed killers emerge from the darkness at a determined pace. They had automatic rifles, Seminovs and double-barrelled hunting rifles. They gathered under the porch facing my house and began firing at us with semi-automatic weapons, shot after shot. Some of them were in dark combat suits resembling those of ninjas, others were in kachabia [the robes favoured by Islamists], some were hooded, some were bearded. I don't know why, but I didn't for one moment believe they were Islamists. People would ask me later why I was so sure. I believe that some of the beards and hair were false.[61]

Instinctively Yous felt that the assailants were in fact members of the armed forces: they were too professional and had been able to slip into the village too easily. Spotted by the assailants, Yous heard bullets whistle around him before losing balance and falling into the alley on the other side of the wall where he lost consciousness. When Yous came to, he was alone in the deserted street. However, it was not the end of the horror:

> The assault began again on a group of women and children who were surrounded. We heard the cries and the tears, the women clutched at each other, their children between their legs or in their arms, and some of them pushed their aggressors. Some of them grabbed some of the women, I suppose those were the ones they wanted to kidnap. Some of the women fought like lionesses to protect their daughters. Those who didn't want to follow the criminals were executed with axe blows or thrust to the ground to have their throats slit. The women cried 'Don't cut our throats, please kill us with your bullets, don't slaughter us' ... suddenly I saw one of the killers tear a child from his mother. The woman tried to hold the child to her, but he hit her with a machete. He took the child by the foot, and making a half turn, smashed its head against a concrete pillar. The others followed suit, gripped with a frenetic laughter. I couldn't stand the sight of it any more, holding my head in my hands.

Yous's suspicions about the attackers' true identities were heightened by the fact that the self-defence militia entrusted with defending the civilians had been invited by the army captain from the local barracks to spend the night at

Fort-de-l'Eau, a pleasure area of bars and night clubs. Only two from the militia, Djeha and Boudjemaa, had stayed at home and they put up a spirited defence around their homes, saving the lives of dozens of inhabitants.

Yous also emphasized the assailants' local knowledge. This was not a random attack. Most of the families whose houses were selected for the assault were originally from the towns of Tablat and Jijel, known for their support of GIA groups. They had fled to Bentalha to find new homes closer to Algiers. Yous speculated whether the massacre was one of revenge, of killing GIA supporters, or of liquidating civilians who might have embarrassing inside information on the counter-insurgency. Other houses containing families originally from Bentalha were spared and, as at Tibhirine, witnesses said the assailants spoke with an Eastern Algerian, not a local, accent.

Yous's book was extremely controversial in Algeria. In *El Watan* Salima Tlemçani claimed that Yous said little or nothing about the militiamen, police and soldiers who did intervene. Equally, Liess Boukra, in a history of armed Islamism, readily admitted that Yous had provided an invaluable insight into the origins of the terorist groups but attacked his failure to put Bentalha into the wider context of the intensification of violence by the GIA groups. Yous, Boukra argued, was just too close to the events to grasp the bigger picture.[62]

In the *Times Literary Supplement* in Britain the veteran Algeria watcher Hugh Roberts produced a balanced and thorough review. For him, even taking into account the book's shortcomings, the sheer depth of detail meant that the regime clearly had a case to answer for.[63] Why, for example, did the authorities refuse requests from Bentalha's residents for more arms to defend themselves? Why were the local Islamist groups given such a free rein by the army? Why did the security forces, stationed on the edge of Bentalha, not intervene? Why did they not pursue the assailants? And, finally, why did searchlights installed by the local police seemingly illuminate the attackers' way?

Such questions explain why the population of the Mitidja felt abandoned by the government and international community in 1997. With their telephone wires cut, their buses no longer running and their schools destroyed, they were left to suffer a horrible fate on their own, confronted with a violence that had no moral compass, no rules, no boundaries. Constantly on edge, constantly afraid they were sleep-walking through a nightmare, they were trapped in a living hell by unknown forces. Many frightened villagers headed for the coast as refugees.

Rumours and speculation changed on a daily, even hourly, basis as the ordinary population tried to make sense of the chaos all around them. Dismayed by the constant contrasts between the regime's rhetoric and the incessant insecurity that had been their daily diet for more than three years, they trusted nobody, least of all the regime itself. Assailed on all sides by ninjas, militias, armed groups, and racketeers, they felt that they were being used and abused by demonic forces beyond their control.

It was all too easy to think of the Algerians as one amorphous mass, to forget that each death was a personal trauma with a lasting impact. Yet, as words lost the power to convey the horror of this endless succession of atrocities, one image did break through the censor to communicate this suffering: the photograph of Oum Saad breaking down upon hearing that all eight of her children had been killed in the massacre. Taken by Hocine of Agence France Presse (AFP), the picture caught the imagination of photo editors around the world and was used on the front pages of most French, Spanish, Italian and Lebanese dailies, plus the *International Herald Tribune*, the *Washington Post* and the *Los Angeles Times*. The photograph did not appear in any of Algeria's ten private dailies but would win the World Press Photograph Prize in February 1998.

The story behind the picture was revealing of the climate of censorship. Alerted to the massacre, Hocine recalled, a few photographers reached the site at around 9 a.m. the following day. Everything was extremely confused. Buildings were charred and there was a smell of burning.

> I was stopped by police in plain clothes four or five times. I couldn't get my camera out. The bodies of the victims had been laid out in a school. There was no way of getting in without running the gauntlet of the people hanging around outside.[64]

His famous shot was taken at Zimirili hospital on the outskirts of Algiers where about a hundred or so people, mainly mothers, had gathered in the hope of discovering survivors. They were not allowed inside the hospital, but searched through the lists of names pinned up at the entrance. After apparently discovering there was no hope for any of her children, Oum Saad crumbled to the ground, almost fainting. Hocine leaned over and snapped while the police were otherwise occupied. As a precaution, he removed the film and jumbled it with others in his bag. Moments later the new film was stripped out of his camera by the police. But the one that mattered survived. Later the pro-government newspaper *Horizons* said that Oum Saad had not lost eight children but was mourning her brother and his family and that the photograph was a montage and manipulation. Oum Saad reportedly went so far as to try to sue the photographer and the AFP, but she is widely believed to have come under government pressure. The AFP amended the caption of the photograph but another photograph of the same scene from a different angle by an *El Watan* photographer authenticated Hocine's shot.

Hocine's work is echoed in the photography of Benyoucef Cherif. Arrested in October 1988, Cherif witnessed for himself the extent of police brutality and became determined to document the explosion of a people 'in search of identity'.[65] His subsequent book of photographs of burnt-out villages, devastated fields and traumatized civilians, published in 2003 as *Algérie: Une Saison en Enfer* (*Algeria: A Season in Hell*), appealed to a common humanity. Those portrayed were individuals, not faceless statistics, and each picture showed an image of unimaginable suffering that had to be multiplied a thousand times.

Inevitably this violence was directly connected to power struggles at the top between the Lamari and Zeroual factions. So Zeroual sacked the chief of police, Abbas Ghezaïel, a well-known pro-Lamari hardliner, and replaced him with one of his own men, Yayeb Derradji. Conversly Lamari, unhappy that his rival was conceding too much, was determined to control the negotiations with the AIS for himself.

This infighting was the origin of continual rumours of plots to oust the president, even whispers of a failed assassination attempt, to such an extent that the United States came out in public support of the beleagured Zeroual. In this atmosphere the massacres in the Mitidja became bound up with the complicated clash between the two camps, and in the lead-up to the June 1997 elections there were huge anti-terrorist sweeps in the area around Bentalha. Yet, in August the army mysteriously disappeared, leaving the terrain to four thousand special troops under Lamari's direct command.[66] (In the afterword to Yous's book the veteran left-wing editor François Gèze argued that these troops were instrumental in orchestrating the massacres in September, either by perpetrating atrocities themselves or by not intervening.) This covert action strengthened Lamari's hand at a crucial phase. First and foremost the massacres gave the AIS no choice but to accept the truce since this was the only way to end the terror that was killing so many former FIS supporters. Furthermore the people, eager for revenge or protection, were forced to accept the hardliners' logic while the international community was once again invited to view the regime as the last bastion against Islamist barbarism.

Behind-the-scenes negotiations with AIS commanders Madani Mezraq and Ahmed Benaicha led to Abedlkader Hachani's release from prison in July 1997. Abassi Madani was released one month later on condition that he took up the offer of dialogue by Kofi Annan, then Secretary General of the United Nations. After much manoeuvring a truce was signed on 21 September between Mezraq and Lamari and the AIS announced a unilateral ceasefire in October 1997. This was undoubtedly a major turning point in the conflict.[67] Little, however, was known about the precise details, such as whether the AIS would be exonerated of its crimes. Nor was the truce accompanied by any attempt at reconciliation.

In the short term the truce led only to renewed violence. The GIA groups wanted to show that the agreement was irrelevant and there was more bloodshed in the run-up to local elections in November 1997 which once again were greeted with widespread accusations of fraud. The killing of 412 people at Relizane in a remote part of western Algeria on 30 December was the harbinger of renewed massacres, which led to the bloodiest Ramadan of the conflict. On 18 January Sidi Hammad, just outside Algiers, was attacked by hooded men who murdered women and children, incinerated the houses and abducted young girls. Again however, despite shrieks, screams and protestations, the army did not intervene.

▨ ▨ ▨

Given its large Algerian population and colonial link, France was the outside country most implicated in the Algerian crisis. Already in early 1997 the former French president, Valéry Giscard d'Estaing, had talked about the need to include Islamists in the electoral process, though he did not specify the FIS. Speculation about what the French should do intensified in the wake of the election of a new socialist-led government on 1 June 1997. With his shock of grey hair and thick-set glasses, the prime minister Lionel Jospin had a reputation as a serious intellectual with a strong interest in the Algerian question who had supported the Rome platform. Interviewed by *Libération* on 27 January 1997, Jospin was adamant that France must not remain silent or give the impression of unconditional support for the regime, but rather condemn its undemocratic nature.[68] However, once in power Jospin took a cautious line, arguing that the situation was so confusing it was unclear what France could or should do. Interviewed on French television on 30 September he commented:

> the great difficulty is that we do not have much idea what is really going on in Algeria … It is not like Chile under Pinochet with the democrats fighting a dictatorial regime. We are confronted with a fanatical and violent opposition fighting against a regime which … has recourse itself to violence and the power of the state, so we have to be careful.[69]

As the government prevaricated, the trade union movement and human rights groups made a stand, organizing on 10 November 1997 a 'day of solidarity' with Algeria that included actors such Gérard Depardieu, Isabelle Adjani (herself half Algerian) and Isabelle Huppert as well as music from Cheb Khaled. The Algerian question also stirred up a heated polemic amongst French intellectuals. In January 1998, for example, Bernard-Henry Lévy visited Algeria and wrote two eyewitness accounts for *Le Monde* in which he argued that it was inconceivable that the army was complicit with the massacres.[70] The following month he likened the methods of the Islamist terror groups to those of the Khmer Rouge in Cambodia.[71] In contrast, the veteran human rights activist Pierre Vidal-Naquet took a much more critical line, calling for an international investigation to establish the truth about the violence.[72]

In the face of this pressure the regime stonewalled. Ahmed Attaf, the foreign minister, told foreign reporters in September that the government would conduct no inquiry into the massacres and would brook no 'interference' from outside the country. 'Those who cast doubts are dishonest,' he claimed. 'We know who the killers are.'[73] The international outcry, however, was just too overwhelming. On 30 September Mary Robinson, former Irish president and now UN Commissioner for Human Rights, made an impassioned plea to stop the bloodshed. Two weeks later four human rights organizations called for a special UN session on Algeria. On 4 January Klaus Kinkel, the German foreign minister, urged the European Union to send in a delegation which, after much negotiation, the regime eventually agreed to allow into the country on 19–20 January 1998. Led by Derek Fatchett, the mission of officials from Britain, Luxembourg and Austria wanted to gauge the situation on the ground. As Robin Cook, the British foreign secretary, said, the objective was 'to convey to the Algerian government the public concern felt in Europe at the massacres and to explore what can be done to end the violence, and what the EU can do'.[74] Lasting under forty-eight hours, the delegation's visit was widely seen as a whitewash. Little was done to put the regime on the spot, although it did put pressure on the authorities to drop resistance to visits by United Nations human rights officials.

In January 1998 an all-party British parliamentary group heard evidence from a former Algerian secret service officer, Captain 'Haroun', that the 'dirty jobs' the secret service carried out involved killing innocent civilians, journalists and even soldiers. Mohammed Larbi Sirtout, a diplomat who had defected in 1995, urged Britain to use its presidency of the European Union to put pressure on Algiers and insisted that the EU should stop deferring to France: 'In Algeria, France has a long tradition of deafness. But many of us hope that Britain and the rest of Europe will listen.'[75] In conclusion Ann Clwyd, the Labour MP chairing the group, stated, 'the evidence is mounting, even if much of it is circumstantial, that the state is highly implicated'.[76]

Finally, after much diplomatic wrangling, a five-member UN fact-finding mission was allowed into the country on 22 July. Headed by Mario Soares, the former Portuguese president, who had lived in exile in Algeria before the fall of the Salazar regime, the mission also included former top ministers from the EU, India, Jordan and Kenya. During its two weeks in Algeria, its members met government officials, political leaders, human rights organizations, lawyers and trade union and management representatives. Testifying under oath five years later, Patrick Baudouin, a lawyer and a leading activist in the International Federation of the Leagues of the Rights of Man who visited Algeria in 1997 and 2002, stated that the UN mission was tightly controlled by the authorities, who carefully selected what the Soares delegation did and did not see. They were also highly adept at playing on post-colonial guilt to blot out difficult questions about abuses in the present.[77] As a result the final report, replicating as it did much of the official line, was widely seen as being too soft on the regime.[78]

Nevertheless, in the run-up to the arrival of the UN mission, the Zeroual regime made a limited attempt to identify human rights outrages within the police and the army. In 1998 ninety-eight soldiers were arrested for individual excesses and much was made of this by the pro-government media – which also emphasized that these were specific cases, men operating on their own account outside the boundaries of the law. At no point did the regime make any admission of *systematic* human-rights abuses. In April the Algiers daily *Liberté* reported that a dozen people from Relizane including two mayors, party members from the president's RND, had been arrested on charges of involvement in the killing by pro-government militias of at least 79 of the 412 killed during the massacres at the end of 1997. The bodies of the dead, some of them believed to have been buried alive, were uncovered in two mass graves, according to police. The two mayors had subjected the local population to a reign of terror for five years.[79] The arrests were initially hailed as a possible breakthrough, but the case was never followed up and the two mayors were released on 15 April. Like the army arrests they were increasingly seen a cynical sop to international opinion and a further way of neutralizing pressure for an international investigation.

In the meantime the violence began to recede. In January 1998 there were twenty-five massacres but this declined to four in March and by April there were none, largely because of a significant number of army victories. At this point Algerians began to breathe a sigh of relief, and began to ask themselves if the worst was now over. In the midst of this respite welcome relief was provided by the World Cup in France as the population avidly followed the fortunes of the mesmeric midfield maestro Zinédine Zidane, born in Marseille of Algerian parents.[80] But violence and controversy were never far from the surface and the country was once again plunged into crisis with the killing of Lounès Matoub, one of Algeria's greatest musicians, on 25 June 1998.

Known as the 'Lion of Kabylia', Lounès Matoub was a big man with a generous smile and jet-black hair. From the outset he was much more than just a singer. Proud that he did not speak Arabic, he saw himself as a bard whose music, militant and uncompromising, reflected the struggles of his people, championing the linguistic and cultural rights of the Kabyles. Successive songs attacked corruption, Islamism and the army, asking hard questions about history and identity whilst fervently advocating democracy, toleration and pluralism. 'The Mute Algerian', for example, attacked the silence and censorship of the Boumediène regime. Similarly, the last album before his death contained a pastiche version of the Algerian national anthem, 'Lettre Ouverte À', dedicated to the memory of Tahar Djaout, the francophone journalist and writer killed on 26 May 1993.

For Matoub the Berber spring in April 1980 was the turning point: the equivalent of November 1954 for the post-independence generation. For the first time the Kabyles were rebelling against an authoritarian regime which, by asserting that the country was ethnically Arab, was trying to eradicate their memory and culture in the quest for a monolithic identity.[81] Henceforth for much of the younger generation this was war and the regime was perceived as an occupying enemy.

Eight years later and Lounès Matoub instinctively identified with the young rioters of Black October. Even if Kabyle identity was not involved he understood their anger and humiliation. So, with two fellow activists, he produced a leaflet calling for a two-day strike in support of the uprising on 9 October 1988. As they stopped cars and buses around the Kabyle capital, Tizi-Ouzou, to distribute the tract all three were arrested by the police but whilst the other two were merely handcuffed Lounès was shot in the arm and the stomach. He was rushed to hospital for an emergency operation and it took him two years to recover. After that the authorities tried desperately to blacken his name claiming that he was homosexual (a major taboo in Algerian culture), a drunkard and even a double agent for the secret services.

Once the violence intensified after 1993, Lounès tried to negotiate, like so many Kabyles, a third course denouncing the army and the Islamist groups in equal measure. It was an attitude which earned him enemies on all sides, and few were surprised when he was kidnapped by a GIA group on 25 September 1994. A furore ensued in Kabylia, with Berber activists threatening war if Lounès was not returned. During his captivity Lounès was sentenced to death on the grounds that, as his songs proved beyond doubt, he was an enemy of God. Also, as his captors continually reminded him, had he not stated on French television that he was not an Arab nor obliged to be a Muslim? There was great joy, therefore, when with no explanation he was freed two weeks later. In Tizi-Ouzou the population danced all night, relieved that the threat of even greater violence had been averted.

During the next three years Lounès went back and forth between France and the family home in the mountain village of Taourirt-Moussa, performing an annual concert in Paris to mark the Berber new year. In October 1997 he married for a third time and then became embroiled in procuring a French visa for his new wife Nadia. Lounès hoped to use his contacts with the RCD leader Saïd Sadi but although promises were made nothing materialized. The authorities dragged their feet and in the meantime Lounès received threats and intimidation, especially over his forthcoming song parodying the national anthem. By this point a Kalashnikov never left his side.

The day of his murder Lounès was returning from lunch in Tizi-Ouzou in his Mercedes with Nadia and her two sisters in the passenger seats. His wife remembered that he was wary about the oncoming traffic.[82] Then at Tala Bouane, a tight bend surrounded by trees, the car was raked with seventy-eight bullets. Lounès was killed but the other three survived with Nadia, covered in blood, playing dead. The authorities immediately blamed the GIA as did many Berber leaders, including the women's rights activist Khalida Messaoudi. Yet there was no ballistic analysis and no autopsy. Nadia Matoub was very suspicious about the killers, whom she thought did not look or act like the GIA.[83] Likewise Lounès's sister, Malika, accused the authorities, even claiming that Saïd Sadi was implicated to some degree.

Matoub's death provoked widespread rioting in the Kabyle region. In Tizi-Ouzou bands of young men wielding iron bars rampaged through the streets attacking the law courts, the offices of Air Algeria, banks and supermarkets and tearing down Arabic street signs. Cars and buildings were set on fire and the security services shot and killed two lycée students as the rioters threw up barricades. Bare-chested protesters chanted, '*Pouvoir assassin, Zeroual assassin*' and '*Ouyahia traître*', leaving no doubt that they blamed the president and prime minister for the killing.

More than fifty thousand people attended Lounès's funeral, only a few days before the government passed a new law making Arabic the country's only official language, a move that the singer himself and other Berber leaders had vehemently opposed. Not surprisingly Zeroual became persona non grata in the eyes of the Kabyle community and the authorities showed a clear lack of zeal in finding the murderers. The government claimed that the singer had been killed by a dissident GIA cell but much of the official version did not add up. Some suspected that Lounès Matoub's death was the result of power struggles at the top with anti-Zeroual factions hoping that this incident, like the massacres, would draw opprobrium on the president and make his position untenable.

■ ■ ■

On 11 September 1998 President Zeroual suddenly announced that he would be stepping down before the end of his term. For most Algerians this was a surprise, although there was a widespread sense that Zeroual had reached the end of his strength. Physically and mentally jaded, he looked worn down by events even if on the face of it the government now had the upper hand in the conflict.

Zeroual's departure was not lamented by the populace, who were mostly indifferent. Their attitude was encapsulated in the following chant, widely sung on the football terraces:

The telephone rang
The president has resigned
It is just another trick
What can I say

If the country was stable for one hour
We would escape on a merchant ship
We would escape from Zeroual's face

I would call myself Michel
And spend the night at the Eiffel Tower.[84]

Feelings of indifference and lack of hope were intermingled with enduring anger against the regime. One other chant in particular was a biting attack on the regime's façade of feigned ignorance.

I did not see anything
I did not do anything
I did not steal from anyone
I did not kill anyone.[85]

It was an unsparing portrait of a regime that was seen as having failed its people. However much it tried to wash its hands of the violence, everybody knew that the *pouvoir* was deeply implicated. Under Zeroual Algeria's standing, both at home and abroad, had reached its lowest ebb.

CHAPTER EIGHT

The New Imperialism and the War on Terror

IN HIS BOOK *Taliban* Ahmed Rashid explains how by the mid-1990s Afghanistan had become a pawn in the new 'Great Game'.[1] Evoking the old-style imperialist rivalry between the British and Russian empires in the later nineteenth century, Rashid's term is an apt description for the new competition between Western companies, Pakistan, Saudi Arabia, Iran and the United States as they vied for the control of new oilfields and transit routes for oil pipe-lines. So, for Rashid the crux of the unfolding Afghan crisis was imperialism and the fight for scarce resources necessary to sustain the West. This was why the Clinton administration initially saw the Taliban in a positive light in 1996; no matter how repressive, in the final analysis the Taliban were securing law and order in an area vital for America's long-term economic interests.

Algeria too must be understood as part of this new 'Great Game'. As the IMF and World Bank opened up Algeria to the world markets there was a scramble for oil, gas and influence. With the deregulation of the all-important energy sector, Western companies and the European Union wooed the regime, signing a series of lucrative contracts to secure a stake in the country's precious resources. Such moves, paving the way for outside control, would have been anathema under Boumediène in the 1960s and 1970s, when Algeria was resolutely anti-imperialist. Striving for economic independence had always been a badge of honour but by the mid-1990s the Algerian regime, desperate for international credit to keep afloat, had no choice but to ingratiate itself with the World Bank and the International Monetary Fund. To reassure would-be investors, fearful about the military situation, the regime created a special exclusion zone around the oil and gas fields in the south. Thus, on

23 December 1995 British Petroleum finalized a contract worth $3 billion giving it the right to exploit gas deposits in Aïn-Salah in the Sahara for the next thirty years. Total completed a similar deal amounting to $1.5 billion one month later and on 15 February 1996 the American firm Arco signed a contract for a joint venture to drill in Rhourd El-Baguel oilfield. In November 1996 a pipeline supplying gas to the EU was opened.

These contracts undoubtedly bolstered the regime at its most perilous point in the war against Islamist insurgents. Tied into Algeria through huge investments, these companies and the EU now had a clear interest in making sure that the regime did not go under. At the same time the deals highlighted the fact that the country's natural resources were a curse as well as a blessing. In theory they made Algeria a rich country but in practice the shadowy economic mafia siphoned off the money through a complex network of private monopolies and import–export companies, even gobbling up much of the 1994 debt rescheduling.[2] Lining their pockets thus, they had no interest in reinvesting this wealth in the population and the result was an investment-starved economy plagued by corruption and bad governance; a state of affairs exacerbated by the Western powers, who were chiefly interested in securing cheap oil and gas resources.

If Algeria was part of the 'Great Game', the country was also a nodal point in the growing 'war' against international Islamist terrorism. Still reeling from the 1995 and 1996 bombings in Port Royal and St Michel in Paris, the French authorities were petrified by the threat of terrorism in the run-up to the World Cup in France in summer 1998. French citizens of Algerian origin were put under intense scrutiny. Visits to their parents' homeland were seen as potentially sinister. The French secret services were particularly concerned by transnational Islamist networks linked to Abu Hamza and Omar Abu Omar, the Jordanian Palestinian better known as Abu Qutada, both of whom were based at the Finsbury Park mosque in north London and issued a regular flow of fatwas to GIA groups operating in France and Algeria, drawing upon a deluge of references from the Qur'an and Salafist theologians to justify all manner of violence, including the killing of women and children. In the eyes of the French, the British government had consistently underestimated the threat posed by this nerve centre of Islamism, and French secret service agents were despatched to London to track the two clerics' every move and infiltrate the Finsbury mosque.[3]

The Central Intelligence Agency (CIA) was also monitoring the Algerian situation closely by the late 1990s. As far back as 1985 the CIA had opened a station in Algiers, producing a regular flow of intelligence, but this operation intensified in the wake of the failed attack on the World Trade Center in New York on 26 February 1993.[4] Then a bomb, composed of 1,200 lbs of explosives, several heavy tanks of hydrogen and two 20-foot fuses and hidden in a van parked beneath the twin towers, had exploded shortly after midday, killing six people and injuring more than a thousand. The attack could have been much worse – one of the ringleaders, the Pakistani militant Ramzi Ahmed Yousef, claimed later that he aimed to kill 250,000 people by toppling one tower into another – and in response the CIA's Counter-Terrorist Center established a seven-day, twenty-four-hour taskforce to collect intelligence on terrorism. One branch tracked extremism in the Sunni world, concentrating on the unfolding situation in Algeria. CIA analysts, in conjunction with station chiefs in Algiers, Cairo and Tunis, studied the Algerian insurgency, deciphering a pattern of international cooperation between Islamist radicals. They were worried by the flow of Saudi Arabian money into these groups, the willingness of Britain, France and Germany to grant asylum to exiled leaders, and the movement of weapons from Sudan to Algeria. And they were alarmed by an upsurge of violence connected to Arab veterans of the Afghan jihad, among whom one name began to loom large: Osama bin Laden, the Saudi millionaire, who was involved in financing these groups.

Drawing up a balance sheet, the CIA Counter-Terrorist Center sought to assess American interests and responsibilities in North Africa.[5] Starting with the assumption that this area was too important strategically to be left to France, CIA chiefs asked a series of related questions: what was the relationship between Algeria and terrorists who might threaten America? What policy should it adopt towards Algerian Islamists? Should it regard all Islamists as fundamentally anti-Western? Was the Algerian government deliberately inflating the threat in order to win American support?

Initially the United States had a foot in both camps. Leading FIS activists, notably Anwar Haddam, were allowed to live in America and had links with the corridors of power in Washington. The Clinton administration had mixed feelings about the Algerian regime, worried by their reluctance to let human rights organizations into the country as well as the news of their growing development of nuclear power.[6] But the more the nineties went on the more the Algerian government was perceived as an ever more important ally in the campaign against Islamic terrorism; a vital source of intelligence, even if this information was tainted by torture. President Zeroual, now seen as 'our man in Algiers', was repeatedly supported in his internal power struggles by the American ambassador Ronald Neumann, and Washington sought to expand military cooperation with Algeria through a series of high-profile visits and joint manoeuvres. In 1998 Admiral Thomas Lopez, then commander of US Naval Forces Europe, headed an official delegation to Algiers, and the destroyer USS *Mitscher* participated in an Algerian navy search and rescue exercise. The United States also doubled its International Military Education and Training programme to Algeria that year. These links were strengthened still further when US Defence Secretary William Cohen announced in February 1999 that America was going to deepen military cooperation and in May there were joint exercises with the US 6th Fleet, thereby making Algeria America's most important strategic partner in North Africa after Egypt and its long-standing ally Morocco.

This muscular American presence undoubtedly alarmed Paris. The Maghreb is France's back yard and the sight of the American military in Algiers fed into insecurities about *grandeur* and the French place in the world. The Algerian authorities, in turn, knew how closely French antennae were tuned to the threat of Anglo-Saxon encroachment. Exploiting this rivalry with great skill, they played one power off against the other, locking both into supporting the regime. Thus, any American visit would invariably be followed by the spectacle of a French official or military man scuttling off to Algiers, desperate to provide a counter-weight to US influence.[7]

Finally, and perhaps most significantly, the Franco-American duel provided the Algerian leadership with a telling insight into Western calculations about international relations. For all their fine words about ethics and human rights, in an increasingly unpredictable post-Cold War world French, American and British priorities would be determined by two factors: the need for cheap resources and the growing war on terror.

■   ■   ■

In the wake of Zeroual's departure presidential elections were set for February 1999. These were then quickly put back to 15 April 1999 as Algeria became embroiled in rumours about who was and who was not putting themselves forward. Backstage there were intense discussions amongst the army barons about who had the capacity to lift the country out of its impasse. Suddenly one name was on everybody's lips: Abdelaziz Bouteflika, Boumediène's foreign minister.

With his short stature and scraped-over hair, Bouteflika, born in 1937, was the nearly man of Algerian politics. He had nearly succeeded Boumediène as president in 1979. He had also nearly taken over in 1994, allegedly turning the post down because he was not promised enough independence. Politically speaking he had a reputation as a canny operator, emerging during the war of liberation as a leading member of Boumediène's Oujda clan before his long service at the United Nations.[8] Well versed in the intricacies of international diplomacy, he was seen as a pro-Western liberal who had always been luke-warm about socialism. In 1981 Bouteflika had gone into self-imposed exile to escape corruption charges that were later dropped. His wilderness years had come to an end when he returned to Algeria in 1987, adding his signature to a letter of protest by eighteen historic Algerian figures condemning the brutality of army troops during October 1988.[9]

This curriculum vitae played a vital role in Bouteflika's political appeal. Not implicated in the violence of the 1990s, he was seen by many as a clean pair of hands who, even if he had a reputation as a liberal modernizer, was a throwback to the halcyon days of Boumediène. Moreover, unlike Zeroual, who had always been stiff and ill at ease on the international stage, Bouteflika was a consum-mate actor. A good speaker in front of the cameras, he projected determination, energy and apparent purpose. Above all he promised to end the violence and restore the Algerians' faith in themselves and their place in the world.

The impetus for Bouteflika's candidature came initially from General Larbi Belkheir who succeeding in winning round the other leading generals, including Smaïn Lamari, the head of counter-intelligence. Lamari was then crucial in winning the endorsement of the RND leadership, some of whom were initially sympathetic to Hamrouche, the former prime minister. Importantly too, Hamas came out in support of Bouteflika when their own leader, Mahfoud Nahnah, was excluded on a technicality, and leading mem-bers of the RCD, including Khalida Messaoudi, also called on Algerians to back him despite their party's policy of a boycott.

Shortly after Zeroual's resignation in September 1998, Khaled Nezzar, supposedly retired but still an extremely influential figure, had set out to stymie any talk of Bouteflika for president.[10] Recalling the way in which Bouteflika had backed out when confronted with the challenges of power in 1994, Nezzar implied that he was temperamentally unsuited for high office. But by January 1999 subtle pressure had been brought to bear on Nezzar and he fell into line. In an interview with *Le Matin* he completely retracted his comments, lavishing praise on Bouteflika as far and away the best candidate.[11]

Such a ringing endorsement typified the bandwagon effect that sur-rounded Bouteflika. Committees of support sprang up in all the major towns, underlining his war of liberation credentials by constantly talking of him as 'al-moudjahid Si Abd el-Kader'. Bouteflika played on this patriotic lineage himself, reminding Algerians that it was he who had campaigned for the return of Abd el-Kader's ashes in 1967 and that he had been one of the coffin bearers.

Although Bouteflika became de facto the official candidate, the regime tried to convince the public that the result was not a foregone conclusion.[12] Zeroual gave what he claimed were personal guarantees to the opposition parties that the elections would be honest and on this basis eleven candidates officially registered for the contest. Of these Hanoune, Ghozali and Boukrouh were excluded because they did not receive enough support from elected representatives, while Nahnah was disqualified because he had no documentation validating his participation in the war of liberation, thereby showing how the memory of the war of liberation continued to be mobilized for political purposes.[13] This left Bouteflika to face Hocine Aït Ahmed, the aging FFS leader dubbed the 'eternal rebel', Mouloud Hamrouche, the reformist prime minister from 1989 to 1991 who was running as an independent, Abdallah Djaballah, the candidate of the new Islamist party, the Movement for National Reform, Mokdad Sifi, prime minister between 1993 and 1995 and backed by the anti-Bouteflika faction in the RND, and Youcef Khatib, a veteran from the internal resistance, imprisoned by Ben Bella, who had organized Zeroual's 1995 election campaign.

Arguably the biggest threat to Bouteflika's ambitions came from Ahmed Taleb Ibrahimi, the education minister in the 1960s who had pioneered Arabization and the closing down of French-language schools, many run by the Catholic Church. Presidential advisor in the 1970s, foreign minister from 1982 to 1988, like Bouteflika he had a long pedigree that was further enhanced by the fact that he was the son of the late Sheik Bachir Al-Ibrahimi, the leader of the Association of Algerian Ulema from 1940 to 1951. Also in favour of dialogue between the different sides, he was backed by many former FIS supporters and many saw him as a bridge between the army and the Islamists.

Despite the regime's assurances, the campaign was not equal from the start. Bouteflika was treated as president-elect by the television and pro-government press while the other candidates were ignored. On 14 April there was fraud during early polling organized for the security forces and the other six candidates withdrew in protest.[14] Undeterred, the regime forged ahead with the election on the following day, whereupon the population registered its disgust through abstention. The turnout was embarrassingly low – an estimated 20 per cent overall and just 5 per cent in Kabylia, where Bouteflika's election posters had been regularly defaced – but state television dutifully announced over 60 per cent, awarding more than 70 per cent of the votes to the duly elected Bouteflika.

By any stretch of the imagination it was a mockery of democracy and the opposition candidates called for a campaign of mass protest. In Tizi-Ouzou, Oran and Algiers thousands flooded into the streets but the regime reacted with repression, banning all demonstrations. Other countries' reactions were carefully calibrated. Both France and the United States declared themselves to be perturbed and disappointed by the election rigging but they stopped well short of an outright condemnation.

Unabashed at the manner of his victory, Bouteflika strode out for his first press conference full of bullish self-confidence. Exuding his characteristic brand of pugnacious charm, he brushed aside difficult questions about the domestic protests and the lukewarm foreign reaction. When a journalist asked who controlled him, he responded by asking who controlled the journalist. Once in office he went about piecing together a coalition composed of the pro-government parties FLN and RND along with Nahnah's party and part of Ennahda. In the meantime the opposition parties, predictably, degenerated into recrimination, each blaming the other for Bouteflika's victory. The new president was left to dominate the political field. In February 2000 Bouteflika replaced six major generals, a significant reshuffle that according to the press headlines demonstrated the president's ascendancy over the army. But on closer inspection things were less clear cut. Yes, Bouteflika had purged the Zeroual faction but this only confirmed the dominance of the former French officers, Lieutenant General Mohammed Lamari, chief of the general staff, Major General Mohammed Médiène, director of intelligence and security, and Major General Smaïn Lamari, director of counter-espionage and internal security, all of them the principal architects of the repression since 1992.[15] These men remained the real power behind the throne, limiting Bouteflika's capacity for independent manoeuvre.

Away from the shadows Bouteflika projected an air of purposeful action, adopting a three-pronged strategy purportedly based on nationalism, honesty and economic recovery that aimed to reconnect with the lost generation of young Algerians. He remembered that under Boumediène Algeria had entered the global limelight, engendering an intangible but real sense of pride in its people. Bouteflika wanted to rekindle this self-belief. He also set out to be honest, acknowledging that the cancellation of elections in January 1992 was one of the origins of the conflict that had led to a hundred thousand deaths; a statement that caused consternation in some military circles.[16] Finally, Bouteflika promised to revitalize the economy, in the hope that the continuing reforms initiated in partnership with Western institutions would at last bear dividends.

Drawing upon his time on the international stage under Boumediène, Bouteflika initially put enormous effort into foreign policy in an attempt to break out of the diplomatic isolation that had bedevilled the country since 1992 and persuade Algeria's principal Western partners to resume normal dealings. He cut a dash at the funeral of Morocco's King Hassan in July 1999, reportedly impressing President Clinton and enraging the Palestinian hardline Hamas movement by shaking hands publicly with prime minister Ehud Barak of Israel. Inevitably, however, France was Bouteflika's main target, and on 15 June 2000 he made a three-day full state visit to Paris. Greeted by a 760-foot red carpet when he touched down at Orly airport, Bouteflika was accorded a big welcome which included personal talks with President Chirac at the Elysée, a speech to the National Assembly, a state dinner and a reception at the Hôtel de Ville as well as lunch with prime minister Lionel Jospin. Thereafter, he met business leaders, members of the Algerian community and the head of the French Jewish community, Henri Hadjenberg.[17] He also travelled to Verdun to pay homage to the 180,000 Algerian Muslims who had fought for France during the First World War. Throughout, Bouteflika stressed the theme of reconciliation and the need for a new era of Franco-Algerian relations and, although he complained that in concrete terms he left empty handed, he knew on another level that the visit was an enormous step forward. He had broken the international quarantine and Algeria was no longer a pariah state. Now that Paris had made a gesture other countries would follow suit and in July Bouteflika received the Spanish prime minister, José Aznar, the first European leader to visit Algeria since 1992.

■ ■ ■

Bouteflika knew that his presidency hinged on his ability to deliver on his election promise to 'extinguish the fire'. On this front he had good reason to be optimistic. The AIS truce had endured and this, in combination with further army victories against the GIA, allowed the authorities to talk more credibly than before about the downward curve of violence. Those insurgents still fighting, officials claimed, were just a residual violence, the final pockets of resistance waiting to be mopped up by the security forces.

But if this assessment was largely true in the area west of Algiers towards the Moroccan border, where a rump of GIA groups had degenerated into smuggling, extortion and rape, it was less so in Kabylia and several regions of eastern Algeria. There the Salafist Group for Preaching and Combat (GSPC), led by Hassan Hattab, the thirty-two-year-old former mechanic and paratrooper, had broken away from the other GIA groups and sought to solder together those groups who had rejected the AIS truce. Accusing the GIA of being infiltrated by the secret services and denigrating the massacre of civilians as murderous and counter-productive, the GSPC concentrated on attacking the security forces. By the end of 1999 its forces numbered between five hundred and one thousand and it had built up some measure of support as Hattab, already blamed by the authorities for the murder of the musician Lounès Matoub, assumed the status of the new public enemy number one.

In rejecting the most extreme forms of violence Hattab was playing a waiting game. He knew that the GSPC activists had to regroup and gather their strength, which in practical terms meant rebuilding the various networks, both within Algeria and without, that the GIA had developed between 1993 and 1998. It also meant approaching Osama bin Laden for logistical support. The Saudi millionaire, eager for access to ready-made networks in Europe and North America, was understood to be only too willing to oblige.[18]

In his book on al-Qaeda, the *Observer* journalist Jason Burke has pieced together the subterranean contacts between the GSPC and bin Laden, showing how, in exchange for money and weapons, the GSPC is thought to have supplied the Saudi with a steady stream of well-trained and well-disciplined militants.[19] In June 2001 bin Laden sent his trusted Yemeni aide Emad Abdelwahid Ahmed Alwan, alias Abu Mohammed, to Algeria, via Ethiopia, the Sudan and Niger, as the latest in a series of initiatives that had been developing since around 1998. Since Alwan had helped Algerian Islamist militants set up camps in the Yemen in the early 1990s he was the perfect emissary and contacts of this nature explain why few of those subsequently arrested in Europe were simply 'al-Qaeda': the majority of them, at least until 2002, were linked to the GSPC or remnants of the GIA, because for bin Laden these men were vital in his gathering campaign against the West. They provided a bridgehead into France and beyond; nodal points in a labyrinthine world of mosques, meeting houses and military camps through which young Muslim men could be recruited and propelled in the direction of Pakistan for weapons training.

Ahmed Ressam, the son of a veteran of the war of liberation, left Algeria in 1992 to look for work in France as an illegal immigrant before getting into trouble with the French authorities and fleeing to Canada. In Montreal Ressam lived on the margins, surviving through petty theft and welfare payments. He had showed no Islamist sympathies when living in Algeria, but now, downtrodden and penniless in the West, he fell under the spell of two fellow countrymen, Fateh Kamel and Abderaouf Hannachi, both of whom frequented the Assuna Annabawiyah mosque in Montreal, well known for its Salafist brand of Islam, and both of whom were linked to the GIA. Fired up by their tales of the struggle in Algeria, as well as by Hannachi's stories of fighting in Afghanistan, Ressam was converted to their hardline brand of Islam and in March 1998 he travelled to Pakistan with a number of other Algerian recruits. At various camps there Ressam received training in sabotage, assassination and explosives, and during this time he and his fellow con-spirators hatched the idea for a huge attack on America.[20] One year later Ressam was arrested at 6 p.m. on 14 December 1999 at the Canadian–American border, his car boot stuffed full of bomb-making equipment whose purpose was to kill hundreds of people at Los Angeles international airport on the eve of the new millennium.[21]

Ressam's biography recalled that of Khaled Kelkhal, the GIA activist assassinated by the French police in 1995. Like Kelkhal, Ressam was living a threadbare existence in the West and, just as for Kelkhal, this experience stimulated a volatile set of reactions. Conscious of being part of an ethnic minority, conscious too of his exclusion from the wealth of mainstream Canadian society, Ressam felt that he was being looked down upon and this nurtured a deep-seated rage. Rootless and alienated, Ressam was easily seduced by Kamel's argument that he had to see Algeria as just one piece in a grand Western plot to humiliate Islam. It was his sacred duty to strike back on behalf of oppressed Muslims everywhere, and violence of the most spectacular kind would enable him to lose his sense of powerlessness and ensure his own martyrdom.

Although Ressam was the most extreme example, many young Algerians, dispersed across Europe and North America either as immigrants or asylum seekers, gravitated towards extremist action. It would of course be wrong to suggest that every member of the Algerian diaspora was a potential terrorist. Nevertheless, the conditions of their lives abroad made a small minority highly susceptible to the lure of armed Islamism.[22]

If some Algerians abroad were willing to take up the call for an inter-national jihad against the West, back in Algeria there was a palpable decline in armed attacks, with 1,500 killed during 1999 as opposed to 3,000 in the previous year. But as violence receded the spotlight moved back on to the system itself. Ordinary Algerians were grateful for an end to chaos and lawless-ness but they were also aware that fundamentally nothing had been resolved since October 1988. With the economy as bleak as ever they were still being humiliated by *le pouvoir*. Algeria had a terrible sameness and people began to suspect that whatever Bouteflika's promises the regime had a vested interest in keeping the violence going, albeit at more tolerable levels, in order to maintain the system.

Many Algerians were sceptical when Antar Zouabri, the GIA leader who according to the regime had been killed in 1997, made a sudden reappearance in 1999 as the alleged murderer of the former FIS leader Abdelkader Hachani, who was killed in broad daylight in central Algiers. Although Zouabri's group was blamed for the murder many saw this as simply too convenient, and suspected that the killers came from within the regime. This was yet another example of a figure of reconciliation, one who had advocated restraint in the face of the 1992 coup and was a possible figure of reconciliation, being assassinated just at the moment when he was poised to return to politics. Moreover, Hachani's death showed how terrorism fulfilled a vital function. Justifying the annual renewal of the state of emergency, it scared people into submission and stifled the emergence of mass political protest.

An experienced political realist, Bouteflika knew that he lacked electoral legitimacy. He wanted to cement his position by putting an end to the violence, and with this aim he put out discreet feelers to the AIS leaders, Madani Mezraq and Ahmed Benaïcha, in an effort to transform the ceasefire into a permanent settlement. The summer months of 1999 witnessed intense behind-the-scenes negotiations which culminated in a series of carefully choreographed responses and counter-responses as both sides, realizing that they had a mutual interest in formally ending the conflict, inched towards a settlement. First, on 1 June, Mezraq announced that he was ready to formalize the truce. On 4 June Bouteflika made a positive reply, signalling the need to enshrine this process in a legal framework. Two days later Mezraq took up his offer, announcing the immediate cessation of all AIS military activity which in turn led the presidential office to issue a statement outlining the 'law on civil concord', duly rubber-stamped by a compliant National Assembly shortly after.

Many ordinary Algerians were genuinely encouraged by this flurry of activity. They looked hopefully to the leading FIS figures at home and abroad who, with the exception of the still imprisoned Belhadj, gave their blessing to the Mezraq-Bouteflika initiative. In contrast two of the former presidential candidates, Aït Ahmed and Taleb Ibrahimi, were critical. They voiced doubts about the civil concord's ability to deliver an enduring peace because the agreement ignored three key issues: the problem of the 'disappeared', the ending of the state of emergency and the future legal status of the FIS.

Sidestepping these issues Bouteflika pressed on regardless, pushing through a model of transition that was rigidly managed from above. The ordinary populace were not involved in any form of consultation; when the civil concord was put to them on 16 September they were simply asked to say reply 'for' or 'against' to the referendum question: 'Are you for or against the initiative of the President of the Republic to establish peace and civil concord?'

Such wording was deliberately vague because Bouteflika had no wish to be constrained. He wanted the referendum to give him a wide room for manoeuvre in his negotiations with the armed groups. Large numbers of Algerians were very aware of the ambiguity but, desperate for any glimmer of hope, they dutifully went to the polls, approving the civil concord with an apparent massive 98.6 per cent approval rate on a turnout of 85 per cent.

This result undoubtedly boosted Bouteflika's prestige. He had seemingly broken the cycle of violence and counter-violence and won himself much-needed legitimacy as he was hailed as the peace maker: the man of consensus who, in offering an outstretched hand to all Algerians, had fulfilled his electoral promise to 'extinguish the fire'. Through him Algeria had taken a big step forward on the road to normalization and to the outside world the civil concord was proclaimed as the basis of a renewed, properly democratic politics.

But behind all the talk of peace and reconciliation Bouteflika had made a cold political calculation. He reasoned that if he was to stop the bloodshed there must be a pact of silence. All the protagonists had to agree to move on by forgetting their murderous divisions and focusing on the future. For this reason there was to be no talk of surrender. In coaxing the insurgents to down arms the regime had to eschew any triumphalism. The guerrillas must be allowed to return to society with their heads held high. They had to be given a tangible reward so that they could proclaim that the fighting had not been in vain and in concrete terms this meant immunity from prosecution, the right to hang on to their spoils of war extracted through racketeering, and the possibility of legalizing the FIS.[23]

Within the civil concord, therefore, truth and justice had to be sacrificed. In the interests of realpolitik the pain and suffering of civilians was ignored. Amnesia was the order of the day as the civil concord in effect came to represent a common pardon for *le pouvoir*, the criminals and the armed groups. So, despite pledges to Amnesty International, nobody was brought to account for violence inflicted upon the population. The government displayed no concern for the families of the victims and the disappeared and this indifference provoked a growing sense of anger from below towards the whole transition process.

As these details became clearer in the subsequent months, the population saw the civil concord more and more as a cynical ploy, a mechanism by which perpetrators on all sides were allowed to escape justice. As Djamel Berrabah, president of the Coordination Committee for Truth and Justice, commented in an interview with *L'Express* on 13 April 2000: 'The ruling class has made a deal with the Islamists: "Be quiet, we know what you have done, you know what we have done – leave us in power and you will get your share."' In response to such criticisms Bouteflika was bluntly realistic. What was the alternative, he asked? How else could the violence be ended without jeopardizing the fragile peace?

In January 2000 the civil concord led to an amnesty whereby six thousand militants from the AIS, as well as groups led by Kertali and by Ali Benhadjar, were pardoned. Theoretically this amnesty was only extended to those not guilty of rape, murder or terrorism but in reality few questions were asked and there was little way of verifying the official figures. The whole process was deliberately opaque, partly, many suspected, because this allowed any double agents to disappear into obscurity. In the weeks following the amnesty hundreds of guerrillas, for the most part young men aged between eighteen and twenty, returned home. Many behaved provocatively. Believing that the amnesty had made them untouchable, they conducted themselves as conquerors, rarely expressing regret. Few gave up their 'Afghan'-type dress and beards, some bragged about their war adventures, enthralling adolescents with accounts of the *mujahidin* exploits. Mezraq paraded around in an armour-plated Mercedes.

In early February Benhadjar and a hundred of his men quit their base in the countryside near Médéa in the 'Triangle of Death'. A former schoolmaster who had been elected as an FIS candidate in the cancelled parliamentary elections, Benhadjar had once been a diehard among diehards, arrested three times before going underground to join the GIA:

> We took up arms to defend ourselves and our right to free speech. The people understand and they've pardoned us. And although the country has paid a heavy toll, our struggle was not in vain because we have recovered the right to free speech.[24]

In 1995 he had left the GIA in protest at their bloodletting to form the Islamic League for Preaching and Jihad (Ligue Islamique de la Daâwa et du Djihad, LIDD), and the following year lost an eighteen-year-old son in a skirmish between the GIA and his breakaway band. He had abided by the AIS ceasefire declared in October 1997 and his group's armed activity was thereafter confined to fighting the GIA, chasing its gunmen out of the region.

Speaking at his home in Médéa in early 2000, Benhadjar showed few signs outwardly of changing. His hennaed beard was still long. But he spoke of reconciliation and reiterated his belief in promises made during negotiations with the AIS, especially one that the FIS would be allowed to re-form: 'We have shown them that we are committed to peace. It is their move now.'[25]

With the likes of Benhadjar's LIDD dissolving themselves, the civil concord did lead to a further significant reduction in guerrilla activity during the first half of 2000. However, this decline stopped in late summer and autumn. Many former guerrillas were dismayed by the refusal to legalize the new political party Wafa (Fidelity) in November 2000 on the grounds that it was the ex-FIS in disguise.[26] For them this showed that the regime was not sincere about engaging with Islamist ideas and that the civil concord was nothing but a ruse to disarm the insurgency. Exploiting this discontent, Hassan Hattab did everything in his power to counteract the Bouteflika effect. Consequently there was a resurgence of violence during the final three months of the year with 250 killed in October alone.

■ ■ ■

A young Algerian asks his father about the colours of the Algerian flag. He knows that the green stands for Islam and the red for the blood of our glorious martyrs but what does the white stand for? 'The blank pages in our history,' replies the father.

(Algerian joke circa 1996)

How best to move on from a traumatic past is a challenge that has confronted a whole series of countries since the 1970s, from Spain, South Africa and Rwanda through to Argentina, Chile and Northern Ireland. Whatever the details of each case, all have been forced to grapple with a common set of questions. Should those with knowledge of killings be legally compelled to talk about them? Should amnesty be available to some? Should names be named in public? Should compensation go to victims? Should perpetrators apologize?

During the 1990s more than fifteen truth commissions were established, with the Guatemalan Historical Clarification Commission being the first and the South African Truth and Reconciliation Commission being the most famous. In the last case Archbishop Desmond Tutu pioneered the model of truth and forgiveness by bringing together victims and perpetrators in an attempt to force a healing process, no matter how raw and painful.[27] In contrast Bouteflika has followed the model of post-Franco Spain, where, after Franco died in 1975, all sides agreed to forget the bloody divisions of the past. By the time of the amnesty in January 2000 it was already possible to see through the calculated vagueness and understand the civil concord as an act of repression. For the sake of peace Bouteflika was determined to bury the 1990s. There was to be no major inquisition about who was behind the violence; no coming to terms with the past. Recent history had to be cast aside.

Bouteflika sought to efface this immediate history by facing up to taboo aspects not of the immediate past but of the war of liberation. So, on 5 July 1999, the thirty-seventh anniversary of independence, Bouteflika announced that Tlemcen, Béjaïa, Hassi Messaoud and Biskra, four of the country's major airports, would carry the names of Messali Hadj, Abane Ramdane, Krim Belkacem and Mohammed Khider: all four controversial historical figures since the last three were assassinated by the secret services whilst Messali, as an opponent of the FLN, died in exile in 1974. At the time Bouteflika's gesture was portrayed as a brave move, an expression of his desire to build a more honest Algeria. Yet the establishment of these sites of public memory was a subtle sleight of hand. By projecting the image of a less regulated attitude to the past, open to pluralism and tolerant of difference, Bouteflika hoped to foster a more inclusive attitude to the present. Through a new public history of the liberation struggle, still the nation's foundation stone, Bouteflika wanted Algerians to put aside their divisions and foster common ideas about politics and compromise.

Bouteflika also looked further back into the past. One day after the rehabilitation of the forgotten leaders, the president gave a speech in Constantine recognizing the Jewish dimension of Algerian culture and the unique contribution of Jews in enriching the country's history and heritage. Equally, in August Bouteflika paid generous tribute to Monsignor Duval, the former archbishop of Algiers, recalling his soubriquet Mohammed Habib Duval and describing him as 'a true Algerian'. In November he proclaimed Saint Augustine as the father of the Algerian nation, telling students at Rome university in November 1999 that the fifth-century theologian was 'a son of Algeria and the most notable of the Fathers of the Church ... a saint as much for Christianity as for Islam'.[28]

Such conciliatory language played well to many Western audiences. By explicitly rejecting those within the Islamist movement who talked of Jews and Christians as an alien presence, it conveyed an image of emancipation and democratization and suggested that Bouteflika's regime was willing to embrace the multifaceted aspects of Algerian culture. In agreeing that Judaism and Christianity were an integral part of Algerian history Bouteflika was laying the basis of a more tolerant national identity, seemingly challenging those historical narratives which had occluded vital aspects of the past.

But paradoxically this new approach came just at the moment when the government was trying to oblige all Algerians to draw a veil over its most recent past by following a policy of silence, evasion and selective memory. Through censorship, the intimidation of journalists and the control of access to paper and printing the government attempted to tightly circumscribe any discussion of the 1990s which departed from the official script of the honourable army versus diabolical terrorists.[29] Unfortunately, what ordinary people had endured was just too traumatic to be swept away.

In the face of official amnesia, grassroots civilian pressure groups refused to be muzzled. As these groups absorbed the implications of the civil concord they did not want their history and experience to be denied or manipulated by the state. They wanted to express their pain and anger and believed that, in denying truth and justice, Bouteflika's transition process was fundamentally flawed.

This issue had been gathering momentum since 1997 when families, desperate to bring their plight to the attention of the national and international media, had organized protests outside barracks, police stations, prisons and detention centres where their relatives had disappeared. The following year these families had sent a letter to the visiting UN fact-finding mission listing in detail the circumstances of 239 cases, meaning that for the first time Algerians were fully confronted with a set of personal identities and precise facts.

The lead was taken by grieving mothers who, determined to give their anger a more effective organizational framework, established the National Association of the Families of the Disappeared and SOS-Disparus in 1998. Led by Nacéra Dutour and Lila Ighil respectively, their cause was also championed by Louisa Hanoune, leader of the Trotskyite Parti des Travailleurs, in the National Assembly.[30] Supported too by the FFS, Hanoune pursued a tireless campaign to break down official silence, and the government, also under intense pressure from international human rights organizations, was eventually forced to face up to the issue and acknowledged that disappearances had taken place on a huge scale. As a result the Office National des Droits de l'Homme (ONDH), a state organization established in 1992 to monitor human rights in the country, pinpointed 4,185 cases by the end of 1999. But it conveniently blamed all the disappearances on the armed groups, making little attempt to examine the role of the security forces, and its establishment was condemned by the civilian protest groups as a ploy to avoid more awkward questions.

The 'mothers of the disappeared' refused to stop their protests. Despite threats, harassment and a hate campaign that sought to stigmatize them as the mothers of 'terrorists and throat cutters', they carried on with their campaign, claiming that the figure of 4,185 was just the tip of the iceberg and that the figure actually ran into tens of thousands.[31] Holding photographs and banners aloft they have held regular vigils outside the National Assembly and the Justice Ministry since 1998. At one point Bouteflika, harangued by placard-waving women during a public meeting, lost his temper and told them to forget their grief for the greater good of the nation.

The government had some ability to silence critical voices at home, but much less abroad. In France in particular there was a steady stream of revelations that the government could not control, led by the left-wing publisher La Découverte under the stewardship of commissioning editor François Gèze. The publisher had previously exposed the crimes of the French army during the war of independence through a series of graphic eyewitness accounts.[32] Now, continuing with this tradition of dissent, La Découverte published two ground-breaking books, Nesroulah Yous's *Qui a Tué à Bentalha?* in October 2000 and *La Sale Guerre* by Habib Souaïdia in February 2001, both of which catalogued in detail the shameful human rights abuses carried out by the Algerian army. Both became media events, with Yous's book serialized in *Le Monde* whilst Souaïdia was extensively interviewed during the course of a special fifty-minute television documentary on La Cinquième on 27 May 2001.

Their revelations about the 'dirty war' were paralleled in the journalist Jean-Baptiste Rivoire's television exposé of the events surrounding the death of Lounès Matoub, screened on 31 October 2000 on Canal Plus. Entitled *Algérie, la Grande Manip* (Algeria, the Great Manipulation) and drawing on a long series of interviews, the documentary challenged the official line that Hattab's groups were the culprits, pointing the finger at shadowy elements within the regime. Algerian exiles in France also confronted the violence through music and novels. On her debut CD, *Raoui*, released in 2000, Souad Massi's haunting acoustic music spoke eloquently about civilian pain and suffering, while Anouar Benmalek, Aziz Chouaki and Boualem Sansal wrote novels that were complex narratives of choices, actions and ambiguities, many miles from the simplistic dichotomies proclaimed by the government.[33]

Away from France, Robert Fisk in the London-based *Independent* also consistently took a scalpel to the Algerian government's version of events, collecting hundreds of pages of evidence from Algerian lawyers and human rights workers that proved beyond doubt that the security services were guilty of torture, extra-judicial killings and 'disappearances'.[34] At the same time the highly controversial Qatar-based Arab satellite station Al-Jazeera, watched by millions across the Arab world, put Algerian human rights in the spotlight through a series of regular documentaries and interviews.[35] Indeed in a desperate attempt to stop Algerians from watching one Al-Jazeera documentary programme in January 1999 examining the role of the security forces in extrajudicial killings, the government shut down power to the major cities, including Algiers, ten minutes into the programme.[36] Thereafter, Bouteflika banned Al-Jazeera journalists indefinitely, after a further programme criticizing the reconciliation initiative.

The Algerian authorities went to great lengths to refute each of these allegations but the Bouteflika regime was forced to grapple with a new dimension: the all-pervasive impact of the internet. By 2001 anybody with web access could study the arguments and counter-arguments at the click of a button. They could not only download highly critical reports from Amnesty International and Human Rights Watch but also look at specific sites set up by Algerian dissidents such as Algeria-Watch, which carried extensive articles on all aspects of government abuses.[37] Of these the most famous and most mysterious site is that of the very well informed Mouvement Algérien des Officiers Libres (MAOL), supposedly based in Madrid and launched in 1997, which seems to be linked to higher echelons in the military. The roots of the MAOL can be traced back to the so-called Hakim Cell, a clandestine group of officers who believed in dialogue with the FIS.[38] Its members included Kasdi Merbah, whose 1993 murder was discussed in Chapter 6.[39] Consistently attacking a clique of criminal generals who are accused of deliberately orchestrating the violence for their economic gain, and calling on honest members of the military to rise up against this corruption, the site has contained a series of revelations about recent Algerian history, including details about state involvement in Boudiaf's assassination. It has also consistently called for a national conference on truth and reconciliation, an independent investigation into the violence and the prosecution of those implicated in the massacres.

In June 2000 the site posted up the secret details of the foreign accounts allegedly held by a number of leading generals, noting that Mohammed Touati had $8 million with Crédit Lyonnais in Monaco; Mohammed Médiène $62 million with UBP in Geneva; and Smaïn Lamari $45 million with Crédit Suisse in Geneva. These figures were subsequently substantiated by the French press.[40] Not surprisingly the Bouteflika regime, unnerved by these revelations, was embarrassed at the site, and accused those behind it of being terrorists trying to manipulate public opinion against the whole transition process.[41] But such mudslinging achieved nothing, and it became increasingly obvious that large numbers of Algerians were unwilling to follow Bouteflika down the road of forgetting.

URBAN ALIENATION

> After all his foreign visits to Canada, Ethiopia and France, Bouteflika should make an official visit to the real Algeria.
>
> (Algerian joke circa 2000)

By the beginning of 2001 there was widespread discontent with Bouteflika. One leading opinion poll noted that less than half of the population approved of the civil concord.[42] Partly this was the result of growing dismay at the civil concord's implications; but partly too it was because throughout 2000 a viable economic programme eluded Bouteflika. He could not find a formula for recovery beyond the belief that liberalization would bring Algeria the benefits of globalization through a trickle-down effect.

For the younger generation in particular there was a glaring discrepancy between Bouteflika's ebullient salesmanship and the truth. Despite his ever-smiling public image, he had palpably failed to connect with them, as evidenced by one memorable incident in June 2000 in Oran when the president, heckled by university students, responded with a fit of pique, throwing out journalists and threatening to confiscate their tapes. The students' contempt reflected the way in which young people lumped the regime, the parties and the democratic process together. In their eyes the exercise of power was all part of the same sordid game, focused on narcissism, money and access to patronage. Caustically referring to the Club des Pins – the protected enclave outside Algiers where many of the elite lived – as 'Jurassic Park', they believed that the country was run by a clique of decrepit old men who had no idea how ordinary Algerians lived.[43]

Such enduring anger reflected the way in which by 2001 the social crisis had taken on an aura of permanence. As the war became more rural, emigration to the major towns and cities had intensified. In Oran alone a hundred thousand people were living in shanty towns by 1996, over one-tenth of the city's total population, with the result that social services and housing provision, already overstretched, now reached breaking point. Of course these newcomers were grateful for the absence of the immediate threat of violence but in trying to eke out a better life they had to contend with non-existent services. Scraping a living on the fringes of society, they felt humiliated by both central and local government which, unable or unwilling to deal with the problem, seemed happy to let them languish in poverty.

Like the rest of the ordinary population, these migrants had to contend not only with the violence of the armed Islamists and the violence of the state but also what they saw as the violence of the IMF's prescriptions. The 1994 Structural Adjustment Programme aimed to demonstrate the benefits of the West's soft power by bringing the population into the virtuous circle of affluence, economic improvement and sound governance. On this measure the regime had managed to balance the books by 1997 and was held up as a success story by the IMF and World Bank.

However, far away from the luxury of the world's leading financial institutions, the reality was that the IMF reforms were heaping humiliation after humiliation on to Algerians. As the state withdrew there was no support to cushion the pain. Subsidies on basic foodstuffs were ended, public spending on social welfare and education was slashed, and state enterprises were either privatized or closed, leading to the loss of 380,000 jobs between 1994 and 1997. Promised redundancy payments never materialized and, as the state failed them, thousands were forced to survive through the black-market economy and family and civil society networks.

The conflict with the Islamists made it much easier to push these reforms through because ordinary people, reeling from an all-pervading violence, were simply too scared to contemplate mass social protest. Moreover there was no leadership from the official trade union organization, the Union Générale des Travailleurs Algériens (UGTA), which maintained that with the Republic in danger it had a duty to side with the government.[44]

Pauperization affected all social classes and by 2001 the statistics made grim reading. On every front life was getting worse. Government budgets on health were savagely cut and, with most medication beyond the pockets of ordinary Algerians, the beginning of the new century witnessed the return of typhoid and meningitis.[45] Education spending was halved between 1985 and 1995 with the result that in 1997 only 39.3 per cent of young people were leaving school with a formal qualification.[46] Between 1991 and 2001 the value of salaries in real terms halved. By this latter date 27 per cent of the population were on less than one dollar a day, the official UN poverty level, and unemployment had reached a catastrophic 35 per cent, of which 80 per cent were aged under thirty. In January and February 1999 La Tribune and Liberté reported that in the Oran area impoverished rural families were selling their young children to survive, and in 2001 UNICEF reported that 1.36 million children between six and fifteen were being forced to work to survive the economic crisis.[47] In 2002 *Liberté* reported on a new and disturbing product of the economic crisis: an epidemic of suicides amongst young men.[48]

Looking at these indices it was difficult not to conclude that between 1980 and 2000 Algeria had not lost one but two generations. However, as the threat of terrorism receded in 2000 people became much less submissive. The downward turn in violence sharpened their sense of antagonism towards the system and gave them renewed energy, leading directly to an upsurge in militancy and social opposition. On 17 May 2000, for example, police used rubber bullets and tear gas to break up a demonstration by nine thousand strikers protesting against the freezing of salaries at the El Hadjar steel works at Annaba; twenty to thirty protestors were seriously injured. Angry at the absence of a socio-economic revival, the mass of Algerians, but particularly the young, laid the blame on Bouteflika, asking why the oil and gas revenues were not being used to create a wealthy and prosperous society for all.

In November 2001 hatred of the regime reached a new high when more than six hundred people died due to flash floods sweeping through the poor districts of the capital. Riots broke out as it became clear that the humanitarian disaster was in large part down to government incompetence. The crucial factor here had been the authorities' decision in 1997 to cement up the ancient drains in Bab el-Oued leading down to the sea, to prevent armed Islamists lurking in the sewers. Nobody had thought to unblock them later, despite the national meteorologist's office warning both the president's office and the interior minister that high winds were on their way.

The fact that the government took no steps to alert the city's 4 million inhabitants of the approaching peril led numerous Algerians to speak subsequently of 'genocide through negligence'. This outrage was intensified when the interior minister, Yazid Zerhouni, blamed the people, arguing that by living in flimsy shanty towns they had left themselves vulnerable and unprotected. Such comments just piled further derision on the government, which was seen as a regime in a generalized state of denial, always seeking to apportion responsibility elsewhere when it was obvious that the disaster was the result of a complete failure to implement city planning or provide adequate housing for the population.

In an effort to assuage public opinion Bouteflika declared three days of national mourning, but in a television appearance he appealed to religious feeling to deflect criticism, claiming, 'This is a test from God, nobody can blame God for what he gives us … neither the government nor any party is responsible, God is testing us.' Such sentiments, terribly misjudged, just inflamed the situation, reinforcing the image of endemic incompetence. As *Le*

Matin sarcastically commented: 'Bouteflika blames God for blocking the drains.'[49] In the same vein *El Watan* accused the president of not liking 'either Algiers or the Algerians', reminding the president that Algerians 'did not elect him, whatever the official election results say'.[50]

Determined to give vent to their anger hundreds of youths from Bab el-Oued gathered in front of the Algiers Government Palace on the evening of 12 November. As they protested they shouted slogans ranging from '*pouvoir assassin*' to the Kabyle cry '*Ulac S'mah Ulac*' ('No forgiveness, none') and the historic rallying cry of the FIS, 'There is no God but God. We live for this profession of faith, we will die for it.'[51] For the first time in Algiers, some demonstrators openly praised Osama bin Laden while others chanted the nicknames of two former Islamist terrorists previously active in the casbah, 'Flicha' and 'Napoli'. The crowd tried to break down the doors of the government building but were beaten back by police, whereupon they turned back in procession to Bab el-Oued, smashing shop windows and wrecking cars as they went. At the base of these protests was the demand to be treated with dignity. Ordinary people were livid at the regime's incompetence and Bouteflika's reputation was badly damaged.

Two years later Bouteflika's image was dented still further when an earthquake struck the region of Boumerdès, east of Algiers, on 23 May 2003, causing the loss of two thousand lives, with thousands more left injured and homeless. Sub-standard state-built housing blocks collapsed, largely because the government had scrimped on materials, while private buildings from the French period survived. The singers Rachid Taha, Cheb Khaled and Faudel released a special CD in France to raise money for the victims but the success of their initiative only underlined the shortcomings of the government's response. Once again too the relief operation was a fiasco and when Bouteflika travelled to Boumerdès to survey the damage an angry crowd kicked and stoned his car, shouting '*pouvoir assassin*'.[52]

Both the floods and the earthquake contributed to the tinder-box atmosphere. By shining the light back on to the system they revealed the continuing gulf between the rulers and the ruled. Ordinary Algerians were dismayed when the state of emergency was prolonged for another year in February 2000, and many began to suspect that this repressive legislation was not the exception but the norm. By keeping the people down, it made them too scared to challenge a liberalization process which in favouring the black market allowed a minority to profit from kickbacks, fraud and tax evasion on a grand scale. As one popular joke put it: 'Why is the Algerian mafia better than the Italian mafia? Because it owns a whole country.'

More than ever, anger, chagrin and consternation were the norm. During the 1980s raï music had given voice to this generational conflict. Now there was a burgeoning rap scene with bands like Intik, an ironic name meaning 'everything going great' in spoken Arabic, T.O.X. and Game Over. Many of the rappers had been involved as teenagers in October 1988 and their street poetry, heavily influenced by Public Enemy in America and IAM in France, but also drawing upon the oral tradition at the heart of Algerian culture, articulated gut-level male anger. Mixing together hip-hop, reggae, soul, chaâbi and raï as well as switching from classical Arabic to spoken Arabic, Berber, French and English, the result was a musical montage whose inner content raged against the *pouvoir*. Disaffection, unemployment and elemental defiance were their themes as these musicians spoke in a language of fearlessness with no reservations or omissions. As one Intik song explained:

Manipulation, aggression, deception
Such is my programme for the day
My only crime is to hope and to dream[53]

The pioneers of the movement were four rappers, Redone, Yacine, Med and Rabah, known collectively as Le Micro Brise le Silence. They organized the first rap concerts in Algiers in 1993 and they produced the first ever Algerian rap album in 1997, the cassette *Ouled El Bahdja* which sold sixty thousand copies; and they enjoyed the first international acclaim, signing up to Island records and releasing their first CD, *Micro Brise le Silence*, in November 1999.

Inspired by the novelist Tahar Djaout, who had been assassinated in May 1993, their starting point was a refusal to be silenced. The spoken word allowed them to struggle against official amnesia and bear witness to the hellish existence of their generation, where Algerians were citizens little more than in name as authority was abused at every level. As such their remarkable music encapsulates the enduring tensions at the heart of Algerian society. On the one side is the system – the police, the military, the politicians – and on the other is the majority who feel downtrodden, despised and disenfranchised.

■ ■ ■

In Kabylia, still seething with anger at Matoub's death, there was a permanent stand-off between the population and the forces of law and order throughout 1999 and 2000. In this volatile atmosphere the traditional parties, the RCD and FFS, were seen as out of date and compromised as Kabylia witnessed the sudden emergence of a new type of grassroots politics based upon village councils.[54] As we saw in Chapter 1, these councils are deeply ingrained in Kabyle culture. Male-dominated and encapsulating traditional codes of honour, they represent the fierce independence of the mountain republics in the face of the intrusion of the plains. Some saw them as archaic while others talked of them as the basis of a citizens' movement. In April 2001, the twenty-first anniversary of the Berber spring, these assemblies bypassed the old parties to challenge the power of central government.

The trigger for the violence was the death of a youth called Massinissah Guermah in police custody. Guermah had been picked up by police, intervening over fighting between rival gangs of youths, on 18 April and badly beaten up. Hauled off to the station at Beni Douala in Tizi-Ouzou, he was shot there at close range and died of his wounds two days later.[55] In a bid to justify the killing the gendarmerie released a communiqué claiming that Guermah had been arrested for theft. The Interior Ministry also tried to dirty Guermah's name by declaring that he was a twenty-six-year-old hooligan. Furious, his family brandished his school report, showing that he was in fact an eighteen-year-old secondary school student with a good academic record.

Such lies, allied to the arrest of three more college students, were highly provocative and throughout the region there were protests attacking the police abuse of power, social injustice and lack of freedom. Shouting the slogan 'Give us work, lodgings and hope', these demonstrations sought to dominate space and opinion but although peaceful they were ferociously repressed by the baton-wielding gendarmerie and the special anti-riot police. Inevitably these crude tactics just produced more violence. Protestors now took out their anger on the symbols of the state, attacking town halls and tax collecting offices while taunting the police by proclaiming 'Hassan Hattab, the People are with you'.[56]

In the weeks that followed, the police violence in Kabylia reached unprecedented levels. During the riots following Matoub's death the police had had strict instructions not to fire on the crowd. Now there was no such restraint. Drawing extensively upon eyewitness accounts gathered at the time, a subsequent report by the Algerian League of the Defence of the Rights of Man produced a damning portrait of an out-of-control police force that revelled in its capacity to inflict pain and terror on the civilian population. Extra-judicial killing became the norm; on 25 April five fleeing protestors were killed by the police (one, Kamel Makhmoukhen, was shot in the back), and three days later in the village of Aït-Yahia local police fired on the crowd killing sixteen-year-old Chaibet Hocine. Police snipers hiding on terraces cold-bloodedly picked off demonstrators, even those trying to help the wounded.[57] Snatch squads, some of which were the elite army units – the 'red berets' – disguised as police, chased youths into hospitals, beating them up and shooting at them on the ground. Suspects were stripped naked and battered with iron bars. Police were also seen spitting on the dead bodies.

Kabylia rapidly became a war zone with the forces of law and order demolishing houses, ransacking shops, and cutting telephone wires, thereby isolating the region from the rest of the country. In El-Kseur a member of the Algerian Red Cross witnessed a day of violence that left 365 casualties as the police surrounded a clinic and barred the wounded from entering: 'The CNS [Compagnie Nationale de Sécurité, the special riot police] and gendarmerie, drunk, let themselves loose on the population. They threw tear gas into houses … they pillaged shops, ransacked a chemist's and attacked a handicapped man, breaking his leg in his own house.'[58] In some cases civilians heard police taunting protestors, 'We are going to do to you what we did at Bentalha.'

Bouteflika was roundly condemned for saying nothing immediately and for remaining in Nigeria on an official visit as the violence spiralled out of control. Only after ten days of rioting and forty-three deaths did he finally intervene on 30 April with an unconvincing television address. Insensitively delivered in classical Arabic, which would not have been understood by large numbers of Algerians and certainly not in Kabylia, Bouteflika's address called on Kabyle youth to remain calm. At the same time he made no attempt to rein in the police. Nobody was sacked and he did not give the order to stop firing on crowds. His one major attempt to assuage the protestors was the announcement of an independent commission of inquiry to be chaired by Professor Mohand Issad, a well-known Kabyle lawyer.

Predictably, Bouteflika's performance led to renewed rioting. In an attempt to channel this anger into a mass movement the village councils organized a march attended by five hundred thousand people on 21 May in Tizi-Ouzou, along with a platform of specific demands. This was followed by a demon-stration against injustice and repression on 14 June in Algiers, which brought together one million marchers, the biggest such protest in the country's history. However, even before the march had begun, *agents provocateurs* tried to turn the march into an ethnic confrontation. Youths perched on the security forces' water cannons chanting 'death to the Kabyles' and threw stones. At least a hundred young people disappeared and many more were badly beaten. Later, in the emergency unit of the Mustapha hospital, youths with knives mingled amongst the doctors and nurses and threatened the injured. For *El Watan* such violence, pushing the country to the brink of civil war, showed just how far the hardliners were willing to stop the establishment of a genuine democracy that will return 'Algeria to Algerians' and purge the country of the 'new colonialists'.[59]

By 30 June the 'black spring' had left an estimated two hundred dead and five thousand injured. In surveying this carnage Professor Issad's report, published on 7 July, was remarkably frank.[60] Although the report refrained from naming individuals it pinpointed faction fighting within the regime as the chief reason for the gendarmes' brutality. The implication was that key figures had deliberately stoked up the violence, playing on the threat of the Kabyles as pro-French fifth columnists, so that Bouteflika would have blood on his hands and hence be discredited. The report was a damning portrait of a government operating without the most basic aspects of democratic control and accountability, in other words a lawless regime. Furthermore, in analysing the wider social causes Issad's diagnosis was bleak: 'Guermah's death ... [was] only the immediate cause of the troubles. The deeper causes rest elsewhere: social, economic, political, identity and abuses of all sorts.'

Such comments recognized that the absence of hope was the true root of the protests. Why else would the rioters show such reckless indifference to the shoot-to-kill policy, shouting, 'You cannot kill us, we are already dead' as they took on the police?[61]

The severity of the repression, widely reported in the European media, meant that the Algerian government was faced with renewed pressure over human rights. In particular the EU, under the Swedish presidency, wanted to call the government to account over the handling of the violence in Kabylia. Seemingly tottering on the edge of chaos, the regime was suddenly once again isolated on the international scene. What was to save it were the extraordinary events of 11 September 2001.

ISLAMIC TERRORISM TAKES CENTRE STAGE

On a clear blue morning on 11 September 2001 nineteen young Arab men, mostly from Saudi Arabia, seized four US airliners, which they crashed into the World Trade Center towers and the Pentagon. These attacks were the most audacious terrorist plot in modern history. Succeeding where all the other precedents – the 1993 attack on the twin towers, the 1994 GIA attempt on the Eiffel Tower, the failed attack on Los Angeles airport in 1999 – had failed, 9/11 was theatrical violence on the grandest scale imaginable, resulting in the death of 2,973 people. Instinctively there was a wave of sympathy with America. Le Monde proclaimed 'We are all Americans now' as flowers piled up outside US embassies from Argentina to Australia. Women in Jordan signed petitions of condolence; candles and banners were held aloft in Bangladesh; the Palestinian leader Yasser Arafat gave blood; and children stood for one minute's silence on the West Bank.

In this moment the international context was changed for ever. As President Bush plotted revenge, he and his inner entourage made swift decisions about who was a friend and who was a foe. They knew that their most precious resource was intelligence, and that in piecing together a global picture of Islamic terrorism they needed the help of those with an inside view into the values, motivations and mindsets of al-Qaeda and its fellow organizations. For this reason the Bouteflika regime was immediately identified as a vital ally in the 'war on terror'.

In the days following 11 September Bush called for a 'crusade' on world terror. For Muslims it was unfortunate choice of words but even so the Algerian leadership immediately grasped the implications of the Bush strategy for them and their regime. Just one month earlier the Algerian government had been facing international opprobrium over the repression in Kabylia, but now they had Washington's backing. In exchange for intelligence they gained all they could desire, in particular the knowledge that the United States would keep the regime afloat financially and militarily. Bouteflika and Mohammed Lamari were invited to Washington in November 2001 for a week-long visit during which they presented the Algerian experience as the major precedent for 11 September. In return Bush unambiguously endorsed the Algerian regime's counter-terrorist strategy while drawing up a plan for Algeria to enter into an association agreement with NATO together with Morocco, Tunisia, Egypt and Jordan.

The Bouteflika government carefully distilled the information it handed over to the CIA. It had a vested interest in portraying the GIA and the GSPC as bin Laden foot soldiers, part of a tightly organized worldwide conspiracy that had been attacking Algeria since 1992. Washington, however, took the Algerians at their word. As the knowledge travelled 'up the chain', policy makers sifting through this intelligence at second-, third- and fourth-hand ignored evidence of secret service manipulation or the fact that some of it had been extracted by torture. Rather than seeing the Algerian information as partial, incomplete and suspect they accepted the existence of the GIA and GSPC as a given and immediately placed them on the list of banned terrorist organizations.

Of course the links between the armed groups in Algeria and bin Laden are not a fiction. They are real and tangible and predate 11 September 2001, even if the actual relationship is more complex than the simplistic identification between the two that the pro-government media now asserted at every possible moment. All Islamist groups became by definition linked to al-Qaeda and on 20 September 2001 the television and radio reported that Algiers had already handed over to Washington a list of 350 Islamist militants known to be abroad whom Algerian intelligence believed were likely to be linked to bin Laden. The Algerian authorities were also reported to have provided a list of two thousand names of 'known members of the GIA and the GSPC'. In response to these measures, a GSPC communiqué on 19 September threatened to target Westerners in Algeria if Afghanistan was attacked, whereupon security was intensified around Western embassies and businesses. This belief in a close link between bin Laden and Algeria was strengthened even further when, less than a month after 11 September, an international friendly between France and Algeria at the Stade de France football stadium near Paris, intended as a gesture of historic reconciliation between the two countries, was dramatically abandoned because young Algerian supporters, mostly French citizens of Algerian descent, invaded the pitch shouting 'Bin Laden, bin Laden' and hurling abuse at the French players.

Bolstered by American support, the army continued to inflict serious reverses on the remnants of armed groups, including most spectacularly the killing of Antar Zouabri in February 2002. To allay suspicion (following the many false claims that he had been liquidated in the past), his bullet-ridden body was displayed to the public. With their infamous emir dead the GIA was said to have been reduced to about a hundred fighters dispersed across the hinterland of Algiers in small units while another small group operated at Sidi-bel-Abbès, the old Foreign Legion headquarters town.

Zouabri's death was heralded as another step on the road to normalization, which was further cemented by the legislative elections held on 30 May 2002. The results gave the FLN a slender majority with 199 of the 389 seats in the new National Assembly. Abdullah Djaballah's Movement for National Reform (MRN) won 43 seats, overtaking Mahfoud Nahnah's Movement of Society for Peace (MSP) which fell from 69 to 38 seats, but the overall Islamist presence in the assembly fell by a fifth. The Worker's Party (Parti des Travailleurs, PT), led by Louisa Hanoune, won the largest secular democratic vote, garnering 21 seats.[62]

On the face of it the results suggested a flourishing pluralism. But the reality was different. The turnout was just over 46 per cent, the lowest since independence, and the Berber parties had boycotted the elections as a result of the continuing violence in Kabylia.[63] Similarly the FLN's astonishing recovery was manufactured by the regime rather than being the expression of the popular will. The decision amongst the elite to resuscitate the FLN was already clear in August 2000 when Ali Benflis, a member of the FLN leadership, was named prime minister. This was deemed necessary because the RND, associated with draconian economic polices and tainted with corruption, was so discredited.

The promotion by the powers that be of the FLN at the expense of the RND demonstrates how pluralism allowed the parties to be played off against each other by a system whose modus operandi is divide and rule. With this aim in mind all the main ideological tendencies are represented in the National Assembly and ideally in the government itself, but to prevent any political party from acquiring too much influence each tendency is represented by at least two parties. So there are the two 'nationalist' parties, the FLN and RND, three Islamist parties, the MSP, MRN and MN (Mouvement Ennahda or 'Resistance Party', also known as the Islamic Resistance Party), two Berber parties, the FFS and RCD, and two parties of the left, the PT and the small but formerly influential Democratic and Social Movement (MDS). Since the parties in each category are rivals rather than allies, the scope which the regime enjoys for exploiting their rivalries is enormous. At the same time, it has been able to take account of changes in public opinion by orchestrating changes in the electoral fortunes of the various rivals at regular intervals.[64]

Understood in this way, the elections were not really elections. They were pseudo-elections based on the exclusion of the electorate because the main results were determined in advance by the regime's 'decision-makers'. The only role the people had was a walk-on role to ratify their choices, which in May 2002 meant the return of the FLN.

THE TRIAL

At midnight on 25 April 2001 Khaled Nezzar, in Paris to reject the claims of army abuses of human rights, was whisked away and put on a special flight back to Algiers. For a man of his military rank it was an unceremonious exit, prompted by the French authorities who were desperate to avoid an embarrassing international incident. Just a few hours before, civil lawsuits had been filed against Nezzar, one by an Algerian family whose son had died in custody and two by ex-prisoners tortured by the army, and under the 1984 International Convention against Torture France would have been obliged to take up their cases in court.

The situation bore strong echoes of the detention of the former Chilean dictator Augusto Pinochet in Britain in 1998. Indeed, in an editorial *Le Monde* likened Nezzar to Pinochet but said that he was worse because he had more blood on his hands.[65] For this reason the Nezzar incident was a political earthquake. It struck fear amongst the other leading generals in Algiers since it showed that they were not safe from prosecution. The spectre of future trials for human rights abuses had been raised.

Incensed by those who called his departure cowardly, Nezzar took it upon himself to defend the Algerian army's honour. On 22 August 2001 he organized a press conference in Algiers where he called on all those who supported the cancellation of the elections in January 1992 to defend him and the army. Specifically Nezzar wished to uphold the honour of the army in the face of charges of dirty tricks made by Habib Souaïdia in his book *La Sale Guerre*, published by La Découverte in February 2001.

Souaïdia had himself been an officer in the feared 'ninjas', created to lead the counter-insurgency in 1993. Fighting in the Mitidja and then Lakhdaria, 75 miles south-east of Algiers, Souaïdia was accused of theft in June 1995 and sentenced by court martial to four years in a military prison. Released in 1999 and believing his life to be in danger he made his way to France where he wrote *La Sale Guerre*. In it he gave a detailed account of the systematic use of torture, napalm and massacres, including soldiers murdering civilians and then attributing these crimes to Islamist armed groups.

It was a damning description of an army out of control, whereby the war against terrorism had long degenerated into racketeering, extortion and financial aggrandisement. In the preface the distinguished anti-Mafia Italian lawyer Ferdinando Imposimato emphasized the book's importance, arguing that by providing an inside picture of the hidden centres of power it showed that the regime had a case to answer under international law.[66]

In France the book was a publishing sensation. It was number one on the bestseller lists for several weeks and widely discussed in the *New York Times*, the *Irish Times*, the *Guardian*, *El Pais* and *La Repubblica*. In Algeria Souaïdia was subjected to a character assassination. As the son of a *harki*, the regime claimed, he was by definition a traitor whose hatred for his country had been sharpened still further by his period in prison. In March 2001, 250 pro-government intellectuals signed a petition claiming that the vast majority of the population supported the army in its difficult struggle against terrorism. Then on 29 April Souaïdia was condemned in absentia to twenty years in prison for attacking the army's integrity.

While the official response was entirely predictable, other anti-government voices raised their concerns about Souaïdia's account. One Algerian journalist,

Mina Kaci, was dubious about parts of the book,[67] and Hugh Roberts, no friend of the military, pointed out some glaring factual errors.[68] In particular, a bomb attack at the cemetery in Sidi Ali was dated as 1992 when it actually occurred two years later, and the author wrongly named General Saïd Bey as commander of the 1st Military Region in 1993 and early 1994. Most of all Roberts was highly sceptical about the massacre at Douar Ez-Zaatria, which Souaïdia claimed took place in March 1993; however, this is much too early and the book is much too vague to be convincing on this point. Reports of civilian massacres, Roberts argued, only came to light in late 1996 and early 1997.

These mistakes apart, however, Roberts was still adamant that Souaïdia's book, in describing an institution that had lost all sense of its proper constitutional role, represented a savage indictment of the army's role. Souaïdia repeated his views when interviewed on the French television channel La Cinquième on 27 May 2001.[69] Pushed by the interviewer, Souaïdia did not hang back, singling out Nezzar and his clique as the men who had wilfully led Algeria to catastrophe:

> It is cowards who profit from it [the war], this is exactly what has happened in our country, it is the former deserters of the French army who have led the country towards anarchy, towards bankruptcy. It is they who are responsible.[70]

When he uttered these words Souaïdia was being deliberately provocative. He was throwing down the gauntlet, challenging both the general's manhood and his sense of place in history, and on 24 August 2001 Nezzar issued a writ for libel.

Lasting from 2 to 5 July 2002 and held in Paris, the ensuing trial, ironically, coincided with the fortieth anniversary of independence. Witnesses for Nezzar included the writer Rachid Boudjedra, the former minister Leïla Aslaoui, and Ali Haroun, formerly a member of the Haut Comité d'Etat. For Souaïdia on the defence side were the historian and former FLN member Mohammed Harbi, the political refugee and former colonel in the Algerian secret services Mohammed Samraoui, and the president of the FFS and war of liberation veteran Hocine Aït Ahmed. Thus many of the dramatis personae of the past decade were present and, as each was called up to the box, at the core of the arguments and cross examinations was the question of justification. Who was responsible for the violence? Was the suspension of the electoral process right? Did it save Algeria from a worse fate? In effect the trial represented the historical inquest on the 1990s that Bouteflika had been so desperate to curtail. For once, rather than forgetting, both sides were intent on addressing blame and culpability head-on.

Through his testimony and subsequent interventions Nezzar was determined to depict the violence of the 1990s through the prism of 11 September 2001. In his opening statement he argued that in terms of ideology and action the FIS were the Algerian equivalent of the Taliban, part of a global plot threatening the whole of humanity.[71] By suspending the elections and fighting this enemy the army had saved the country from barbarity, anticipating the post-9/11 'war on terror'. Such was the language in which Nezzar and many of his key witnesses constructed their arguments, echoing the polarized vocabulary of President Bush.

Much of the evidence called upon by Nezzar's lawyers was undeniably harrowing. When two women, Attika Hadjrissa and Saâdia Hadjrissa, described their ordeals at the hands of GIA groups, everybody in the courtroom recognized the depth of their suffering.[72] The problem, however, was that the prosecution's argument – an army defending a population under brutal terrorist attacks– did not fit all the facts. When Nezzar tried to call the disappeared 'martyrs in the war on terror' other narratives were just too resistant. What, the defence countered, about the victims of state terrorism? What too about the role of the system? One of the defence witnesses, the economist Omar Bendarra, who possessed enormous inside knowledge since he had managed the national debt between 1989 and 1991, explained how a minority had been able to exploit the violence to accrue massive fortunes.[73] Another defence witness, Mohammed Harbi, compared Algeria since 1962 to Prussia in the eighteenth century, describing it as a military regime where the army controlled the state rather than the other way round.[74]

Bringing so many of the key figures head to head, the debate was conducted in an atmosphere of simmering rage, producing moments of real drama. When Nezzar argued that it was normal for secret services to use infiltration, Samraoui retorted angrily 'But not massacres, my general.'[75] The intensity of the arguments meant that the level of detail was uniquely illuminating, exposing much of the inner workings of a secretive system for the first time.

At the end of the four days Nezzar lost the case. In different circumstances such a verdict might have dealt a major international blow against the system. But the regime could afford to dismiss the Nezzar trial as irrelevant when compared to the bigger international picture. Given the legitimacy bestowed on them by the Bush administration their self-confidence was impossible to stem. By 2003 previously secretive figures like Mohammed Lamari were prepared to come out and declare openly that they had won. The bloody decade 1993–2003, he declared, was now over. The country had not gone the way of Afghanistan and was now returning to normal, as was evident by the resumption of Air France and British Airways flights to Algiers after their boycotting of Algerian airports for years, and the fact that 2003 was designated 'the year of Algeria' in France with a series of exhibitions and special events. The final symbol of this victory came when on 2 July 1993 the regime released Abassi Madani and Ali Belhadj, now that they had finished their twelve-year prison sentences. Now aged seventy-two and forty-seven respectively, they were banned from all forms of political activity and not allowed to vote. Significantly, their freedom did not provoke a huge public reaction, with Madani going into exile while Belhadj remained as a brooding presence, constantly harassed by the authorities.

■ ■ ■

Although Bouteflika had unflinchingly endorsed the Bush administration's campaign against terrorism he conducted a delicate balancing act in the run-up to the Second Gulf War, which began in 2003. Not wishing to jeopardize the American alliance but mindful too of the population's instinctive anti-imperialism, he chose his words with care. Stopping well short of any outright condemnation, he criticized Washington for not following international law and said that the war 'would not be something for humanity to be proud of'.[76]

Remembering how the First Gulf War had destabilized Algerian politics, he was careful to contain public anger. Despite the media's strident attacks on American imperialism, he did not permit protests against the war in Iraq. He wanted to keep a tight rein on anti-American sentiment lest this anger should spill over into criticism of his own regime. The one moment of public outpouring came with the visit on 2 March of President Chirac, whose opposition to the Iraq invasion, fitting into the long tradition of Gaullist anti-Americanism, was rapturously acclaimed in Algiers.

Back in Britain the activities of Algerians supposedly linked to bin Laden played a crucial role in the lead-up to the Iraq invasion in March 2003. Until the 1990s Algerians had been almost unknown in Britain, with only twenty-five asylum applications in 1990. By 1995 this number had risen to 1,865. Most were genuine asylum-seekers, but not all. One regular visitor to the Finsbury Park mosque and the Four Feathers community centre, a makeshift place of worship near Baker Street, was Abu 'The Doctor' Doha, a thirty-seven-year-old Algerian who was identified by French secret services as a senior

GSPC member involved in establishing terror networks in London.[77] In February 2001 he was arrested at Heathrow trying to board a flight to Saudi Arabia. Another was Rachid Ramda, editor of the paper *Al-Ansar* which glorified GIA atrocities. The French accused him of being the mastermind behind the 1995 Paris Métro bombing and began a lengthy extradition process to get him to stand trial in France.

These two examples explain why the Algerian community in Britain, numbering twelve thousand by 2003, was coming under increasing surveillance. The domestic security agency MI5 had information that GSPC cells were about to launch a huge attack using ricin, one of the most lethal poisons known to humanity, and as a result the Algerian population became the focus of one of the biggest anti-terrorist operations ever mounted in Britain. Four North Africans, named as Mustapha Taleb, Mouloud Feddag, Sidali Feddag and Samir Feddag, and all thought to be Algerian, were arrested in January 2003 and charged under the UK's Chemical Weapons Act of 1996 after police discovered traces of ricin in a North London flat in Wood Green following a protracted Anglo-French surveillance operation. In Manchester a group of Algerians were cornered by the police and during the course of their arrests a policeman, DC Stephen Oake, was killed. The two operations were presented by the British secret services as a radical new departure, suggesting that Algerian Islamist terrorism had moved on to a new level. Previously content to use the country as a logistical base for attacks in France and Algeria, procuring forged passports and credit cards, the Algerians now wanted to attack Britain itself.

The precise nature of their activities, particularly an alleged plan to attack the London Underground, provoked a furore amongst the press and politicians, which prime minister Tony Blair played up to the hilt as tangible evidence of the link between the threat of terrorism and weapons of mass destruction; if the terrorists had no qualms about deploying ricin, what would they do with nuclear or chemical weapons? Such language conjured up untold horrors. Playing on people's fears, it was intended to overcome widespread public scepticism and opposition to the coming invasion of Iraq.

The Second Gulf War led to the rapid fall of Saddam Hussein but post-victory euphoria was short-lived and soon British and American forces were engaged in savage wars of violence and counter-violence, much of it evoking Algeria both in 1950s and the 1990s. However, in the frantic forward rush of events many forgot the role of the Algerian ricin threat in the justifications for the war, which was relegated to footnote status. But in April 2005 the four were acquitted, embarrassing the British government, police and security services. Their trial revealed that no traces of ricin had been found in the Wood Green flat occupied by the suspects. Indeed the 2003 Algerian panic led to only one conviction, of Kamel Bourgass, who was given a life sentence for the murder of DC Stephen Oake in Manchester.

Three jurors from the trial in October 2005 condemned the British government's new anti-terrorism legislation. One juror told the BBC's *Panorama* programme: 'Before the trial I had a lot of faith in the authorities to be making the right decisions on my behalf … having been through this trial I'm very sceptical now as to the real reasons why this new legislation is being pushed through.'[78]

The case underlined the danger of demonizing Algerians as potential terrorists, and showed how the war on terror was shot through with the potential for mistakes, shortcomings and potential miscarriages of justice.[79] A related issue concerned security evidence from Algeria, which was often tainted by torture. The Director General of MI5, Dame Eliza Manningham-Buller, was adamant that evidence extracted by torture in Algeria could save lives, citing the example of Bourgass, whom MI5 had been informed about by Algerian secret services.

Elsewhere Algerians and French people of Algerian origin became subject to intense surveillance, especially after the Madrid train bombings on 11 March 2004, which killed 191. The security services tracked their movements throughout Europe and America, resulting in a steady flurry of trials and arrests. In February 2005 the French police rounded up more than twenty suspects in the La Courneuve suburb of Paris. One of the group's ringleaders allegedly confessed that they were making chemical weapons, using knowledge gleaned from training camps run by al-Qaeda in Afghanistan and at secret bases in the Panski Gorge, a lawless region linking Georgia with war-torn Chechnya. Similarly, on 15 March a French court sentenced a French Algerian man to ten years in prison for plotting a suicide attack on the US Embassy in Paris in 2001 and jailed five accomplices, all also of Algerian origin, for one to nine years. Djamel Beghal received the toughest term possible under French law as the ringleader of the failed plot.[80]

The panic about Algerian terrorism further strengthened Western support for Bouteflika's regime. In particular the Bush administration welcomed the reversals inflicted by the army on the GSPC, notably the killing of 150 militants in September 2003 near Sétif and the seizing of a major weapons arsenal along Algeria's southern border with Mali in January 2004.

By this point the GSPC seemed to be on the verge of defeat, especially after reports of Hattab's resignation as leader and his subsequent death in August

2003. However, Hattab's successor, Nabil Sahrawi, continued to spit defiance, telling the *Al-Hayat* newspaper in January: 'The Islamic state will not arise through means of slogans, demonstrations, parties and electioneering but through blood, body parts, and [sacrifice of] lives.'[81] But he too was killed on 19 June 2004 during a three-day gun battle with the Algerian armed forces as they conducted a huge search and destroy sweep in the El-Kseur region in Bejaia province two hundred miles east of Algiers.

As the net tightened one GSPC group, led by Abderrezak 'El-Para', was credited in June 2003 with staging the spectacular kidnapping of thirty-two European tourists, most of them German, travelling across the Sahara. One hostage was freed in a raid by Algerian soldiers but the rest were forced to trek from wadi to wadi on the way into Mali; an ordeal which led to the death of a German woman. Eventually they were released on 18 August following payment of a $5 million ransom by Austria, Germany and Switzerland. Interviewed on German television, one of the hostages, Gerhard Wintersteller, commented:

> The Salafists were well aware of what was about to happen. They marched us twenty kilometres through the desert to a predetermined location, a geographically suitable venue for our 'liberation'. It occurred to me much later that the whole thing might have been staged by the Algerian military. I still wonder if there are links between the Salafists and the army.[82]

Writing in *Le Monde Diplomatique*, Selima Mellah and Jean-Baptiste Rivoire revealed that 'El-Para', otherwise known as Amari Saifi, was chief bodyguard to Khaled Nezzar, from 1990 to 1993, an unusual background for a terrorist leader, whilst a video passed on to the CIA claiming him as 'a lieutenant of bin Laden' was shown to be a fake. For these reasons they suggested that the abduction may have been concocted by the Algerian secret services or sponsored by them to help the campaign for more post-9/11 American support.[83]

Certainly the kidnapping of the Western tourists, as well as the news that the GSPC were planning to kidnap competitors on the 2004 Paris–Dakar rally as they drove through Mali, gave added urgency to the American offensive against al-Qaeda in the region, the so-called Pan-Sahel Initiative.[84] Fearing that the impoverished southern fringe of the Sahara – the intersection between North and West Africa – could become a safe haven for terrorism, American special forces set out to impose order. Working with Algeria, Chad, Mali, Mauritania, Niger and Senegal, they sent in small, highly mobile units that could defeat the GSPC on the ground. In March 2004 the American

European Command sent a Navy P-3 Orion surveillance aircraft to sweep the area, relaying Saifi's position to soldiers from Chad, Niger and Nigeria in the region. In the resultant fighting forty-three GSPC members were killed as Saifi was pursued into Mali, Niger and Chad, only to be captured by a Chadian anti-government group, the Movement for Democracy and Justice, who after much negotiation handed him over to Algeria at the end of October 2004.

Two months later Saifi was reportedly backing Bouteflika's plan for a general amnesty and this led many to wonder whether he was a DRS agent who, by keeping the al-Qaeda threat in place, had ensured the continuation of the 'war on terrorism' dividend.[85] As a result of all this counter-insurgency action, the budget for pan-Sahel agreement increased from $7 million to $125 million in 2005.

BOUTEFLIKA: FRIEND AND ALLY

'Washington has much to learn from Algeria on ways to fight terrorism,' commented William Burns, the American Deputy Secretary of State for North African Affairs, speaking on 9 December 2002 at the end of an official visit to Algeria, which concluded with an agreement to sell counter-terrorist military equipment to Algiers, thereby ending an embargo in place since the cancellation of elections in 1992. Such endorsements continued throughout 2003 with the Bush administration describing the regime as the 'most democratic in the Arab world' while the American Secretary of State, Colin Powell, visiting Algiers briefly in December, praised Algeria's 'exceptional cooperation in the war on terrorism'.

This fulsome support also meant that the Bush administration warmly welcomed Bouteflika's re-election on 9 April 2004, at which the incumbent president supposedly secured 83 per cent of the vote. However, his main challenger, Ali Benflis – the prime minister from 2000 until Bouteflika replaced him with Ahmed Ouyahia in May 2003, who came second with a distant 8 per cent – derided the election as a sham.[86] He alleged that there were irregularities 'in thousands of polling stations across the country', and vowed to appeal to the Constitutional Council which validates results. In the same vein Abdel Monem Said, director of the Al-Ahram Centre for Political and Strategic Studies in Cairo, said he found such a landslide deeply worrying, adding: 'Any president who can win re-election with a score of 83 per cent is a sign that there was a heavy government presence in the voting process.'

The US State Department poured scorn on these claims, saying

Bouteflika's re-election was 'free from fraud' and Algeria's first democratic presidential contest. On 3 July President Bush backed this up with a personal message, declaring: 'America continues to rely on Algeria as its partner in the fight against terrorism as well as in the crucial role of spreading democracy and promoting prosperity in the world.' Not to be outdone, President Chirac also congratulated Bouteflika and said the campaign had 'allowed the Algerian people to show its willingness to move forward on the path of democratic pluralism'. Likewise Anne-Marie Lizin, head of the foreign affairs commission of Belgium's Senate, stated: 'We have the feeling of an enormous step forward ... this vote has reached European standards.'[87]

This external legitimacy strengthened Bouteflika's hand as he continued to preside over changes that were hailed as hopeful in the West, in particular his commitment to clear and transparent government.[88] Most significantly he made apparent inroads towards making the military accountable to civilian authority as the portly Mohammed Lamari retired in 2004 from his post as *de facto* defence minister, ostensibly for reasons of ill-health. This was followed by the sidelining of Larbi Belkheir, widely seen as a gamekeeper for the military in his position as head of the president's office, who was appointed Ambassador to Morocco from 26 August 2005. This left only three supporters of the January 1992 coup still in power – Abdelmalek Guenaizia, the minister delegate for defence, and the two ruthless heads of the intelligence services, Major General Mohammed Médiène and Major General Smaïn Lamari – and seemed to signal that Bouteflika had the upper hand over the army.

Away from international politics and away from this court intrigue, the regime still had a fundamental problem of legitimacy amongst the young. With unemployment still endemic the generational divide was as great as ever, especially in Kabylia. The village council movement, still seething with rage, re-started talks with the government in January 2005 but these broke down shortly afterwards. The divide was worsened by the climate of censorship which Bouteflika introduced after his re-election. Editors, journalists and cartoonists critical of the president and his government were ruthlessly repressed. Mohammed Benchicou, the editor of *Le Matin*, was imprisoned in 2004 for attacking Bouteflika in print. In December 2005 Benchicou's sentence was extended by six months and the paper, forced to cease publication, was ordered to pay a fine of 2.5 million dinars. *Le Matin* journalists Sid Ahmed Semiane and Ghada Hamrouche and the daily's cartoonist Ali Dilem were also sentenced to six more months in prison. Equally, Bouteflika kept a tight rein on any form of Islamist dissent. Ali Belhadj was under constant surveillance and in July 2005 he was arrested and imprisoned for seven months for making a statement on Al-Jazeera that praised Iraqi insurgents in their fight against the 'American occupation', shortly after two Algerian diplomats had been kidnapped in Iraq.

Bouteflika clearly wanted to silence debate as he sought to bring final closure to the reconciliation process and in this tense atmosphere a peace charter was put to a referendum on 29 September 2005.[89] Continuing along the path of the 1999 civil concord, the charter enshrined a broad amnesty for past abuses that covered members of the state security forces and armed groups who were in prison or about to surrender. This supposedly did not extend to those who had committed 'acts of collective massacre, rape, or the use of explosives in public places', but, given the lack of any serious investigation into these crimes, the Algerian public knew that such promises were a dead letter. The opposition, led by the FFS, called for a boycott of the referendum on the grounds that the charter glorified force, inscribed immunity from prosecution, negotiated away suffering and represented a denial of truth and justice to hundreds of thousands of victims and their families. Unsurprisingly the state-controlled television and radio gave scant coverage to such criticism, and independent journalists and organizations were intimidated; the Algerian League for the Defence of Human Rights was prevented from holding public meetings as the government continued to draw upon the state of emergency legislation despite claiming that the war was over.

Officials claimed that the charter was approved by 97 per cent on a turnout of 79 per cent. Independent estimates, however, put the numbers voting in the big cities at some 20–30 per cent lower. *Le Soir d'Algérie* estimated a participation rate of 50 per cent in Sétif whilst in Kabylia polling stations were attacked and ballots destroyed. Undeterred, Bouteflika pressed ahead, and on 1 November 6,778 prisoners were amnestied as the government set about transforming the charter into law.

Back on the international stage Bouteflika continued to cultivate strong relations with the West. For example, he attended the G8 summit in Gleneagles at which Tony Blair unveiled a major international initiative to deal with debt relief. This meant that he was in Britain at the time of the 7 July 2005 bombings in London, which were greeted with sighs of 'now you know' by the pro-government Algerian media. 'Londonistan', as one *El-Moudjahid* journalist explained, was finally blowing back in British faces.[90]

During the autumn of 2005 Bouteflika was bedevilled with serious health problems. He was rushed to France for treatment as Algeria became awash with rumours that he was about to die. By the beginning of 2006 he had returned, all smiles, to his position, as the Blair government, determined to crack down on religious extremism but sensitive to the issue of human rights, tried to conclude an agreement that detainees sent back to Algeria would not be tortured. Talks led to the offer of an official state visit, the first by an Algerian head of state to Britain, which Bouteflika knew would further enhance his external legitimacy. On 11–12 July 2006 he was accorded the full red-carpet treatment. Following an audience with the Queen he had one-to-one talks and lunch with Blair at 10 Downing Street. He also met the Leaders of the House of Commons and the House of Lords, and had discussions with the Lord Mayor of London and leading British investment and commercial representatives.

The meeting between Bouteflika and Blair concluded with a joint statement in which the two underlined the growing importance of relations, especially given that Algeria was a key supplier of gas to Europe. Algeria and Britain signed an agreement to establish a Joint Commission with ministerial talks about investment, debt repayment, and trade to be held on an annual basis. Finally and most importantly the two countries agreed to deepen security and judicial cooperation in the fight against terrorism. In practical terms this meant joint military exercises, training visits and weapons sales. It also meant the signing of four legal treaties between Britain and Algeria on Extradition, Mutual Legal Assistance in Criminal Matters, Judicial Cooperation in Civil and Commercial Matters, and the Re-admission and Circulation of Persons, which theoretically ensured that no detainees would suffer human rights abuses, a commitment further sealed by letters between the president and the prime minister that outlined the precise framework for returning suspects.

Armed with such assurances, Kim Howells, Secretary for State for Foreign and Commonwealth Affairs, deflected questions in the House of Commons about the human rights of individuals deported back to Algeria. Replying to the MP Jeremy Corbyn's concerns, voiced in the Chamber on 13 September 2006, Howells admitted that there was no memorandum of understanding with the Algerian government nor indeed was the government seeking one. Nevertheless, he announced:

> The government are satisfied that these arrangements and the changing circumstances in Algeria allow the UK to deport individuals in a manner consistent with its domestic and international human rights obligations. The Special Immigration Appeals Commission recently dismissed an appeal against deportation by terrorist suspect 'Y', ruling that he would not face a real risk of inhuman or degrading treat-

ment if he were returned to Algeria. Algeria is a signatory to the United Nations Convention Against Torture.

Howells' replies illustrate just how much the post-11 September and post-7 July context has transformed attitudes to the Algerian regime. By July 2006 we are light years away from 1998 when the international community, led by the then UK foreign secretary Robin Cook, sought to call the Zeroual regime to account on human rights abuses. Now the criticisms voiced by Amnesty International and Human Rights Watch are met with a muted response. Why? Because Algeria is a pivot in the 'war on terror' and this turn of events in international relations has allowed the regime to weather the storm for the time being. Bouteflika is officially viewed as a friend in the Muslim world and neither the American or British governments want to pose awkward questions that might destabilize his regime.

The Anger That Will Not Go Away

ALGERIA 2007. IT is fifty-three years since the beginning of the war of liberation, forty-five years since independence and ten years since the worst massacres. Bouteflika has been president since April 1999 and his official internet site, www.el-mouradia.dz, projects transparency, modernity and democratic accountability. At the click of a button you can access a biography of the president, pictures of the past heads of state, documents, an historical timeline and Bouteflika's speeches. One can even email the president.

However, this depiction of Algeria as a successful twenty-first-century state evades some awkward questions. The coups of 1965 and 1992 do not merit a mention, and although we are told that Boudiaf was assassinated the details of why and how are omitted. In terms of the violence of the 1990s Algeria is cast as victim, one of the countries that has suffered most from the scourge of terrorism. Nothing is said about the vast human-rights abuses carried out by the forces of law and order.

Now, it is claimed, Algeria has shaken off this bloodshed. As a result of Bouteflika's transition process the country is striding forward and is resolutely orientated towards the future. Algiers is the Arab cultural capital for 2007. There were national elections in May and in July the country hosted the ninth All-Africa Games. Confidence and stability have been restored. Unlike in 1997, Algeria no longer has the hallmarks of a failed state.

This is the official façade: what is the reality? His website might exude confidence but in practice Bouteflika's government, led since May 2006 by Abdelhaziz Belkhadem, is beset by permanent tensions, the first of which is the need to deliver a better economy. In this respect there are some positive signs. Digital terrestrial television is about to be rolled out across the three national channels. The windfall from the increase in oil prices means that, in theory at least, the government has a huge fiscal reserve to invest in renewing the country's dilapidated roads and railways. The country's first bank, Crédit Populaire d'Algérie, is about to be privatized and foreign investors are queuing up to get a further share of Algeria's gas riches, the sixth largest in the world.[1] As in much of Africa and the Middle East, there is also a growing Chinese presence which has poured huge amounts of money into building and construction over the last five years.[2] On top of this Algeria continues to develop a civilian nuclear programme as a symbol of its desire to be the major power in North Africa, signing a cooperation agreement with the United States on 9 June 2007. Yet the country remains blighted by unemployment, particularly amongst the young. Official statistics in 2006 put the unemployment rate at 13 per cent but this figure is challenged by Louisa Hanoune, leader of the Trotskyist Parti des Travailleurs, who claims that it is 30 per cent.[3] Elsewhere *The Economist* advances a figure of 17.3 per cent.[4]

Whichever figure is correct, the truth is that unemployment is the daily backdrop to day-to-day life, which explains why the government is encouraging the younger population to become involved in private enterprise. 'Commerce not politics' is the regime's slogan, and it has introduced a series of schemes to help under-thirties to establish their own businesses, resulting in an explosion of pizzerias, cybercafés and international call centres.[5] Unemployment is also the reason why the government turns a blind eye not only to the black market but also to clandestine immigration as thousands try to leave in search of a better economic life, usually in France. It knows that both, by channelling away social discontent, are in effect safety valves for the system.

In the meantime, Bouteflika, mindful of the need for American support to prop up the regime, knows that he must aid the United States in its 'war on terror' despite widespread anger at the war in Iraq. It is a delicate balancing act which has led both governments to be increasingly discreet about the exact nature of their collaboration within the framework of the Pan-Sahel Counter-Terrorist Initiative set up in 2004. The establishment in 2006 of a new Algerian-US military base at Tamanrasset, the administrative capital of the country's extreme south, was cloaked in secrecy, lest it provoke popular uproar.[6] However, flight records of planes reveal that two US military flights, transporting 100 Special Force personnel and their dogs, landed at the base on 16 February 2006, followed by a third flight, carrying surveillance and listening equipment on the next day. Local people saw these troops travelling overland into northern Mali in search of pro-al-Qaeda Islamist guerrillas reportedly operating across Chad, Niger, Mali and Mauritania.

To bolster support and deflect criticism away from his pro-US policy Bouteflika has been very willing to resort to traditional nationalist discourse attacking the French. In an emotional speech in May 2005, opening an historical conference to mark the sixtieth anniversary of the French repression in Sétif in eastern Algeria, Bouteflika set out to expose the hypocrisy of French liberal values. Just at the moment when huge numbers of Algerians were giving their lives in the liberation of Europe from Nazism, he argued, the French were carrying out a massacre of unspeakable horror.[7] Conveniently forgetting the grave human-rights abuses carried out by the Algerian regime since independence, Bouteflika readily assumed the mantle of victim, attacking France as a country in denial about the colonial past and even making an explicit link between the Holocaust and colonialism. Bouteflika's vitriol was coloured by the recent Franco-Algerian polemic stirred up by French government legislation in February 2005 which decreed that the colonial mission must be taught in schools in a positive fashion.[8] His polemic undoubtedly blighted public relations between the two countries, preventing the long-mooted treaty of reconciliation, though behind the scenes they continued to cooperate on economic and security issues. Crucially, however, it allowed Bouteflika, like Boumediène before him, to look strong by standing up to the old colonial power.

Bouteflika was also confronted with power struggles within the regime. In the wake of the 2004 presidential elections he seemed to have the upper hand, but in November 2005 the inner circle of the military, fearful of continuing scares about the president's health, met in secret to discuss the crisis. The Algerian press, tightly controlled and fearful of censorship, said nothing about the event. However, the *Gazette du Maroc* reported that the proceedings were dominated by the heads of the DRS, generals Mohammed Médiène and Smaïn Lamari, who talked about Lakdar Brahimi, presidential candidate in 1999, former foreign-affairs minister and former UN envoy in Afghanistan and Iraq, as Bouteflika's most likely successor.[9] For the veteran human-rights activist Ali-Yahia Abdennour, the meeting illustrated the continuing strength of the DRS:

> The DRS has never been as powerful as during Bouteflika's second term. Neither he nor the generals dare oppose it. The DRS has six or seven ministers in the government ... and it has placed in each department a colonel whose function is to spy on the minister and his personnel. This system paralyzes the State and deprives its institutions of any authority. The real president is not Bouteflika, it is general Médiène. The youth in Algiers call Bouteflika the 'president-Taïwan', in reference to the fake goods that come from South-East Asia. For them, he is the fake president.[10]

Of course, behind each of these issues – the economy, US support and the internal power struggles – the security question looms large. Bouteflika's presidency stands or falls by his ability to bring a final end to the violence, but many believe that the terrorist threat is manipulated by the government to maintain the state of emergency and limit freedom. As one young Algerian, who wished to remain anonymous, claimed, 'They know where the GSPC are. They could finish them off in a week but terrorism is useful because it makes people scared and keeps them down.'[11]

On 11 April 2007 a series of coordinated bombs exploded in Algiers, killing at least thirty-three people and wounding more than 222, according to official sources.[12] It was the first time since the late 1990s that the capital had been targeted by such a spate of violence. The symbolic target of the main attack in central Algiers, seemingly carried out by a suicide bomber, was the Prime Minister's office, which was left with a gaping hole in the six-storey building. In the eastern outskirts of the city three car bombs hit a police station in Bab Ezzouar. The attacks, whose media impact across the world was enormous, were immediately claimed by the al-Qaeda Organization in the Islamic Magrheb which posted photographs of the three suicide bombers on the Internet.

For months the Algerian press had been awash with speculation ever since the news, released by videotape on the fifth anniversary of the 11 September attacks, that Al Qa'eda's second in command, Ayman Al Zawahiri, had recruited the GSPC as the group's North African emissary. In January 2007 the GSPC officially changed its name to the al-Qaeda Organization in the Islamic Maghreb, a recognition of the recruiting power of the al-Qaeda brand name. The 11 April attacks were the most powerful expression of a climate of violence that had been palpable for months. On 30 October 2006, for example, two booby-trap bombs had killed three and wounded twenty-four in the suburbs of Algiers. On 10 December a bus carrying workers for the US company Halliburton was attacked. The US and British media had already picked up on this, pondering for some time whether Algeria and North Africa represented a new front for al-Qaeda.[13] However, with the exception of Simon Tisdale at the *Guardian*, journalists accepted such stories as a given, without considering how the Algerian government might be exploiting the al-Qaeda threat to muffle criticism and enlist international support.[14]

The bombs underlined Algeria's fragility. As *Le Monde*'s editorial the following day emphasized, Bouteflika might not be directly responsible for the outrage but, by failing to provide real hope for the young and installing a pseudo-democracy, he, like many other leaders in the Arab world, has provided a pretext for such violence.[15] By pointing the finger at Bouteflika, *Le*

Monde drew attention to the unstable pillars of the regime. His transition process might have promised to turn the page but in reality it has generated huge anger. Although the regime has offered compensation to the families of the disappeared, has closed down counter-insurgency centres such as the one at Blida, and has enshrined a law making it impossible to prosecute the forces of law and order for human rights abuses, in the long term such official amnesia is unsustainable.[16] The family of one of the murdered monks, Father Christophe Lebreton, is trying to bring a legal action against the Algerian government through the French courts, and there is continued pressure from international human rights groups. Amnesty International has closely monitored the case of the two Algerians detainees, 'Q' and 'K', who were deported by Britain back to Algeria in January 2007 on the grounds that they were a threat to national security. Despite guarantees given by Bouteflika during his official visit to Britain in July 2006, Amnesty claims that both were immediately picked up by the DRS in Algiers. Scrutiny of this nature, in conjunction with the arrest and trial of former leaders such as General Pinochet and Slobodan Milošević, means that many generals, whether still serving or retired, fear that they could be prosecuted outside the country for atrocities committed inside Algeria, and there are persistent rumours that they are seeking immunity from prosecution.[17]

There is also anger at the authoritarian nature of the Bouteflika regime. What, many Algerians ask, is the point of voting now that Bouteflika has altered the law so that he can run for a third term as president in 2009? Where is the democratic choice? And doesn't the regime's concerted attack on the freedom of speech reflect its fundamental priorities? The political cartoonist Ali Dilem has been constantly harassed because his images, testament to the subversive power of humour, mock the president and the regime. One cartoon, published in *Le Matin* on 8 September 2003, depicted the president being chased by an angry Algerian population with the caption 'Bouteflika we are all behind you'; in conjunction with a series, published in *Liberté* in October and November 2003, that cast him as a puppet of the generals, this led to a one-year prison sentence for Dilem and a fine of 50,000 dinars (500 euros).

However, what fuels this anger more than anything else is generalized economic disaffection. Algerians feel angry and frustrated because the system offers no future. The wealth that flows from the oil and gas reserves, and the continuing demand from foreign companies to exploit these resources, mean the regime can disregard the wishes of the vast majority of Algerian citizens. With no need to tax them to raise revenue it has no financial incentive to enter into a genuine political and social relationship with the population. For this reason Algerians in general and the young in particular feel politically, socially and economically dispossessed. '*Hogra*', 'humiliation', is the keyword that still sums up the existence of millions of Algerians. As one contemporary joke puts it: 'Is there such a thing as hope in Algeria? Yes, a visa. In Algeria, hope is called a visa.'

Bouteflika: 'I am not a dictator!'
Algerian: 'Modest, too!'

Ali Dilem's cartoons have constantly mocked Bouteflika, earning him numerous fines and prison sentences.

In 1989 this anger was channelled by the FIS. To vote for the FIS was a way of expressing disaffection with the system. Significantly though, much of the FIS language evoked the sharply polarized categories of the wartime FLN. During the war of liberation the FLN had presented the anti-colonial struggle as a battle of opposites. Justice and injustice; brothers and enemies; coloniser and colonised: the FLN categorized the world into sharply divided choices, a logic of violence that was powerfully expressed by Frantz Fanon in *The Wretched of the Earth*. In the early 1990s the FIS took over this rhetoric and transformed it into a self-righteous anger of the dispossessed. This was the key to their electoral success, and it highlighted one of the major problems of the post-independence era, namely the preponderance of a political culture that cannot imagine dialogue, pluralism or constructive dissent.

The anger that produced the FIS is still there. Now, however, this alienation does not express itself through organized politics but by hostility to the electoral process which is widely perceived as a sham. The legislative elections on 17 May, which saw the victory of the ruling coalition FLN, RND and MSP under the banner of Presidential Alliance, were marked by huge abstention. Only 35 per cent of the electorate turned out to vote, the lowest number of any election since the establishment of multi-party politics in 1989, and this despite calls by the government to vote as a way of rejecting al-Qaeda. The Minister of the Interior, Yazid Zerhouni, tried to put a brave face on the results, even claiming that there was no reason to be 'ashamed', but in reality the turn-out was a damning verdict on a political system that in the eyes of large parts of the population is riddled with corruption.[18] There was also widespread resentment at the way in which the threat of al-Qaeda was exploited to pressurise Algerians into voting. As Selim Khayami, editor of the daily *Quotidien d'Oran*, argued:

> Not voting does not mean that we are in favour of Al-Qaeda. This blackmail is unacceptable. We reject terrorism unambiguously. Nevertheless that does not solve the crisis of political representation in Algeria.[19]

If voting apathy is one expression of anger at the system, the other is directionless violence and juvenile delinquency. Throughout Algeria riots, largely unreported by the press, take place on a regular basis, often as many as five a week. As the daily *Liberté* reported in September 2006, in a fascinating exploration of youth attitudes in Bab el-Oued in Algiers entitled 'Being twenty in Algeria', these riots are a telling comment on the lack of a civil society.[20] Instead there is a wall of incomprehension between the government and the young, as the latter finds solace in a burgeoning street culture of break-dancing, capoera and rapping, as well as a new world of cybercafés, internet chatrooms and text messaging. This generation also expresses a strong distrust of official history. Disappointed by the post-independence state, many believe that the war of liberation was in vain and that the revolution has been betrayed. As one schoolboy puts it provocatively: 'The Algerian War is a tissue of lies.'[21] Many feel that the regime has sold the country out to US imperialism, and this is why football crowds chant bin Laden's name. They know that this is a provocation which will inspire fear in the West.

In 1952 the French demographer, Alfred Sauvy, in a seminal article in the left-wing magazine *L'Observateur*, coined the term 'Third World'.[22] Drawing an explicit comparison not only with the two-bloc politics of the Cold War but also with the role of the third estate during the French Revolution, Sauvy wanted to convey the colossal transformation represented by decolonization. For Sauvy this was the most significant revolution of the twentieth century: the arrival of Africa, Asia and Latin America as actors on the international stage. The key question then was: what did these countries and populations aspire to?

After independence Algeria was in the vanguard of the third-world movement. Algerians had brought an end to colonial oppression and won their right to self-determination. Yet by the 1980s the new post-colonial generation was being humiliated by a post-colonial regime presiding over endemic corruption and a failing economy. These contradictions produced October 1988, the pivotal event in post-independence Algeria, and nineteen years on the same problems are still there. Ordinary Algerians still feel humiliated. They still want to be treated as citizens. They still want good government, the rule of law and use of the oil and gas wealth for the benefit of the majority, not the minority.

Ever a tireless opponent of the regime, the dissident historian Mohammed Harbi sees this as the fundamental model of Algerian politics. To understand Algeria today, he explains, you must start with the massive exclusion of people from power, the rejection of pluralism and the absence of any long-term meaningful political blueprint from the political elite. For this reason he is pessimistic about the future:

> The regime has stabilized and with United States support they can do what they want. They are untouchable. But the regime has nothing to offer for the long term. It is not interested in asking where Algeria and Algerians will be in twenty years' time.[23]

Of course, Harbi's remarks could apply to a whole host of countries, especially given that Algeria is strategically positioned at the tip of the arc of insecurity stretching from Morocco through Africa and the Middle East to Pakistan and Indonesia. Living under regimes characterized by corruption and poor government, hundreds of millions of people feel downtrodden at home and ignored by the West, which is only too willing to turn a blind eye on the grounds of strategic interests.

For this reason Sauvy's question is just as relevant at the beginning of the twenty-first century. What these populations aspire to and how they perceive the West is *the* major issue in international politics, because the brutal truth is that the anger of the post-colonial dispossessed will not go away. This is a fury that has the potential to endure for decades to come.

NOTES

Introduction: The Role of the Past in Algerian History

1 Joseph-François Michaud produced a six-volume history of the Crusades which was published in Paris between 1812 and 1822. On the impact of Michaud see Kim Munholland, 'Michaud's *History of the Crusades* and the French Crusade in Algeria under Louis-Philippe' in Petre ten-Doesschate Chu and Gabriel P. Weisberg (eds), *The Popularization of Images: Visual Culture under the July Monarchy*, Princeton, NJ: Princeton University Press, 1994.

2 On this point see Chu and Weisberg (eds), *The Popularization of Images* (op. cit.) and Andrew Wheatcroft, *Infidels: The Conflict Between Christendom and Islam 638–2002*, London: Viking, 2003.

3 John Ruedy, *Modern Algeria: The Origins and Development of a Nation*, Bloomington: Indiana University Press, 1992, pp. 47–8.

4 It was a mythology which explains why, during the death throes of French Algeria in 1962, diehard settlers operated a 'scorched earth' policy. Hospitals and universities were dynamited because, so the logic went, nothing could be left to the Arabs. Algeria had to be left as it was before 1830.

5 For an analysis of the significance of this expedition see Roger Benjamin, *Orientalism: Delacroix to Klee*, Sydney: The Art Gallery of New South Wales, 1997.

6 Ibid.

7 On this argument see Edward Said, *Orientalism*, London: Routledge & Kegan Paul, 1978, and Rana Kabbani, *Europe's Myths of the Orient*, London: Macmillan, 1986.

8 On this see Azzedine Haddour, *Colonial Myths, History and Narrative*, Manchester: Manchester University Press, 2000, and Jean-François Guilhaume, *Les Mythes Fondateurs de l'Algérie Française*, Paris: L'Harmattan, 1993.

9 Emile Félix Gautier, *L'Islamisation de l'Afrique du Nord*, Paris: Payot, 1927.

10 On this point see Benjamin Stora, *La Gangrène et l'Oubli: La Mémoire de la Guerre d'Algérie*, Paris: La Découverte, 1991. See also Charles-Robert Ageron, *La Guerre d'Algérie et les Algériens*, Paris: Armand Colin, 1997.

11 This was very significant because the colonial authorities had everything in their power to cut Algeria off from the rest of the Muslim world.

12 Abassi Madani was a veteran of the war of liberation. He was directly involved in the wave of attacks against the French launched by the FLN on 1 November 1954.

13 The novel which made Mouloud Mammeri's literary reputation is *La Colline Oubliée*, Paris: Seuil, 1952. For a fascinating insight into Mouloud Mammeri see *Mouloud Mammeri: Entretien avec Tahar Djaout*, Algiers: Laphomic, 1987.

14 On the 'Berber spring' see Salem Chaker, *Berbères Aujourd'hui*, Paris: L'Harmattan, 1989.

15 On the Kabyle myth see Patricia Lorcin, *Imperial Identities: Stereotyping, Prejudice and Race in Colonial Algeria*, London: I.B. Tauris, 1995.

16 These narratives are not monolithic. Within them there were conflicting tendencies, even if there was agreement on the broad interpretative framework.

17 Renan's insights were the starting point for Eric Hobsbawm and Terrence Ranger's edited collection, *The Invention of Tradition*, Cambridge: Cambridge University Press, 1983. See also Homi Bhabha (ed.) *Nation and Narration*, London: Routledge, 1996. The transmission of historical memory is now a major subject of research for historians. On this see Pierre

Nora (ed.) *Les Lieux de Mémoire*, Paris: Gallimard, seven volumes, 1984–1992, and the journal *History and Memory* which is produced by the Eva and Marc Besen Institute for Historical Consciousness, Tel Aviv University, and published twice a year by Indiana University Press. See also Martin Evans and Ken Lunn (eds), *War and Memory in the Twentieth Century*, Oxford: Berg, 1997, and Immanuel Sivan and Jay Winter, *War and Remembrance in the Twentieth Century*, Cambridge: Cambridge University Press, 1999. On the specific issue of Algeria see Gilles Manceron and Hassan Remaoun, *D'une Rive à l'Autre. La Guerre d'Algérie de la Mémoire à l'Histoire*, Paris: Syros, 1993. On the general issue of colonial memory see Robert Aldrich, *Vestiges of the Colonial Empire in France: Monuments, Museums and Colonial Memories*, Basingstoke: Macmillan, 2005. On the gender aspects of the transmission of memory, in this case those of Britain and the Second World War, see Lucy Noakes, *War and the British*, London: I.B. Tauris, 1998.

18 Mohammed Harbi is one of the most important historians of Algeria. See Mohammed Harbi, *Le FLN: Mirage et Réalité*, Paris: Editions Jeune Afrique, 1980, and *Les Archives de la Révolution Algérienne*, Paris: Editions Jeune Afrique, 1981. See also his fascinating personal memoirs *Une Vie Debout: Mémoires Politiques*, Paris: La Découverte, 2001.

19 Abdelmalek Sayad, *Histoire et Recherche Identitaire*, Paris: Bouchène, 2002. See also Mohammed Harbi and Benjamin Stora (eds), *La Guerre d'Algérie 1954–2004: La Fin de l'Amnésie*, Paris: Robert Laffont, 2004. On 20–22 June 2006 Gilbert Meynier and Frédéric Abécassis organized a conference on the Algerian War at the Ecole Normale Supérieure in Lyon. Bringing together over a hundred historians, its explicit intention was to go beyond official myths and memory to produce a critically conscious history of Franco-Algerian relations. On this see http://ens-web3.ens–lsh.fr/colloques/france-algerie.

Chapter 1: Dissident Landscape

1 On this see James McDougall, *History and the Culture of Nationalism in Algeria*, Cambridge: Cambridge University Press, 2006. Within this book McDougall provides a detailed and highly perceptive analysis of the politicization of the past in Algeria.

2 Traditionally in Kabylia the switch from summer to winter is known as the gates of the year because this determines if the weather will bring bread or famine.

3 On this see Michael Brett and Elizabeth Fentress, *The Berbers*, Oxford: Blackwell, 1996.

4 Noel Malcolm, *Kosovo: A Short History*, London: Macmillan, 1998.

5 Sallust, *The Jugurthine War/The Conspiracy of Catiline*, London: Penguin, 1963.

6 Kateb Yacine, *Nedjma*, Paris: Seuil, 1956.

7 For an outline of the personal biography of André Mandouze see Martin Evans, *Memory of Resistance: French Opposition to the Algerian War 1954–62*, Oxford: Berg, 1997. See also his autobiography, *Mémoires d'Outre Siècle: D'une Résistance à l'Autre*, Paris: Viviane Hamy, 1998.

8 Mandouze made this point in the conclusion to a conference on 'The French Army and the Algerian War' at the University of Salford in October 1996. His testimony appears in Martin S. Alexander, Martin Evans and J.F.V. Keiger (eds), *The Algerian War and the French Army, 1954–62: Experiences, Images, Testimonies*, Basingstoke: Macmillan, 2002.

9 Kateb Yacine engaged in a critical dialogue with St Augustine. His first collection of poems, published in 1946, was entitled *Soliloques* – a clear reference to St Augustine's work of the same title. Assia Djebar used excerpts from Saint Augustine's *Confessions* in the preface to *L'Amour, La Fantasia*, Paris: Jean-Claude Lattès, 1985.

10 Brett and Fentress, *The Berbers*, p. 83.

11 Samy Hadad, *Algérie: Autopsie d'une Crise*, Paris: L'Harmattan, 1998.

12 Kharijism, meaning 'seceders', was highly puritanical. Supporters believed in the creation of a virtuous society through the purging of unbelievers. For this reason Kharijism became a reference point for some of the armed Islamist groups during the 1990s.

13 On this see Michael Brett, 'The Fatimid revolution (861–973) and its aftermath in North Africa' in J.D. Fage (ed.), *The Cambridge History of Africa*, vol. 2, Cambridge: Cambridge University Press, 1978, pp. 631–6.

14 Ibn Khaldoun, *Kitab al-'ibar wa diwan al-mubtada wa'l-khabar*, Bulaq, 1867–8. For an overview on Ibn Khaldoun see A. al-Azmeh, *Ibn Khaldoun: An Essay in Reinterpretation*, London: Routledge, 1982.

15 Maghreb is the Arabic word which denotes the western Arab world (Algeria, Libya, Mauritania, Morocco, Tunisia and the Western Sahara). Mashriq denotes the eastern Arab world (Egypt, Palestine, Syria, etc.).

16 Fatima Mernissi, *Islam and Democracy: Fear of the Modern World*, London: Virago, 1993, p. 30.

17 How many Arabs arrived in North Africa is a highly contentious issue because it raises questions about how the present-day population should be defined ethnically.

18 The word 'Sufi' means 'wool' in Arabic.

19 The four Sunni schools of law are Hanafi, Maliki, Shafi'i and Hanbali. These four share most of their rulings but differ on the due weight given to reason and analogy in resolving issues of Islamic law.

20 Linda Colley, *Captives: Britain, Empire and the World 1600–1850*, London: Jonathan Cape, 2002.

21 On this point see McDougall, *History and the Culture of Nationalism in Algeria*, pp. 172–3.

22 Luis Martinez, *The Algerian Civil War 1990–1998*, London: Hurst & Company, 2000, pp. 12–13.

Chapter 2: Forced Marriage: French Algeria 1830–1962

1 *South Bank* documentary on Rachid Taha and Khaled, broadcast on ITV in March 2005.

2 Mohammed Harbi, *Une Vie Debout*.

3 Three African leaders, Senegal's Léopold Senghor, Tunisia's Habib Bourguiba and Niger's Hamani Diori, were the moving force behind the establishment of the Francophone movement. For an overview of the organization go to www.francophone.org.

4 On Abd el-Kader see Raphael Danziger, *Abd el-Kader and the Algerians: Resistance to the French and Internal Consolidation*, New York: Africana Publishing Company, 1977; Ismail al-Arabi, *Al muqawama al jaza'iriyya that liwa' al amir Abd al Qadir*, Algiers: Société Nationale d'Edition, 1982; Bruno Etienne, *Abd-el-Kader*, Paris: Hachette, 1994; and Julia Clancy-Smith, *Rebel and Saint*, California: University of California Press, 1994.

5 Quoted in Alistair Horne, *A Savage War of Peace: Algeria 1954–1962*, London: Macmillan, 1977, p. 30.

6 For an example of how colonial historians lionized Bugeaud see Augustin Bernard, *L'Algérie*, Paris: Larousse, 1931, p. 89.

7 Harbi, *Une Vie Debout*, p. 10.

8 This romanticization was especially pronounced after he protected Christians in Damascus from Muslim attacks in 1860.

9 Kateb Yacine, *Abd el-Kader et l'Indépendance Algérienne*, Algiers: Enahda, 1947. In this pamphlet Kateb Yacine holds up Abd el-Kader as the founding father of the Algerian nation who has been denigrated by French propaganda.

10 Inevitably political Islamists have challenged this official memory. By portraying Abd el-

Kader as a nationalist the FLN memory has forgotten that first and foremost he was a theocrat who wanted to create a state based upon sharia law.

11 Jean Graniage, *Histoire Contemporaine du Maghreb*, Paris: Fayard, 1994, p. 223.
12 On this see David Prochaska, *Making Algeria French*, Cambridge: Cambridge University Press, 1990. See also Charles-Robert Ageron, *L'Algérie Algérienne de Napoléon III à de Gaulle*, Paris: Sinbad, 1980.
13 Louis Gardel, *Fort Saganne*, Paris: Editions du Seuil, 1980. He also wrote the screenplay for the 1984 film of the novel.
14 For a history of the Foreign Legion see Douglas Porch, *The French Foreign Legion*, New York: Harper Collins, 1991.
15 Foreign Legion song.
16 Even by 1956 only eight out of 864 higher administrative posts were held by Muslims.
17 On this see Jean-François Guilhaume, *Les Mythes Fondateurs de l'Algérie Française*, Paris: L'Harmattan, 1992.
18 To become citizens Jews did not have to renounce their rights under Mosaic law and this stirred up Muslim resentment.
19 Edouard Drumont, *La France Juive*, Paris: La France, 1886.
20 On this see Patricia Lorcin, *Imperial Identities*.
21 On this see Graniage, *Histoire Contemporaine du Maghreb*, p. 205.
22 By 1841 the number of native troops fighting for the French had risen to 8,700.
23 On this point see Daniel Lefeuvre, *Chère Algérie 1930–1962*, Paris: Société Française d'Histoire d'Outre Mer, 1997.
24 On the history of Algerian immigration see Benjamin Stora, *Ils Venaient de l'Algérie: L'Immigration Algérienne en France, 1912–1992*, Paris: Fayard, 1992, and Neil Macmaster, *Colonial Migrants and Racism: Algerians in France, 1900–62*, London: Macmillan, 1997.
25 Aline Charby interviewed by Martin Evans, 13 November 1989, Paris.
26 Marie Cardinal, *Les Pieds Noirs*, Paris: Place Furstenberg Editeurs, 1994.
27 For a fascinating insight into this see Leila Sebbar, *Une Enfance Algérienne*, Paris: Gallimard, 1997.
28 For an example of this type of optimism see Bernard, *L'Algérie*, p. 104.
29 Archives Nationales, Section D'Outre Mer, 8 H 61, Rapport de M. le Gouverneur Général de l'Algérie au Haut Comité Méditerranéen, *Situation de l'Algérie au 1 octobre 1937*.
30 In 1988 the French comic Guy Bedos made a documentary about his childhood in Algeria in the late 1940s. Within it he vividly remembered the nightmares he used to have about Arabs invading his house and attacking his family.
31 On Albert Camus see Olivier Todd, *Albert Camus: Une Vie*, Paris: Gallimard, 1996.
32 These articles are reproduced in Albert Camus, *Chroniques Algériennes 1939–1958*, Paris: Gallimard, 1958.
33 From Patrick Eveno and Jean Planchais, *La Guerre d'Algérie*, Paris: La Découverte, 1989, pp. 196–7.
34 Gilbert Meynier, *L'Algérie Révélée: La Guerre de 1914–1918 et le Premier Quart du Vingtième Siècle*, Geneva: Librairie Droz, 1981.
35 Le Manifeste Jeune Algérien, 8 June 1912.
36 See Ferhat Abbas, *Le Jeune Algérien: De la Colonie vers la Province*, Paris: La Jeune Parque, 1931, and *La Nuit Coloniale*, Paris: Julliard, 1962.
37 Ferhat Abbas, 'En marge du nationalisme. La France c'est moi', *L'Entente Franco-Musulmane*, 27 February 1936, no. 24, p.1.
38 Jamal al-Din al-Afghani was born in Afghanistan in 1838. In 1853 he visited India where he studied Western science before travelling to Egypt, Turkey, Russia, Britain and France.

In 1871 he met Mohammed Abduh in Egypt. They moved to Paris in 1884 where they published a journal *Al-Urwah al-Wuthqa* ('The Strongest Bond') which preached the unity of the *umma* and a return to the purity of early Islam. Although impressed by the strength of the French nation, al-Afghani was certain that it would eventually fall because the Third Republic, by championing reason and materialism, had repudiated religious values. Al-Afghani died in 1897 but his ideas continued to exert an influence through Mohammed Adbuh and Mohammed Rashid Rida. Mohammed Abduh's views are encapsulated in his major work *Risalat al-Tawhid* ('Epistle of Unity'), Cairo, 1963.

39 On the Egyptian Brotherhood see Malise Ruthven, *Islam*, Oxford: Oxford University Press, 1997.

40 Shiekh Ben Badis, *Ash-Shihab*, April 1936.

41 Ibid., p. 44.

42 Quoted by Brahim S. Nali, 'The Berber Issue in Algeria' in Reza Shah-Kazemi (ed.), *Algeria: Revolution Revisited*, London: Islamic World Report, 1997, p. 139.

43 On this point see Mohammed Harbi, *Le FLN: Mirage et Réalité*, Paris: Jeune Afrique, 1980.

44 On the French Communist Party and Algeria see Daniele Joly, *The French Communist Party and the Algerian War*, London: Macmillan, 1991.

45 Charte revendicative du peuple algérien musulman', *La Défense*, 26 June 1936, p. 1.

46 Abbas, *La Nuit Coloniale*, p. 151.

47 'Message des représentants des musulmans algériens aux autorités, 20 December 1942' in Claude Collot and Jean-Robert Henry, *Le Mouvement National Algérien*, Paris: L'Harmattan, p. 154.

48 'Manifeste du peuple algérien, 31 March 1943', in Collot and Henry, *Le Mouvement National Algérien*, pp. 155–65.

49 This was a declaration by Abbas on 3 January 1944 before a committee established by de Gaulle to set out a programme of reform for Algeria. The committee's recommendations would lay the basis for the reforms of 7 March 1944. 'Commission chargée d'établir un programme de réformes politiques, sociales et économiques en faveur des musulmans français d'Algérie', Algiers: Imprimérie officielle, 1944, pp. 56–8.

50 Statuts de l'Association des Amis du Manifeste et de la Liberté, 14 March 1944, article 4, p. 1.

51 On Sétif see Radouane Ainad-Tabet, *Le Mouvement du 8 Mai 1945 en Algérie*, Algiers: Offices des Publications Universitaires, 1985.

52 Quoted in Horne, *A Savage War of Peace*, p. 27.

53 Guy Monnerot died, whilst his wife was later picked up by a French patrol sent out from Batna.

54 On these grounds, given that Messali opposed the FLN, the reconstituted PPA was forbidden.

55 It was an undeclared war because there was no formal declaration of hostilities. The French referred to the conflict as a law and order issue in an effort to minimize the problem.

56 For a history of the war see Benjamin Stora, *Histoire de la Guerre d'Algérie, 1954–1962*, Paris: La Découverte, 1994.

57 The Algerian Communist Party (PCA) did establish an armed resistance movement in 1956, the *maquis rouge*. On 1 July this was dissolved and integrated into the FLN.

58 The Socialist Party was known as the Section Française de l'Internationale Ouvrière and the Christian Democrats were the Mouvement Républicain Populaire.

59 This was the figure put forward by Paul Teitgen, secretary general of the Algiers police, when he resigned in protest at Massu's methods on 12 September 1957.

60 Interview with Jean Lacouture in *The Algerian War*, Channel Four television series directed by Peter Batty, 1984.

61 Simon Murray, *Legionnaire: An Englishman in the French Foreign Legion*, London: Macmillan, 2000, p. 157. His memoir was originally published in 1978.

62 Gilbert Meynier, *Histoire Intérieure du FLN*, Paris: Fayard, 2003.

63 Ben Bella's capture by the French on 22 October 1956 averted a major split which would have set the internal resistance against the external leadership.

64 How Abane was killed has been shrouded in mystery. It seems that he was killed in Morocco in 1957. On 29 May 1958 the FLN daily *El Moudjahid* claimed that he had been killed heroically in the *maquis*, a blatant lie.

Chapter 3: Darling of the Non-Aligned Movement, 1962–78

1 For a perceptive biography of Fanon see David Macey, *Frantz Fanon: A Life*, London: Granta, 2000. See also Robert J.C. Young, *Postcolonialism*, Oxford: Oxford University Press, 2003.

2 Reproduced in *Towards An African Revolution*, New York: Monthly Press Review, 1967. Orginally published as *Pour la Révolution Africaine*, Paris: Maspero, 1964.

3 *The Wretched of the Earth*, London: Penguin, 1967. Orginally published as *Les Damnés de la Terre*, Paris: Maspero, 1961.

4 Fanon was posthumously awarded the Prix National des Lettres in December 1964.

5 Assia Djebar, *Les Enfants du Nouveau Monde*, Paris: Julliard, 1962.

6 On the *harkis* see Mohand Hamoumou, *Et Ils Sont Devenus Harkis*, Paris: Fayard, 1993, and Abd-El-Aziz Méliani, *Le Drame des Harkis*, Paris: Perrin, 1993. See also Martin Evans 'The *harkis*: the experience and memory of France's Muslim auxiliaries' in Alexander, Evans and Keiger (eds), *The Algerian War and the French Army, 1954–62*.

7 On the issue of who killed who and how many were killed see Martin S. Alexander, Martin Evans and J.F.V. Keiger, 'The "War without a Name", the French Army and the Algerians: Recovering Experiences, Images and Testimonies' in Alexander, Evans and Keiger (eds), *The Algerian War and the French Army, 1954–62*.

8 On FLN attitudes to Jews and settlers see the remarkable collection of orginal documents gathered together by Mohammed Harbi and Gilbert Meynier, *Le FLN: Documents et Histoire 1954–1962*, Paris: Fayard, 2004.

9 Although the settlers were shabbily treated, soon many made a huge contribution to the French economic miracle during the 1960s.

10 Ben Khedda quoted in Horne, *A Savage War of Peace*.

11 Harbi, *Le FLN: Mirage et Réalité*.

12 Edward Behr, 'Algeria's Bitter Peace', *Sunday Times,* 7 July 1963.

13 Quoted by Mohamed Gharib, 'The Algerian Islamist Movement' in Reza Shah-Kazemi, *Algeria: Revolution Revisited*, London: Islamic World Report, 1997, p. 79.

14 Sayid Qutb, *Milestones on the Road,* Cairo: Kazi Publications, 1964.

15 On this see Hugh Roberts, *The Battlefield Algeria, 1988–2002*, London: Verso, 2003.

16 Quoted in Arslan Humbaraci, *Algeria: A Revolution that Failed*, London: Pall Mall, 1966, p. 227.

17 In 1997 Benyoucef Benkhedda, the former president of the GPRA, claimed that the pro-French francophone Algerian minority had taken over key parts of the state and were defending their privileges against the Islamic majority much as the settler minority had defended their privileges under colonialism. On this see Benyoucef Benkhedda, *La Crise de 1962*, Algiers: Dahlab, 1997. In his memoirs *Une Vie Debout*, Mohammed Harbi is

sceptical about any sort of premeditated francophone plot. Nonetheless, he draws attention to the class background of many of the DAF. Many were sons of *caïds* who generally looked down on the ordinary Algerian people.

18 Ahmed Taleb-Ibrahimi, *De la Décolonisation à la Révolution Naturelle*, Algiers: NPDC, 1973.

19 Kateb Yacine claimed that he was using the French language in a very different way from the former colonial power. In a sense he had made the language his own and was imbuing it with new, subversive meanings. On the question of language see C. Achour, *Abécédaires en Devenir. Idéologie et Langue Française*, Algiers: ENAP, 1985.

20 On this see P. Balta and C. Rulleau, *La Stratégie de Boumediène*, Paris: Sinbad, 1978.

21 Speech accessed from the *Castro Speech Data Base*, http://lanic.utexas.edu/lla/cb/cuba/castro.html on 28 April 2005.

22 Ibid.

23 One Algerian colleague at the University of Portsmouth, Houria Hammoudi-Honey, vividly recalls the popular enthusiasm that Castro's visits generated. The crowds, she remembers, were not shepherded by the regime; this was a spontaneous reaction. Oral evidence recounted to Martin Evans, Portsmouth, 14 February 2005.

24 On this point see Roberts, *The Battlefield Algeria, 1988–2002*.

25 On the relationship between Islam and Greek philosophy see Majid Fakhry, *Philosophy, Dogma and the Impact of Greek Thought in Islam*, Aldershot: Variorum, 1994, and F.E. Peters, *Aristotle and the Arabs*, New York: New York University Press, 1968.

26 The most important book by Kateb Yacine and indeed possibly the most significant book of modern Algerian literature is the novel *Nedjma*, Paris: Seuil, 1956.

27 By 1977, 2,064,360 hectares were in the socialist sector whilst 4,472,220 hectares were still in private hands.

28 By 1980, private farms produced 95 per cent of livestock, 60 per cent of vegetables, 44 per cent of winter cereals and 18 per cent of industrial crops.

29 These figures are taken from the official census which was published in February 1977.

30 Eldridge Cleaver was the press officer of the Black Panther Party. On the run from the American police on charges stemming from a shoot-out with the Oakland police, he, along with several Panther comrades, were delegates to the First Pan-African Cultural Festival under way in Algiers. The Algerian government later gave him political asylum.

31 The live recording, originally released in 1969, is entitled *Archie Shepp Live at the Pan-African Festival*. Those playing with Shepp included Lester Bowie and Alan Silva.

32 In 1962 thousands of *harkis* escaped to France despite the hostility of de Gaulle. They have continued to define themselves as *harkis* and at present the *harki* community in France stands at 400,000.

33 Editorial, *Le Méridonial*, 26 August 1973.

Chapter 4: Black October

1 For an analysis of 'Black October' see Abed Charef, *Dossier Octobre*, Algiers: Laphomic, 1989.

2 Najet Khadda and Monique Gadant, 'Mots et choses de la révolte', *Peuples Méditerranéens* 52–53 July–August 1990, p. 22. Khadda and Gadant remark that the slang phrases used had a strong homosexual connotation which, given the hostility to homosexuality in Algerian society, further stigmatized these policemen as separate from the local community.

3 Khadda and Gadant, 'Mots et choses de la révolte', p. 20.

4 On the use of Edward Thompson's concept of the moral economy of the crowd see Hugh

Roberts, 'Moral Economy or Moral Polity? The political anthropology of Algerian riots', Working Paper no. 17, Crisis States Research Centre, London School of Economics, which can be accessed at www.crisisstates.com/Publications/wp/wp.17.htm.

5 Frédéric Fritscher, 'Au moins deux cent morts depuis le début des émeutes', *Le Monde*, 11 October 1988. Figures on deaths from Benjamin Stora, *Algeria 1830–2000*, Ithaca and London: Cornell University Press, 2001, p. 196.

6 *Le Monde* reprinted substantial parts of Chadli's 10 October speech on 12 October 1988.

7 Rabah Bouaziz interviewed by Martin Evans, 16 October Algiers, 1989.

8 In personal adverts housing is stipulated as a condition of marriage. Such adverts in the press are a testament to the general level of frustration; most used a coded language to talk about illicit sexual encounters.

9 On the National Front see Peter Davies, *The National Front in France: Ideology, Discourse and Power*, London: Routledge, 1999.

10 The new government was led by Jacques Chirac, who as prime minister tried to appropriate many of the themes of the National Front.

11 By 1989 whole blocks of flats were able to receive French channels by satellite. This was a major development since it broke the monopoly of the government-controlled media.

12 On immigration see Benjamin Stora, *Ils Venaient de l'Algérie: L'Immigration Algérienne en France, 1912–1992*, Paris: Fayard, 1992, and A.G. Hargreaves, *Immigration, 'Race' and Ethnicity in Contemporary France*, London: Routledge, 1995.

13 *Zaguet*, though it looks like it might be Arabic, is a corruption of the French 'ça se gâte'.

14 Joke recounted to Martin Evans, Algiers, November 1990.

15 Rachid Taha's 1998 album *Diwan* is a modern reworking of traditional songs from 1920s onwards. As such it provides a fascinating insight into how music has sustained Algerian society right up to the present day, articulating the hopes and aspirations of ordinary people.

16 *Le Drame Algérien*, p. 41.

17 '*Beraka*' was the big summer hit of 1987, selling a million cassettes. For a history of raï see Bouziane Daoudi and Hadj Miliani, *L'Aventure du Rai: Musique et Société*, Paris: Seuil, 1992.

18 Many of the officers who owed allegiance to Nezzar were trained at the most prestigious military academy, the former French officer school at Cherchell. With impressive facilities, Cherchell was pivotal in developing an *esprit de corps* by which officers looked down on the masses.

19 Joke recounted to Martin Evans, Algiers, October 1989.

20 On this see Mohammed Harbi, *L'Algérie et Son Destin*, Paris: Arcantère, 1992.

21 On this see Phillip C. Naylor, *France and Algeria: A History of Decolonization and Transformation*, Gainesville: University Press of Florida, 2000.

22 The term *beurs* refers to the descendants of Algerian, Moroccan and Tunisian migrants born or raised in France. The origin of the term is confused although it seems to be a slang word derived from a reversal of the French word *Arabe*. On this see A.G. Hargreaves, *Immigration and Identity in Beur Fiction: Voices from the North African Community in France*, Oxford: Berg, 1997.

23 On this see Hocine Aït Ahmed, *L'Affaire Mecili*, Paris: La Découverte, 1987.

24 On this see Phillip C. Naylor, *France and Algeria*.

25 On this specific point see Roberts, *The Battlefield Algeria, 1988–2002*.

26 Saïd Sadi, *Algérie: L'Heure de Vérité*, Paris: Flammarion, 1996, p. 82.

27 'Interview de Ali Yahia Abdenour', *La Tribune d'Octobre*, 1 July 1989.

28 Khalida Messaoudi, *Unbowed*, Philadelphia: University of Pennsylvania Press, 1998, p. 55. Originally published as *Une Algérienne Debout*, Paris: Flammarion, 1995.

29 Children of immigrants who had French nationality in particular noticed the change. Sabrea Oughton, visiting her relatives in Algeria in 1985, vividly remembers the new atmosphere. She was told to be careful about what she wore: jeans and T-shirts were no longer appropriate. Her right to travel back to France without the authorization of a male relative was also questioned by the authorities.

30 Quoted in Stora, *Algeria 1830–2000*, p. 191.

31 Quoted in Ahmed Rouadjia, *Les Frères et la Mosquée: Enquête sur le Mouvement Islamiste en Algérie*, Paris: Karthala, 1990, pp. 171–2.

32 Quoted in Jason Burke, *Al-Qaeda*, London: I.B. Tauris, 2003, p. 29.

33 Malise Ruthven, *A Fury for God: The Islamist Attack on America*, London: Granta, 2002, p. 127.

34 In Belhadj's view, God must remain beyond the reach of human formulation. Making God into some sort of thing, giving God a definite shape, is to supplant the essentially mysterious with a dangerous human fabrication; we should distrust all images lest we fall in love with them. This explains why Belhadj disliked the Sufi tradition of saints and tombs.

35 Quoted in Rouadjia, *Les Frères et la Mosquée*, p. 180. Clo-Clo (Claude François), Salvatore Adamo and Enrico Macias are well-known popular French singers. Enrico Macias is of Jewish Algerian origin.

36 Olivier Mongin and Olivier Roy, *Islam, le Grand Malentendu*, Paris: Autrement, 1987, p. 52.

37 Messaoudi, *Unbowed*, p. 78.

38 Some journalists have claimed that in the 1980s the head of the Saudi Arabian secret service, Prince Turki bin Faysal, entered into an alliance with the Pakistani Secret Services, the ISI directorate and the CIA to coordinate the recruitment of Sunni volunteers, laying the foundation for what was to become Al-Qaeda. Prince Turki has vigorously denied this, and in December 2004 he accepted substantial libel damages and an apology from *Paris Match* over claims made in the magazine that he was linked to the 9/11 attacks and had funded Al-Qaeda.

39 On this see John Cooley, *Unholy Wars: Afghanistan, America and International Terrorism*, London: Pluto, 2001; Michael Griffin, *Reaping the Whirlwind*, London: Pluto, 2001; and Ahmed Rashid, *Taliban*, London: I.B. Tauris, 2000.

40 There were in fact an enormous amount of tensions between Afghans and the Arab fighters. On this see Burke, *Al-Qaeda*.

41 On this see Khalida Messaoudi, 'Les Algériennes et la lutte', *Les Temps Modernes*, July–August 1982. See also Leïla Aslaoui, *Les Années Rouges*, Algiers: Casbah Editions, 2000.

42 Messaoudi, *Unbowed*, p. 50.

43 Tahar Djaout, *Les Chercheurs d'Os*, Paris: Seuil, 1984.

44 Assia Djebar, *Femmes d'Alger*, Paris: Des Femmes, 1980, and Fettouma Touati, *Le Printemps Désespéré*, Paris: L'Harmattan, 1984.

45 The papers from the conference were published as M. Touili (ed.), *Le Retentissement de la Révolution Algérienne: Colloque International d'Alger (24–28 novembre 1984)*, Algiers: Entreprise Nationale du Livre, 1985.

46 Ali Haroun, *La Septième Wilaya: La Guerre du FLN en France 1954–1962*, Paris: Seuil, 1986.

47 The fact that Algerians visiting France could buy Harbi's and Haroun's books reflected how globalization, a phenomenon that would accelerate with the spread of the internet and satellite television, was undermining attempts to police the boundaries of history and memory.

48 Frédéric Fritscher, 'Le président Chadli récuse le concept de binationalité' *Le Monde*, 21 September 1988.

49 Messaoudi, *Unbowed*, p. 89.
50 Salim Guendouz interviewed by Martin Evans, 12 October 1989.

Chapter 5: Political Islam

 1 Ali Haroun interviewed by Martin Evans, Algiers, 9 October 1989.
 2 New laws on press freedom were introduced in January 1990.
 3 Algerians referred to Hamrouche as 'the umbrella man', an allusion to his years spent as head of protocol at the presidency, where he would carry the umbrella for President Boumediène. On the football terraces supporters would pull out their umbrellas as a sign of ridicule.
 4 Through this legislation the Strict Investment Codes of 1963 and 1966 were swept aside.
 5 One is reminded of the famous dictum of Don Fabrizio Corbera, Prince of Salina, in Giuseppe Tomasi di Lampedusa's famous novel *The Leopard* (1958), that for everything to remain the same everything must seem to change.
 6 Quoted by A. Djilali, 'Islamistes: En quête d'unité', *Algérie-Actualité*, 2 March 1989, p. 9.
 7 Ibid.
 8 Ibid.
 9 'Annonce officielle de la création du Front islamique du salut', *El Moudjahid*, 10–11 March 1989.
10 This was the day the FIS leadership filed an official request for recognition with the interior ministry.
11 From an interview with Abassi Madani in *Parcours Maghrébin*, 26 March 1990.
12 By June 1991 the *Majlis al-Shura* had expanded to thirty-five members.
13 They also liked the alternative markets developed by the FIS.
14 The FIS press included *El Mounquid*, which was mostly Arabic language, and *El Forkane* and *El Hadaya*, which were written in French. *El Balagh* and *El Inkad* were produced in Arabic. The sermons of Ali Belhadj, reproduced on cassette, were also widely disseminated.
15 Ali Belhadj sermon, 12 November 1989.
16 Martin Evans gave a paper at this conference analysing the impact of Kateb Yacine on the French anti-colonial left between 1947 and 1962. The conference proceedings were published as N. Khader (ed.), *Kateb Yacine*, Algiers: Algiers University Press, 1992.
17 On this see Ahmed Rouadjia, *Les Frères et la Mosquée: Enquête sur le Mouvement Islamiste en Algérie*, Paris: Karthala, 1990, p. 233.
18 Comment to Martin Evans, Algiers, 30 October 1990.
19 Cited by Lahouari Addi, *L'Algérie et la Démocratie: Pouvoir et Crise du Politique dans l'Algérie contemporaine*, Paris: La Découverte, 1995, p. 203.
20 See Khalida Messaoudi, *Unbowed*, Philadelphia: University of Pennsylvania Press, 1998.
21 See Rouadjia, *Les Frères et la Mosquée*, p. 275.
22 Hugh Roberts, *The Battlefield Algeria, 1988–2002*.
23 'Dieu est grand et le laser est son prophète', *Le Monde*, 7 July 1990.
24 Ali Belhadj, sermon, Kouba mosque, 15 June 1990.
25 Comment to Martin Evans, Algiers, 29 October 1990.
26 Anne-Marie Louanchi interviewed by Martin Evans, Algiers, 26 October 1990.
27 Gilles Kepel, *Jihad: The Trail of Political Islam*, London: I.B. Tauris, 2001.
28 Nesroulah Yous, *Qui a Tué à Bentalha?*, Paris: La Découverte, 2000.
29 Habib Souaïdia, *La Sale Guerre*, Paris: La Découverte, 2001.
30 Ibid.
31 The speech was reproduced in *El Mounquid*, 8 November 1990.

32 Ahmed Ben Bella quoted by Phillip C. Naylor, *France and Algeria*, Gainesville: University of Florida Press, 2000, p. 182.

33 Roberts, *The Battlefield Algeria, 1988–2002*.

34 Ali Belhadj, sermon, Tipaza, 5 April 1991.

35 Ibid.

36 The letter dated 3 September 1991 was entitled *Es-Sâ'ida el-fâtia mîn wara'i es-soudjoûn el-'askâriyya* ('The Coming Generation in the Military Prisons').

37 Alfred Hermida, 'The face of the modern woman that fundamentalist Algeria would veil', *Observer,* 12 January 1992.

38 She told one of the authors (John Phillips) that they asked her mother: 'Don't you think that you are too old to show your legs?'

39 Interview with Martin Evans, Paris, 30 June 2003.

40 The PAGS did not participate in the elections and the RCD won just 2.9 per cent of the vote.

41 Interview with John Phillips, Algiers, January 1992.

42 Interview with John Phillips, Algiers, January 1992.

43 José Garçon's preface to Djallal Malti, *La Nouvelle Guerre d'Algérie*, Paris: La Découverte, 1999, p. 18.

44 FIS tract.

45 Interview with John Phillips, Algiers, January 1992.

46 Ibid.

47 Quote from *Al-Sabah* in Jill Smolowe, 'North Africa, a prelude to civil war?', *Time* magazine, 27 January 1992.

48 Quoted by Naylor, *France and Algeria*, p. 186.

49 Smolowe, op. cit.

50 Interview with John Phillips, Algiers, January 1992.

51 Abdelkader interviewed by Martin Evans, Portsmouth, 2004.

52 The full text of Boudiaf's speech was reproduced in *El Moudjahid*, 23 April 1992.

53 Ibid.

Chapter 6: Algeria's Agony

1 The inquiry found Saad Djallal, whose job was to protect the president's back and carry his bullet-proof vest ready for him to wear if necessary, was 12 yards from his charge. Lahouali Mohammed and Balaib Aissa also had strayed from their allotted positions behind onstage curtains.

2 Nacer Boudiaf made these comments during a series of interviews with major Algerian daily newspapers, including *El Watan* on 30 June 2003.

3 Boumaarafi was sentenced to death in 1995 on charges of the murder and of plotting to overthrow Algeria's government. From 2002 he was held at the Serkadji prison in Algiers and subsequently at Blida prison.

4 Ignacio Cembrero, 'Fatiha Budiaf: Viuda del asesinado presidente de Argelia', *El Pais*, 14 June 1998.

5 Ibid.

6 Y.B. and Samy Mouhoubi, 'Algérie: Un colonel dissident accuse', *Le Monde*, 27 November 1999.

7 The three aides who accompanied him were shot within a fortnight.

8 The MAOL claimed that he persuaded the commission to accept as authentic a fake letter purportedly linking Boumaarafi to Islamists. See www.anp.org/affaireboudiaf/engaffboudiaf.html (last accessed 8 June 2007).

9 Al-Jazeera, 1 August 2001.

10 On 24 June 2006 in Lyon, Martin Evans was in conversation with a number of younger Algerian academics. All subscribed to the view that Boudiaf was murdered by elements within the regime.

11 Quoted in John W. Kiser, *The Monks of Tibhirine: Faith, Love and Terror in Algeria*, New York: St Martin's Griffin, 2003.

12 Yous, *Qui a Tué à Bentalha?*, pp. 32–3.

13 Souaïdia, *La Sale Guerre*, p. 61.

14 Sheikh Cherati, *Appel aux Tyrans: Le soulèvement contre les gouvernants*, sermon on cassette circulated in summer 1992.

15 Quoted by Jane Korlan, 'The fires of Islamic revolt kindle in Algerian cellars', *Sunday Times*, 21 June 1992.

16 Gilles Millet, 'Les Afghans, des groupes paramilitaries aux marges du FIS', *Libération*, 11 February 1992.

17 Figures cited by Luis Martinez in *The Algerian Civil War*, London: Hurst & Company, 2000, p. 215. Martinez draws his figures from a report in *Algérie-Actualité*, 1–7 November 1993.

18 The Belhadj letter was photocopied and circulated amongst some of the armed groups.

19 On this basis the government broke off diplomatic relations with both countries on 28 March 1993.

20 On casualty rates for the police and army see Jocelyne Césari, 'Algérie, chronique intérieure', in Kacen Basfao and Jean-Robert Henry (eds), *Annuaire de l'Afrique du Nord*, Aix-en-Provence: CNRS, 1992.

21 But it was modified from 11 p.m. to 5.30 a.m. at the start of Ramadan.

22 *Djamaate islamiyya mousallaha* was the Arabic term although all became known by the blanket French acronym GIA.

23 Martinez, *The Algerian Civil War*, p. 215.

24 To cut the throat was seen as an insulting way to kill someone because it was like slaughtering sheep.

25 Yous, *Qui a Tué à Bentalha?*, p. 81.

26 Amnesty International Report on Algeria, 1994.

27 Martinez, *The Algerian Civil War*, pp. 83–4.

28 On the symbolic meaning of violence in Algeria in the 1990s see Abderrahmane Moussaoui, *De la Violence en Algérie*, Paris: Actes Sud, 2006. On the more general question of how killing is related to pleasure and power see Joanna Bourke, *An Intimate History of Killing: Face-to-Face Killing in 20th Century Warfare*, London: Granta, 1999.

29 On the impact of these films see Martinez, *The Algerian Civil War*.

30 Aziz Chouaki, *The Star of Algiers*, London: Serpent's Tail, 2006. This charts how a 36-year-old man, frustrated in his dream to become a pop star and humiliated at every turn, ends up in prison before rediscovering Islam; he eventually becomes a GIA emir. Yasmina Khadra is the nom de plume of a former Algerian police officer, Mohammed Moulessehoul, born in 1955; see Yasmina Khadra, *À quoi Rêvent les Loups*, Paris: Julliard, 1999. Luis Martinez too is a pseudonym; his work has provided a remarkable insight into how and why young men became drawn into violence; see Martinez, *The Algerian Civil War*.

31 This quote comes from Rachid, a 31-year-old jailed in Algeria for his beliefs and by March 2003 living illegally in London: 'Inside the mind of a terrorist', *Observer*, 9 March 2003.

32 Interview with John Phillips, Algiers, 1996.

33 Aslaoui was Minister for Youth and Sport from June 1991 to July 1992.

34 Death sentence for Khalida Messaoudi sent by the Mouvement pour l'Etat Islamique on 12 June 1993.

35 Qu'ran, Sura 36, *Ya Sin*, verses 8–10, pp. 308–9.

36 Quoted in 'Outlaw Blues', *Melody Maker*, 26 September 1992, p. 7.

37 Rachid Mimouni, *De la Barbarie en Général et de l'Intégrisme en Particulier*, Paris: Le Pré aux Clercs, 1992.

38 Séverine Labat, 'Les Islamistes, nouvelle barbarie' in *Le Drame Algérien*, Reporters Sans Frontières, Paris: La Découverte, 1994, p. 180.

39 GIA statement, 30 October 1993.

40 As one Algerian explained to Martin Evans, people were suspicious of official accounts blaming the GIA since surely only highly trained troops with specialist skills would have been able to swim the 50 yards to the ship.

41 At the end of February 1994, Djaffar El-Afghani was cornered and killed, possibly as a result of an AIS tip off.

42 Y.B. and Samy Mouhoubi, 'Algérie: Un colonel dissident accuse'.

43 Philippe Bernard and Nathaniel Herberg, *Lettres d'Algérie*, Paris: Gallimard 1997.

44 Ibid. pp. 34–5.

45 The work of Gyps and Ali Dilem can be seen at www.louzine.net. Extracts of Mahfouf's stand-up act can be accessed on YouTube. See Gyps, *FIS and Love*, Paris: Editions de l'Auteur, 1996; *Algé-Rien*, Editions de l'Auteur, 1998; and *L'Algérie, C'est Comme Ca*, Editions de l'Auteur, 2003. See also the collection of contemporary Algerian political artists in *Vive la Démocratie: La Vie des Algériens Vue par les Caricaturistes*, Paris: Pour, 1987.

46 Cited by Christopher Walker, 'Algerian militant onslaught claims more foreign lives', *The Times*, 12 July 1994.

47 They made it clear that in return for any aid they wanted assurances about the supply of specialist military equipment.

48 Agence France Presse, '<< L'extrême sauvagerie>> du chef Yahia', *Libération*, 28 December 1994.

49 Ferhat Mehenni, 'Un pays sans horizon politique valable', *Libération*, 28 December 1994.

50 Ahmed Ben Bella, interviewed on TF1 on 28 December 1994.

51 Martin Alexander, Martin Evans and J.F.V. Keiger (eds), *The French Army and the Algerian War*, London: Macmillan, 2002.

52 The claim was that many of the GIA emirs, such as Saïd Makhloufi, were the sons of *harki*s.

53 Aslaoui, p. 115.

54 *Mots de vérité*, a collection of AIS/FIS texts dated April 1995. The SAS was a reference to the specialized units, *Sections Administratives Spécialisées*, set up by the French army in 1955 to win over Muslim hearts and minds by working with the Algerian population, administering justice, teaching health education and building houses.

55 The Clinton administration put pressure on the regime to renew invitations to Amnesty International and Human Rights Watch. Amnesty International in London, the International Committee of the Red Cross in Geneva and Human Rights Watch/Middle East of New York all said that despite their repeated efforts to get into the country the authorities had been reluctant to cooperate on the grounds that it could not guarantee the security of any mission. In the meantime no other country in the Arab world except Iraq executed as many people for politically motivated offences.

56 It was subsequently transmitted on the French television channel Canal + on 17 December. Benjamin Stora, *La Guerre Invisible, Algérie, Années 90*, Paris: Presses de Sciences Po, 2001.

57 Interview by John Phillips with Abdelhamid Aoun, September 1998.

58 The pro-government Algerian press also sought to stoke up anti-Roman Catholic

sentiment, reflecting evident irritation in the regime's upper echelons with the Sant'Egidio mediation.

59 Khaled Kelkal, 'Moi, j'espère, Inch Allah, retourner dans mon pays', *Libération*, 7 October 1995. The interview was originally carried out by German research student on 3 October 1992 during his fieldwork for a thesis on the politics of integration.

60 Quoted by Phillip C. Naylor, *France and Algeria*, p. 225.

61 John Sweeney and Leonard Doyle, 'Algeria regime was behind Paris bombs', *Observer*, 16 November 1997.

62 'Deux Français sur trois souhaitent le << status quo >> avec Alger', *Le Monde*, 24 October 1995.

63 Sant'Egidio statement, November 1995.

64 For an overview of the whole Euro-Med agreement, go to http://ec.europa.eu/external_relations/euromed/.

Chapter 7: The Algerian Question

1 Born Henri Salem in London in 1921 he emigrated to France and then to Algeria. He joined underground militant communists in 1941 and the PCA in 1942. Whilst living clandestinely he adopted the pseudonym Alleg to disguise his Anglo-Jewish origins.

2 Officially the army claimed that Audin managed to escape but the historian Pierre Vidal-Naquet came to the conclusion that he had been murdered by his captors, setting out his arguments in *L'Affaire Audin*, Paris: Editions de Minuit, 1958. Vidal-Naquet was instrumental in the establishment of the Audin Committee which set out to find out about Audin's disappearance.

3 In *La Question* he describes how 'my jaws were soldered to the electrode by the current, and it was impossible for me to unlock my teeth, no matter what effort I made. My eyes, under their spasmed lids, were crossed with images of fire, and geometric luminous patterns flashed in front of them.'

4 On the systematic use of torture by the French army during the war of liberation, see Pierre Vidal-Naquet, *Torture: Cancer of Democracy*, London: Penguin, 1963. See also the excellent Raphaëlle Branche, *La Torture et l'Armée pendant la Guerre d'Algérie 1954–1962*, Paris: Gallimard, 2001.

5 Nesroulah Yous, *Qui a Tué à Bentalha?* and Souaïdia, *La Sale Guerre*. See also Mohammed Samraoui, *Chroniques des Années de Sang*, Paris, 2003, and Amnesty International, *Algeria: Civilian Population Caught in a Spiral of Violence*, 18 November 1997.

6 In a move to distance itself from Zeroual the French government also doubled aid to Tunisia and wiped out a billion francs of Moroccan debt.

7 Between 1 October 1997 and 30 January 1998 40 per cent of terrorist acts were committed in the *wilaya* of Relizane and 25 per cent in the *wilaya* of Blida.

8 As Mohammed Lamari pointed out in 1998 to a meeting of fellow officers: 'We are not going to fight a flea with a hammer.'

9 As an inducement to down arms, the clemency law of February 1995 meant that any member of any armed group who surrendered would be in effect pardoned of any crimes if they did not involve murder.

10 Yous, *Qui a Tué à Bentalha?*, p. 42.

11 GIA communiqué 41, dated 18 January 1996, threatened military conscripts; communiqué 42, dated 31 January 1996, threatened those working on the hydrocarbon sector.

12 *Zaouedj el moutaa* was an Iranian phenomenon used to justify prostitution. Within the armed groups it was a forced temporary marriage to sanctify rape.

13 Amnesty International report in Reporters sans Frontières, *Algérie: Le Livre Noir*, Paris: La Découverte, 2003.

14 Ibid., p. 16.

15 On this see Yous, *Qui a Tué à Bentalha?*, p. 85.

16 Martinez, *The Algerian Civil War*, p. 215.

17 On this see the interviews with FIS leaders in exile in Patrick Denaud, *Algérie – Le FIS: Sa Direction Parle*, Paris: L'Harmattan, 1997, p. 106.

18 'Déchaînons nos foudres contre la Djaz'ara Renegate, Au nom de dieu', le Groupe Islamique Armé, communiqué, 5 January 1996.

19 Zitouni was seen as theologically unsophisticated and not well versed in the Qur'an.

20 On the nature of Islamist activity in London see Jason Burke, *Al-Qaeda*. See also Louis Aggoun and Jean-Baptiste Rivoire, *Françalgérie, Crimes et Mensonges d'Etats*, Paris: La Découverte, 2004.

21 Within Patrick Denaud, *Algérie – Le FIS: Sa Direction Parle*, one exiled FIS leader, Ould Adda Abdelkrim, denounces the violence and hatred contained within *Al Ansar* as anti-Muslim. He found it astonishing that the paper had not been banned or the publishers arrested by the British police: Denaud, p. 96.

22 In 1993 the local police were placed under the direct control of the DRS which then developed this network of counter-insurgency centres.

23 See Algeria Watch, *Les Centres de détention secrète, de torture et d'exécutions*, report published on the website www.Algeria-watch.org and reproduced in Reporters sans Frontières, *Algérie: Le Livre Noir*, pp. 49–69.

24 See comments by exiled FIS leader Djaffar El Houar in Denaud, *Algérie – Le FIS: Sa Direction Parle*, p. 221.

25 Arnaud Dubus, 'Les sept moines de Tibehirine enlevés sur ordre d'Alger', *Libération*, 23 December 2002.

26 On this see also Algeria Watch, *Les Centres de détention secrète, de torture et d'exécutions*, p. 62.

27 Mohammed Samraoui, *Chroniques des Années de Sang*.

28 Ibid., p. 162.

29 Roberts, *The Battlefield Algeria*, p. 260.

30 The first Cistercian monastery in Algeria was founded at Staoueli in 1843. It was a hazardous place to pursue the monastic vocation of silence, prayer and labour. In 1848 alone malaria killed ten monks. In the anti-clerical Third Republic, at the end of the nineteenth century, the Trappists, fearing expulsion, took refuge in Slovenia. In 1934, amid threats by the Yugoslav government, five monks returned to Algeria.

31 Interview of Archbishop Duval by Martin Evans, 15 October 1989.

32 Quoted by Stora, *Algeria, 1830–2000*, p. 225.

33 Robert Masson, who wrote a book about the monks and their fate, suggests that it was the day after the harrowing visit, as the monastery bells pealed for Christmas services (they were the only Christian bells still rung in Algeria), that de Chergé wrote a passage of his Testament denying he sought martyrdom: 'I would not have known how to wish for such a death. It seemed important to me to profess this. I do not see, in effect, how I could rejoice that this people that I love be accused indiscriminately of my murder.' Robert Masson, *Tibhirine: Les Veilleurs de l'Atlas*, Paris: Editions du Cerf, 1997.

34 Ibid., p. 32.

35 Ibid., p. 33.

36 Ibid., p. 49.

37 Reproduced in Denaud, *Algérie – Le FIS: Sa Direction Parle*, pp. 130–1.

38 Ibid., p. 131.

39 Interviewed by Denuad, one of the leading FIS exiles, Rabah Kebir, claimed that the murders of the monks and Claverie were the work of the DRS. *Algérie – Le FIS: Sa Direction Parle*, p. 129.

40 Arnaud Dubus, 'Les sept moines de Tibehirine enlevés sur ordre d'Alger', *Libération*, 23 December 2002.

41 Ibid.

42 Ibid.

43 Article 1 stated that Islam was the state religion. Article 2 stated that Arabic was the national and official language.

44 To reinforce this, the authorities reintroduced the 1990 law on Arabization which forbade, under threat of punishment, the official use of any language other than Arabic.

45 The introduction of a second chamber in the national legislature – known as the Council of the Nation – was designed to limit the powers of the elected lower house – the National Popular Assembly. One-third of the Council was to be appointed by the president whilst the remaining two-thirds would be made up of indirectly elected local and regional assembly members. The constitution stated that no bill voted by the National Popular Assembly could become law unless it was approved by three-quarters of the Council of the Nation. In this way the president wielded enormous powers through appointees in the Council and the power to veto National Assembly decisions. The president was also given the authority to appoint the governors of the country's forty-eight administrative regions, along with the power to appoint judges, the governor of the Central Bank, the secretary general of the government and the heads of all the security organs.

46 On 4 January 1997 the Conseil National Transitoire (CNT) passed law recognizing these local militias, henceforth known as Legitimate Defence Groups. This became another complex factor in the violence since if many were sincerely committed to fighting Islamist violence others were fronts for racketeering and extortion.

47 Statement issued to the media signed by foreign journalists (including John Phillips) covering referendum in Algiers, 29 November 1996.

48 José Garçon, 'Algérie: scepticisme après le vote', *Libération*, 30 November 1996 and A.L. Chabane 'Louisa Hanoune: La Constitution est une machine de guerre', *El Watan*, 3 December 1996. In Kabylia the turnout was only 22.7 per cent in the *wilaya* of Tizi-Ouzou.

49 On 12 December 1996 the European Parliament debated the situation in Algeria. At the end of the debate a composite resolution was voted on and passed. It condemned 'in the strongest possible terms all terrorist acts in Algeria and the resulting massacres'. It also condemned any moves to restrict freedom of expression and called on the Algerian authorities to 'launch an initiative for dialogue between all members of Algerian civil society in order to reach a consensus on true democratic reform in the country'. The resolution was forwarded to the European Commission, the Council of Ministers and the Algerian government. The full resolution is reproduced in the *Journal of Algerian Studies*, London: Frank Cass, vol. 2, 1997, pp. 138–9.

50 Quoted in Benyoucef Cherif, *Algérie: Une Saison en Enfer*, Paris: L'Aventurine, 2003, p. 68.

51 The full text of his televised address is reproduced in the *Journal of Algerian Studies*, London: Frank Cass, vol. 2, 1997, pp. 140–2.

52 In 2000 Amnesty International would cast grave doubts over responsibility for the killing.

53 Interviewed by John Phillips, 30 August 1997.

54 Interviewed by John Phillips, 23 September 1997.

55 Yous, *Qui a Tué à Bentalha?*, p. 205.

56 Interviewed by John Phillips, 23 September 1997.

57 Interviewed by John Phillips, 23 September 1997.

58 John Phillips, 'Army link to Algeria slaughter', *Sunday Times*, 26 October 1997.

59 Thomas Ferenczi, 'Proche et lointaine Algérie', *Le Monde*, 15 September 1997.

60 'Une nuit d'horreur à Bentalha', *Le Monde*, 10 October 2000.

61 Yous, *Qui a Tué à Bentalha?*, p. 169.

62 Liess Boukra, *Algérie la Terreur Sacrée*, Lausanne: Favre, 2002.

63 Roberts, *The Battlefield Algeria*.

64 Quoted in Michel Guerrin, 'Algerian icon', Index on Censorship 6, 1997. Original article in *Le Monde*, 26 September 1997.

65 Cherif, *Algérie: Une Saison en Enfer*, p. 8.

66 There were rumours that this was 192 Squadron, the members of which had been drugged up as a way of making them insensitive to violence. The number of the Squadron is a reference to the date of the coup of January 1992.

67 The AIS provided vital information on the GIA.

68 José Garçon and Pierre Haski, 'Lionel Jospin s'exprime sur la crise en Algérie', *Libération*, 27 January 1997.

69 Quoted in Phillip C. Naylor, *France and Algeria*, p. 239.

70 Bernard-Henri Lévy, 'Choses vues en Algérie', *Le Monde,* 8 and 9 January 1998.

71 Bernard-Henri Lévy, 'Algérie: gare au syndrome Timisoara', *Le Monde*, 12 February 1998.

72 François Gèze and Pierre Vidal-Naquet, 'L'Algérie et les intellectuels français' *Le Monde*, 4 February 1998.

73 Interviewed by John Phillips, quoted in Phillips, 'Army link to Algeria slaughter'.

74 Robin Cook, quoted in 'Algeria agrees to EU visit', http://news.bbc.co.uk, 15 January 1998.

75 Quoted in 'Zeroual agents accused of massacres', *The Times*, 23 January 1998.

76 Ibid.

77 Testimony of Patrick Baudouin in Habib Souaïdia, *Le Procès de la 'Sale Guerre'*, Paris: La Découverte, 2002, p. 159.

78 On critical reactions to the report see Ligue Algérienne de Défense des Droits de l'Homme, 'Contredit au rapport du panel onusien sur la situation des droits de l'homme en Algérie', at www.algeria-watch.org/farticle/aa/laddh2.htm.

79 The suspects were arrested after a civil servant's widow recognized the alleged murderer of her husband among the militia. On this whole episode see Mohammed Smaïn, *Relizane dans la Tourmente: Silence! On tue*, Paris: Bouchène, 2006.

80 Zidane scored twice in the final where France beat Brazil three goals to nil. Algerian newspapers acclaimed the victory at least as enthusiastically as those in France.

81 Lounès Matoub, *Rebelle*, Paris: Stock, 1995.

82 Nadia Matoub, *Pour l'Amour d'un Rebelle*, Paris: Robert Laffont, 2000.

83 Ibid., p. 17.

84 Quoted in *Algeria's Bloody Years*, the 2003 documentary by Thiery Leclère, Malek Bensmail and Patrice Barrat which charts the violence in Algeria between 1993 and 2003. The documentary was financed by the BBC and Canal Plus.

85 The chant *Aiya Aiya* is reproduced on Rachid Taha's 1998 CD *Diwân*.

Chapter 8: The New Imperialism and the War on Terror

1 Ahmed Rashid, *Taliban*, London: I.B. Tauris, 2000. See also his article 'The new Great Game – the battle for Central Asia's oil', *Far Eastern Economic Review*, 10 April 1997.

2 For example, 3,000 import-export companies were set up post-1994.

3 Reda Hassaine, 'Undercover Agent', *Sunday Times*, 17 July 2005.

4 The failed attack on 26 February 1993 was carried out by a small group proclaiming itself

to be the 'Liberation Army, Fifth Battalion'. On this see Steve Coll, *Ghost Wars*, New York: Penguin, 2004, pp. 249–51.

5 On this see Coll, *Ghost Wars*, p. 258.

6 In 1996 Algeria signed a nuclear cooperation agreement with China, and the country now has two experimental reactors. The United States has closely monitored the situation and under pressure from the United States the Algerian government accepted International Atomic Energy Agency (IAEA) safeguards in February 1992. Algeria signed up to the Nuclear Non-Proliferation Treaty in January 1995 and is regularly inspected by the IAEA.

7 On this see Roberts, *The Battlefield Algeria*, p. 239.

8 On the Oujda clan see Chapter 3.

9 This was sent to President Chadli on 29 October 1988; the other signatories included three senior FLN wartime leaders, Lakhdar Ben Tobbal, Tahar Zbiri and Mohammedi Said and other prominent former ministers such as Belaid Abdesselam. The declaration called for democracy, the convening of a national conference to elaborate the necessary programme of political reform in a consensual manner, and the postponement of the scheduled presidential election until new democratic rules were agreed.

10 M. Bh, 'Nezzar conteste Bouteflika', *El Watan*, 16 September 1998.

11 Khaled Nezzar, 'Nezzar répond à Benbaïbèche', *Le Matin*, 11 January 1999.

12 The daily *El Watan* was not convinced by these assurances and on 9 February 1999 published a cartoon of a handcuffed ballot box.

13 The law excluded all those born before 1942 who did not participate in the war of liberation. In effect this was a subtle way of bolstering Bouteflika's campaign since Nahnah could have taken votes away from him.

14 In some barracks the only voting slip available was for Bouteflika and there were no independent observers present. Aït Ahmed suffered a heart attack towards the end of the campaign and was flown to Switzerland for treatment. He had intended to return for polling day but given the circumstances did not.

15 Roberts, *The Battlefield Algeria*, p. 273.

16 Some parts of the military began to wonder whether, like Boudiaf, Bouteflika would have to be 'reined in'.

17 Roberts, *The Battlefield Algeria*, p. 283.

18 In Sudan in 1994 the GIA had repelled advances from bin Laden on the grounds that he was not pious enough.

19 Burke, *Al-Qaeda*. As such Algeria is a perfect example of the way in which bin Laden fed off specific national struggles to develop an international network of affiliated groups.

20 Burke, *Al-Qaeda*, p. 208. The initiative came from Ressam who went to bin Laden's intermediaries for money.

21 On this see Burke, *Al-Qaeda*, pp. 198–212.

22 The violence in Algeria led to a growing number of asylum seekers. Many looked for asylum not just in France but also Britain, Canada, Germany and America as the Algerian diaspora was dispersed across the globe.

23 Mezraq kept his fortune and was seen parading around in a brand new Mercedes. In 2002 he called on people to vote for the FLN.

24 'Islamic Guerrilla Emir keeps low profile', *Algeria Interface*, 10 February 2000.

25 Ibid.

26 On 13 April 2000 *El Watan* claimed that a large number of the founder members were ex-FIS. This was vehemently denied by Wafa leaders.

27 On this theme see the *History Today* series entitled 'Coming to Terms With the Past' which began in November 2003. See specifically Rachel Seider on Guatemala.

28 Quoted in 'In the steps of Augustine', *30 Days* magazine, No. 1, Rome, 2001.

29 For example, acute housing shortages meant that journalists in state television and radio could easily be bought off, since they did not want to face the sack and loss of their livelihood by asking difficult questions.

30 On Louisa Hanoune see Louisa Hanoune, *Une Autre Voix pour l'Algérie: Entretiens avec Ghania Mouffouk*, Paris: La Découverte, 1996.

31 On the debate about the precise figures of the number of disappeared see Habib Souaïdia, *Le Procès de la 'Sale Guerre'*, pp. 175–87. See also '1000 cas de disparations forcées', www.algeria.watch.org/mrv/2002/1000_disparitions_A.htm.

32 La Découverte was previously know as Maspero; during the Algerian War it published Maurice Maschino, *Le Refus*, Paris: Maspero, 1960, and Jacques Vergès, Mourad Oussedik and Abdessamed Benabdallah, *Nuremberg pour l'Algérie*, Paris: Maspero, 1961.

33 Anour Benmalek, *Les Amants Désunis*, Paris: Calmann-Lévy, 1998 (translated as *The Lovers of Algeria*, London: Harvill, 2001); Aziz Chouaki, *L'Etoile d'Alger*, Paris: Balland, 2002 (translated as *The Star of Algiers*, London: Serpent's Tail, 2005); Boualem Sansal, *Le Serment des Barbares*, Paris: Gallimard, 1999. See also novels written under the pseudonym Yasmina Khadra.

34 Robert Fisk, *The Great War for Civilisation*, London: Fourth Estate, 2005, pp. 631–719.

35 On 1 August 2001 Al-Jazeera included a lengthy interview with Mohammed Samraoui, the former colonel in the DRS, who reiterated his accusation that Boudiaf was assassinated by insiders in the regime.

36 On this see Hugh Miles, *Al-Jazeera*, London: Abacus, 2005, pp. 59-60.

37 For example, Amnesty International and Human Rights Watch have expressed grave reservations about the transition process on the grounds that human rights abuses have not been investigated.

38 Y.B. and Samy Mouhoubi, 'Algérie: un colonel dissident accuse', *Le Monde*, 27 November 1999, pp. 14–15.

39 On this see José Garçon, 'Maol, un bug dans l'armée algérienne', *Libération*, 17 May 2001. By May 2001 the MAOL site had received 720,000 hits.

40 *Le Figaro*, 15 June 2000.

41 Bouteflika interviewed on the radio station Europe 1, 7 November 1999.

42 Salima Tlemçani, 'Les jeunes contre la grâce amnistiante', *El Watan*, 14 April 2001.

43 For example, many Algerians were disgusted by the argument in the new National Assembly about salaries for its members. The argument reinforced the image that all politicians were in politics for the money and personal enrichment.

44 On this see Reporters sans Frontières, *Algérie: Le Livre Noir*.

45 Most had access to only 75 litres of water a day, often very polluted, when double that was required to meet minimum needs. Homes and businesses kept water in cans, buckets and saucepans.

46 On this see *Une Population Précarisée*, a report for Fédération des Ligues des Droits de l'Homme by Sophie Bessis, Smaïl Goumeziane and Ahmed Dahmani, November 2001. Extracts of the report are reproduced in *Algérie: Le Livre Noir*, pp. 177–202.

47 The United Nations International Children's Emergency Fund (UNICEF) report, as well as a country profile of Algeria, can be accessed at www.unicef.org. The website also contains a detailed report from October 2003 on how Algerian children have been coping with the impact of the violence entitled 'Psychological rehabilitation of children traumatized by terrorist violence'.

48 'Pourquoi les Algériens se suicident?', *Liberté*, 18 July 2002. On the phenomenon of youth suicide see also Sid Ahmed Semiane, 'La mort au bout du suicide', *Le Matin*, 17 January

2002. In the article Sid Ahmed Semiane talks about the case of a young man who had set fire to himself in broad daylight. In the letter explaining to his family why he simply wrote: 'No jobs, no housing, no hope. Goodbye and long live Algeria.'

49 Sid Ahmed Semiane, 'La main de Dieu à Bab el-Oued', *Le Matin*, 12 November 2001.

50 T.B., 'Visite tardive', *El Watan*, 13 November 2001.

51 *Le Monde*, 12 November 2001.

52 Asked by a housing association leader if people would have to riot to underline their need for help, the interior minister, Yazid Zerhouni, said, 'You will have neither tent nor any help … if you want to demonstrate, do so and you'll see.' The CD *Abdelkader* by Faudel, Khaled and Taha was a track take from their CD *1,2,3 Soleils – Taha, Khaled, Faudel in Concert*, 2000. This was a live recording of their concert at the Bercy Stadium in Paris on 26 September 1998.

53 Taken from their debut CD *Intik*, released on Sony in 2000.

54 The young had nothing but contempt for the RCD. They saw it treating Kabylia as a fiefdom with which to do deals with the government.

55 Reporters sans Frontières, *Algérie: Le Livre Noir*, p. 138.

56 The rioting was not directionless. Smaïl Mira's house was attacked because as the head of the local anti-terrorist militia he had used his position as a front for extortion and racketeering.

57 Reporters sans Frontières, *Algérie: Le Livre Noir*, p. 127.

58 Ibid.

59 A. Samil, 'Le message', *El Watan*, 14 June 2001.

60 He had been promised unprecedented access to government records by Bouteflika but the DRS did not cooperate with the commission, some indication of tensions at the top.

61 José Garçon, 'Trois manifestants tués en Kabylie', *Libération*, 26 April 2001. The International Crisis Group (ICG) argued that the young were animated by despair and anger. On this see the ICG report 'Algeria: Anger and Unrest in Kabylie', June 2003, which can be accessed at www.crisisgroup.org.

62 In 1997 Hanoune's Trotskyites won four seats. Like Djaballah, Hanoune also signed the Rome platform which major opposition parties drew up in 1995 calling for a negotiated solution to the conflict. But with the main architect on the Algerian side of the Rome platform, Hocine Aït Ahmed's FFS, not participating in the election and with Bouteflika trying to promote his own version of national reconciliation it has been suggested the regime was happy to see Hanoune being given the ostensible leadership of the regime's democratic critics at the expense of Aït Ahmed.

63 The village councils used intimidation to stop people voting.

64 On this see Roberts, *The Battlefield Algeria*.

65 Claire Tréan, 'Un general algérien et la justice française', *Le Monde*, 26 April 2001.

66 Preface to Souaïdia, *La Sale Guerre*.

67 Interviewed by Martin Evans, Paris, 23 May 2003.

68 Roberts, *The Battlefield Algeria*.

69 The programme *Droit d'Auteurs* was a special edition about Algeria.

70 Quoted in Souaïdia, *Le Procès de la 'Sale Guerre'*, p. 20.

71 Ibid., p. 61.

72 Ibid., pp. 210–13.

73 Ibid., p. 266.

74 Ibid., p. 144.

75 Ibid., p. 241.

76 *New York Times*, 11 February 2004.

77 Disciples included Zacarias Moussaoui, a French citizen of Moroccan descent, who was involved in the 11 September 2001 attacks. On this see the account by his brother Abd Samad Moussaoui, *Zacarias Moussaoui, Mon Frère*, Paris: Denoël, 2002. See also Frédéric Chambon, 'La part d'ombre de Zacarias Moussaoui', *Le Monde*, 30 March 2002.

78 Quoted in 'Ricin jurors attack new terror laws', *Observer*, 9 October 2005.

79 This was underlined by the case of Lotfi Raissi, who had always wanted to be a pilot and left his family home in Algeria to pursue his dream in the United States. Twelve days after the attacks on New York and Washington he was accused of plotting the 9/11 attacks and interned in London's Belmarsh prison. Five months later the case against Raissi collapsed and he was released but is still battling to clear his name.

80 Beghal was extradited to France from the United Arab Emirates in late September 2001 after he told police in the Gulf state that he had helped plan a foiled suicide attack on the American Embassy just off the Champs Elysées. He later retracted his statement, saying that he had confessed under 'methodical torture'.

81 *Al-Hayat*, January 2004.

82 Selima Mellah and Jean-Baptiste Rivoire, 'Enquete sur l'étrange <<Ben Laden du Sahara>>', *Le Monde Diplomatique*, 4 February 2005.

83 Ibid.

84 The tenth and eleventh stages of the event were cancelled at the time for 'security reasons'. The leading French driver, Stéphane Peterhansel, and the Spanish motorcyclist Nani Roma were among those targeted.

85 If his links to bin Laden were as strong as Algeria claimed, it is curious that American authorities did not request his extradition. Suspicion over El-Para's status was heightened further when he was convicted on terrorism charges on 25 June 2005, and sentenced to death at the end of a trial that was held formally in his absence even though he had been back in the country for more than six months. 'This is the first time in the annals of Algerian justice that an accused person has been condemned in his absence when the authorities say that he is in the hands of the police,' *Liberté* newspaper commented.

86 The Islamic candidate Abdallah Djaballah won slightly less than 5 per cent of the vote. The others, each gaining less than 2 per cent, were Said Sadi, whose base was in the ethnic Berber region east of Algiers, Louise Hanoune, the Trotskyist, and Ali Faouzi Rebaine, a little-known politician from the tiny Algeria of Patriots Party.

87 Minister Ahmed Ouyahia, Bouteflika's top ally, claimed that the military had kept its promise not to interfere. 'This is proof of a new democratic maturity.' The Army had allowed soldiers to vote for the first time at regular polling stations and not their barracks, a move seen as curbing military influence over the outcome.

88 Algeria is one of the leading countries, along with Egypt, Nigeria, Senegal and South Africa, behind a pan-African initiative, New Partnership for African Development (Nepad), to monitor corruption and encourage good governance. The initiative was launched by the Organization for African Unity in July 2001. On this see www.nepad.org.

89 During the referendum fifty people were killed.

90 Conversation with Martin Evans, Lyon, 23 June 2006.

Afterword: The Anger That Will Not Go Away

1 On this see *The Economist: The World in 2007*, 2007.

2 On the growing role of China in Algeria see Ali Bisri, 'Chinatown couscous', *Afrique-Asie*, February 2007.

3 Lahouari Addi, 'En Algérie, du conflit armé à la violence sociale', *Le Monde Diplomatique*, April 2006.

4 Xan Smiley, 'Algeria Forecast', *The Economist: The World in 2007*, 2007.

5 Lahouari Addi 'En Algérie, du conflit armé à la violence sociale'.

6 On this see Jeremy Keenan, 'A sift through the sand reveals no grain of truth', *Times Higher Education Supplement*, 15 December 2006.

7 Bouteflika's speech can be found at www.algeria-watch.org.

8 Dozens of historians signed a petition opposing the law led by Claude Liauzu, emeritus professor at Paris VII and a distinguished specialist of colonialism.

9 On this see Lahouari Addi 'En Algérie, du conflit armé à la violence sociale'.

10 Quoted by Lahouari Addi 'En Algérie, du conflit armé à la violence sociale'.

11 Interview with Martin Evans, Paris, 9 March 2007.

12 Piotr Smolar, 'Al-Qaida démontre son implantation dans les pays du Maghreb', *Le Monde*, 13 April 2007.

13 On this see Jeremy Keenan, 'A sift through the sand reveals no grain of truth'.

14 Simon Tisdale, 'Fears grow of a radical Islamist Maghreb', *Guardian*, 14 February 2007.

15 Editorial, 'Al-Qaida à Alger', *Le Monde*, 13 April 2007.

16 Even in Spain the 'pact of silence' has not endured, with the generations of grandsons and granddaughters of the civil war generation now wanting truth and justice. On this see Giles Tremlett, *Ghosts of Spain: Travels Through a Country's Hidden Past*, London: Faber and Faber, 2007.

17 See *Jane's Sentinel Security Assessment*, March 2004, which reported that in talks with France Algeria agreed to give ground on the Western Sahara issue: 'In compensation, France will guarantee that Algeria's generals do not face prosecution before the International Criminal Court or other European tribunals for crimes committed during the civil war.'

   Middle East Online of 19 December 2005 quoted an NGO report saying 'a strong rumour in Algeria says there has been a pact between the generals and the presidency: the former will withdraw from power in exchange for impunity from crimes committed by the army during the Sale Guerre; it says that the generals are haunted by the threat of having to appear before a national or international court of justice, particularly over the issue of the "disappeared". The condemnation to death of Fouad Boulema, for alleged participation in the major massacres of Rais and Bentalha, is seen by some as the beginning of the whitewashing of the army, which has been accused of complicity in the massacres.'

18 The main oppostion party, the FFS, boycotted the elections, while the al-Qaeda Organization in the Islamic Maghreb called on Algerians not to vote. In terms of results the FLN lost its overall majority, falling from 199 to 136 deputies. However, this was compensated by the progress of the other two parties in the ruling coalition as the RND gained 61 seats and the MSP 52.

19 Quoted by Florence Beaugé, 'La menace terroriste n'a pas pesé sur la campagne électorale en Algérie', *Le Monde*, 18 May 2007.

20 Mustapha Benfodil, 'Politique, sexe, Internet, violence, portable, visa, Nasrallah ... Avoir 20 ans en Algérie, *Liberté*, 5 September 2006.

21 Ibid.

22 Alfred Sauvy, 'Trois mondes, une planète', *L'Observateur*, August 1952.

23 Interview with Martin Evans, Paris, 9 March 2007.

BIBLIOGRAPHY

Websites

www.algeria-watch.org
Very well-informed independent Algerian website which monitors human rights issues in the country

http://amnesty.org.uk
Amnesty International website, which carries articles about human rights in Algeria

www.anp.org
Website for the dissident Movement of Free Algerian Officers, which has continually embarrassed the government by posting up inside information on the regime

www.cg.gov.dz
The Algerian government's website

www.elmoudjahid.com
Website for the daily *El Moudjahid*

www.el-mouradia.dz
President Bouteflika's official website with speeches, official documents and the constitution

www.elwatan.com
Website for the daily *El Watan*

http://ens-web3.ens-lsh.fr/colloques/france-algerie/
Website devoted to up-to-date research on Franco-Algerian history, based upon conference organized in Lyon 20–22 June 2006

http://ffs-dz.com
Official website for the Front des Forces Socialistes

http://icg.org
Website for the International Crisis Group based in Cairo, which closely monitors the unfolding political situation in Algeria

www.liberte-algerie.com
Website for the daily *Liberté*

http://rcd-algerie.org
Official website for the Rassemblement pour la Culture and la Démocratie

Newspapers and Magazines

Algérie-Actualité (Algiers weekly, now defunct)
The Economist
Esprit
L'Express
Le Figaro
The Guardian
Al-Hayat
The Independent
International Herald Tribune
Le Matin (Algiers daily)
Le Monde
Le Monde Diplomatique
Libération
Liberté (Algiers daily)
El Moudjahid (Algiers daily)
El Mounquid (FIS newspaper, now defunct)
Le Nouvel Observateur
The Observer
El Pais
Le Quotidien d'Oran (Oran daily)
The Sunday Times
Les Temps Modernes
The Times
La Tribune (Algiers daily)
La Tribune d'Octobre (Algerian weekly, now defunct)
El Watan (Algiers daily)

Books and Articles

Abbas, Ferhat, *La Nuit Coloniale*, Paris: Julliard, 1962
——, *L'Indépendance Confisquée, 1962–1968*, Paris: Flammarion, 1984
Abdullatif Ahmida, Ali (ed.), *Beyond Colonialism and Nationalism in the Maghrib*, Basingstoke: Palgrave, 2000
Aboud, Hichem, *La Mafia des Généraux*, Paris: JC Lattès, 2002
Addi, Lahouari, *L'Impasse du Populisme: L'Algérie, Collectivité Politique et Etat en Construction*, Algiers: ENAL, 1990
——, *L'Algérie et la Démocratie: Pouvoir et Crise du Politique dans l'Algérie Contemporaine*, Paris: La Découverte, 1994
——, 'Les intellectuals qu'on assassine', *Esprit*, January–February, 1995
Ageron, Charles-Robert, *La Décolonisation Française*, Paris: Armand Colin, 1991

———, *Modern Algeria: A History from 1830 to the Present*, London: Hurst, 1991

———, *L'Algérie des Français*, Paris: Seuil, 1993

———, *La Guerre d'Algérie et les Algériens*, Paris: Armand Colin, 1997

Aggoun, Lounis and Jean-Baptiste Rivoire, *Françalgérie, Crimes et Mensonges d'Etats*, Paris: La Découverte, 2004

Ahmed, Akbar S. and Hastings Donnan (eds), *Islam, Globalization and Postmodernity*, London: Routledge, 1994

Aït Ahmed, Hocine, *Mémoires d'un Combattant*, Paris: Messinger, 1983

———, *L'Affaire Mecili*, Paris: La Découverte, 1989

Aldrich, Robert, *Vestiges of the Colonial Empire in France: Monuments, Museums and Colonial Memories*, Basingstoke: Macmillan, 2005

Alexander, Martin, Martin Evans and J.F.V. Keiger (eds), *The Algerian War and the French Army: Experiences, Images, Testimonies*, Basingstoke: Macmillan, 2002

Ali, Youcef Hadj, *Lettre Ouverte aux Français qui ne Comprennent Décidément rien à l'Algérie*, Paris: Albin Michel, 1998

Ali Yahia, Abdennou, *Algérie, Raison et Déraison d'une Guerre*, Paris: L'Harmattan, 1996

Alleg, Henri, *La Question*, Paris: Editions de Minuit, 1958

——— (ed.), *La Guerre d'Algérie*, 3 volumes, Paris: Temps Actuel, 1981

Allouache, Merzak and Vincent Colonna, *Algérie, 30 Ans*, Paris: Autrement, 1992

Amrane-Minne, Danièle Djamila, *Des Femmes dans la Guerre d'Algérie*, Paris: Karthala, 1994

al-Arabi, Ismail, *Al muqawama al jaza'iriyya that liwa' al amir Abd al Qadir*, Algiers: Société Nationale d'Edition, 1982

Aslaoui, Leïla, *Les Années Rouges*, Algiers: Casbah Editions, 2000

Behr, Edward, *The Algerian Problem*, London: Penguin, 1961

Belhadj, Ali, *Al-Irchad wal-Nosho fi Bayani Ahkam al-Riddat wa Suluh [Guidance and Advice in Understanding the Judgements on Apostasy and Reconciliation]*, FIS pamphlet, 1991

Bendjedid, Chadli, *Discours du president Chadli Bendjedid*, 5 volumes, Algiers: Ministère de l'Information, 1980–83

Benkhedda, Benyoucef, *La Crise de 1962*, Algiers: Dahlab, 1997

Bennoune, Mahfoud, *The Making of Contemporary Algeria: Colonial Upheavals and Post-Independence Development*, Cambridge: Cambridge University Press, 1988

Benrabah, Mohammed, *Langue et Pouvoir en Algérie*, Paris: Editions Séguier, 1999

Benrabah, Mohammed, Abdenour Djellouli, Nabile Farès, Gilbert Grandguillaume, Abdelwahab Meddeb, Olivier Mongin, Lucile Provost,

Benjamin Stora, Paul Thibaud and Pierre Vidal-Naquet, *Les Violences en Algérie*, Paris: Editions Odile Jacob, 1998

Bernard, Philippe and Nathaniel Herberg (eds), *Lettres d'Algérie*, Paris: Gallimard, 1997

Bhabha, Homi, *Nation and Narration*, London: Routledge, 1996

Boudjedra, Rachid, *FIS de la Haine*, Paris: Denoël, 1992

Boumediène, Houari, *Discours du President Boumediène*, 8 volumes, Algiers: Ministère de l'Information et de la Culture, 1966–79

Bourke, Joanna, *An Intimate History of Killing*, London: Granta, 1998

Branche, Raphaëlle, *La Torture et l'Armée pendant la Guerre d'Algérie 1954–1962*, Paris: Gallimard, 2001

——, *La Guerre d'Algérie: Une Histoire Apaisée*, Paris: Seuil, 2005

Brett, Michael and Elizabeth Fentress, *The Berbers*, Oxford: Blackwell, 1996

Burgat, François, *L'Islamism au Maghreb*, Paris: Editions Karthala, 1988

——, 'Algérie: l'AIS et le GIA, itineraries de constitution et relations', *Monde Arabe Maghreb-Machrek*, No. 149, 1995

Burke, Jason, *Al-Qaeda*, London: I.B. Tauris, 2003

Camus, Albert, *Chroniques Algériennes 1939–1958*, Paris: Gallimard, 1958

Carlier, Omar, *Entre Nation et Jihad: Histoire Sociale des Radicalismes Algériens*, Paris: Presses de Science Po, 1995

Chaker, Salem, *Berbères Aujourd'hui*, Paris: L'Harmattan, 1989

Charef, Abd, *Algérie: Le Grand Dérapage*, Paris: Editions de l'Aube, 1994

Chaliand, Gérard, *L'Algérie est-elle Socialiste?*, Paris: Maspero, 1964

Chaliand, Gérard and Juliette Minces, *L'Algérie Indépendante*, Paris: Maspero, 1972

Cherif, Benyoucef, *Algérie: Une Saison en Enfer*, Paris: L'Aventurine, 2003

Cherif, Hachemi, *Algérie: Modernité Enjeux en Jeu*, Algiers: ENAG Editions, 1996

Clancy-Smith, Julia A., *Rebel and Saint: Muslim Notables, Populist Protests, Colonial Encounters (Algeria and Tunisia, 1800–1904)*, Berkeley: University of California Press, 1994

Coll, Steve, *Ghost Wars*, New York: Penguin, 2004

Cooley, John, *Unholy Wars: Afghanistan, America and International Terrorism*, London: Pluto Press, 2001

Cubertafond, Bernard, *L'Algérie Contemporaine*, Paris: Presses Universitaires de France, 1981

Denaud, Patrick, *Algérie – Le FIS: Sa Direction Parle*, Paris: L'Harmattan, 1997

Dévoluy, Pierre and Duteil, Mireille, *La Poudrière Algérienne*, Paris: Calmann-Lévy, 1994

Djebar, Assia, *Femmes d'Alger*, Paris: Des Femmes, 1980

Droz, Bernard and Evelyne Lever, *Histoire de la Guerre d'Algérie*, Paris: Seuil, 1982

Entelis, John P., 'State-society relations: Algeria as a case study', in M. Tessler, J. Nachtwey and A. Banda (eds), *Area Studies and Social Sciences: Strategies for Understanding Middle East Politics*, Bloomington: Indiana University Press, 1999

Esposito, John, *The Islamic Threat: Myth or Reality*, Oxford: Oxford University Press, 1992

————, *Islam and Democracy*, Oxford: Oxford University Press, 1996

Evans, Martin, *The Memory of Resistance: French Opposition to the Algerian War 1954–62*, Oxford: Berg, 1997

———— (ed.), *Empire and Culture: The French Experience 1830–1940*, Basingstoke: Macmillan, 2004

Evans, Martin and Ken Lunn (eds), *War and Memory in the Twentieth Century*, Oxford: Berg, 1997

Eveno, Patrick and Jean Planchais, *La Guerre d'Algérie*, Paris: La Découverte, 1989

Fanon, Frantz, *The Wretched of the Earth*, London: Penguin, 1967

————, *Towards an African Revolution*, New York: Monthly Press Review, 1967

Fisk, Robert, *The Great War for Civilisation*, London: Fourth Estate, 2005

Fleming, Fergus, *The Sword and the Cross*, London: Granta, 2003

Francos, Ania and Jean-Pierre Séréni, *Un Algérien Nommé Boumediène*, Paris: Stock, 1976

Gadant, Monique, *Islam et Nationalisme en Algérie*, Paris: L'Harmattan, 1988

————, *Le Nationalisme Algérien et les Femmes*, Paris: L'Harmattan, 1995

Graffenried, Michael von, *Inside Algeria*, New York: Aperture, 1998

Graniage, Jean, *Histoire Contemporaine du Maghreb*, Paris: Fayard, 1994

Guilhaume, Jean-François, *Les Mythes Fondateurs de l'Algérie Française*, Paris: L'Harmattan, 1992

Hadad, Samy, *Algérie: Autopsie d'une Crise*, Paris: L'Harmattan, 1998

Haddour, Azzedine, *Colonial Myths, History and Narrative*, Manchester: Manchester University Press, 2000

Hadjadj, Djillali, *Corruption et Démocratie en Algérie*, Paris: Editions La Dispute, 1998

Hamoumou, Mohand, *Ets Ils Sont Devenus Harkis*, Paris: Fayard, 1993

Hanoune, Louisa, *Une Autre Voix pour l'Algérie: Entretiens avec Ghania Mouffouk*, Paris: La Découverte, 1996

Harbi, Mohammed, *Aux Origins du FLN: Le Populisme Révolutionnaire en Algérie*, Paris: Christian Bourgois, 1975

————, *Le FLN: Mirage et Réalité*, Paris: Editions Jeune Afrique, 1980

———, *La Guerre Commence en Algérie*, Bruxelles: Complexe, 1984

———, *L'Algérie et Son Destin: Croyants et Citoyens*, Paris: Arcantère, 1992

———, *Une Vie Debout: Mémoires Politiques*, Paris: La Découverte, 2001

——— (ed.), *Les Archives de la Revolution Algérienne*, Paris: Editions Jeune Afrique, 1981

Harbi, Mohammed and Gilbert Meynier (eds), *Le FLN: Documents et Histoire 1954–62*, Paris: Fayard, 2004

Harbi, Mohammed and Benjamin Stora (eds), *La Guerre d'Algérie 1954–2004: La Fin de l'Amnésie*, Paris: Robert Laffont, 2004

Hidouci, Ghazi, *Algérie: La Libération Inachevée*, Paris: La Découverte, 1995

Hobsbawm, Eric and Terrence Ranger (ed.), *The Invention of Tradition*, Cambridge: Cambridge University Press, 1983

Horani, Albert, *A History of the Arab Peoples*, London: Faber and Faber, 1991

Horne, Alistair, *A Savage War of Peace: Algeria 1954-1962*, London: Macmillan, 1977

Irwin, Robert, *The Mysteries of Algiers*, London: Penguin, 1988

Jeanson, Francis, *Algéries, de Retour en Retour*, Paris: Seuil, 1991

Joffe, George (ed.), *North Africa: Nation, State and Region*, London: Routledge, 1993

Kedward, Roderick, *La Vie en Bleu: France and the French since 1900*, London: Allen Lane, 2005

Kepel, Gilles, *Jihad: Expansion et Déclin de l'Islamisme*, Paris: Gallimard, 2000

King, John, *Algeria: A Society Divided*, Cheltenham: Understanding Global Issues, 1999

Kiser, John W., *The Monks of Tibhirine: Faith, Love and Terror in Algeria*, New York: St Martin's Griffin, 2003

Labat, Séverine, *Les Islamistes Algériens: Entre les Urnes et le Maquis*, Paris: Seuil, 1995

Le Sueur, James D., *Uncivil War, Intellectuals and Identity Politics during the Decolonization of Algeria*, Philadelphia: University of Pennsylvania Press, 2001

Leveau, Remy (ed.), *L'Algérie dans la Guerre*, Bruxelles: Editions Complexes, 1995

Lorcin, Patricia, *Imperial Identities: Stereotyping, Prejudice and Race in Colonial Algeria*, London: I.B. Tauris, 1995

McDougall, James, *History and the Culture of Nationalism in Algeria*, Cambridge: Cambridge University Press, 2006

——— (ed.), *Nation, Society and Culture in North Africa*, London: Frank Cass, 2003

Majumdar, Margaret A. and Mohammed Saad, *Transition and Development in Algeria*, Bristol: Intellect, 2005

Malti, Djallal, *La Nouvelle Guerre d'Algérie*, Paris: La Découverte, 1999

Manceron, Gilles and Remaoun, Hassan, *D'une Rive à l'Autre: La Guerre d'Algérie de la Mémoire à l'Histoire*, Paris: Syros, 1993

Martinez, Luis, *La Guerre Civile en Algérie, 1990–1998*, Paris: Editions Karthala, 1998

Matoub, Lounès, *Rebelle*, Paris: Stock, 1995

Matoub, Nadia, *Pour l'Amour d'un Rebelle*, Paris: Robert Laffont, 2000

Messaoudi, Khalida, *Unbowed*, Philadelphia: University of Pennsylvania Press, 1998

Meynier, Gilbert, *L'Algérie Révélée: La Guerre de 1914–1918 et le Premier Quart du Vingtième Siècle*, Geneva: Librairie Droz, 1981

———, *Histoire Intérieure du FLN, 1954–1962*, Paris: Fayard, 2002

———, *L'Algérie des Origines*, Paris: La Découverte, 2007

Mimouni, *De la Barbarie en Général et de l'Intégrisme en Particulier*, Paris: Le Pré aux Clercs, 1992

Mouffok, Ghania, *Etre Journaliste en Algérie*, Paris: Reporters sans Frontières, 1996

Moussaoui, Abderrahmane, *De la Violence en Algérie*, Paris: Actes Sud, 2006

Naylor, Phillip C., *France and Algeria: A History of Decolonization and Transformation*, Gainesville: University Press of Florida, 2000

Nezzar, Khaled, *Mémoires du Khaled Nezzar*, Algiers: Chihab Editions, 1999

Provost, Lucile, *La Seconde Guerre d'Algérie*, Paris: Flammarion, 1996

Quandt, William B., *Revolution and Political Leadership: Algeria, 1954–1968*, Cambridge, Mass: MIT Press, 1969

———, *Between Ballots and Bullets*, Washington: Brookings Institution Press, 1998

Rashid, Ahmed, *Taliban*, London: I.B. Tauris, 2000

Redjala, Ramdane, *L'Opposition en Algérie depuis 1962*, Paris: L'Harmattan, 1988

Reporters sans Frontières, *Le Drame Algérien*, Paris: La Découverte, 1996

Rioux, Jean-Pierre (ed.), *La Guerre d'Algérie et les Français*, Paris: Fayard, 1990

Roberts, Hugh, *The Battlefield Algeria, 1988–2002*, London: Verso, 2003

Rouadjia, Ahmed, *Les Frères et la Mosquée*, Paris: Editions Karthala, 1989

———, *Grandeur et Decadence de l'Etat Algérien*, Paris: Editions Karthala, 1994

Roy, Olivier, *The Failure of Political Islam*, London: I.B. Tauris, 1994

Ruedy, John, *Modern Algeria: The Origins and Development of a Nation*, Bloomington: Indiana University Press, 1992

Ruthven, Malise, *Islam*, Oxford: Oxford University Press, 1997

———, *A Fury for God: The Islamist Attack on America*, London: Granta, 2002

Sadi, Saïd, *Algérie: L'Heure de Vérité*, Paris: Flammarion, 1996

Samraoui, Mohammed, *Chroniques des Années de Sang*, Paris: Denoël, 2003

Sayad, Abdelmalek, *Histoire et Recherche Identitaire*, Paris: Bouchène, 2002

Semiane, Sid Ahmed, *Au Refuge des Balles Perdues*, Paris: La Découverte, 2005

Smaïn, Mohammed, *Relizane dans la Tourmente: Silence! On Tue*, Paris: Bouchène, 2006

Souaïdia, Habib, *La Sale Guerre*, Paris: La Découverte, 2001

———, *Le Procès de la 'Sale Guerre'*, Paris: La Découverte, 2003

Spencer, Claire, 'Algeria: France's Disarray and Europe's Conundrum', in B.A. Roberson (ed.), *The Middle East and Europe: The Power Deficit*, London: Routledge, 1998

Stone, Martin, *The Agony of Algeria*, London: Hurst, 1997

Stora, Benjamin, *Messali Hadj (1898–1974), Pionnier du Nationalisme Algérien*, Paris: L'Harmattan, 1986

———, *La Gangrène et l'Oubli: La Mémoire de la Guerre d'Algérie*, Paris: La Découverte, 1991

———, *Ils Venaient d'Algérie: L'Immigration Algérienne en France, 1912–1992*, Paris: Fayard, 1992

———, *L'Algérie en 1995: La Guerre, l'Histoire, la Politique*, Paris: Editions Michalon, 1995

———, *Algeria 1830–2000*, Ithaca: Cornell University Press, 2001

Thénault, Sylvie, *Une Drôle de Justice: Les Magistrats dans la Guerre d'Algérie*, Paris: La Découverte, 2001

———, *Histoire de la Guerre d'Indépendance Algérienne*, Paris: Flammarion, 2005

Vidal-Naquet, Pierre, *Torture: Cancer of Democracy*, London: Penguin, 1963

Volpi, Frédéric, 'Democratisation and its enemies: the Algerian transition to authoritarianism 1988–2001', in Robin Luckham and Gavin Cawthra (eds), *Governing Security: Democratic Control of Military and Security Establishments in Transitional Democracies*, London: Zed Books, 2003

———, *Islam and Democracy: The Failure of Dialogue in Algeria*, London: Pluto Press, 2003

Wheatcroft, Andrew, *Infidels: The Conflict Between Christendom and Islam 638–2002*, London: Viking, 2003

Willis, Michael, *The Islamist Challenge in Algeria*, London: Ithica, 1996

Yacine, Kateb, *Nedjma*, Paris: Seuil, 1956

Yous, Nesroulah, *Qui a Tué à Bentalha?*, Paris: La Découverte, 2000

Zaharaoui, Saïd, *Entre l'Horreur et l'Espoir: Chronique de la Nouvelle Guerre d'Algérie*, Paris: Robert Laffont, 2000

Zirem, Youcef, *Algérie la Guerre des Ombres*, Bruxelles: Editions Complexes, 2002

INDEX